VINTAGE

INTERNATIONAL

Also by W. H. Auden

City Without Walls

Collected Shorter Poems

The English Auden

Epistle to a Godson

Forewords and Afterwords

Homage to Clio

Selected Poems

Thank You, Fog: Last Poems

W. H. Auden: Collected Poems

W. H. AUDEN

The Dyer's Hand
and Other Essays

Selected by Edward Mendelson

VINTAGE INTERNATIONAL
VINTAGE BOOKS
A DIVISION OF RANDOM HOUSE, INC.
NEW YORK

First Vintage International Edition, December 1989

Published in the United States by Vintage Books, a division of Random House, Inc., New York, and simultaneously in Canada by Random House of Canada Limited, Toronto. Originally published, in hardcover, by Random House, Inc., in 1962.

Library of Congress Cataloging-in-Publication Data
Auden, W. H. (Wystan Hugh), 1907–1973.
The dyer's hand and other essays / W.H. Auden—1st Vintage international ed.
p. cm.—(Vintage international)
Originally published: New York: Random House, 1962.
ISBN 0-679-72484-2:$12.95
I. Title.
PR6001.U4D9 1989
814'.52—dc20 89-40057
CIP

The article on page 209 appeared originally in *The New Yorker.*

Manufactured in the United States of America
10 9 8 7 6 5 4 3 2 1

The author wishes to thank the following for permission to reprint material included in these essays:

Harcourt, Brace & World—and Jonathan Cape Ltd. for selection from "Chard Whitlow" from *A Map of Verona and Other Poems* by Henry Reed.

Harvard University Press—and Basil Blackwell & Mott Ltd. for selection from *The Discovery of the Mind* by Bruno Snell.

Holt, Rinehart and Winston, Inc.—for selections from *Complete Poems of Robert Frost.* Copyright 1916, 1921, 1923, 1928, 1930, 1939, 1947, 1949, by Holt, Rinehart and Winston, Inc.

Alfred A. Knopf, Inc.—for selections from *The Borzoi Book of French Folk Tales,* edited by Paul Delarue.

The Macmillan Company—for selections from *Collected Poems* of Marianne Moore. Copyright 1935, 1941, 1951 by Marianne Moore; —and The Macmillan Company of Canada and Mrs. W. B. Yeats for lines from "Nineteen Hundred and Nineteen" from *Collected Poems* of William Butler Yeats. Copyright 1928 by The Macmillan Company, copyright 1956 by Bertha Georgie Yeats;—for "The Scholars" from *Collected Poems* of William Butler Yeats. First published in *Poetry* in 1916. Copyright 1944 by Bertha Georgie Yeats;—and for "Ben Jonson Entertains a Man from Stratford" from *Collected Poems* of Edward Arlington Robinson. Copyright 1916 by The Macmillan Company, copyright 1944 by Ruth Nivison.

John Murray Ltd.—and Houghton Mifflin, Inc., for lines from "In Westminster Abbey" from *Collected Poems* of John Betjeman.

New Directions—for selections from *Miss Lonelyhearts* by Nathanael West. Copyright 1933 by Nathanael West;—and for *The Day of*

For

NEVILL COGHILL

Three grateful memories:

a home full of books,
a childhood spent in country provinces,
a tutor in whom one could confide.

We have Art
in order that we may not perish from Truth

F. W. NIETZSCHE

FOREWORD

It is a sad fact about our culture that a poet can earn much more money writing or talking about his art than he can by practicing it. All the poems I have written were written for love; naturally, when I have written one, I try to market it, but the prospect of a market played no role in its writing.

On the other hand, I have never written a line of criticism except in response to a demand by others for a lecture, an introduction, a review, etc.; though I hope that some love went into their writing, I wrote them because I needed the money. I should like to thank the various publishers, editors, college authorities and, not least, the ladies and gentlemen who voted me into the Chair of Poetry at Oxford University, but for whose generosity and support I should never have been able to pay my bills.

The trouble about writing commissioned criticism is that the relation between form and content is arbitrary; a lecture must take fifty-five minutes to deliver, an introduction must be so and so many thousand, a review so and so many hundred words long. Only rarely do the conditions set down conform exactly with one's thought. Sometimes one feels cramped, forced to omit or oversimplify arguments; more often, all one really has to say could be put down in half the allotted space, and one can only try to pad as inconspicuously as possible.

Moreover, in a number of articles which were not planned as a series but written for diverse occasions, it is inevitable that one will often repeat oneself.

A poem must be a closed system, but there is something, in my opinion, lifeless, even false, about systematic criticism. In going over my critical pieces, I have reduced them, when possible, to sets of notes because, as a reader, I prefer a critic's notebooks to his treatises. The order of the chapters, however, is deliberate, and I would like them to be read in sequence.

W. H. A.

CONTENTS

IV

THE SHAKESPEARIAN CITY

V

TWO BESTIARIES

VI

AMERICANA

VII

THE SHIELD OF PERSEUS

VIII

HOMAGE TO IGOR STRAVINSKY

PART ONE

Prologue

READING

A book is a mirror: if an ass peers into it, you can't expect an apostle to look out.

C. G. LICHTENBERG

One only reads well that which one reads with some quite personal purpose. It may be to acquire some power. It can be out of hatred for the author.

PAUL VALÉRY

The interests of a writer and the interests of his readers are never the same and if, on occasion, they happen to coincide, this is a lucky accident.

In relation to a writer, most readers believe in the Double Standard: they may be unfaithful to him as often as they like, but he must never, never be unfaithful to them.

To read is to translate, for no two persons' experiences are the same. A bad reader is like a bad translator: he interprets literally when he ought to paraphrase and paraphrases when he ought to interpret literally. In learning to read well, scholarship, valuable as it is, is less important than instinct; some great scholars have been poor translators.

We often derive much profit from reading a book in a different way from that which its author intended but only (once childhood is over) if we know that we are doing so.

As readers, most of us, to some degree, are like those urchins who pencil mustaches on the faces of girls in advertisements.

One sign that a book has literary value is that it can be read in a number of different ways. Vice versa, the proof that pornography has no literary value is that, if one attempts to read it in any other way than as a sexual stimulus, to read it, say, as a psychological case-history of the author's sexual fantasies, one is bored to tears.

Though a work of literature can be read in a number of ways, this number is finite and can be arranged in a hierarchical order; some readings are obviously "truer" than others, some doubtful, some obviously false, and some, like reading a novel backwards, absurd. That is why, for a desert island, one would choose a good dictionary rather than the greatest literary masterpiece imaginable, for, in relation to its readers, a dictionary is absolutely passive and may legitimately be read in an infinite number of ways.

We cannot read an author for the first time in the same way that we read the latest book by an established author. In a new author, we tend to see either only his virtues or only his defects and, even if we do see both, we cannot see the relation between them. In the case of an established author, if we can still read him at all, we know that we cannot enjoy the virtues we admire in him without tolerating the defects we deplore. Moreover, our judgment of an established author is never simply an aesthetic judgment. In addition to any literary merit it may have, a new book by him has a historic interest for us as the act of a person in whom we have long been interested. He is not only a poet or a novelist; he is also a character in our biography.

A poet cannot read another poet, nor a novelist another novelist, without comparing their work to his own. His judgments as he reads are of this kind: *My God! My Great-Grandfather! My Uncle! My Enemy! My Brother! My imbecile Brother!*

In literature, vulgarity is preferable to nullity, just as grocer's port is preferable to distilled water.

Good taste is much more a matter of discrimination than of exclusion, and when good taste feels compelled to exclude, it is with regret, not with pleasure.

Pleasure is by no means an infallible critical guide, but it is the least fallible.

A child's reading is guided by pleasure, but his pleasure is undifferentiated; he cannot distinguish, for example, between aesthetic pleasure and the pleasures of learning or daydreaming. In adolescence we realize that there are different kinds of pleasure, some of which cannot be enjoyed simultaneously, but we need help from others in defining them. Whether it be a matter of taste in food or taste in literature, the adolescent looks for a mentor in whose authority he can believe. He eats or reads what his mentor recommends and, inevitably, there are occasions when he has to deceive himself a little; he has to pretend that he enjoys olives or *War and Peace* a little more than he actually does. Between the ages of twenty and forty we are engaged in the process of discovering who we are, which involves learning the difference between accidental limitations which it is our duty to outgrow and the necessary limitations of our nature beyond which we cannot trespass with impunity. Few of us can learn this without making mistakes, without trying to become a little more of a universal man than we are permitted to be. It is during this period that a writer can most easily be led astray by another writer or by some ideology. When someone between twenty and forty says, apropos of a work of art, "I know what I like," he is really saying "I have no taste of my own but accept the taste of my cultural milieu," because, between twenty and forty, the surest sign that a man has a genuine taste of his own is that he is uncertain of it. After forty, if we have not lost our authentic selves altogether, pleasure can again become what it was when we were children, the proper guide to what *we* should read.

Though the pleasure which works of art give us must not be confused with other pleasures that we enjoy, it is related to all of them simply by being *our* pleasure and not someone else's. All the judgments, aesthetic or moral, that we pass, however objective we try to make them, are in part a rationalization and in part a corrective discipline of our subjective wishes. So long as a man writes poetry or fiction, his dream of Eden is his own business, but the moment he starts writing literary criticism, honesty demands that he describe it to his readers, so that they may be in the position to judge his judgments. Accordingly, I must now give my answers to a questionnaire I once made up which provides the kind of information I should like to have myself when reading other critics.

EDEN

Landscape

Limestone uplands like the Pennines plus a small region of igneous rocks with at least one extinct volcano. A precipitous and indented sea-coast.

Climate

British.

Ethnic origin of inhabitants

Highly varied as in the United States, but with a slight nordic predominance.

Language

Of mixed origins like English, but highly inflected.

Weights & Measures

Irregular and complicated. No decimal system.

Religion

Roman Catholic in an easygoing Mediterranean sort of way. Lots of local saints.

Size of Capital

Plato's ideal figure, 5004, about right.

Form of Government

Absolute monarchy, elected for life by lot.

Sources of Natural Power

Wind, water, peat, coal. No oil.

Economic activities

Lead mining, coal mining, chemical factories, paper mills, sheep farming, truck farming, greenhouse horticulture.

Means of transport

Horses and horse-drawn vehicles, narrow-gauge railroads, canal barges, balloons. No automobiles or airplanes.

Architecture

State: Baroque. Ecclesiastical: Romanesque or Byzantine. Domestic: Eighteenth Century British or American Colonial.

Domestic Furniture and Equipment

Victorian except for kitchens and bathrooms which are as full of modern gadgets as possible.

Formal Dress

The fashions of Paris in the 1830's and '40's.

Sources of Public Information

Gossip. Technical and learned periodicals but no newspapers.

Public Statues

Confined to famous defunct chefs.

Public Entertainments

Religious Processions, Brass Bands, Opera, Classical Ballet. No movies, radio or television.

If I were to attempt to write down the names of all the poets and novelists for whose work I am really grateful because I know that if I had not read them my life would be poorer, the list would take up pages. But when I try to think of all the critics for whom I am really grateful, I find myself with a list of thirty-four names. Of these, twelve are German and only two French. Does this indicate a conscious bias? It does.

If good literary critics are rarer than good poets or novelists, one reason is the nature of human egoism. A poet or a novelist has to learn to be humble in the face of his subject matter which is life in general. But the subject matter of a critic, before which he has to learn to be humble, is made up of authors, that is to say, of human individuals, and this kind of humility is much more difficult to acquire. It is far easier to say—"Life is more important than anything I can say about it"—than to say—"Mr. A's work is more important than anything I can say about it."

There are people who are too intelligent to become authors, but they do not become critics.

Authors can be stupid enough, God knows, but they are not always quite so stupid as a certain kind of critic seems to think. The kind of critic, I mean, to whom, when he condemns a work or a passage, the possibility never occurs that its author may have foreseen exactly what he is going to say.

What is the function of a critic? So far as I am concerned, he can do me one or more of the following services:

1) Introduce me to authors or works of which I was hitherto unaware.
2) Convince me that I have undervalued an author or a work because I had not read them carefully enough.
3) Show me relations between works of different ages and cultures which I could never have seen for myself because I do not know enough and never shall.
4) Give a "reading" of a work which increases my understanding of it.
5) Throw light upon the process of artistic "Making."

6) Throw light upon the relation of art to life, to science, economics, ethics, religion, etc.

The first three of these services demand scholarship. A scholar is not merely someone whose knowledge is extensive; the knowledge must be of value to others. One would not call a man who knew the Manhattan Telephone Directory by heart a scholar, because one cannot imagine circumstances in which he would acquire a pupil. Since scholarship implies a relation between one who knows more and one who knows less, it may be temporary; in relation to the public, every reviewer is, temporarily, a scholar, because he has read the book he is reviewing and the public have not. Though the knowledge a scholar possesses must be potentially valuable, it is not necessary that he recognize its value himself; it is always possible that the pupil to whom he imparts his knowledge has a better sense of its value than he. In general, when reading a scholarly critic, one profits more from his quotations than from his comments.

The last three services demand, not superior knowledge, but superior insight. A critic shows superior insight if the questions he raises are fresh and important, however much one may disagree with his answers to them. Few readers, probably, find themselves able to accept Tolstoi's conclusions in *What Is Art?*, but, once one has read the book, one can never again ignore the questions Tolstoi raises.

The one thing I most emphatically do not ask of a critic is that he tell me what I *ought* to approve of or condemn. I have no objection to his telling me what works and authors he likes and dislikes; indeed, it is useful to know this for, from his expressed preferences about works which I have read, I learn how likely I am to agree or disagree with his verdicts on works which I have not. But let him not dare to lay down the law to me. The responsibility for what I choose to read is mine, and nobody else on earth can do it for me.

The critical opinions of a writer should always be taken with a large grain of salt. For the most part, they are manifestations of his debate with himself as to what he should do next and what he should avoid. Moreover, unlike a scientist, he is usually even more ignorant of what his colleagues are doing than is the general public. A poet over thirty may still be a voracious reader, but it is unlikely that much of what he reads is modern poetry.

Very few of us can truthfully boast that we have never condemned a book or even an author on hearsay, but quite a lot of us that we have never praised one we had not read.

The injunction "Resist not evil but overcome evil with good" may in many spheres of life be impossible to obey literally, but in the sphere of the arts it is common sense. Bad art is always with us, but any given work of art is always bad in a period way; the particular kind of badness it exhibits will pass away to be succeeded by some other kind. It is unnecessary, therefore, to attack it, because it will perish anyway. Had Macaulay never written his review of Robert Montgomery, we would not today be still under the illusion that Montgomery was a great poet. The only sensible procedure for a critic is to keep silent about works which he believes to be bad, while at the same time vigorously campaigning for those which he believes to be good, especially if they are being neglected or underestimated by the public.

Some books are undeservedly forgotten; none are undeservedly remembered.

Some critics argue that it is their moral duty to expose the badness of an author because, unless this is done, he may corrupt other writers. To be sure, a young writer can be led astray, deflected, that is, from his true path, by an older, but he is much more likely to be seduced by a good writer than by a bad one. The more powerful and original a writer, the more dangerous he is to lesser talents who are trying to find themselves. On the other hand, works which were in themselves poor have often proved a stumulus to the imagination and become the indirect cause of good work in others.

You do not educate a person's palate by telling him that what he has been in the habit of eating—watery, overboiled cabbage, let us say—is disgusting, but by persuading him to try a dish of vegetables which have been properly cooked. With some people, it is true, you seem to get quicker results by telling them—"Only vulgar people like overcooked cabbage; the best people like cabbage as the Chinese cook it"—but the results are less likely to be lasting.

If, when a reviewer whose taste I trust condemns a book, I feel a certain relief, this is only because so many books are published that it is a relief to think—"Well, here, at least, is one I do not have to bother about." But had he kept silent, the effect would have been the same.

Attacking bad books is not only a waste of time but also bad for the character. If I find a book really bad, the only interest I can derive from writing about it has to come from myself, from such display of intelligence, wit and malice as I can contrive. One cannot review a bad book without showing off.

There is one evil that concerns literature which should never be passed over in silence but be continually publicly attacked, and that is corruption of the language, for writers cannot invent their own language and are dependent upon the language they inherit so that, if it be corrupt, they must be corrupted. But the critic who concerns himself with this evil must attack it at its source, which is not in works of literature but in the misuse of language by the man-in-the-street, journalists, politicians, etc. Furthermore, he must be able to practice what he preaches. How many critics in England or America today are masters of their native tongue as Karl Kraus was a master of German?

One cannot blame the reviewers themselves. Most of them, probably, would much prefer to review only those books which, whatever their faults, they believe to be worth reading but, if a regular reviewer on one of the big Sunday papers were to obey his inclination, at least one Sunday in three his column would be empty. Again, any conscientious critic who has ever had to review a new volume of poetry in a limited space knows that the only fair thing to do would be to give a series of quotations without comment but, if he did so, his editor would complain that he was not earning his money.

Reviewers may justly be blamed, however, for their habit of labeling and packaging authors. At first critics classified authors as Ancients, that is to say, Greek and Latin authors, and Moderns, that is to say, every post-Classical Author. Then they classified them by eras, the Augustans, the Victorians, etc., and now they classify them by decades, the writers of the '30's, '40's, etc. Very soon, it seems, they will be labeling authors, like automobiles, by the year. Already the decade classification is absurd, for it suggests that authors conveniently stop writing at the age of thirty-five or so.

"Contemporary" is a much abused term. My contemporaries are simply those who are on earth while I am alive, whether they be babies or centenarians.

A writer, or, at least, a poet, is always being asked by people who should know better: "Whom do you write for?" The question is, of course, a silly one, but I can give it a silly answer. Occasionally I come across a book which I feel has been written especially for me and for me only. Like a jealous lover, I don't want anybody else to hear of it. To have a million such readers, unaware of each other's existence, to be read with passion and never talked about, is the daydream, surely, of every author.

WRITING

It is the author's aim to say once and emphatically, "He said."

H. D. THOREAU

The art of literature, vocal or written, is to adjust the language so that it embodies what it indicates.

A. N. WHITEHEAD

All those whose success in life depends neither upon a job which satisfies some specific and unchanging social need, like a farmer's, nor, like a surgeon's, upon some craft which he can be taught by others and improve by practice, but upon "inspiration," the lucky hazard of ideas, live by their wits, a phrase which carries a slightly pejorative meaning. Every "original" genius, be he an artist or a scientist, has something a bit shady about him, like a gambler or a medium.

Literary gatherings, cocktail parties and the like, are a social nightmare because writers have no "shop" to talk. Lawyers and doctors can entertain each other with stories about interesting cases, about experiences, that is to say, related to their professional interests but yet impersonal and outside themselves. Writers have no impersonal professional interests. The literary equivalent of talking shop would be writers reciting their own work at each other, an unpopular procedure for which only very young writers have the nerve.

No poet or novelist wishes he were the only one who ever lived, but most of them wish they were the only one alive, and quite a number fondly believe their wish has been granted.

In theory, the author of a good book should remain anonymous, for it is to his work, not to himself, that admiration is due. In practice, this seems to be impossible. However, the praise and public attention that writers sometimes receive does not seem to be as fatal to them as one might expect. Just as a good man forgets his deed the moment he has done it, a genuine writer forgets a work as soon as he has completed it and starts to think about the next one; if he thinks about his past work at all, he is more likely to remember its faults than its virtues. Fame often makes a writer vain, but seldom makes him proud.

Writers can be guilty of every kind of human conceit but one, the conceit of the social worker: "We are all here on earth to help others; what on earth the others are here for, I don't know."

When a successful author analyzes the reasons for his success, he generally underestimates the talent he was born with, and overestimates his skill in employing it.

Every writer would rather be rich than poor, but no genuine writer cares about popularity as such. He needs approval of his work by others in order to be reassured that the vision of life he believes he has had is a true vision and not a self-delusion, but he can only be reassured by those whose judgment he respects. It would only be necessary for a writer to secure universal popularity if imagination and intelligence were equally distributed among all men.

When some obvious booby tells me he has liked a poem of mine, I feel as if I had picked his pocket.

Writers, poets especially, have an odd relation to the public because their medium, language, is not, like the paint of the painter or the notes of the composer, reserved for their use but is the common property of the linguistic group to which they belong. Lots of people are willing to admit that they don't understand painting or music, but very few indeed who have been to school and learned to read advertisements will admit that they don't understand English. As Karl Kraus said: "The public doesn't understand German, and in Journalese I can't tell them so."

How happy the lot of the mathematician! He is judged solely by his peers, and the standard is so high that no colleague or rival can ever win a reputation he does not deserve. No cashier writes a letter to the press complaining about the incomprehensibility of Modern Mathematics and comparing it unfavorably with the good old days when mathematicians were content to paper irregularly shaped rooms and fill bathtubs without closing the waste pipe.

To say that a work is inspired means that, in the judgment of its author or his readers, it is better than they could reasonably hope it would be, and nothing else.

All works of art are commissioned in the sense that no artist can create one by a simple act of will but must wait until what he believes to be a good idea for a work "comes" to him. Among those works which are failures because their initial conceptions were false or inadequate, the number of self-commissioned works may well be greater than the number commissioned by patrons.

The degree of excitement which a writer feels during the process of composition is as much an indication of the value of the final result as the excitement felt by a worshiper is an indication of the value of his devotions, that is to say, very little indication.

The Oracle claimed to make prophecies and give good advice about the future; it never pretended to be giving poetry readings.

If poems could be created in a trance without the conscious participation of the poet, the writing of poetry would be so boring or even unpleasant an operation that only a substantial reward in money or social prestige could induce a man to be a poet. From the manuscript evidence, it now appears that Coleridge's account of the composition of "Kubla Khan" was a fib.

It is true that, when he is writing a poem, it seems to a poet as if there were two people involved, his conscious self and a Muse whom he has to woo or an Angel with whom he has to wrestle, but, as in an ordinary wooing or wrestling match, his role is as important as Hers. The Muse, like Beatrice in *Much Ado,* is a spirited girl who has as little use for an abject suitor as she has for a vulgar brute. She appreciates chivalry and good manners, but she despises those who will not stand up to her and takes a cruel delight in telling them nonsense and lies which the poor little things obediently write down as "inspired" truth.

> *When I was writing the chorus in G Minor, I suddenly dipped my pen into the medicine bottle instead of the ink; I made a blot, and when I dried it with sand (blotting paper had not been invented then) it took the form of a natural, which instantly gave me the idea of the effect which the change from G minor to G major would make, and to this blot all the effect—if any—is due.*
>
> (Rossini to Louis Engel.)

Such an act of judgment, distinguishing between Chance and Providence, deserves, surely, to be called an inspiration.

To keep his errors down to a minimum, the internal Censor to whom a poet submits his work in progress should be a Censorate. It should include, for instance, a sensitive only child, a practical housewife, a logician, a monk, an irreverent buffoon and even, perhaps, hated by all the others and returning their dislike, a brutal, foul-mouthed drill sergeant who considers all poetry rubbish.

In the course of many centuries a few laborsaving devices have been introduced into the mental kitchen—alcohol, coffee, tobacco, Benzedrine, etc.—but these are very crude, constantly breaking down, and liable to injure the cook. Literary composition in the twentieth century A.D. is pretty much what it was in the twentieth century B.C.: nearly everything has still to be done by hand.

Most people enjoy the sight of their own handwriting as they enjoy the smell of their own farts. Much as I loathe the typewriter, I must admit that it is a help in self-criticism. Typescript is so impersonal and hideous to look at that, if I type out a poem, I immediately see defects which I missed when I looked through it in manuscript. When it comes to a poem by somebody else, the severest test I know of is to write it out in longhand. The physical tedium of doing this ensures that the slightest defect will reveal itself; the hand is constantly looking for an excuse to stop.

Most artists are sincere and most art is bad, though some insincere (sincerely insincere) works can be quite good. (STRAVINSKY.) Sincerity is like sleep. Normally, one should assume that, of course, one will be sincere, and not give the question a second thought. Most writers, however, suffer occasionally from bouts of insincerity as men do from bouts of insomnia. The remedy in both cases is often quite simple: in the case of the latter, to change one's diet, in the case of the former, to change one's company.

The schoolmasters of literature frown on affectations of style as silly and unhealthy. Instead of frowning, they ought to laugh indulgently. Shakespeare makes fun of the Euphuists in *Love's Labour's Lost* and in *Hamlet,* but he owed them a great deal and he knew it. Nothing, on the face of it, could have been more futile than the attempt of Spenser, Harvey and others to be good little humanists and write English verse in classical meters, yet, but for their folly, many of Campion's most beautiful songs and the choruses in *Samson Agonistes* would never have been written. In literature, as in life, affectation, passionately adopted and loyally persevered in, is one of the chief forms of self-discipline by which mankind has raised itself by its own bootstraps.

A mannered style, that of Góngora or Henry James, for example, is like eccentric clothing: very few writers can carry it off, but one is enchanted by the rare exception who can.

When a reviewer describes a book as "sincere," one knows immediately that it is a) insincere (insincerely insincere) and b) badly written. Sincerity in the proper sense of the word, meaning authenticity, is, however, or ought to be, a writer's chief preoccupation. No writer can ever judge exactly how good or bad a work of his may be, but he can always know, not immediately perhaps, but certainly in a short while, whether something he has written is authentic—in his handwriting—or a forgery.

The most painful of all experiences to a poet is to find that a poem of his which he knows to be a forgery has pleased the public and got into the anthologies. For all he knows or cares, the poem may be quite good, but that is not the point; *he* should not have written it.

The work of a young writer—*Werther* is the classic example—is sometimes a therapeutic act. He finds himself obsessed by certain ways of feeling and thinking of which his instinct tells him he must be rid before he can discover his authentic interests and sympathies, and the only way by which he can be rid of them forever is by surrendering to them. Once he has done this, he has developed the necessary antibodies which will make him immune for the rest of his life. As a rule, the disease is some spiritual malaise of his generation. If so, he may, as Goethe did, find himself in an embarrassing situation. What he wrote in order to exorcise certain feelings is enthusiastically welcomed by his contemporaries because it expresses just what they feel but, unlike him, they are perfectly happy to feel in this way; for the moment they regard him as their spokesman. Time passes. Having gotten the poison out of his system, the writer turns to his true interests which are not, and never were, those of his early admirers, who now pursue him with cries of "Traitor!"

The intellect of man is forced to choose
Perfection of the life or of the work. (YEATS.)
This is untrue; perfection is possible in neither. All one can say is that a writer who, like all men, has his personal weaknesses and limitations, should be aware of them and try his best to keep them out of his work. For every writer, there are certain subjects which, because of defects in his character and his talent, he should never touch.

What makes it difficult for a poet not to tell lies is that, in poetry, all facts and all beliefs cease to be true or false and become interesting possibilities. The reader does not have to share the beliefs expressed in a poem in order to enjoy it. Knowing this, a poet is constantly tempted to make use of an idea or a belief, not because he believes it to be true, but because he sees it has interesting poetic possibilities. It may not, perhaps, be absolutely necessary that he *believe* it, but it is certainly necessary that his emotions be deeply involved, and this they can never be unless, as a man, he takes it more seriously than as a mere poetic convenience.

The integrity of a writer is more threatened by appeals to his social conscience, his political or religious convictions, than by appeals to his cupidity. It is morally less confusing to be goosed by a traveling salesman than by a bishop.

Some writers confuse authenticity, which they ought always to aim at, with originality, which they should never bother about. There is a certain kind of person who is so dominated by the desire to be loved for himself alone that he has constantly to test those around him by tiresome behavior; what he says and does must be admired, not because it is intrinsically admirable, but because it is *his* remark, *his* act. Does not this explain a good deal of avant-garde art?

Slavery is so intolerable a condition that the slave can hardly escape deluding himself into thinking that he is choosing to obey his master's commands when, in fact, he is obliged to. Most slaves of habit suffer from this delusion and so do some writers, enslaved by an all too "personal" style.

> *"Let me think: was I the same when I got up this morning? . . . But if I'm not the same, the next question is 'Who in the world am I?' . . . I'm sure I'm not Ada . . . for her hair goes in such long ringlets and mine doesn't go in ringlets at all; and I'm sure I can't be Mabel, for I know all sorts of things, and she, oh! she knows such a very little! Beside* she's *she and* I'm *I and—oh dear, how puzzling it all is! I'll try if I know all the things I used to know. . . ." Her eyes filled with tears . . . : "I must be Mabel after all, and I shall have to go and live in that poky little house, and have next to no toys to play with, and oh!—ever so many lessons to learn! No, I've made up my mind about it: if I'm Mabel, I'll stay down here!"*
>
> *(Alice in Wonderland.)*

> *At the next peg the Queen turned again and this time she said: "Speak in French when you can't think of the English for a thing—turn your toes out as you walk—and remember who you are."*
>
> *(Through the Looking-Glass.)*

Most writers, except the supreme masters who transcend all systems of classification are either Alices or Mabels. For example:

Alice	*Mabel*
Montaigne	Pascal
Marvell	Donne
Burns	Shelley
Jane Austen	Dickens
Turgenev	Dostoievski
Valéry	Gide
Virginia Woolf	Joyce
E. M. Forster	Lawrence
Robert Graves	Yeats

"Orthodoxy," said a real Alice of a bishop, "is reticence."

Except when used as historical labels, the terms *classical* and *romantic* are misleading terms for two poetic parties, the Aristocratic and the Democratic, which have always existed and to one of which every writer belongs, though he may switch his party allegiance or, on some specific issue, refuse to obey his Party Whip.

The Aristocratic Principle as regards subject matter:
No subject matter shall be treated by poets which poetry cannot digest. It defends poetry against didacticism and journalism.

The Democratic Principle as regards subject matter:
No subject matter shall be excluded by poets which poetry is capable of digesting. It defends poetry against limited or stale conceptions of what is "poetic."

The Aristocratic Principle as regards treatment:
No irrelevant aspects of a given subject shall be expressed in a poem which treats it. It defends poetry against barbaric vagueness.

The Democratic Principle as regards treatment:
No relevant aspect of a given subject shall remain unexpressed in a poem which treats it. It defends poetry against decadent triviality.

Every work of a writer should be a first step, but this will be a false step unless, whether or not he realize it at the time, it is also a further step. When a writer is dead, one ought to be able to see that his various works, taken together, make one consistent *oeuvre*.

It takes little talent to see clearly what lies under one's nose, a good deal of it to know in which direction to point that organ.

The greatest writer cannot see through a brick wall but, unlike the rest of us, he does not build one.

Only a minor talent can be a perfect gentleman; a major talent is always more than a bit of a cad. Hence the importance of minor writers—as teachers of good manners. Now and again, an exquisite minor work can make a master feel thoroughly ashamed of himself.

The poet is the father of his poem; its mother is a language: one could list poems as race horses are listed—*out of L by P.*

A poet has to woo, not only his own Muse but also Dame Philology, and, for the beginner, the latter is the more important. As a rule, the sign that a beginner has a genuine original talent is that he is more interested in playing with words than in saying something original; his attitude is that of the old lady, quoted by E. M. Forster—"How can I know what I think till I see what I say?" It is only later, when he has wooed and won Dame Philology, that he can give his entire devotion to his Muse.

Rhymes, meters, stanza forms, etc., are like servants. If the master is fair enough to win their affection and firm enough to command their respect, the result is an orderly happy household. If he is too tyrannical, they give notice; if he lacks authority, they become slovenly, impertinent, drunk and dishonest.

The poet who writes "free" verse is like Robinson Crusoe on his desert island: he must do all his cooking, laundry and darning for himself. In a few exceptional cases, this manly independence produces something original and impressive, but more often the result is squalor—dirty sheets on the unmade bed and empty bottles on the unswept floor.

There are some poets, Kipling for example, whose relation to language reminds one of a drill sergeant: the words are taught to wash behind their ears, stand properly at attention and execute complicated maneuvers, but at the cost of never being allowed to think for themselves. There are others, Swinburne, for example, who remind one more of Svengali: under their hypnotic suggestion, an extraordinary performance is put on, not by raw recruits, but by feeble-minded schoolchildren.

Due to the Curse of Babel, poetry is the most provincial of the arts, but today, when civilization is becoming monotonously the same all the world over, one feels inclined to regard this as a blessing rather than a curse: in poetry, at least, there cannot be an "International Style."

My language is the universal whore whom I have to make into a virgin. (KARL KRAUS.) It is both the glory and the shame of poetry that its medium is not its private property, that a poet cannot invent his words and that words are products, not of nature, but of a human society which uses them for a thousand different purposes. In modern societies where language is continually being debased and reduced to nonspeech, the poet is in constant danger of having his ear corrupted, a danger to which the painter and the composer, whose media are their private property, are not exposed. On the other hand he is more protected than they from another modern peril, that of solipsist subjectivity; however esoteric a poem may be, the fact that all its words have meanings which can be looked up in a dictionary makes it testify to the existence of other people. Even the language of *Finnegans Wake* was not created by Joyce *ex nihilo;* a purely private verbal world is not possible.

The difference between verse and prose is self-evident, but it is a sheer waste of time to look for a definition of the difference between poetry and prose. Frost's definition of poetry as the untranslatable element in language looks plausible at first sight but, on closer examination, will not quite do. In the first place, even in the most rarefied poetry, there are some elements which are translatable. The sound of the words, their rhythmical relations, and all meanings and association of meanings which depend upon sound, like rhymes and puns, are, of course, untranslatable, but poetry is not, like music, pure sound. Any elements in a poem which are not based on verbal experience are, to some degree, translatable into another tongue, for example, images, similes and metaphors which are drawn from sensory experience. Moreover, because one characteristic that all men, whatever their culture, have in common is uniqueness—every man is a member of a class of one—the unique perspective on the world which every genuine poet has survives translation. If one takes a poem by Goethe and a poem by Hölderlin and makes literal prose cribs of them, every reader will recognize that the two poems were written by two different people. In the second place, if speech can never become music, neither can it ever become algebra. Even in the most "prosy" language, in informative and technical prose, there is a personal element because language is a personal creation. *Ne pas se pencher au dehors* has a different feeling tone from *Nichthinauslehnen*. A purely poetic language would be unlearnable, a purely prosaic not worth learning.

Valéry bases his definitions of poetry and prose on the difference between the gratuitous and the useful, play and work, and uses as an analogy the difference between dancing and walking. But this will not do either. A commuter may walk to his suburban station every morning, but at the same time he may enjoy the walk for its own sake; the fact that his walk is necessary does not exclude the possibility of its also being a form of play. Vice versa, a dance does not cease to be play if it is also believed to have a useful purpose like promoting a good harvest.

If French poets have been more prone than English to fall into the heresy of thinking that poetry ought to be as much like music as possible, one reason may be that, in traditional French verse, sound effects have always played a much more important role than they have in English verse. The English-speaking peoples have always felt that the difference between poetic speech and the conversational speech of everyday should be kept small, and, whenever English poets have felt that the gap between poetic and ordinary speech was growing too wide, there has been a stylistic revolution to bring them closer again. In English verse, even in Shakespeare's grandest rhetorical passages, the ear is always aware of its relation to everyday speech. A good actor must—alas, today he too seldom does—make the audience hear Shakespeare's lines as verse not prose, but if he tries to make the verse sound like a different language, he will make himself ridiculous.

But French poetry, both in the way it is written and the way it is recited, has emphasized and gloried in the difference between itself and ordinary speech; in French drama, verse and prose *are* different languages. Valéry quotes a contemporary description of Rachel's powers of declamation; in reciting she could and did use a range of two octaves, from F below Middle C to F in alt; an actress who tried to do the same with Shakespeare as Rachel did with Racine would be laughed off the stage.

One can read Shakespeare to oneself without even mentally *hearing* the lines and be very moved; indeed, one may easily find a performance disappointing because almost anyone with an understanding of English verse can speak it better than the average actor and actress. But to read Racine to oneself, even, I fancy, if one is a Frenchman, is like reading the score of an opera when one can hardly play or sing; one can no more get an adequate notion of *Phèdre* without having heard a great performance, than one can of *Tristan und Isolde* if one has never heard a great Isolde like Leider or Flagstad.

(Monsieur St. John Perse tells me that, when it comes to everyday speech, it is French which is the more monotonous and English which has the wider range of vocal inflection.)

I must confess that French classical tragedy strikes me as being opera for the unmusical. When I read the *Hippolytus*, I can recognize, despite all differences, a kinship between the world of Euripides and the world of Shakespeare, but the world of Racine, like the world of opera, seems to be another planet altogether. Euripides' Aphrodite is as concerned with fish and fowl as she is with human beings; Racine's Venus is not only unconcerned with animals, she takes no interest in the Lower Orders. It is impossible to imagine any of Racine's characters sneezing or wanting to go to the bathroom, for in his world there is neither weather nor nature. In consequence, the passions by which his characters are consumed can only exist, as it were, on stage, the creation of the magnificent speech and the grand gestures of the actors and actresses who endow them with flesh and blood. This is also the case in opera, but no speaking voice, however magnificent, can hope to compete, in expressiveness through sound, with a great singing voice backed by an orchestra.

Whenever people talk to me about the weather, I always feel certain that they mean something else. (OSCAR WILDE.) The only kind of speech which approximates to the symbolist's poetic ideal is polite tea table conversation, in which the meaning of the banalities uttered depends almost entirely upon vocal inflections.

Owing to its superior power as a mnemonic, verse is superior to prose as a medium for didactic instruction. Those who condemn didacticism must disapprove *a fortiori* of didactic prose; in verse, as the Alka-Seltzer advertisements testify, the didactic message loses half its immodesty. Verse is also certainly the equal of prose as a medium for the lucid exposition of ideas; in skillful hands, the form of the verse can parallel and reinforce the steps of the logic. Indeed, contrary to what most people who have inherited the romantic conception of poetry believe, the danger of argument in verse —Pope's *Essay on Man* is an example—is that the verse may make the ideas *too* clear and distinct, more Cartesian than they really are.

On the other hand, verse is unsuited to controversy, to proving some truth or belief which is not universally accepted, because its formal nature cannot but convey a certain skepticism about its conclusions.

Thirty days hath September,
April, June and November

is valid because nobody doubts its truth. Were there, however, a party who passionately denied it, the lines would be powerless to convince him because, formally, it would make no difference if the lines ran:

Thirty days hath September,
August, May and December.

Poetry is not magic. In so far as poetry, or any other of the arts, can be said to have an ulterior purpose, it is, by telling the truth, to disenchant and disintoxicate.

"The unacknowledged legislators of the world" describes the secret police, not the poets.

Catharsis is properly effected, not by works of art, but by religious rites. It is also effected, usually improperly, by bull-fights, professional football matches, bad movies, military bands and monster rallies at which ten thousand girl guides form themselves into a model of the national flag.

The condition of mankind is, and always has been, so miserable and depraved that, if anyone were to say to the poet: "For God's sake stop singing and do something useful like putting on the kettle or fetching bandages," what just reason could he give for refusing? But nobody says this. The self-appointed unqualified nurse says: "You are to sing the patient a song which will make him believe that I, and I alone, can cure him. If you can't or won't, I shall confiscate your passport and send you to the mines." And the poor patient in his delirium cries: "Please sing me a song which will give me sweet dreams instead of nightmares. If you succeed, I will give you a penthouse in New York or a ranch in Arizona."

Why the hell [illegible]
[illegible]

[illegible] is not [illegible] or any [illegible] of [illegible] can be [illegible] it [illegible] to [illegible]

[illegible] of the [illegible]

[illegible] in [illegible] of [illegible] but [illegible] the [illegible] and [illegible] by [illegible] and [illegible] such as [illegible] into [illegible] of [illegible] national flag.

[illegible] of [illegible] has been [illegible] If [illegible] what [illegible] the [illegible] and [illegible] that [illegible] I [illegible] that [illegible] to the [illegible] of [illegible] of [illegible] in [illegible]

PART TWO

The Dyer's Hand

MAKING, KNOWING AND JUDGING*

The art of life, of a poet's life, is, not having anything to do, to do something.

H. D. THOREAU

Even the greatest of that long line of scholars and poets who have held this chair before me—when I recall the names of some, I am filled with fear and trembling—must have asked themselves: "What *is* a Professor of Poetry? How can Poetry be *professed?*"

I can imagine one possible answer, though unfortunately it is not the right one. I should be feeling less uneasy at this moment than I do, if the duties of the Professor of Poetry were to produce, as occasion should demand, an epithalamium for the nuptials of a Reader in Romance Languages, an

* An Inaugural Lecture delivered before the University of Oxford on 11 June 1956.

elegy on a deceased Canon of Christ Church, a May-day Masque for Somerville or an election ballad for his successor. I should at least be working in the medium to which I am accustomed.

But these are not his duties. His primary duty is to give lectures—which presupposes that he knows something which his audience does not. You have chosen for your new Professor someone who has no more right to the learned garb he is wearing than he would have to a clerical collar. One of his secondary duties is to deliver every other year on oration in Latin. You have chosen a barbarian who cannot write in that tongue and does not know how to pronounce it. Even barbarians have their sense of honor and I must take this public opportunity to say that, for the alien sounds I shall utter at Encaenia, my "affable familiar ghost" has been Mr. J. G. Griffith of Jesus.

But it is my primary duty which I must attempt to do this afternoon. If I am in any way to deserve your extraordinary choice for what one of the noblest and most learned of my predecessors so aptly called *The Siege Perilous,* then I must find some topic about which I cannot help knowing something simply because I have written some poems, and, for an inaugural lecture, this topic should be of general and, if possible, central concern to the verbal Art of Numbers.

Many years ago, there appeared in *Punch* a joke which I have heard attributed to the scholar and poet A. E. Housman. The cartoon showed two middle-aged English examiners taking a country stroll in spring. And the caption ran:

FIRST E. E. O cuckoo shall I call thee bird
Or but a wandering voice?
SECOND E. E. State the alternative preferred
With reasons for your choice.

At first reading this seems to be a satire on examiners. But is it? The moment I try to answer the question, I find myself thinking: "It has an answer and if Wordsworth had put the question to himself instead of to the reader, he would have deleted *bird* as redundant. His inner examiner must have been asleep at the time."

Even if poems were often written in trances, poets would still accept responsibility for them by signing their names and taking the credit. They cannot claim oracular immunity. Admirers of "Kubla Khan," the only documented case of a trance poem which we possess, should not lightly dismiss what Coleridge, who was, after all, a great critic, says in his introductory note:

> The following fragment is here published at the request of a poet of great and deserved celebrity (Lord Byron) and, as far as the Author's own opinions are concerned, rather as a psychological curiosity, than on the grounds of any supposed poetic merits.

It has, of course, extraordinary poetic merits, but Coleridge was not being falsely modest. He saw, I think, as a reader can see, that even the fragment that exists is disjointed and would have had to be worked on if he ever completed the poem, and his critical conscience felt on its honor to admit this.

It seems to me, then, that this might be a possible topic. Anyone who writes poetry ought to have something to say about this critic who is only interested in one author and only concerned with works that do not yet exist. To distinguish him from the critic who is concerned with the already existing works of others, let us call him the Censor.

How does the Censor get his education? How does his attitude towards the literature of the past differ from that of the scholarly critic? If a poet should take to writing criticism, what help to him in that activity are the experiences of his Censor? Is there any truth in Dryden's statement: "Poets themselves are the most proper, though not, I conclude, the only critics"?

In trying to answer these questions, I shall be compelled, from time to time, to give autobiographical illustrations. This is regrettable but unavoidable. I have no other guinea pig.

I

I began writing poetry myself because one Sunday afternoon in March 1922, a friend suggested that I should: the thought had never occurred to me. I scarcely knew any poems—*The English Hymnal,* the Psalms, *Struwwelpeter* and the mnemonic rhymes in *Kennedy's Shorter Latin Primer* are about all I remember—and I took little interest in what is called Imaginative Literature. Most of my reading had been related to a private world of Sacred Objects. Aside from a few stories like George Macdonald's *The Princess and the Goblin* and Jules Verne's *The Child of the Cavern,* the subjects of which touched upon my obsessions, my favorite books bore such titles as *Underground Life, Machinery for Metalliferous Mines, Lead and Zinc Ores of Northumberland and Alston Moor,* and my conscious purpose in reading them had been to gain information about my sacred objects. At the time, therefore, the suggestion that I write poetry seemed like a revelation from heaven for which nothing in my past could account.

Looking back, however, I now realize that I had read the technological prose of my favorite books in a peculiar way. A word like *pyrites,* for example, was for me, not simply an indicative sign; it was the Proper Name of a Sacred Being, so that, when I heard an aunt pronounce it *pirrits,* I was shocked. Her pronunciation was more than wrong, it was ugly. Ignorance was impiety.

It was Edward Lear, I believe,* who said that the true test of imagination is the ability to name a cat, and we are told in the first chapter of Genesis that the Lord brought to unfallen Adam all the creatures that he might name them and whatsoever Adam called every living creature, that was the name thereof, which is to say, its Proper Name. Here Adam plays the role of the Proto-poet, not the Proto-prosewriter. A Proper Name must not only refer, it must refer aptly and this aptness must be publicly recognizable. It is curious to observe, for instance, that when a person has been christened

* I was wrong: it was Samuel Butler.

inaptly, he and his friends instinctively call him by some other name. Like a line of poetry, a Proper Name is untranslatable. Language is prosaic to the degree that "It does not matter what particular word is associated with an idea, provided the association once made is permanent." Language is poetic to the degree that it does matter.

> The power of verse [writes Valéry] is derived from an indefinable harmony between what it *says* and what it *is*. Indefinable is essential to the definition. The harmony ought not to be definable; when it can be defined it is imitative harmony and that is not good. The impossibility of defining the relation, together with the impossibility of denying it, constitutes the essence of the poetic line.

The poet is someone, says Mallarmé, who *"de plusieurs vocables refait un mot total,"* and the most poetical of all scholastic disciplines is, surely, Philology, the study of language in abstraction from its uses, so that words become, as it were, little lyrics about themselves.

Since Proper Names in the grammatical sense refer to unique objects, we cannot judge their aptness without personal acquaintance with what they name. To know whether *Old Foss* was an apt name for Lear's cat, we should have had to have known them both. A line of poetry like

A drop of water in the breaking gulf

is a name for an experience we all know so that we can judge its aptness, and it names, as a Proper Name cannot, relations and actions as well as things. But Shakespeare and Lear are both using language in the same way and, I believe, for the same motive, but into that I shall go later. My present point is that, if my friend's suggestion met with such an unexpected response, the reason may have been that, without knowing it, I had been enjoying the poetic use of language for a long time.

A beginner's efforts cannot be called bad or imitative. They are imaginary. A bad poem has this or that fault which can be pointed out; an imitative poem is a recognizable imitation of this or that poem, this or that poet. But about an imaginary poem no criticism can be made since it is an imitation of poetry-in-general. Never again will a poet feel so inspired, so certain of genius, as he feels in these first days as his pencil flies across the page. Yet something is being learned even now. As he scribbles on he is beginning to get the habit of noticing metrical quantities, to see that any two-syllable word in isolation must be either a *ti-tum,* a *tum-ti* or, occasionally, a *tum-tum,* but that when associated with other words it can sometimes become a *ti-ti;* when he discovers a rhyme he has not thought of before, he stores it away in his memory, a habit which an Italian poet may not need to acquire but which an English poet will find useful.

And, though as yet he can only scribble, he has started reading real poems for pleasure and on purpose. Many things can be said against anthologies, but for an adolescent to whom even the names of most of the poets are unknown, a good one can be an invaluable instructor. I had the extraordinary good fortune to be presented one Christmas with the De la Mare anthology *Come Hither*. This had, for my purposes, two great virtues. Firstly, its good taste. Reading it today, I find very few poems which I should have omitted and none which I should think it bad taste to admire. Secondly, its catholic taste. Given the youthful audience for which it was designed, there were certain kinds of poetry which it did not represent, but within those limits the variety was extraordinary. Particularly valuable was its lack of literary class consciousness, its juxtaposition on terms of equality of unofficial poetry, such as counting-out rhymes, and official poetry such as the odes of Keats. It taught me at the start that poetry does not have to be great or even serious to be good, and that one does not have to be ashamed of moods in which one feels no desire whatsoever to read *The Divine Comedy* and a great desire to read

> When other ladies to the shades go down,
> Still Flavia, Chloris, Celia stay in town.
> These Ghosts of Beauty ling'ring there abide,
> And haunt the places where their Honour died.

Matthew Arnold's notion of Touchstones by which to measure all poems has always struck me as a doubtful one, likely to turn readers into snobs and to ruin talented poets by tempting them to imitate what is beyond their powers.

A poet who wishes to improve himself should certainly keep good company, but for his profit as well as for his comfort the company should not be too far above his station. It is by no means clear that the poetry which influenced Shakespeare's development most fruitfully was the greatest poetry with which he was acquainted. Even for readers, when one thinks of the attention that a great poem demands, there is something frivolous about the notion of spending every day with one. Masterpieces should be kept for High Holidays of the Spirit.

I am not trying to defend the aesthetic heresy that one subject is no more important than any other, or that a poem has no subject or that there is no difference between a great poem and a good one—a heresy which seems to me contrary to human feeling and common sense—but I can understand why it exists. Nothing is worse than a bad poem which was intended to be great.

So a would-be poet begins to learn that poetry is more various than he imagined and that he can like and dislike different poems for different reasons. His Censor, however, has still not yet been born. Before he can give birth to him, he has to pretend to be somebody else; he has to get a literary transference upon some poet in particular.

If poetry were in great public demand so that there were overworked professional poets, I can imagine a system under which an established poet would take on a small number of apprentices who would begin by changing his blotting paper, advance to typing his manuscripts and end up by ghostwriting poems for him which he was too busy to start or finish. The apprentices might really learn something for, knowing that he would get the blame as well as the credit for their work, the Master would be extremely choosy about his apprentices and do his best to teach them all he knew.

In fact, of course, a would-be poet serves his apprenticeship in a library. This has its advantages. Though the Master is deaf and dumb and gives neither instruction nor criticism, the apprentice can choose any Master he likes, living or dead, the Master is available at any hour of the day or night, lessons are all for free, and his passionate admiration of his Master will ensure that he work hard to please him.

To please means to imitate and it is impossible to do a recognizable imitation of a poet without attending to every detail of his diction, rhythms and habits of sensibility. In imitating his Master, the apprentice acquires a Censor, for he learns that, no matter how he finds it, by inspiration, by potluck or after hours of laborious search, there is only one word or rhythm or form that is the *right* one. The right one is still not yet the *real* one, for the apprentice is ventriloquizing, but he has got away from poetry-in-general; he is learning how *a* poem is written. Later in life, incidentally, he will realize how important is the art of imitation, for he will not infrequently be called upon to imitate himself.

My first Master was Thomas Hardy, and I think I was very lucky in my choice. He was a good poet, perhaps a great one, but not *too* good. Much as I loved him, even I could see that his diction was often clumsy and forced and that a lot of his poems were plain bad. This gave me hope where a flawless poet might have made me despair. He was modern without being too modern. His world and sensibility were close enough to mine—curiously enough his face bore a striking resemblance to my father's—so that, in imitating him, I was being led towards not away from myself, but they were not so close as to obliterate my identity. If I looked through his spectacles, at least I was conscious of a certain eyestrain. Lastly, his metrical variety, his fondness for complicated stanza forms, were an invaluable training in the craft of making. I am also thankful that my first Master did not write in free verse or I might then have been tempted to believe that free verse is easier to write than stricter forms, whereas I now know it is infinitely more difficult.

Presently the curtain rises on a scene rather like the finale to Act II of *Die Meistersinger*. Let us call it The Gathering of the Apprentices. The apprentices gather together from all over and discover that they are a new generation; somebody shouts the word "modern" and the riot is on. The New Iconoclastic Poets and Critics are discovered—when I was an undergraduate a critic could still describe Mr. T. S. Eliot, O.M., as "a drunken helot"—the poetry which these new authorities recommend becomes the Canon, that on which they frown is thrown out of the window. There are gods whom it is blasphemy to criticize and devils whose names may not be mentioned without execrations. The apprentices have seen a great light while their tutors sit in darkness and the shadow of death.

Really, how do the dons stand it, for I'm sure this scene repeats itself year after year. When I recall the kindness of my tutors, the patience with which they listened, the courtesy with which they hid their boredom, I am overwhelmed by their sheer goodness. I suppose that, having arrived there, they knew that the road of excess can lead to the palace of Wisdom, though it frequently does not.

An apprentice discovers that there is a significant relation between the statement "Today I am nineteen" and the statement "Today is February the twenty-first, 1926." If the discovery goes to his head, it is, nevertheless, a discovery he must make, for, until he realizes that all the poems he has read, however different they may be, have one common characteristic—they have all been written—his own writing will never cease to be imitative. He will never know what he himself *can write* until he has a general sense of what *needs to be written.* And this is the one thing his elders cannot teach him, just because they are his elders; he can only learn it from his fellow apprentices with whom he shares one thing in common, youth.

The discovery is not wholly pleasant. If the young speak of the past as a burden it is a joy to throw off, behind their words may often lie a resentment and fright at realizing that the past will not carry them on its back.

The critical statements of the Censor are always polemical advice to his poet, meant, not as objective truths, but as pointers, and in youth which is trying to discover its own identity, the exasperation at not having yet succeeded naturally tends to express itself in violence and exaggeration.

If an undergraduate announces to his tutor one morning that Gertrude Stein is the greatest writer who ever lived or that Shakespeare is no good, he is really only saying something like this: "I don't know what to write yet or how, but yesterday while reading Gertrude Stein, I thought I saw a clue" or "Reading Shakespeare yesterday, I realized that one of the faults in what I write is a tendency to rhetorical bombast."

Fashion and snobbery are also valuable as a defense against literary indigestion. Regardless of their quality, it is always better to read a few books carefully than skim through many, and, short of a personal taste which cannot be formed overnight, snobbery is as good a principle of limitation as any other.

I am eternally grateful, for example, to the musical fashion of my youth which prevented me from listening to Italian Opera until I was over thirty, by which age I was capable of really appreciating a world so beautiful and so challenging to my own cultural heritage.

The apprentices do each other a further mutual service which no older and sounder critic could do. They read each other's manuscripts. At this age a fellow apprentice has two great virtues as a critic. When he reads your poem, he may grossly overestimate it, but if he does, he really believes what he is saying; he never flatters or praises merely to encourage. Secondly, he reads your poem with that passionate attention which grown-up critics only give to masterpieces and grown-up poets only to themselves. When he finds fault, his criticisms are intended to help you to improve. He really wants your poem to be better.

It is just this kind of personal criticism which in later life, when the band of apprentices has dispersed, a writer often finds it so hard to get. The verdicts of reviewers, however just, are seldom of any use to him. Why should they be? A critic's duty is to tell the public what a work is, not tell its author what he should and could have written instead. Yet this is the only kind of criticism from which an author can benefit. Those who could do it for him are generally, like himself, too elsewhere, too busy, too married, too selfish.

We must assume that our apprentice does succeed in becoming a poet, that, sooner or later, a day arrives when his Censor is able to say truthfully and for the first time: "All the words are right, and all are yours."

His thrill at hearing this does not last long, however, for a moment later comes the thought: "Will it ever happen again?" Whatever his future life as a wage-earner, a citizen, a family man may be, to the end of his days his life as a poet will be without anticipation. He will never be able to say: "Tomorrow I will write a poem and, thanks to my training and experience, I already know I shall do a good job." In the eyes of others a man is a poet if he has written one good poem. In his own he is only a poet at the moment when he is making his last revision to a new poem. The moment, before, he was still only a potential poet; the moment after, he is a man who has ceased to write poetry, perhaps forever.

II

It is hardly surprising, then, if a young poet seldom does well in his examinations. If he does, then, either he is also a scholar in the making, or he is a very good boy indeed. A medical student knows that he must study anatomy in order to become a doctor, so he has a reason for study. A future scholar has a reason, because he knows more or less what he wants to know. But there is nothing a would-be poet knows he has to know. He is at the mercy of the immediate moment because he has no concrete reason for not yielding to its demands and, for all he knows now, surrendering to his immediate desire may turn out later to have been the best thing he could have done. His immediate desire can even be to attend a lecture. I remember one I attended, delivered by Professor Tolkien. I do not remember a single word he said but at a certain point he recited, and magnificently, a long passage of *Beowulf*. I was spellbound. This poetry, I knew, was going to be my dish. I became willing, therefore, to work at Anglo-Saxon because, unless I did, I should never be able to read this poetry. I learned enough to read it, however sloppily, and Anglo-Saxon and Middle English poetry have been one of my strongest, most lasting influences.

But this was something which neither I nor anybody else could have foreseen. Again, what good angel lured me into Blackwell's one afternoon and, from such a wilderness of volumes, picked out for me the essays of W. P. Ker? No other critic whom I have subsequently read could have granted me the same vision of a kind of literary All Souls Night in which the dead, the living and the unborn writers of every age and in every tongue were seen as engaged upon a common, noble and civilizing task. No other could have so instantaneously aroused in me a fascination with prosody, which I have never lost.

You must not imagine, however, that being a bad boy is all fun. During my three years as an undergraduate, I had a high old time, I made some lifelong friends and I was more unhappy than I have ever been before or since. I might or might not be wasting my time—only the future would show—I was certainly wasting my parents' money. Nor must you think that, because he fails to study, a young poet looks down his nose at all the scholarly investigations going on around him. Unless he is very young indeed, he knows that these lines by Yeats are rather silly.

> Bald heads forgetful of their sins,
> Old, learned, respectable bald heads
> Edit and annotate the lines
> That young men, tossing on their beds,
> Rhymed out in their despair
> To flatter beauty's ignorant ear.
>
> All shuffle there; all cough in ink;
> All wear the carpet with their shoes;
> All think what other people think;
> All know the man their neighbour knows.

Lord, what would they say
Did their Catullus walk that way?

Ignoring the obvious libel—that all dons are bald and respectable—the sentiments are still nonsense. Edit indeed; Thank God they do. If it had not been for scholars working themselves blind copying and collating manuscripts, how many poems would be unavailable, including those of Catullus, and how many others full of lines that made no sense? Nor has the invention of printing made editors unnecessary. Lucky the poet whose collected works are not full of misprints. Even a young poet knows or very soon will realize that, but for scholars, he would be at the mercy of the literary taste of a past generation, since, once a book has gone out of print and been forgotten, only the scholar with his unselfish courage to read the unreadable will retrieve the rare prize. How much Donne, even, would he have read, had it not been for Professor Grierson? What would he know of Clare or Barnes or Christopher Smart but for Messrs. Blunden, Grigson, Forcestead and Bond? Nor is editing all that scholars have already done for him. There is that blessed combination of poet and scholar, the translator. How, for example, without the learning and talent of Sir Arthur Waley, could he have discovered, and without the slightest effort on his part, an entirely new world of poetry, that of the Chinese?

No, what prevents the young poet from academic study is not conceited ingratitude but a Law of mental growth. Except in matters of life and death, temporal or spiritual, questions must not be answered until they have been asked, and at present he has no questions. At present he makes little distinction between a book, a country walk and a kiss. All are equally experiences to store away in his memory. Could he look into a memory, the literary historian would find many members of that species which he calls books, but they are curiously changed from the books he finds in his library. The dates are all different. *In Memoriam* is written before *The Dunciad,* the thirteenth century comes after the sixteenth. He always thought Robert Burton wrote a big book about melancholy.

Apparently he only wrote ten pages. He is accustomed to the notion that a book can only be written once. Here some are continually rewritten. In his library books are related to each other in an orderly way by genre or subject. Here the commonest principle of association seems to be by age groups. *Piers Ploughman III* is going about with Kierkegaard's *Journals, Piers Ploughman IV* with *The Making of the English Landscape.* Most puzzling of all, instead of only associating with members of their own kind, in this extraordinary democracy every species of being knows every other and the closest friend of a book is rarely another book. *Gulliver's Travels* walks arm in arm with a love affair, a canto of *Il Paradiso* sits with a singularly good dinner, *War and Peace* never leaves the side of a penniless Christmas in a foreign city, the tenth *The Winter's Tale* exchanges greetings with the first complete recording of *La Favorita.*

Yet this is the world out of which poems are made. In a better and more sensible poem than "The Scholars" Yeats describes it as a "rag and bone shop." Let me use the less drab but no less anarchic image of a Mad Hatter's Tea-Party.

In so reading to stock his memory with images upon which later he may be able to draw in his own work, there is no critical principle by which a poet can select his books. The critical judgment "This book is good or bad" implies good or bad at all times, but in relation to a reader's future a book is good now if its future effect is good, and, since the future is unknown, no judgment can be made. The safest guide, therefore, is the naïve uncritical principle of personal liking. A person at least knows one thing about his future, that however different it may be from his present, it will be his. However he may have changed he will still be himself, not somebody else. What he likes now, therefore, whether an impersonal judgment approve or disapprove, has the best chance of becoming useful to him later.

A poet is all the more willing to be guided by personal liking because he assumes, I think with reason, that, since he wants to write poetry himself, his taste may be limited but it will not be so bad as to lead him astray. The chances are that most of the books he likes are such as a critic would approve of. Should it come to a quarrel between liking and approving, however, I think he will always take the side of liking, and he enjoys baiting the critic with teasers like the problem of the comically bad poem.

> Go, Mary, to the summer house
> And sweep the wooden floor,
> And light the little fire, and wash
> The pretty varnished door;
> For there the London gentleman,
> Who lately lectured here,
> Will smoke a pipe with Jonathan,
> And taste our home-brewed beer.
>
> Go bind the dahlias, that our guest
> May praise their fading dyes;
> But strip of every fading bloom
> The flower that won the prize!
> And take thy father's knife, and prune
> The roses that remain,
> And let the fallen hollyhock
> Peep through the broken pane.
>
> I'll follow in an hour or two;
> Be sure I will not fail
> To bring his flute and spying glass,
> The pipes and bottled ale;
> And that grand music that he made
> About the child in bliss,
> Our guest shall hear it sung and played,
> And feel how grand it is!*

Had this poem appeared last week under the title "Mr. Ebenezer Elliott Entertains a Metropolitan Visitor" and been

* Ebenezer Elliott, quoted by Aldous Huxley in *Texts and Pretexts.*

signed by Mr. John Betjeman, would it be good? Since it was not written by Mr. Betjeman as a comic dramatic monologue but by Mr. Elliott himself as a serious lyric, is it bad? What difference do the inverted commas make?

In judging a work of the past, the question of the historical critic—"What was the author of this work trying to do? How far did he succeed in doing it?"—important as he knows it to be, will always interest a poet less than the question—"What does this work suggest to living writers now? Will it help or hinder them in what they are trying to do?"

A few years ago I came across the following lines:

> Wherewith Love to the harts forest he fleeth
> Leaving the enterprise with pain and cry,
> And there him hideth and not appeareth.
> What may I do? When my master feareth,
> But in the field with him to live and die,
> For good is the life ending faithfully.

I found the rhythm of these lines strangely beautiful, they haunted me and I know that they have had an influence upon the rhythm of certain lines of my own.

Of course I know that all the historical evidence suggests that Wyatt was trying to write regular iambics, that the rhythm he was after would have his lines run thus:

> And there him hideth and not appeareth
> What may I do? When my master feareth
> But in the field with him to live and die
> For good is the life ending faithfully.

Since they cannot be read this way without sounding monstrous, one must say that Wyatt failed to do what he was trying to do, and a literary historian of the sixteenth century will have to censure him.

Luckily I am spared this duty and can without reservation approve. Between Wyatt and the present day lie four hundred years of prosodic practice and development. Thanks to the work of our predecessors any schoolboy can today write the regular iambics which Wyatt, struggling to escape from the metrical anarchy of the fifteenth and early sixteenth centuries, found so difficult. Our problem in the twentieth century is not how to write iambics but how not to write in them from automatic habit when they are not to our genuine purpose. What for Wyatt was a failure is for us a blessing. Must a work be censored for being beautiful by accident? I suppose it must, but a poet will always have a sneaking regard for luck because he knows the role which it plays in poetic composition. Something unexpected is always turning up, and though he knows that the Censor has to pass it, the memory of the lucky dip is what he treasures.

A young poet may be conceited about his good taste, but he is under no illusions about his ignorance. He is well aware of how much poetry there is that he would like but of which he has never heard, and that there are learned men who have read it. His problem is knowing which learned man to ask, for it is not just more good poetry that he wants to read, but more of the kind he likes. He judges a scholarly or critical book less by the text than by the quotations, and all his life, I think, when he reads a work of criticism, he will find himself trying to guess what taste lies behind the critic's judgment. Like Matthew Arnold I have my Touchstones, but they are for testing critics, not poets. Many of them concern taste in other matters than poetry or even literature, but here are four questions which, could I examine a critic, I should ask him:

"Do you like, and by like I really mean like, not approve of on principle:

1) Long lists of proper names such as the Old Testament genealogies or the Catalogue of ships in the *Iliad*?
2) Riddles and all other ways of not calling a spade a spade?
3) Complicated verse forms of great technical difficulty, such as Englyns, Drott-Kvaetts, Sestinas, even if their content is trivial?

4) Conscious theatrical exaggeration, pieces of Baroque flattery like Dryden's welcome to the Duchess of Ormond?"

If a critic could truthfully answer "yes" to all four, then I should trust his judgment implicitly on all literary matters.

III

It is not uncommon, it is even usual, for a poet to write reviews, compile anthologies, compose critical introductions. It is one of his main sources of income. He may even find himself lecturing. In such chores he has little to offset his lack of scholarship, but that little he has.

His lazy habit of only reading what he likes will at least have taught him one lesson, that to be worth attacking a book must be worth reading. The greatest critical study of a single figure that I know of, *The Case of Wagner,* is a model of what such an attack should be. Savage as he often is, Nietzsche never allows the reader to forget for one instant that Wagner is an extraordinary genius and that, for all which may be wrong with it, his music is of the highest importance. Indeed it was this book which first taught me to listen to Wagner, about whom I had previously held silly preconceived notions. Another model is D. H. Lawrence's *Studies in Classic American Literature*. I remember my disappointment, when, after reading the essay on Fenimore Cooper which is highly critical, I hurried off to read him. Unfortunately, I did not find Cooper nearly as exciting as Lawrence had made him sound.

The second advantage which a poet possesses is that such satisfactions to the ego as the writing of poetry can provide have been taken care of in his case. I should not expect a poet turned critic to become either a prig, a critic's critic, a romantic novelist or a maniac. By the prig, I mean the critic for whom no actual poem is good enough since the only one that would be is the poem he would like to write himself but cannot. Reading his criticism, one gets the impression that he would rather a poem were bad than good. His twin, the critic's critic, shows no obvious resentment; indeed, on the surface he appears to idolize the poet about whom he is writing; but his critical analysis of his idol's work is so much more complicated and difficult than the work itself as to deprive someone who has not yet read it of all wish to do so. He, too, one suspects, has a secret grievance. He finds it unfortunate and regrettable that before there can be criticism there has to be a poem to criticize. For him a poem is not a work of art by somebody else; it is his own discovered document.

The romantic novelist is a much jollier figure. His happy hunting ground is the field of unanswerable questions, particularly if they concern the private lives of authors. Since the questions to which he devotes his life—he is often an extremely learned gentleman—can never be answered, he is free to indulge his fancies without misgivings. And why shouldn't he? How much duller the Variorum edition of the Shakespeare sonnets would be without him. Jolliest of all is the maniac. The commonest of his kind is the man who believes that poetry is written in cyphers—but there are many other kinds. My favorite is the John Bellendon Ker who set out to prove that English nursery rhymes were originally written in a form of Old Dutch invented by himself.

Whatever his defects, a poet at least thinks a poem more important than anything which can be said about it, he would rather it were good than bad, the last thing he wants is that it should be like one of his own, and his experience as a maker should have taught him to recognize quickly whether a critical question is important, unimportant but real, unreal because unanswerable or just absurd.

He will know, for example, that knowledge of an artist's life, temperament and opinions is unimportant to an understanding of his art, but that a similar knowledge about a critic may be important to an understanding of his judgments. If we knew every detail of Shakespeare's life, our reading of his plays would be little changed, if at all; but how much less interesting *The Lives of the Poets* would be if we knew nothing else about Johnson.

He will know, to take an instance of an unanswerable question, that if the date of the Shakespeare sonnets can ever be fixed, it will not be fixed by poring over Sonnet CVII. His experience as a maker of poems will make him reason something like this: "The feeling expressed here is the not uncommon feeling—All's well with my love and all's well with the world at large. The feeling that all is well with the world at large can be produced in many ways. It *can* be produced by an occasion of public rejoicing, some historical event like the defeat of the Armada or the successful passing of the Queen's climacteric, but it does not have to be. The same feeling can be aroused by a fine day. The figures employed in the lines

> The mortal moon hath her eclipse endured
> And the sad augurs mock their own presage,
> Incertainties now crown themselves assured
> And peace proclaims olives of endless age

come from literature and contain no specific historical reference. They could have been suggested to Shakespeare by some historical event, but he could have written them without one. Further, even if they were so prompted, the date of the event does not have to be contemporary with the occasion celebrated in the sonnet. A present instance of a feeling always recalls past instances and their circumstances, so that it is possible, if the poet chooses, to employ images suggested by the circumstances of a past occasion to describe the present if the feeling is the same. What Shakespeare has written contains no historical clue."

Because of his limited knowledge, a poet would generally be wise, when talking about poetry, to choose either some general subject upon which if his conclusions are true in a few cases, they must be true in most, or some detailed matter which only requires the intensive study of a few works. He may have something sensible to say about woods, even about leaves, but you should never trust him on trees.

Speaking for myself, the questions which interest me most when reading a poem are two. The first is technical: "Here is a verbal contraption. How does it work?" The second is, in the broadest sense, moral: "What kind of a guy inhabits this poem? What is his notion of the good life or the good place? His notion of the Evil One? What does he conceal from the reader? What does he conceal even from himself?"

And you must not be surprised if he should have nothing but platitudes to say; firstly because he will always find it hard to believe that a poem needs expounding, and secondly because he doesn't consider poetry quite that important: any poet, I believe, will echo Miss Marianne Moore's words: *"I, too, dislike it."*

IV

Away back we left a young poet who had just written his first real poem and was wondering if it would be his last. We must assume that it was not, that he has arrived on the literary scene in the sense that now people pass judgment on his work without having read it. Twenty years have gone by. The table of his Mad Hatter's Tea-Party has gotten much longer and there are thousands of new faces, some charming, some quite horrid. Down at the far end, some of those who used to be so amusing have turned into crashing bores or fallen asleep, a sad change which has often come over later guests after holding forth for a few years. Boredom does not necessarily imply disapproval; I still think Rilke a great poet though I cannot read him any more.

Many of the books which have been most important to him have not been works of poetry or criticism but books which have altered his way of looking at the world and himself, and a lot of these, probably, are what an expert in their field would call "unsound." The expert, no doubt, is right, but it is not for a poet to judge; his duty is to be grateful.

And among the experiences which have influenced his writing, a number may have been experiences of other arts. I know, for example, that through listening to music I have learned much about how to organize a poem, how to obtain variety and contrast through change of tone, tempo and rhythm, though I could not say just how. Man is an analogy-drawing animal; that is his great good fortune. His danger is of treating analogies as identities, of saying, for instance, "Poetry should be as much like music as possible." I suspect that the people who are most likely to say this are the tone-deaf. The more one loves another art, the less likely it is that one will wish to trespass upon its domain.

During these twenty years, one thing has never changed since he wrote his first poem. Every time he writes a new one, the same question occurs to him: "Will it ever happen again," but now he begins to hear his Censor saying: "It must never happen again." Having spent twenty years learning to be himself, he finds that he must now start learning not to be himself. At first he may think this means no more than keeping a sharper look out for obsessive rhythms, tics of expression, privately numinous words, but presently he discovers that the command not to imitate himself can mean something harder than that. It can mean that he should refrain from writing a poem which might turn out to be a good one, and even an admired one. He learns that, if on finishing a poem he is convinced that it is good, the chances are that the poem is a self-imitation. The most hopeful sign that it is not is the feeling of complete uncertainty: "Either this is quite good or it is quite bad, I can't tell." And, of course, it may very well be quite bad. Discovering oneself is a passive process because the self is already there. Time and attention are all that it takes. But changing oneself means changing in one direction rather than another, and towards one goal rather than another. The goal may be unknown but movement is impossible without a hypothesis as to where it lies. It is at this point, therefore, that a poet often begins to take an interest in theories of poetry and even to develop one of his own.

I am always interested in hearing what a poet has to say about the nature of poetry, though I do not take it too seriously. As objective statements his definitions are never accurate, never complete and always one-sided. Not one would stand up under a rigorous analysis. In unkind moments one is almost tempted to think that all they are really saying is: "Read me. Don't read the other fellows." But, taken as critical admonitions addressed by his Censor to the poet himself, there is generally something to be learned from them.

Baudelaire has given us an excellent account of their origin and purpose.

> I pity the poets who are guided solely by instinct; they seem to me incomplete. In the spiritual life of the former there must come a crisis when they would think out their art, discover the obscure laws in consequence of which they have produced, and draw from this study a series of precepts whose divine purpose is infallibility in poetic production.

The evidence, that is to say, upon which the poet bases his conclusions consists of his own experiences in writing and his private judgments upon his own works. Looking back, he sees many occasions on which he took a wrong turning or walked up a blind alley, mistakes which, it seems to him now, he could have avoided, had he been more conscious at the time of the choice he was making. Looking over the poems he has written, he finds that, irrespective of their merits, there are some which he particularly dislikes and some which are his favorites. Of one he may think: "This is full of faults, but it is the kind of poem I ought to write more of"; of another: "This may be all right in itself but it's exactly the sort of thing I must never do again." The principles he formulates, therefore, are intended to guard himself against making unnecessary mistakes and provide him with a guesswork map of the future. They are fallible, of course—like all guesses—the word *infallibility* in Baudelaire's description is typical poet's fib. But there is a difference between a project which may fail and one which must.

In trying to formulate principles, a poet may have another motive which Baudelaire does not mention, a desire to justify his writing poetry at all, and in recent years this motive seems to have grown stronger. The Rimbaud Myth—the tale of a great poet who ceases writing, not because, like Coleridge, he has nothing more to say, but because he chooses to stop

—may not be true, I am pretty sure it is not, but as a myth it haunts the artistic conscience of this century.

Knowing all this, and knowing that you know it, I shall now proceed to make some general statements of my own. I hope they are not nonsense, but I cannot be sure. At least, even as emotive noises, I find them useful to me. The only verifiable facts I can offer in evidence are these.

Some cultures make a social distinction between the sacred and the profane, certain human beings are publicly regarded as numinous, and a clear division is made between certain actions which are regarded as sacred rites of great importance to the well-being of society, and everyday profane behavior. In such cultures, if they are advanced enough to recognize poetry as an art, the poet has a public—even a professional status—and his poetry is either public or esoteric.

There are other cultures, like our own, in which the distinction between the sacred and the profane is not socially recognized. Either the distinction is denied or it is regarded as an individual matter of taste with which society is not and should not be concerned. In such cultures, the poet has an amateur status and his poetry is neither public nor esoteric but intimate. That is to say, he writes neither as a citizen nor as a member of a group of professional adepts, but as a single person to be read by other single persons. Intimate poetry is not necessarily obscure; for someone not in the know, ancient esoteric poetry can be more obscure than the wildest modern. Nor, needless to say, is intimate poetry necessarily inferior to other kinds.

In what follows, the terms Primary and Secondary Imagination are taken, of course, from the thirteenth chapter of *Biographia Literaria*. I have adopted them because, though my description may differ from Coleridge's, I believe we are both trying to describe the same phenomena.

Herewith, then, what I might describe as a literary dogmatic psalm, a kind of private *Quicunque vult*.

The concern of the Primary Imagination, its only concern, is with sacred beings and sacred events. The sacred is that to which it is obliged to respond; the profane is that to which it cannot respond and therefore does not know. The profane is known to other faculties of the mind, but not to the Primary Imagination. A sacred being cannot be anticipated; it must be encountered. On encounter the imagination has no option but to respond. All imaginations do not recognize the same sacred beings or events, but every imagination responds to those it recognizes in the same way. The impression made upon the imagination by any sacred being is of an overwhelming but undefinable importance—an unchangeable quality, an Identity, as Keats said: I-am-that-I-am is what every sacred being seems to say. The impression made by a sacred event is of an overwhelming but undefinable significance. In his book *Witchcraft,* Mr. Charles Williams has described it thus:

> One is aware that a phenomenon, being wholly itself, is laden with universal meaning. A hand lighting a cigarette is the explanation of everything; a foot stepping from the train is the rock of all existence. . . . Two light dancing steps by a girl appear to be what all the Schoolmen were trying to express . . . but two quiet steps by an old man seem like the very speech of hell. Or the other way round.

The response of the imagination to such a presence or significance is a passion of awe. This awe may vary greatly in intensity and range in tone from joyous wonder to panic dread. A sacred being may be attractive or repulsive—a swan or an octopus—beautiful or ugly—a toothless hag or a fair young child—good or evil—a Beatrice or a Belle Dame Sans Merci—historical fact or fiction—a person met on the road or an image encountered in a story or a dream—it may be noble or something unmentionable in a drawing room, it may be anything it likes on condition, but this condition is absolute, that it arouse awe. The realm of the Primary Imagination is without freedom, sense of time or humor. Whatever determines this response or lack of response lies below consciousness and is of concern to psychology, not art.

Some sacred beings seem to be sacred to all imaginations

at all times. The Moon, for example, Fire, Snakes and those four important beings which can only be defined in terms of nonbeing: Darkness, Silence, Nothing, Death. Some, like kings, are only sacred to all within a certain culture; some only to members of a social group—the Latin language among humanists—and some are only sacred to a single imagination. Many of us have sacred landscapes which probably all have much in common, but there will almost certainly be details which are peculiar to each. An imagination can acquire new sacred beings and it can lose old ones to the profane. Sacred beings can be acquired by social contagion but not consciously. One cannot be taught to recognize a sacred being, one has to be converted. As a rule, perhaps, with advancing age sacred events gain in importance over sacred beings.

A sacred being may also be an object of desire but the imagination does not desire it. A desire can be a sacred being but the imagination is without desire. In the presence of the sacred, it is self-forgetful; in its absence the very type of the profane, "The most unpoetical of all God's creatures." A sacred being may also demand to be loved or obeyed, it may reward or punish, but the imagination is unconcerned: a law can be a sacred being, but the imagination does not obey. To the imagination a sacred being is self-sufficient, and like Aristotle's God can have no need of friends.

The Secondary Imagination is of another character and at another mental level. It is active not passive, and its categories are not the sacred and the profane, but the beautiful and ugly. Our dreams are full of sacred beings and events—indeed, they may well contain nothing else, but we cannot distinguish in dreams—or so it seems to me, though I may be wrong—between the beautiful and the ugly. Beauty and ugliness pertain to Form not to Being. The Primary Imagination only recognizes one kind of being, the sacred, but the Secondary Imagination recognizes both beautiful and ugly forms. To the Primary Imagination a sacred being is that which it is. To the Secondary Imagination a beautiful form is as it ought to be, an ugly form as it ought not to be. Observing the beautiful, it has the feeling of satisfaction, pleasure, absence of conflict; observing the ugly, the contrary feelings. It does not desire the beautiful, but an ugly form arouses in it a desire that its ugliness be corrected and made beautiful. It does not worship the beautiful; it approves of it and can give reasons for its approval. The Secondary Imagination has, one might say, a bourgeois nature. It approves of regularity, of spatial symmetry and temporal repetition, of law and order: it disapproves of loose ends, irrelevance and mess.

Lastly, the Secondary Imagination is social and craves agreement with other minds. If I think a form beautiful and you think it ugly, we cannot both help agreeing that one of us must be wrong, whereas if I think something is sacred and you think it is profane, neither of us will dream of arguing the matter.

Both kinds of imagination are essential to the health of the mind. Without the inspiration of sacred awe, its beautiful forms would soon become banal, its rhythms mechanical; without the activity of the Secondary Imagination the passivity of the Primary would be the mind's undoing; sooner or later its sacred beings would possess it, it would come to think of itself as sacred, exclude the outer world as profane and so go mad.

The impulse to create a work of art is felt when, in certain persons, the passive awe provoked by sacred beings or events is transformed into a desire to express that awe in a rite of worship or homage, and to be fit homage, this rite must be beautiful. This rite has no magical or idolatrous intention; nothing is expected in return. Nor is it, in a Christian sense, an act of devotion. If it praises the Creator, it does so indirectly by praising His creatures—among which may be human notions of the Divine Nature. With God as Redeemer, it has, so far as I can see, little if anything to do.

In poetry the rite is verbal; it pays homage by naming. I suspect that the predisposition of a mind towards the poetic medium may have its origin in an error. A nurse, let us suppose, says to a child, "Look at the moon!" The child looks and for him this is a sacred encounter. In his mind the word "moon" is not a name of a sacred object but one of its most important properties and, therefore, numinous. The notion of writing poetry cannot occur to him, of course, until he has realized that names and things are not identical and that there cannot be an intelligible sacred language, but I wonder if, when he has discovered the social nature of language, he would attach such importance to one of its uses, that of naming, if he had not previously made this false identification.

The pure poem, in the French sense of *la poésie pure* would be, I suppose, a celebration of the numinous-in-itself in abstraction from all cases and devoid of any profane reference whatsoever—a sort of *sanctus, sanctus, sanctus.* If it could be written, which is doubtful, it would not necessarily be the best poem.

A poem is a rite; hence its formal and ritualistic character. Its use of language is deliberately and ostentatiously different from talk. Even when it employs the diction and rhythms of conversation, it employs them as a deliberate informality, presupposing the norm with which they are intended to contrast.

The form of a rite must be beautiful, exhibiting, for example, balance, closure and aptness to that which it is the form of. It is over this last quality of aptness that most of our aesthetic quarrels arise, and must arise, whenever our sacred and profane worlds differ.

> To the Eyes of a Miser, a Guinea is far more beautiful than the Sun & a bag worn with the use of Money has more beautiful proportions than a Vine filled with Grapes.

Blake, it will be noticed, does not accuse the Miser of lacking imagination.

The value of a profane thing lies in what it usefully does, the value of a sacred thing lies in what it *is:* a sacred thing may also have a function but it does not have to. The apt name for a profane being, therefore, is the word or words that accurately describe his function—a Mr. Smith, a Mr. Weaver. The apt name for a sacred being is the word or words which worthily express his importance—Son of Thunder, The Well-Wishing One.

Great changes in artistic style always reflect some alteration in the frontier between the sacred and profane in the imagination of a society. Thus, to take an architectural example, a seventeenth-century monarch had the same function as that of a modern State official—he had to govern. But in designing his palace, the Baroque architect did not aim, as a modern architect aims when designing a government building, at making an office in which the king could govern as easily and efficiently as possible; he was trying to make a home fit for God's earthly representative to inhabit; in so far as he thought at all about what the king would do in it as a ruler, he thought of his ceremonial not his practical actions.

Even today few people find a functionally furnished living room beautiful because, to most of us, a sitting room is not merely a place to sit in; it is also a shrine for father's chair.

Thanks to the social nature of language, a poet can relate any one sacred being or event to any other. The relation may be harmonious, an ironic contrast or a tragic contradiction like the great man, or the beloved, and death; he can relate them to every other concern of the mind, the demands of desire, reason and conscience, and he can bring them into contact and contrast with the profane. Again the consequences can be happy, ironic, tragic and, in relation to the profane, comic. How many poems have been written, for example, upon one of these three themes:

> This was sacred but now it is profane. Alas, or thank goodness!
> This is sacred but ought it to be?
> This is sacred but is that so important?

But it is from the sacred encounters of his imagination that a poet's impulse to write a poem arises. Thanks to the language, he need not name them directly unless he wishes; he can describe one in terms of another and translate those that are private or irrational or socially unacceptable into such as are acceptable to reason and society. Some poems are directly *about* the sacred beings they were written *for*: others are not, and in that case no reader can tell what was the original encounter which provided the impulse for the poem. Nor, probably, can the poet himself. Every poem he writes involves his whole past. Every love poem, for instance, is hung with trophies of lovers gone, and among these may be some very peculiar objects indeed. The lovely lady of the present may number among her predecessors an overshot waterwheel. But the encounter, be it novel or renewed by recollection from the past, must be suffered by a poet before he can write a genuine poem.

Whatever its actual content and overt interest, every poem is rooted in imaginative awe. Poetry can do a hundred and one things, delight, sadden, disturb, amuse, instruct—it may express every possible shade of emotion, and describe every conceivable kind of event, but there is only one thing that all poetry must do; it must praise all it can for being and for happening.

THE VIRGIN & THE DYNAMO

There is a square. There is an oblong. The players take the square and place it upon the oblong. They place it very accurately. They make a perfect dwelling-place. The structure is now visible. What was inchoate is here stated. We are not so various or so mean. We have made oblongs and stood them upon squares. This is our triumph. This is our consolation.

VIRGINIA WOOLF

The Two Real Worlds

1) The Natural World of the Dynamo, the world of masses, identical relations and recurrent events, describable, not in words but in terms of numbers, or rather, in algebraic terms. In this world, Freedom is the consciousness of Necessity and Justice the equality of all before natural law. (*Hard cases make bad law.*)

2) The Historical World of the Virgin, the world of faces, analogical relations and singular events, describable only in terms of speech. In this World, Necessity is the consciousness of Freedom and Justice the love of my

neighbor as a unique and irreplaceable being. (*One law for the ox and the ass is oppression.*)

Since all human experience is that of conscious persons, man's realization that the World of the Dynamo exists in which events happen of themselves and cannot be prevented by anybody's art, came later than his realization that the World of the Virgin exists. Freedom is an immediate datum of consciousness; Necessity is not.

The Two Chimerical Worlds

1) The magical polytheistic nature created by the aesthetic illusion which would regard the world of masses as if it were a world of faces. The aesthetic religion says prayers to the Dynamo.

2) The mechanized history created by the scientific illusion which would regard the world of faces as if it were a world of masses. The scientific religion treats the Virgin as a statistic. "Scientific" politics is animism stood on its head.

Without Art, we could have no notion of Liberty; without Science no notion of Equality; without either, therefore, no notion of Justice.

Without Art, we should have no notion of the sacred; without Science, we should always worship false gods.

By nature we tend to endow with a face any power which we imagine to be responsible for our lives and behavior; vice versa, we tend to deprive of their faces any persons whom we believe to be at the mercy of our will. In both cases, we are trying to avoid responsibility. In the first case, we wish to say: "I can't help doing what I do; someone else, stronger than I, is making me do it"—in the second: "I can do what I like to N because N is a thing, an x with no will of its own."

The pagan gods of nature do not have real faces but rather masks, for a real face expresses a responsibility for itself, and the pagan gods are, by definition, irresponsible. It is permissible, and even right, to endow Nature with a real face, e.g., the face of the Madonna, for by so doing we make nature remind us of our duty towards her, but we may only do this after we have removed the pagan mask from her, seen her as a world of masses and realized that she is not responsible for us.

Vice versa, the saint can employ the algebraic notion of *any* in his relation to others as an expression of the fact that his neighbor is not someone of whom he is personally fond, but anybody who happens to need him; but he can only do this because he has advanced spiritually to the point where he sees nobody as a faceless cypher.

Henry Adams thought that Venus and the Virgin of Chartres were the same persons. Actually, Venus is the Dynamo in disguise, a symbol for an impersonal natural force, and Adam's nostalgic preference for Chartres to Chicago was nothing but aestheticism; he thought the disguise was prettier than the reality, but it was the Dynamo he worshiped, not the Virgin.

Pluralities

Any world is comprised of a plurality of objects and events. Pluralities are of three kinds; crowds, societies and communities.

1) *A Crowd*

A crowd is comprised of $n > 1$ members whose only relation is arithmetical, they can only be counted. A crowd loves neither itself nor anything other than itself; its existence is chimerical. Of a crowd it may be said, either that it is not real but only apparent, or that it should not be.

2) *A Society*

A society is comprised of a definite or an optimum number of members, united in a specific manner into a whole with a characteristic mode of behavior which is different from the modes of behavior of its component members in isolation. A society cannot come into being until its component members are present and properly related; add or subtract a member, change their relations, and the society either ceases to exist or is transformed into another society. A society is a system which loves itself; to this self-love, the self-love of its members is totally subordinate. Of a society it may be said that it is more or less efficient in maintaining its existence.

3) *A Community*

A community is comprised of n members united, to use a definition of Saint Augustine's, by a common love of something other than themselves. Like a crowd and unlike a society, its character is not changed by the addition or subtraction of a member. It exists, neither by chance, like a crowd, nor actually, like a society, but potentially, so that it is possible to conceive of a community in which, at present, $n=1$. In a community all members are free and equal. If, out of a group of ten persons, nine prefer beef to mutton and one prefers mutton to beef, there is not a single community containing a dissident member; there are two communities, a large one and a small one. To achieve an actual existence, it has to embody itself in a society or societies which can express the love which is its *raison d'être*. A community of music lovers, for example, cannot just sit around loving music like anything, but must form itself into societies like choirs, orchestras, string quartets, etc., and make music. Such an embodiment of a community in a society is an order. Of a community it may be said that its love is more or less good. Such a love presupposes choice, so that, in the natural world of the Dynamo, communities do not exist, only societies which are submembers of the total system of nature, enjoying their self-occurrence. Communities can only exist in the historical world of the Virgin, but they do not necessarily exist there.

Whenever rival communities compete for embodiment in the same society, there is either unfreedom or disorder. In the chimerical case of a society embodying a crowd, there would be a state of total unfreedom and disorder; the traditional term for this chimerical state is Hell. A perfect order, one in which the community united by the best love is embodied in the most self-sustaining society, could be described, as science describes nature, in terms of laws-of, but the description would be irrelevant, the relevant description being, "Here, love is the fulfilling of the law" or "In His Will is our peace"; the traditional term for this ideal order is Paradise. In historical existence where no love is perfect, no society immortal, and no embodiment of the one in the other precise, the obligation to approximate to the ideal is felt as an imperative "Thou shalt."

Man exists as a unity-in-tension of four modes of being: soul, body, mind and spirit.

As soul and body, he is an individual, as mind and spirit a member of a society. Were he only soul and body, his only relation to others would be numerical and a poem would be comprehensible only to its author; were he only mind and spirit, men would only exist collectively as the system Man, and there would be nothing for a poem to be about.

As body and mind, man is a natural creature, as soul and spirit, a historical person. Were he only body and mind, his existence would be one of everlasting recurrence, and only one good poem could exist; were he only soul and spirit, his existence would be one of perpetual novelty, and every new poem would supersede all previous poems, or rather a poem would be superseded before it could be written.

Man's consciousness is a unity-in-tension of three modes of awareness:

1) A consciousness of the self as self-contained, as embracing all that it is aware of in a unity of experiencing. This mode is undogmatic, amoral and passive; its good is the enjoyment of being, its evil the fear of nonbeing.
2) A consciousness of beyondness, of an ego standing as a spectator over against both a self and the external world. This mode is dogmatic, amoral, objective. Its good is the perception of true relations, its evil the fear of accidental or false relations.
3) The ego's consciousness of itself as striving-towards,

as desiring to transform the self, to realize its potentialities. This mode is moral and active; its good is not present but propounded, its evil, the present actuality.

Were the first mode absolute, man would inhabit a magical world in which the image of an object, the emotion it aroused and the word signifying it were all identical, a world where past and future, the living and the dead were united. Language in such a world would consist only of proper names which would not be words in the ordinary sense but sacred syllables, and, in the place of the poet, there would be the magician whose task is to discover and utter the truly potent spell which can compel what-is-not to be.

Were the second mode absolute, man would inhabit a world which was a pure system of universals. Language would be an algebra, and there could exist only one poem, of absolute banality, expressing the system.

Were the third mode absolute, man would inhabit a purely arbitrary world, the world of the clown and the actor. In language there would be no relation between word and thing, *love* would rhyme with *indifference,* and all poetry would be nonsense poetry.

Thanks to the first mode of consciousness, every good poem is unique; thanks to the second, a poet can embody his private experiences in a public poem which can be comprehended by others in terms of their private experiences; thanks to the third, both poet and reader desire that this be done.

The subject matter of the scientist is a crowd of natural events at all times; he presupposes that this crowd is not real but apparent, and seeks to discover the true place of events in the system of nature. The subject matter of the poet is a crowd of historical occasions of feeling recollected from the past; he presupposes that this crowd is real but should not be, and seeks to transform it into a community. Both science and art are primarily spiritual activities, whatever practical applications may be derived from their results. Disorder, lack of meaning, are spiritual not physical discomforts, order and sense spiritual not physical satisfactions.

It is impossible, I believe, for any poet, while he is writing a poem, to observe with complete accuracy what is going on, to define with any certainty how much of the final result is due to subconscious activity over which he has no control, and how much is due to conscious artifice. All one can say with certainty is negative. A poem does not compose itself in the poet's mind as a child grows in its mother's womb; *some* degree of conscious participation by the poet is necessary, *some* element of craft is always present. On the other hand, the writing of poetry is not, like carpentry, simply a craft; a carpenter can decide to build a table according to certain specifications and know before he begins that the result will be exactly what he intended, but no poet can know what his poem is going to be like until he has written it. The element of craftsmanship in poetry is obscured by the fact that all men are taught to speak and most to read and write, while very few men are taught to draw or paint or write music. Every poet, however, in addition to the everyday linguistic training he receives, requires a training in the poetic use of language. Even those poets who are most vehemently insistent upon the importance of the Muse and the vanity of conscious calculation must admit that, if they had never read any poetry in their lives, it is unlikely that they would have written any themselves. If, in what follows, I refer to the poet, I include under that both his Muse and his mind, his subconscious and conscious activity.

The subject matter of a poem is comprised of a crowd of recollected occasions of feeling, among which the most important are recollections of encounters with sacred beings or events. This crowd the poet attempts to transform into a community by embodying it in a verbal society. Such a society, like any society in nature, has its own laws; its laws of prosody and syntax are analogous to the laws of physics and chemistry. Every poem must presuppose—sometimes mistakenly—that the history of the language is at an end.

One should say, rather, that a poem is a natural organism, not an inorganic thing. For example, it is rhythmical. The temporal recurrences of rhythm are never identical, as the metrical notation would seem to suggest. Rhythm is to time what symmetry is to space. Seen from a certain distance, the features of a human face seem symmetrically arranged, so that a face with a nose a foot long or a left eye situated two inches away from the nose would appear monstrous. Close up, however, the exact symmetry disappears; the size and position of the features vary slightly from face to face and, indeed, if a face could exist in which the symmetry were mathematically perfect, it would look, not like a face, but like a lifeless mask. So with rhythm. A poem may be described as being written in iambic pentameters, but if every foot in every line were identical, the poem would sound intolerable to the ear. I am sometimes inclined to think that the aversion of many modern poets and their readers to formal verse may be due to their association of regular repetition and formal restrictions with all that is most boring and lifeless in modern life, road drills, time-clock punching, bureaucratic regulations.

It has been said that a poem should not mean but be. This is not quite accurate. In a poem, as distinct from many other kinds of verbal societies, meaning and being are identical. A poem might be called a pseudo-person. Like a person, it is unique and addresses the reader personally. On the other hand, like a natural being and unlike a historical person, it cannot lie. We may be and frequently are mistaken as to the meaning or the value of a poem, but the cause of our mistake lies in our own ignorance or self-deception, not in the poem itself.

The nature of the final poetic order is the outcome of a dialectical struggle between the recollected occasions of feeling and the verbal system. As a society the verbal system is actively coercive upon the occasions it is attempting to embody; what it cannot embody truthfully it excludes. As a potential community the occasions are passively resistant to all claims of the system to embody them which they do not recognize as just; they decline all unjust persuasions. As members of crowds, every occasion competes with every other, demanding inclusion and a dominant position to which they are not necessarily entitled, and every word demands that the system shall modify itself in its case, that a special exception shall be made for it and it only.

In a successful poem, society and community are one order and the system may love itself because the feelings which it embodies are all members of the same community, loving each other and it. A poem may fail in two ways; it may exclude too much (banality), or attempt to embody more than one community at once (disorder).

In writing a poem, the poet can work in two ways. Starting from an intuitive idea of the kind of community he desires to call into being, he may work backwards in search of the system which will most justly incarnate that idea, or, starting with a certain system, he may work forward in search of the community which it is capable of incarnating most truthfully. In practice he nearly always works simultaneously in both directions, modifying his conception of the ultimate nature of the community at the immediate suggestions of the system, and modifying the system in response to his growing intuition of the future needs of the community.

A system cannot be selected completely arbitrarily nor can one say that any given system is absolutely necessary. The poet searches for one which imposes just obligations on the feelings. "Ought" always implies "can" so that a system whose claims cannot be met must be scrapped. But the poet has to beware of accusing the system of injustice when what is at fault is the laxness and self-love of the feelings upon which it is making its demands.

Every poet, consciously or unconsciously, holds the following absolute presuppositions, as the dogmas of his art:

1) A historical world exists, a world of unique events and unique persons, related by analogy, not identity. The number of events and analogical relations is potentially infinite. The existence of such a world is a good, and every addition to the number of events, persons and relations is an additional good.

2) The historical world is a fallen world, i.e., though it is good that it exists, the way in which it exists is evil, being full of unfreedom and disorder.

3) The historical world is a redeemable world. The unfreedom and disorder of the past can be reconciled in the future.

It follows from the first presupposition that the poet's activity in creating a poem is analogous to God's activity in creating man after his own image. It is not an imitation, for were it so, the poet would be able to create like God *ex nihilo*; instead, he requires pre-existing occasions of feeling and a pre-existing language out of which to create. It is analogous in that the poet creates not necessarily according to a law of nature but voluntarily according to provocation.

It is untrue, strictly speaking, to say that a poet should not write poems unless he must; strictly speaking it can only be said that he should not write them unless he can. The phrase is sound in practice, because only in those who can and when they can is the motive genuinely compulsive.

In those who profess a desire to write poetry, yet exhibit an incapacity to do so, it is often the case that their desire is not for creation but for self-perpetuation, that they refuse to accept their own mortality, just as there are parents who desire children, not as new persons analogous to themselves, but to prolong their own existence in time. The sterility of this substitution of identity for analogy is expressed in the myth of Narcissus. When the poet speaks, as he sometimes does, of achieving immortality through his poem, he does not mean that he hopes, like Faust, to live for ever, but that he hopes to rise from the dead. In poetry as in other matters the law holds good that he who would save his life must lose it; unless the poet sacrifices his feelings completely to the poem so that they are no longer his but the poem's, he fails.

It follows from the second presupposition, that a poem is a witness to man's knowledge of evil as well as good. It is not the duty of a witness to pass moral judgment on the evidence he has to give, but to give it clearly and accurately; the only crime of which a witness can be guilty is perjury. When we say that poetry is beyond good and evil, we simply mean that a poet can no more change the facts of what he has felt than, in the natural order, parents can change the inherited physical characteristics which they pass on to their children. The judgment good-or-evil applies only to the intentional movements of the will. Of our feelings in a given situation which are the joint product of our intention and the response to the external factors in that situation it can only be said that, given an intention and the response, they are appropriate or inappropriate. Of a recollected feeling it cannot be said that it is appropriate or inappropriate because the historical situation in which it arose no longer exists.

Every poem, therefore, is an attempt to present an analogy to that paradisal state in which Freedom and Law, System and Order are united in harmony. Every good poem is very nearly a Utopia. Again, an analogy, not an imitation; the harmony is possible and verbal only.

It follows from the third presupposition that a poem is beautiful or ugly to the degree that it succeeds or fails in reconciling contradictory feelings in an order of mutual propriety. Every beautiful poem presents an analogy to the forgiveness of sins; an analogy, not an imitation, because it is not evil intentions which are repented of and pardoned but contradictory feelings which the poet surrenders to the poem in which they are reconciled.

The effect of beauty, therefore, is good to the degree that, through its analogies, the goodness of created existence, the historical fall into unfreedom and disorder, and the possibility of regaining paradise through repentance and forgiveness are recognized. Its effect is evil to the degree that beauty is taken, not as analogous to, but identical with goodness, so that the artist regards himself or is regarded by others as God, the pleasure of beauty taken for the joy of Paradise, and the conclusion drawn that, since all is well in the work of art, all is well in history. But all is not well there.

THE POET & THE CITY

. . . Being everything, let us admit that is to be something,
Or give ourselves the benefit of the doubt . . .

WILLIAM EMPSON

There is little or nothing to be remembered written on the subject of getting an honest living. Neither the New Testament nor Poor Richard speaks to our condition. One would never think, from looking at literature, that this question had ever disturbed a solitary individual's musings.

H. D. THOREAU

It is astonishing how many young people of both sexes, when asked what they want to do in life, give neither a sensible answer like "I want to be a lawyer, an innkeeper, a farmer" nor a romantic answer like "I want to be an explorer, a racing motorist, a missionary, President of the United States." A surprisingly large number say "I want to be a writer," and by writing they mean "creative" writing. Even if they say "I want to be a journalist," this is because they are under the illusion that in that profession they will be able to create; even if their genuine desire is to make money, they will select some highly paid subliterary pursuit like Advertising.

Among these would-be writers, the majority have no marked literary gift. This in itself is not surprising; a marked gift for any occupation is not very common. What is surprising is that such a high percentage of those without any marked talent for any profession should think of writing as the solution. One would have expected that a certain number would imagine that they had a talent for medicine or engineering and so on, but this is not the case. In our age, if a young person is untalented, the odds are in favor of his imagining he wants to write. (There are, no doubt, a lot without any talent for acting who dream of becoming film stars but they have at least been endowed by nature with a fairly attractive face and figure.)

In accepting and defending the social institution of slavery, the Greeks were harder-hearted than we but clearer-headed; they knew that labor as such is slavery, and that no man can feel a personal pride in being a laborer. A man can be proud of being a worker—someone, that is, who fabricates enduring objects, but in our society, the process of fabrication has been so rationalized in the interests of speed, economy and quantity that the part played by the individual factory employee has become too small for it to be meaningful to him as work, and practically all workers have been reduced to laborers. It is only natural, therefore, that the arts which cannot be rationalized in this way—the artist still remains personally responsible for what he makes—should fascinate those who, because they have no marked talent, are afraid, with good reason, that all they have to look forward to is a lifetime of meaningless labor. This fascination is not due to the nature of art itself, but to the way in which an artist works; he, and in our age, almost nobody else, is his own master. The idea of being one's own master appeals to most human beings, and this is apt to lead to the fantastic hope that the capacity for artistic creation is universal, something nearly all human beings, by virtue, not of some special talent, but of their humanity, could do if they tried.

Until quite recently a man was proud of not having to earn his own living and ashamed of being obliged to earn it, but today, would any man dare describe himself when applying for a passport as *Gentleman,* even if, as a matter of fact, he has independent means and no job? Today, the question "What do you do?" means "How do you earn your living?" On my own passport I am described as a "Writer"; this is not embarrassing for me in dealing with the authorities, because immigration and customs officials know that some kinds of writers make lots of money. But if a stranger in the train asks me my occupation, I never answer "writer" for fear that he may go on to ask me what I write, and to answer "poetry" would embarrass us both, for we both know that nobody can earn a living simply by writing poetry. (The most satisfactory answer I have discovered, satisfactory because it withers curiosity, is to say *Medieval Historian.*)

Some writers, even some poets, become famous public figures, but writers as such have no social status, in the way that doctors and lawyers, whether famous or obscure, have.

There are two reason for this. Firstly, the so-called fine arts have lost the social utility they once had. Since the invention of printing and the spread of literacy, verse no longer has a utility value as a mnemonic, a device by which knowledge and culture were handed on from one generation to the next, and, since the invention of the camera, the draughtsman and painter are no longer needed to provide visual documentation; they have, consequently, become "pure" arts, that is to say, gratuitous activities. Secondly, in a society governed by the values appropriate to Labor (capitalist America may well be more completely governed by these than communist Russia) the gratuitous is no longer regarded—most earlier cultures thought differently—as sacred, because, to Man the Laborer, leisure is not sacred but a respite from laboring, a time for relaxation and the pleasures of consumption. In so far as such a society thinks about the gratuitous at all, it is suspicious of it—artists do not labor, therefore, they are probably parasitic idlers—or, at best, regards it as trivial—to write poetry or paint pictures is a harmless private hobby.

In the purely gratuitous arts, poetry, painting, music, our century has no need, I believe, to be ashamed of its achievements, and in its fabrication of purely utile and functional articles like airplanes, dams, surgical instruments, it surpasses any previous age. But whenever it attempts to combine the gratuitous with the utile, to fabricate something which shall be both functional and beautiful, it fails utterly. No previous age has created anything so hideous as the average modern automobile, lampshade or building, whether domestic or public. What could be more terrifying than a modern office building? It seems to be saying to the white-collar slaves who work in it: "For labor in this age, the human body is much more complicated than it need be: you would do better and be happier if it were simplified."

In the affluent countries today, thanks to the high per capita income, small houses and scarcity of domestic servants, there is one art in which we probably excel all other societies that ever existed, the art of cooking. (It is the one art which Man the Laborer regards as sacred.) If the world population continues to increase at its present rate, this cultural glory will be short-lived, and it may well be that future historians will look nostalgically back to the years 1950-1975 as The Golden Age of Cuisine. It is difficult to imagine a *haute cuisine* based on algae and chemically treated grass.

A poet, painter or musician has to accept the divorce in his art between the gratuitous and the utile as a fact for, if he rebels, he is liable to fall into error.

Had Tolstoi, when he wrote *What Is Art?*, been content with the proposition, "When the gratuitious and the utile are divorced from each other, there can be no art," one might have disagreed with him, but he would have been difficult to refute. But he was unwilling to say that, if Shakespeare and himself were not artists, there was no modern art. Instead he tried to persuade himself that utility alone, a spiritual utility maybe, but still utility without gratuity, was sufficient to produce art, and this compelled him to be dishonest and praise works which aesthetically he must have despised. The notion of *l'art engagé* and art as propaganda are extensions of this heresy, and when poets fall into it, the cause, I fear, is less their social conscience than their vanity; they are nostalgic for a past when poets had a public status. The opposite heresy is to endow the gratuitous with a magic utility of its own, so that the poet comes to think of himself as the god who creates his subjective universe out of nothing—to him the visible material universe *is* nothing. Mallarmé, who planned to write the sacred book of a new universal religion, and Rilke with his notion of *Gesang ist Dasein,* are heresiarchs of this type. Both were geniuses but, admire them as one may and must, one's final impression of their work is of something false and unreal. As Erich Heller says of Rilke:

> In the great poetry of the European tradition, the emotions do not interpret; they respond to the interpreted world: in Rilke's mature poetry the emotions do the interpreting and then respond to their own interpretation.

In all societies, educational facilities are limited to those activities and habits of behavior which a particular society considers important. In a culture like that of Wales in the Middle Ages, which regarded poets as socially important, a would-be poet, like a would-be dentist in our own culture, was systematically trained and admitted to the rank of poet only after meeting high professional standards.

In our culture a would-be poet has to educate himself; he may be in the position to go to a first-class school and university, but such places can only contribute to his poetic education by accident, not by design. This has its drawbacks; a good deal of modern poetry, even some of the best, shows just that uncertainty of taste, crankiness and egoism which self-educated people so often exhibit.

A metropolis can be a wonderful place for a mature artist to live in, but, unless his parents are very poor, it is a dangerous place for a would-be artist to grow up in; he is confronted with too much of the best in art too soon. This is like having a liaison with a wise and beautiful woman twenty years older than himself; all too often his fate is that of *Chéri*.

In my daydream College for Bards, the curriculum would be as follows:

1) In addition to English, at least one ancient language, probably Greek or Hebrew, and two modern languages would be required.
2) Thousands of lines of poetry in these languages would be learned by heart.
3) The library would contain no books of literary criticism, and the only critical exercise required of students would be the writing of parodies.
4) Courses in prosody, rhetoric and comparative philology would be required of all students, and every student would have to select three courses out of courses in mathematics, natural history, geology, meteorology, archaeology, mythology, liturgics, cooking.
5) Every student would be required to look after a domestic animal and cultivate a garden plot.

A poet has not only to educate himself as a poet, he has also to consider how he is going to earn his living. Ideally, he should have a job which does not in any way involve the manipulation of words. At one time, children training to become rabbis were also taught some skilled manual trade, and if only they knew their child was going to become a poet, the best thing parents could do would be to get him at an early age into some Craft Trades Union. Unfortunately, they cannot know this in advance, and, except in very rare cases, by the time he is twenty-one, the only nonliterary job for which a poet-to-be is qualified is unskilled manual labor. In earning his living, the average poet has to choose between being a translator, a teacher, a literary journalist or a writer of advertising copy and, of these, all but the first can be directly detrimental to his poetry, and even translation does not free him from leading a too exclusively literary life.

There are four aspects of our present *Weltanschauung* which have made an artistic vocation more difficult than it used to be.

1) *The loss of belief in the eternity of the physical universe.* The possibility of becoming an artist, a maker of things which shall outlast the maker's life, might never have occurred to man, had he not had before his eyes, in contrast to the transitoriness of human life, a universe of things, earth, ocean, sky, sun, moon, stars, etc., which appeared to be everlasting and unchanging.

Physics, geology and biology have now replaced this everlasting universe with a picture of nature as a process in which nothing is now what it was or what it will be. Today, Christian and Atheist alike are eschatologically minded. It is difficult for a modern artist to believe he can make an enduring object when he has no model of endurance to go by; he is more tempted than his predecessors to abandon the search for perfection as a waste of time and be content with sketches and improvisations.

2) *The loss of belief in the significance and reality of sensory phenomena.* This loss has been progressive since Luther, who denied any intelligible relation between subjective Faith and objective Works, and Descartes, with his doctrine of primary and secondary qualities. Hitherto, the traditional conception of the phenomenal world had been one of sacramental analogies; what the senses perceived was an outward and visible sign of the inward and invisible, but both were believed to be real and valuable. Modern science has destroyed our faith in the naïve observation of our senses: we cannot, it tells us, ever know what the physical universe is *really* like; we can only hold whatever subjective notion is appropriate to the particular human purpose we have in view.

This destroys the traditional conception of *art* as *mimesis,* for there is no longer a nature "out there" to be truly or falsely imitated; all an artist can be *true* to are his subjective sensations and feelings. The change in attitude is already to be seen in Blake's remark that some people see the sun as a round golden disc the size of a guinea but that he sees it as a host crying Holy, Holy, Holy. What is significant about this is that Blake, like the Newtonians he hated, accepts a division between the physical and the spiritual, but, in opposition to them, regards the material universe as the abode of Satan, and so attaches no value to what his physical eye sees.

3) *The loss of belief in a norm of human nature which will always require the same kind of man-fabricated world to be at home in.* Until the Industrial Revolution, the way in which men lived changed so slowly that any man, thinking of his great-grandchildren, could imagine them as people living the same kind of life with the same kind of needs and satisfactions as himself. Technology, with its ever-accelerating transformation of man's way of living, has made it impossible for us to imagine what life will be like even twenty years from now.

Further, until recently, men knew and cared little about cultures far removed from their own in time or space; by human nature, they meant the kind of behavior exhibited in their own culture. Anthropology and archaeology have destroyed this provincial notion: we know that human nature is so plastic that it can exhibit varieties of behavior which, in the animal kingdom, could only be exhibited by different species.

The artist, therefore, no longer has any assurance, when he makes something, that even the next generation will find it enjoyable or comprehensible.

He cannot help desiring an immediate success, with all the danger to his integrity which that implies.

Further, the fact that we now have at our disposal the arts of all ages and cultures, has completely changed the meaning of the word tradition. It no longer means a way of working handed down from one generation to the next; a sense of tradition now means a consciousness of the whole of the past as present, yet at the same time as a structured whole the parts of which are related in terms of before and after. Originality no longer means a slight modification in the style of one's immediate predecessors; it means a capacity to find in any work of any date or place a clue to finding one's authentic voice. The burden of choice and selection is put squarely upon the shoulders of each individual poet and it is a heavy one.

4) *The disappearance of the Public Realm as the sphere of revelatory personal deeds.* To the Greeks the Private Realm was the sphere of life ruled by the necessity of sustaining life, and the Public Realm the sphere of freedom where a man could disclose himself to others. Today, the significance of the terms private and public has been reversed; public life is the necessary impersonal life, the place where a man fulfills his social function, and it is in his private life that he is free to be his personal self.

In consequence the arts, literature in particular, have lost their traditional principal human subject, the man of action, the doer of public deeds.

The advent of the machine has destroyed the direct relation between a man's intention and his deed. If St. George meets the dragon face to face and plunges a spear into its heart, he may legitimately say "I slew the dragon," but, if he drops a bomb on the dragon from an altitude of twenty thousand feet, though his intention—to slay it—is the same, his act consists in pressing a lever and it is the bomb, not St. George, that does the killing.

If, at Pharaoh's command, ten thousand of his subjects toil for five years at draining the fens, this means that Pharaoh commands the personal loyalty of enough persons to see that his orders are carried out; if his army revolts, he is powerless. But if Pharaoh can have the fens drained in six months by a hundred men with bulldozers, the situation is changed. He still needs some authority, enough to persuade a hundred men to man the bulldozers, but that is all: the rest of the work is done by machines which know nothing of loyalty or fear, and if his enemy, Nebuchadnezzar, should get hold of them, they will work just as efficiently at filling up the canals as they have just worked at digging them out. It is now possible to imagine a world in which the only human work on such projects will be done by a mere handful of persons who operate computers.

It is extremely difficult today to use public figures as themes for poetry because the good or evil they do depends less upon their characters and intentions than upon the quantity of impersonal force at their disposal.

Every British or American poet will agree that Winston Churchill is a greater figure than Charles II, but he will also know that he could not write a good poem on Churchill, while Dryden had no difficulty in writing a good poem on Charles. To write a good poem on Churchill, a poet would have to know Winston Churchill intimately, and his poem would be about the man, not about the Prime Minister. All attempts to write about persons or events, however important, to which the poet is not intimately related in a personal way are now doomed to failure. Yeats could write great poetry about the Troubles in Ireland, because most of the protagonists were known to him personally and the places where the events occurred had been familiar to him since childhood.

The true men of action in our time, those who transform the world, are not the politicians and statesmen, but the scientists. Unfortunately poetry cannot celebrate them because their deeds are concerned with things, not persons, and are, therefore, speechless.

When I find myself in the company of scientists, I feel like a shabby curate who has strayed by mistake into a drawing room full of dukes.

The growth in size of societies and the development of mass media of communication have created a social phenomenon which was unknown to the ancient world, that peculiar kind of crowd which Kierkegaard calls The Public.

> A public is neither a nation nor a generation, nor a community, nor a society, nor these particular men, for all

> these are only what they are through the concrete; no single person who belongs to the public makes a real commitment; for some hours of the day, perhaps, he belongs to the public—at moments when he is nothing else, since when he really is what he is, he does not form part of the public. Made up of such individuals at the moments when they are nothing, a public is a kind of gigantic something, an abstract and deserted void which is everything and nothing.

The ancient world knew the phenomenon of the crowd in the sense that Shakespeare uses the word, a visible congregation of a large number of human individuals in a limited physical space, who can, on occasions, be transformed by demagogic oratory into a mob which behaves in a way of which none of its members would be capable by himself, and this phenomenon is known, of course, to us, too. But the public is something else. A student in the subway during the rush hour whose thoughts are concentrated on a mathematical problem or his girl friend is a member of a crowd but not a member of the public. To join the public, it is not necessary for a man to go to some particular spot; he can sit at home, open a newspaper or turn on his TV set.

A man has his distinctive personal scent which his wife, his children and his dog can recognize. A crowd has a generalized stink. The public is odorless.

A mob is active; it smashes, kills and sacrifices itself. The public is passive or, at most, curious. It neither murders nor sacrifices itself; it looks on, or looks away, while the mob beats up a Negro or the police round up Jews for the gas ovens.

The public is the least exclusive of clubs; anybody, rich or poor, educated or unlettered, nice or nasty, can join it: it even tolerates a pseudo revolt against itself, that is, the formation within itself of clique publics.

In a crowd, a passion like rage or terror is highly contagious; each member of a crowd excites all the others, so that passion increases at a geometric rate. But among members of the Public, there is no contact. If two members of the public meet and speak to each other, the function of their words is not to convey meaning or arouse passion but to conceal by noise the silence and solitude of the void in which the Public exists.

Occasionally the Public embodies itself in a crowd and so becomes visible—in the crowd, for example, which collects to watch the wrecking gang demolish the old family mansion, fascinated by yet another proof that physical force is the Prince of this world against whom no love of the heart shall prevail.

Before the phenomenon of the Public appeared in society, there existed naïve art and sophisticated art which were different from each other but only in the way that two brothers are different. The Athenian court may smile at the mechanics' play of Pyramus and Thisbe, but they recognize it as a play. Court poetry and Folk poetry were bound by the common tie that both were made by hand and both were intended to last; the crudest ballad was as custom-built as the most esoteric sonnet. The appearance of the Public and the mass media which cater to it have destroyed naïve popular art. The sophisticated "highbrow" artist survives and can still work as he did a thousand years ago, because his audience is too small to interest the mass media. But the audience of the popular artist is the majority and this the mass media must steal from him if they are not to go bankrupt. Consequently, aside from a few comedians, the only art today is "highbrow." What the mass media offer is not popular art, but entertainment which is intended to be consumed like food, forgotten, and replaced by a new dish. This is bad for everyone; the majority lose all genuine taste of their own, and the minority become cultural snobs.

The two characteristics of art which make it possible for an art historian to divide the history of art into periods, are, firstly, a common style of expression over a certain period and, secondly, a common notion, explicit or implicit, of the hero, the kind of human being who most deserves to be celebrated, remembered and, if possible, imitated. The characteristic style of "Modern" poetry is an intimate tone of voice, the speech of one person addressing one person, not a large audience; whenever a modern poet raises his voice he sounds phony. And its characteristic hero is neither the "Great Man" nor the romantic rebel, both doers of extraordinary deeds, but the man or woman in any walk of life who, despite all the impersonal pressures of modern society, manages to acquire and preserve a face of his own.

Poets are, by the nature of their interests and the nature of artistic fabrication, singularly ill-equipped to understand politics or economics. Their natural interest is in singular individuals and personal relations, while politics and economics are concerned with large numbers of people, hence with the human average (the poet is bored to death by the idea of the Common Man) and with impersonal, to a great extent involuntary, relations. The poet cannot understand the function of money in modern society because for him there is no relation between subjective value and market value; he may be paid ten pounds for a poem which he believes is very good and took him months to write, and a hundred pounds for a piece of journalism which costs him but a day's work. If he is a successful poet—though few poets make enough money to be called successful in the way that a novelist or playwright can—he is a member of the Manchester school and believes in absolute *laisser-faire;* if he is unsuccessful and embittered, he is liable to combine aggressive fantasies about the annihilation of the present order with impractical day-dreams of Utopia. Society has always to beware of the utopias being planned by artists *manqués* over cafeteria tables late at night.

All poets adore explosions, thunderstorms, tornadoes, conflagrations, ruins, scenes of spectacular carnage. The poetic imagination is not at all a desirable quality in a statesman.

In a war or a revolution, a poet may do very well as a guerilla fighter or a spy, but it is unlikely that he will make a good regular soldier, or, in peace time, a conscientious member of a parliamentary committee.

All political theories which, like Plato's, are based on analogies drawn from artistic fabrication are bound, if put into practice, to turn into tyrannies. The whole aim of a poet, or any other kind of artist, is to produce something which is complete and will endure without change. A poetic city would always contain exactly the same number of inhabitants doing exactly the same jobs for ever.

Moreover, in the process of arriving at the finished work, the artist has continually to employ violence. A poet writes:

The mast-high anchor dives through a cleft

changes it to

The anchor dives through closing paths

changes it again to

The anchor dives among hayricks

and finally to

The anchor dives through the floors of a church.

A *cleft* and *closing paths* have been liquidated, and hayricks deported to another stanza.

A society which was really like a good poem, embodying the aesthetic virtues of beauty, order, economy and subordination of detail to the whole, would be a nightmare of horror for, given the historical reality of actual men, such a society could only come into being through selective breeding, extermination of the physically and mentally unfit, absolute obedience to its Director, and a large slave class kept out of sight in cellars.

Vice versa, a poem which was really like a political democracy—examples, unfortunately, exist—would be formless, windy, banal and utterly boring.

There are two kinds of political issues, Party issues and Revolutionary issues. In a party issue, all parties are agreed as to the nature and justice of the social goal to be reached, but differ in their policies for reaching it. The existence of different parties is justified, firstly, because no party can offer irrefutable proof that its policy is the only one which will achieve the commonly desired goal and, secondly, because no social goal can be achieved without some sacrifice of individual or group interest and it is natural for each individual and social group to seek a policy which will keep its sacrifice to a minimum, to hope that, if sacrifices must be made, it would be more just if someone else made them. In a party issue, each party seeks to convince the members of its society, primarily by appealing to their reason; it marshals facts and arguments to convince others that its policy is more likely to achieve the desired goal than that of its opponents. On a party issue it is essential that passions be kept at a low temperature: effective oratory requires, of course, some appeal to the emotions of the audience, but in party politics orators should display the mock-passion of prosecuting and defending attorneys, not really lose their tempers. Outside the Chamber, the rival deputies should be able to dine in each other's houses; fanatics have no place in party politics.

A revolutionary issue is one in which different groups within a society hold different views as to what is just. When this is the case, argument and compromise are out of the question; each group is bound to regard the other as wicked or mad or both. Every revolutionary issue is potentially a *casus belli*. On a revolutionary issue, an orator cannot convince his audience by appealing to their reason; he may convert some of them by awakening and appealing to their conscience, but his principal function, whether he represent the revolutionary or the counterrevolutionary group, is to arouse its passion to the point where it will give all its energies to achieving total victory for itself and total defeat for its opponents. When an issue is revolutionary, fanatics are essential.

Today, there is only one genuine world-wide revolutionary issue, racial equality. The debate between capitalism, socialism and communism is really a party issue, because the goal which all seek is really the same, a goal which is summed up in Brecht's well-known line:

Erst kommt das Fressen, dann kommt die Moral.

I.e., Grub first, then Ethics. In all the technologically advanced countries today, whatever political label they give themselves, their policies have, essentially, the same goal: to guarantee to every member of society, as a psychophysical organism, the right to physical and mental health. The positive symbolic figure of this goal is a naked anonymous baby, the negative symbol, a mass of anonymous concentration camp corpses.

What is so terrifying and immeasurably depressing about most contemporary politics is the refusal—mainly but not, alas, only by the communists—to admit that this is a party issue to be settled by appeal to facts and reason, the insistence that there is a revolutionary issue between us. If an African gives his life for the cause of racial equality, his death is meaningful to him; but what is utterly absurd, is that people should be deprived every day of their liberties and their lives, and that the human race may quite possibly destroy itself over what is really a matter of practical policy like asking whether, given its particular historical circumstances, the health of a community is more or less likely to be secured by Private Practice or by Socialized Medicine.

What is peculiar and novel to our age is that the principal goal of politics in every advanced society is not, strictly speaking, a political one, that is to say, it is not concerned with human beings as persons and citizens but with human bodies, with the precultural, prepolitical human creature. It is, perhaps, inevitable that respect for the liberty of the individual should have so greatly diminished and the authoritarian powers of the State have so greatly increased from what they were fifty years ago, for the main political issue today is concerned not with human liberties but with human necessities.

As creatures we are all equally slaves to natural necessity; we are not free to vote how much food, sleep, light and air we need to keep in good health; we all need a certain quantity, and we all need the same quantity.

Every age is one-sided in its political and social preoccupation and in seeking to realize the particular value it esteems most highly, it neglects and even sacrifices other values. The relation of a poet, or any artist, to society and politics is, except in Africa or still backward semifeudal countries, more difficult than it has ever been because, while he cannot but approve of the importance of *everybody* getting enough food to eat and enough leisure, this problem has nothing whatever to do with art, which is concerned with *singular persons,* as they are alone and as they are in their personal relations. Since these interests are not the predominant ones in his society; indeed, in so far as it thinks about them at all, it is with suspicion and latent hostility—it secretly or openly thinks that the claim that one is a singular person, or a demand for privacy, is putting on airs, a claim to be superior to other folk—every artist feels himself at odds with modern civilization.

In our age, the mere making of a work of art is itself a political act. So long as artists exist, making what they please and think they ought to make, even if it is not terribly good, even if it appeals to only a handful of people, they remind the Management of something managers need to be reminded of, namely, that the managed are people with faces, not anonymous numbers, that *Homo Laborans* is also *Homo Ludens.*

If a poet meets an illiterate peasant, they may not be able to say much to each other, but if they both meet a public official, they share the same feeling of suspicion; neither will trust one further than he can throw a grand piano. If they enter a government building, both share the same feeling of apprehension; perhaps they will never get out again. Whatever the cultural differences between them, they both sniff in any official world the smell of an unreality in which persons are treated as statistics. The peasant may play cards in the evening while the poet writes verses, but there is one political principle to which they both subscribe, namely, that among the half dozen or so things for which a man of honor should be prepared, if necessary, to die, the right to play, the right to frivolity, is not the least.

PART THREE

The Well of Narcissus

HIC ET ILLE

A mirror has no heart but plenty of ideas.
MALCOLM DE CHAZAL

A

Every man carries with him through life a mirror, as unique and impossible to get rid of as his shadow.

A parlor game for a wet afternoon—imagining the mirrors of one's friends. A has a huge pier glass, gilded and baroque, B a discreet little pocket mirror in a pigskin case with his initials stamped on the back; whenever one looks at C, he is in the act of throwing his mirror away but, if one looks in his pocket or up his sleeve, one always finds another, like an extra ace.

Most, perhaps all, our mirrors are inaccurate and uncomplimentary, though to varying degrees and in various ways.

Some magnify, some diminish, others return lugubrious, comic, derisive, or terrifying images.

But the properties of our own particular mirror are not so important as we sometimes like to think. We shall be judged, not by the kind of mirror found on us, but by the use we have made of it, by our *riposte* to our reflection.

The psychoanalyst says: "Come, my good man, I know what is the matter with you. You have a distorting mirror. No wonder you feel guilty. But cheer up. For a slight consideration I shall be delighted to correct it for you. There! Look! A perfect image. Not a trace of distortion. Now you are one of the elect. That will be five thousand dollars, please."

And immediately come seven devils, and the last state of that man is worse than the first.

The politician, secular or clerical, promises the crowd that, if only they will hand in their private mirrors to him, to be melted down into one large public mirror, the curse of Narcissus will be taken away.

Narcissus does not fall in love with his reflection because it is beautiful, but because it is *his*. If it were his beauty that enthralled him, he would be set free in a few years by its fading.

"After all," sighed Narcissus the hunchback, "on *me* it looks good."

The contemplation of his reflection does not turn Narcissus into Priapus: the spell in which he is trapped is not a desire for himself but the satisfaction of not desiring the nymphs.

"I prefer my pistol to my p . . . ," said Narcissus; "it cannot take aim without my permission"—and took a pot shot at Echo.

Narcissus (drunk): "I shouldn't look at me like that, if I were you. I suppose you think you know who I am. Well, let me tell *you*, my dear, that one of these days you are going to get a very big surprise *indeed*!"

A vain woman comes to realize that vanity is a sin and in order not to succumb to temptation, has all the mirrors removed from her house. Consequently, in a short while she cannot remember how she looks. She remembers that vanity is sinful but she forgets that she is vain.

He who despises himself, nevertheless esteems himself as a self-despiser. (NIETZSCHE.) A vain person is always vain *about* something. He overestimates the importance of some quality or exaggerates the degree to which he possesses it, but the quality has some real importance and he does possess it to some degree. The fantasy of overestimation or exaggeration makes the vain person comic, but the fact that he cannot be vain about nothing makes his vanity a venial sin, because it is always open to correction by appeal to objective fact.

A proud person, on the other hand, is not proud *of* anything, he *is* proud, he exists proudly. Pride is neither comic nor venial, but the most mortal of all sins because, lacking any basis in concrete particulars, it is both incorrigible and absolute: one cannot be more or less proud, only proud or humble.

Thus, if a painter tries to portray the Seven Deadly Sins, his experience will furnish him readily enough with images symbolic of Gluttony, Lust, Sloth, Anger, Avarice, and Envy, for all these are qualities of a person's relations to others and the world, but no experience can provide an image of Pride, for the relation it qualifies is the subjective relation of a person to himself. In the seventh frame, therefore, the painter can only place, in lieu of a canvas, a mirror.

Le Moi est toujours haïssable. (PASCAL.) True enough, but it is equally true that only *le Moi* is lovable in itself, not merely as an object of desire.

B

The absolutely banal—my sense of my own uniqueness. How strange that one should treasure this more than any of the exciting and interesting experiences, emotions, ideas that come and go, leaving it unchanged and unmoved.

The ego which recalls a previous condition of a now changed Self cannot believe that it, too, has changed. The Ego fancies that it is like Zeus who could assume one bodily appearance after another, now a swan, now a bull, while all the time remaining Zeus. Remembering some wrong or foolish action of the past, the Ego feels shame, as one feels ashamed of having been seen in bad company, at having been associated with a Self whom it regards as responsible for the act. Shame, not guilt: guilt, it fancies, is what the Self should feel.

Every autobiography is concerned with two characters, a Don Quixote, the Ego, and a Sancho Panza, the Self. In one kind of autobiography the Self occupies the stage and narrates, like a Greek Messenger, what the Ego is doing off stage. In another kind it is the Ego who is narrator and the Self who is described without being able to answer back. If the same person were to write his autobiography twice, first in one mode and then in the other, the two accounts would be so different that it would be hard to believe that they referred to the same person. In one he would appear as an obsessed creature, a passionate Knight forever serenading Faith or Beauty, humorless and over-life-size: in the other as coolly detached, full of humor and self-mockery, lacking in a capacity for affection, easily bored and smaller than life-size. As Don Quixote seen by Sancho Panza, he never prays; as Sancho Panza seen by Don Quixote, he never giggles.

An honest self-portrait is extremely rare because a man who has reached the degree of self-consciousness presupposed by the desire to paint his own portrait has almost always also developed an ego-consciousness which paints himself painting himself, and introduces artificial highlights and dramatic shadows.

As an autobiographer, Boswell is almost alone in his honesty.

> I determined, if the Cyprian Fury should seize me, to participate my amorous flame with a genteel girl.

Stendhal would never have dared write such a sentence. He would have said to himself: "Phrases like *Cyprian Fury* and *amorous flame* are clichés; I must put down in plain words exactly what I mean." But he would have been wrong, for the Self thinks in clichés and euphemisms, not in the style of the Code Napoléon.

History is, strictly speaking, the study of questions; the study of answers belongs to anthropology and sociology. To ask a question is to declare war, to make some issue a *casus belli*; history proper is the history of battles, physical, intellectual or spiritual and, the more revolutionary the outcome, the greater the historical interest. Culture is history which has become dormant or extinct, a second nature. A good historian is, of course, both a historian in the strict sense and a sociologist. So far as the life of an individual is concerned, an autobiography probably gives a truer picture of a man's history than even the best biography could have done. But a biographer can perceive what an autobiographer cannot, a man's culture, the influence upon his life of the presuppositions which he takes for granted.

It is possible to imagine oneself as rich when one is poor, as beautiful when ugly, as generous when stingy, etc., but it is impossible to imagine oneself as either more or less imaginative than, in fact, one is. A man whose every thought was commonplace could never know this to be the case.

I cannot help believing that my thoughts and acts are my own, not inherited reflexes and prejudices. The most I can say is: "Father taught me such-and-such and I agree with him." My prejudices must be right because, if I knew them to be wrong, I could no longer hold them.

Subjectively, my experience of life is one of having to make a series of choices between given alternatives and it is this experience of doubt, indecision, temptation, that seems more important and memorable than the actions I take. Further, if I make a choice which I consider the wrong one, I can never believe, however strong the temptation to make it, that it was inevitable, that I could not and should not have made the opposite choice. But when I look at others, I cannot see them making choices; I can only see what they actually do and, if I know them well, it is rarely that I am surprised, that I could not have predicted, given his character and upbringing, how so-and-so would behave.

Compared with myself, that is, other people seem at once less free and stronger in character. No man, however tough he appears to his friends, can help portraying himself in his autobiography as a sensitive plant.

To peek is always an unfriendly act, a theft of knowledge; we all know this and cannot peek without feeling guilty. As compensation we demand that what we discover by peeking shall be surprising. If I peer through the keyhole of a bishop's study and find him saying his prayers, the "idleness" of my curiosity is at once rebuked, but if I catch him making love to the parlor-maid I can persuade myself that my curiosity has really achieved something.

In the same way, the private papers of an author must, if they are to satisfy the public, be twice as unexpected and shocking as his published books.

Private letters, entries in journals, etc., fall into two classes, those in which the writer is in control of his situation—what he writes about is what he chooses to write—and those in which the situation dictates what he writes. The terms personal and impersonal are here ambiguous: the first class is impersonal in so far as the writer is looking at himself in the world as if at a third person, but personal in so far as it is his personal act so to look—the signature to the letter is really his and he is responsible for its contents. Vice versa, the second class is personal in that the writer is identical with what he writes, but impersonal in that it is the situation, not he, which enforces that identity.

The second class are what journalists call "human documents" and should be published, if at all, anonymously.

Rejoice with those that do rejoice. Certainly. But *weep* with them that weep? What good does that do? It is the decent side of us, not our hardness of heart, that is bored and embarrassed at having to listen to the woes of others because, as a rule, we can do nothing to alleviate them. To be curious about suffering which we cannot alleviate—and the sufferings of the dead are all beyond our aid—is *Schadenfreude* and nothing else.

Literary confessors are contemptible, like beggars who exhibit their sores for money, but not so contemptible as the public that buys their books.

One ceases to be a child when one realizes that telling one's trouble does not make it any better. (CAESARE PAVESE.) Exactly. Not even telling it to oneself. Most of us have known shameful moments when we blubbered, beat the wall with our fists, cursed the power which made us and the world, and wished that we were dead or that someone else was. But at such times, the *I* of the sufferer should have the tact and decency to look the other way.

Our sufferings and weaknesses, in so far as they are personal, *our* sufferings, *our* weaknesses, are of no literary interest whatsoever. They are only interesting in so far as we can see them as typical of the human condition. A suffering, a weakness, which cannot be expressed as an aphorism should not be mentioned.

The same rules apply to self-examination as apply to confession to a priest: *be brief, be blunt, be gone.* Be brief, be blunt, forget. The scrupuland is a nasty specimen.

C

If we were suddenly to become disembodied spirits, a few might behave better than before, but most of us would behave very much worse.

The Body is a born Aristotelian, its guiding principle, the Golden Mean. The most "fleshly" of the sins are not Gluttony and Lust, but Sloth and Cowardice: on the other hand, without a body, we could neither conceive of nor practice the virtue of Prudence.

You taught me language and my profit on't Is, I know how to curse. In the debate between the Body and Soul, if the former could present its own case objectively, it would always win. As it is, it can only protest the Soul's misstatement of its case by subjective acts of rebellion, coughs, belches, constipation, etc., which always put it in the wrong.

All bodies have the same vocabulary of physical symptoms to select from, but the way in which they use it varies from one body to another: in some, the style of bodily behavior is banal, in some highly mannered, in some vague, in some precise, and, occasionally, to his bewilderment, a physician encounters one which is really witty.

Anxiety affects the Body and the Mind in different ways: it makes the former develop compulsions, a concentration on certain actions to the exclusion of others; it makes the latter surrender to daydreaming, a lack of concentration on any thought in particular.

In a state of panic, a man runs round in circles by himself. In a state of joy, he links hands with others and they dance round in a circle together.

In the judgment of my nose, some of my neighbors are bad, but none is my inferior.

The ear tends to be lazy, craves the familiar, and is shocked by the unexpected: the eye, on the other hand, tends to be impatient, craves the novel and is bored by repetition. Thus, the average listener prefers concerts confined to works by old masters and it is only the highbrow who is willing to listen to new works, but the average reader wants the latest book and it is the classics of the past which are left to the highbrow.

Similarly, so long as a child has to be read to or told stories, he insists on the same tale being retold again and again, but, once he has learned to read for himself, he rarely reads the same book twice.

As seen reflected in a mirror, a room or a landscape seems more solidly there in space than when looked at directly. In that purely visual world nothing can be hailed, moved, smashed, or eaten, and it is only the observer himself who, by shifting his position or closing his eyes, can change.

From the height of 10,000 feet, the earth appears to the human eye as it appears to the eye of the camera; that is to say, all history is reduced to nature. This has the salutary effect of making historical evils, like national divisions and political hatreds, seem absurd. I look down from an airplane upon a stretch of land which is obviously continuous. That, across it, marked by a tiny ridge or river or even by no topographical sign whatever, there should run a frontier, and that the human beings living on one side should hate or refuse to trade with or be forbidden to visit those on the other side, is instantaneously revealed to me as ridiculous. Unfortunately, I cannot have this revelation without simultaneously having the illusion that there are no historical values either. From the same height I cannot distinguish between an outcrop of rock and a Gothic cathedral, or between a happy family playing in a backyard and a flock of sheep, so that I am unable to feel any difference between dropping a bomb upon one or the other. If the effect of distance upon the observed and the observer were mutual, so that, as the objects on the ground shrank in size and lost their uniqueness, the observer in the airplane felt himself shrinking and becoming more and more generalized, we should either give up flying as too painful or create a heaven on earth.

Those who accuse the movies of having a deleterious moral effect may well be right but not for the reasons they usually give. It is not what movies are about—gangsters or adultery—which does the damage, but the naturalistic nature of the medium itself which encourages a fantastic conception of time. In all narrative art, the narration of the action takes less time than it would in real life, but in the epic or the drama or the novel, the artistic conventions are so obvious that a confusion of art with life is impossible. Suppose that there is a scene in a play in which a man woos a woman; this may take forty minutes by the clock to play, but the audience will have the sense of having watched a scene which really took, let us say, two hours.

The absolute naturalism of the camera destroys this sense and encourages the audience to imagine that, in real life as on the screen, the process of wooing takes forty minutes.

When he grows impatient, the movie addict does not cry "Hurry!" he cries "Cut!"

A daydream is a meal at which images are eaten. Some of us are gourmets, some gourmands, and a good many take their images precooked out of a can and swallow them down whole, absent-mindedly and with little relish.

Even if it be true that our primary interest is in sexual objects only, and that all our later interests are symbolic transferences, we could never make such a transference if the new objects of interest did not have a real value of their own. If all round hills were suddenly to turn into breasts, all caves into wombs, all towers into phalloi, we should not be pleased or even shocked: we should be bored.

Between the ages of seven and twelve my fantasy life was centered around lead mines and I spent many hours imagining in the minutest detail the Platonic Idea of all lead mines. In planning its concentrating mill, I ran into difficulty: I had to choose between two types of a certain machine for separating the slimes. One I found more "beautiful" but the other was, I knew from my reading, the more efficient. My feeling at the time, I remember very clearly, was that I was confronted by a moral choice and that it was my duty to choose the second.

Like all polemical movements, existentialism is one-sided. In their laudable protest against systematic philosophers, like Hegel or Marx, who would reduce all individual existence to general processes, the existentialists have invented an equally imaginary anthropology from which all elements, like man's physical nature, or his reason, about which general statements can be made, are excluded.

A task for an existentialist theologian: to preach a sermon on the topic *The Sleep of Christ.*

One of the most horrible, yet most important, discoveries of our age has been that, if you really wish to destroy a person and turn him into an automaton, the surest method is not physical torture, in the strict sense, but simply to keep him awake, i.e., in an existential relation to life without intermission.

All the existentialist descriptions of choice, like Pascal's wager or Kierkegaard's leap, are interesting as dramatic literature, but are they true? When I look back at the three or four choices in my life which have been decisive, I find that, at the time I made them, I had very little sense of the seriousness of what I was doing and only later did I discover that what had then seemed an unimportant brook was, in fact, a Rubicon.

For this I am very thankful since, had I been fully aware of the risk I was taking, I should never have dared take such a step.

In a reflective and anxious age, it is surely better, pedagogically, to minimize rather than to exaggerate the risks involved in a choice, just as one encourages a boy to swim who is afraid of the water by telling him that nothing can happen.

D

Under the stress of emotion, animals and children "make" faces, but they do not have one.

So much countenance and so little face. (HENRY JAMES.) Every European visitor to the United States is struck by the comparative rarity of what he would call a face, by the frequency of men and women who look like elderly babies. If he stays in the States for any length of time, he will learn that this cannot be put down to a lack of sensibility—the American feels the joys and sufferings of human life as keenly as anybody else. The only plausible explanation I can find lies in his different attitude to the past. To have a face, in the European sense of the word, it would seem that one must not only enjoy and suffer but also desire to preserve the memory of even the most humiliating and unpleasant experiences of the past.

More than any other people, perhaps, the Americans obey the scriptural injunction: "Let the dead bury their dead."

When I consider others I can easily believe that their bodies express their personalities and that the two are inseparable. But it is impossible for me not to feel that my body is other than I, that I inhabit it like a house, and that my face is a mask which, with or without my consent, conceals my real nature from others.

It is impossible consciously to approach a mirror without composing or "making" a special face, and if we catch sight of our reflection unawares we rarely recognize ourselves. I cannot read my face in the mirror because I am already obvious to myself.

The image of myself which I try to create in my own mind in order that I may love myself is very different from the image which I try to create in the minds of others in order that they may love me.

Most faces are asymmetric, i.e., one side is happy, the other sad, one self-confident, the other diffident, etc. By cutting up photographs it is possible to make two very different portraits, one from the two left sides, the other from the two rights. If these be now shown to the subject and to his friends, almost invariably the one which the subject prefers will be the one his friends dislike.

We can imagine loving what we do not love a great deal more easily than we can imagine fearing what we do not fear. I can sympathize with a man who has a passion for collecting stamps, but if he is afraid of mice there is a gulf between us. On the other hand, if he is unafraid of spiders, of which I am terrified, I admire him as superior but I do not feel that he is a stranger. Between friends differences in taste or opinion are irritating in direct proportion to their triviality. If my friend takes up Vedanta, I can accept it, but if he prefers his steak well done, I feel it to be a treachery.

When one talks to another, one is more conscious of him as a listener to the conversation than of oneself. But the moment one writes anything, be it only a note to pass down the table, one is more conscious of oneself as a reader than of the intended recipient.

Hence we cannot be as false in writing as we can in speaking, nor as true. The written word can neither conceal nor reveal so much as the spoken.

Two card players. A is a good loser when, holding good cards, he makes a fatal error, but a bad loser when he is dealt cards with which it is impossible to win. With B it is the other way round; he cheerfully resigns himself to defeat if his hand is poor, but becomes furious if defeat is his own fault.

Almost all of our relationships begin and most of them continue as forms of mutual exploitation, a mental or physical barter, to be terminated when one or both parties run out of goods.

But if the seed of a genuine disinterested love, which is often present, is ever to develop, it is essential that we pretend to ourselves and to others that it is stronger and more developed than it is, that we are less selfish than we are. Hence the social havoc wrought by the paranoid to whom the thought of indifference is so intolerable that he divides others into two classes, those who love him for himself alone and those who hate him for the same reason.

Do a paranoid a favor, like paying his hotel bill in a foreign city when his monthly check has not yet arrived, and he will take this as an expression of personal affection—the thought that you might have done it from a general sense of duty towards a fellow countryman in distress will never occur to him. So back he comes for more until your patience is exhausted, there is a row, and he departs convinced that you are his personal enemy. In this he is right to the extent that it is difficult not to hate a person who reveals to you so clearly how little you love others.

Two cyclic madmen. In his elated phase, A feels: "I am God. The universe is full of gods. I adore all and am adored by all." B feels: "The universe is only a thing. I am happily free from all bonds of attachment to it." In the corresponding depressed phase, A feels: "I am a devil. The universe is full of devils. I hate all and am hated by all." B feels: "I am only a thing to the universe which takes no interest in me." This difference is reflected in their behavior. When elated A does not wash and even revels in dirt because all things are holy. He runs after women, after whores in particular whom he intends to save through Love. But B in this mood takes a fastidious pride in his physical cleanliness as a mark of his superiority and is chaste for the same reason. When depressed A begins to wash obsessively to cleanse himself from guilt and feels a morbid horror of all sex, B now neglects his appearance because "nobody cares how I look," and tries to be a Don Juan seducer in an attempt to compel life to take an interest in him.

A's God—Zeus-Jehovah: B's God—The Unmoved Mover.

BALAAM AND HIS ASS

Am I not thine ass, upon which thou hast ridden ever since I was thine unto this day?

NUMBERS: XXII, 30

Friend, I do thee no wrong: didst thou not agree with me for a penny?

MATTHEW: XX, 13

I

The relation between Master and Servant is not given by nature or fate but comes into being through an act of conscious volition. Nor is it erotic; an erotic relationship, e.g., between man and wife or parent and child, comes into being in order to satisfy needs which are, in part, given by nature; the needs which are satisfied by a master-servant relationship are purely social and historical. By this definition, a wet nurse is not a servant, a cook may be. Thirdly, it is contractual. A contractual relationship comes into being through the free decision of both parties, a double commitment. The liberty of decision need not be, and indeed very rarely is, equal on both sides, but the weaker party must possess *some* degree of sovereignty. Thus, a slave is not a servant because he has no sovereignty whatsoever; he cannot even say, "I would rather starve than work for you." A contractual relationship not only involves double sovereignty, it is also asymmetric; what the master contributes, e.g., shelter, food and wages, and what the servant contributes, e.g., looking after the master's clothes and house, are qualitatively different and there is no objective standard by which one can decide whether the one is or is not equivalent to the other. A contract, therefore, differs from a law. In law all sovereignty lies with the law or with those who impose it and the individual has no sovereignty. Even in a democracy where sovereignty is said to reside in the people, it is as one of the people that each citizen has a share in that, not as an individual. Further, the relationship of all individuals to a law is symmetric; it commands or prohibits the same thing to all who come under it. Of any law one can ask the aesthetic question, "Is it enforceable?" and the ethical question, "Is it just?" An individual has the aesthetic right to break the law if he is powerful enough to do so with impunity, and it may be his ethical duty to break it if his conscience tells him that the law is unjust. Of a contract, on the other hand, one can only ask the historical question, "Did both parties pledge their word do it?" Its justice or its enforceability are secondary to the historical fact of mutual personal commitment. A contract can only be broken or changed by the mutual consent of both parties. It will be my ethical duty to insist on changing a contract when my conscience tells me it is unfair only if I am in the advantageous position; if I am in the weaker position I have a right to propose a change but no right to insist on one.

When the false oracle has informed Don Quixote that Dulcinea can only be disenchanted if Sancho Panza will receive several thousand lashes, the latter agrees to receive them on condition that he inflict them himself and in his own good time. One night Don Quixote becomes so impatient for the release of his love that he attempts to become the whipper, at which point Sancho Panza knocks his master down.

DON QUIXOTE: So you would rebel against your lord and master, would you, and dare to raise your hand against the one who feeds you.

SANCHO: I neither make nor unmake a king, but am simply standing up for myself, for I am my own lord.

Similarly, when Mr. Pickwick, on entering the Debtors' Prison, attempts to dismiss Sam Weller because it would be unjust to the latter to expect him to accompany his master, Sam Weller refuses to accept dismissal and arranges to get sent to jail himself.

Lastly, the master-servant relationship is between real persons. Thus we do not call the employees of a factory or a store servants because the factory and the store are corporate, i.e., fictitious, persons.

II

Who is there?
I.
Who is I?
Thou.
And that is the awakening—the Thou and the I.

—PAUL VALÉRY

Man is a creature who is capable of entering into Thou-Thou relationships with God and with his neighbors because he has a Thou-Thou relationship to himself. There are other social animals who have signal codes, e.g., bees have signals for informing each other about the whereabouts and distance of flowers, but only man has a language by means of which he can disclose himself to his neighbor, which he could not do and could not want to do if he did not first possess the capacity and the need to disclose himself to himself. The communication of mere objective fact only requires monologue and for monologue a language is not necessary, only a code. But subjective communication demands dialogue and dialogue demands a real language.

A capacity for self-disclosure implies an equal capacity for self-concealment. Of an animal it is equally true to say that it is incapable of telling us what it *really* feels, and that it is incapable of hiding its feelings. A man can do both. For the animal motto is that of the trolls in Ibsen's *Peer Gynt*—"To thyself be enough"—while the human motto is, "To thyself by true." Peer is perfectly willing, if it is convenient, to swear that the cow he sees is a beautiful young lady, but when the Troll-King suggests an operation which will take away from Peer the power of distinguishing between truth and falsehood so that if he wishes that a cow were a beautiful girl, the cow immediately appears to him as such, Peer revolts.

To present artistically a human personality in its full depth, its inner dialectic, its self-disclosure and self-concealment, through the medium of a single character is almost impossible. The convention of the soliloquy attempts to get around the difficulty but it suffers from the disadvantage of *being* a convention; it presents, that is, what is really a dialogue in the form of a monologue. When Hamlet soliloquizes, we hear a single voice which is supposed to be addressed to himself but, in fact, is heard as addressed to us, the audience, so that we suspect that he is not disclosing to himself what he conceals from others, but only disclosing to us what he thinks it is good we should know, and at the same time concealing from us what he does not choose to tell us.

A dialogue requires two voices, but, if it is the inner dialogue of human personality that is to be expressed artistically, the two characters employed to express it and the relationship between them must be of a special kind. The pair must in certain respects be similar, i.e., they must be of the same sex, and in others, physical and temperamental, polar opposites—identical twins will not do because they inevitably raise the question, "Which is the real one?"—and they must be inseparable, i.e., the relationship between them must be of a kind which is not affected by the passage of time or the fluctuations of mood and passion, and which makes it plausible that wherever one of them is, whatever he is doing, the other should be there too. There is only one relationship which satisfies all these conditions, that between master and personal servant. It might be objected at this point that the Ego-self relationship is given while the master-servant relationship, as defined above, is contractual. The objection would be valid if man, like all other finite things, had only the proto-history of coming into being and then merely sustaining that being. But man has a real history; having come into being, he has then through his choices to become what he is not yet, and this he cannot do unless he first chooses himself as he is now with all his finite limitations. To reach "the age of consent" means to arrive at the point where the "given" Ego-self relationship is changed into a contractual one. Suicide is a breach of contract.

III

CRICHTON: *There must always be a master and servants in all civilized communities, for it is natural, and whatever is natural is right.*

LORD LOAMSHIRE: *It's very unnatural for me to stand here and allow you to talk such nonsense.*

CRICHTON: *Yes, my lord, it is. That is what I have been striving to point out to your lordship.*

—J. M. BARRIE, *The Admirable Crichton*

Defined abstractly, a master is one who gives orders and a servant is one who obeys orders. This characteristic makes the master-servant relationship peculiarly suitable as an expression of the inner life, so much of which is carried on in imperatives. If a large lady carelessly, but not intentionally, treads on my corn during a subway rush hour, what goes on in my mind can be expressed dramatically as follows:

SELF: *(in whom the physical sensation of pain has become the mental passion of anger):*
"Care for my anger! Do something about it!"

COGNITIVE EGO: "You are angry because of the pain caused by this large lady who, carelessly but not intentionally, has trodden on your corn. If you decide to relieve your feelings, you can give her a sharp kick on the ankle without being noticed."

SELF: "Kick her."

SUPER-EGO: *(to simplify matters, let us pretend that super-ego and conscience are identical, which they are not):*
"Unintentional wrongs must not be avenged. Ladies must not be kicked. Control your anger!"

LADY: *(noticing what she has done):*
"I beg your pardon! I hope I didn't hurt you."

SELF: "Kick her!"

SUPER-EGO: "Smile! Say 'Not at all, Madam.' "

VOLITIONAL EGO: *(to the appropriate voluntary muscles):*
either "Kick her!"
or "Smile! Say 'Not at all, Madam!' "

Of my five "characters," only one, my cognitive ego, really employs the indicative mood. Of the others, my self and my super-ego cannot, either of them, be a servant. Each is a master who is either obeyed or disobeyed. Neither can take orders. My body, on the other hand (or rather its "voluntary muscles"), can do nothing but what it is told; it can never be a master, nor even a servant, only a slave. While my volitional ego is always both, a servant in relation to either my self or my super-ego and a master in relation to my body.

The "demands" of reason are not imperatives because, although it is possible not to listen to them and to forget them, as long as we listen and remember, it is impossible to disobey them, and a true imperative always implies the possibility of either obeying or disobeying. In so far as we listen to reason, we are its slaves, not its servants.

IV

I care for nobody, no, not I
And nobody cares for me.
—The Miller of Dee

But my five wits nor my five senses can
Dissuade one foolish heart from serving thee,
Who leaves unswayed the likeness of a man
Thy proud heart's slave and vassal wretch to be.
—SHAKESPEARE, *Sonnet CXLI*

Because of its double role the volitional ego has two wishes which, since the Fall, instead of being dialectically related, have become contradictory opposites. On the one hand it wishes to be free of all demands made upon it by the self or the conscience or the outer world. As Kierkegaard wrote:

> If I had a humble spirit in my service, who, when I asked for a glass of water, brought me the world's costliest wines blended in a chalice, I should dismiss him, in order to teach him that pleasure consists not in what I enjoy, but in having my own way.

When Biron, the hero of *Love's Labour's Lost*, who has hitherto been free of passion, finds himself falling in love, he is annoyed.

This senior junior, giant dwarf, Dan Cupid,
Sole emperator and great general
Of trotting paritors (Oh my little heart)
And I to be a corporal of his field
And wear his colours like a tumbler's hoop.

On the other hand, the same ego wishes to be important, to find its existence meaningful, to have a *telos*, and this *telos* it can only find in something or someone outside itself. To have a *telos* is to have something to obey, to be the servant of. Thus all lovers instinctively use the master-servant metaphor.

MIRANDA: To be your fellow
You may deny me; but I'll be your servant,
Whether you will or no.
FERDINAND: My Mistress, dearest,
And I thus humble ever.
MIRANDA: My husband then?

FERDINAND: Aye, with a heart as willing
As bondage e'er of freedom.

And so, with calculation, speaks every seducer.

BERTRAM: I prithee do not strive against my vows.
I was compelled to her, but I love thee
By love's own sweet constraint, and will for ever
Do thee all rights of service.

DIANA: Ay, so you serve us
Till we serve you.

To be loved, to be the *telos* of another, can contribute to the ego's sense of importance, provided that it feels that such giving of love is a free act on the part of the other, that the other is not a slave of his or her passion. In practice, unfortunately, if there is an erotic element present as distinct from *philia*, most people find it hard to believe that another's love for them is free and not a compulsion, unless they happen to reciprocate it.

Had man not fallen, the wish of his ego for freedom would be simply a wish not to find its *telos* in a false or inferior good, and its wish for a *telos* simply a longing for the true good, and both wishes would be granted. In his fallen state, he oscillates between a wish for absolute autonomy, to be as God, and a wish for an idol who will take over the whole responsibility for his existence, to be an irresponsible slave. The consequence of indulging the first is a sense of loneliness and lack of meaning; the consequence of indulging the second, a masochistic insistence on being made to suffer. John falls in love with Anne who returns his love, is always faithful and anxious to please. Proud and self-satisfied, he thinks of *my Anne*, presently of *my wife* and finally of *my well-being*. Anne as a real other has ceased to exist for him. He does not suffer in any way that he can put his finger on, nevertheless he begins to feel bored and lonely.

George falls in love with Alice who does not return his love, is unfaithful and treats him badly. To George she remains

Alice, cruel but real. He suffers but he is not lonely or bored, for his suffering is the proof that another exists to cause it.

The futility of trying to combine both wishes into one, of trying, that is, to have a *telos*, but to find it within oneself not without, is expressed in the myth of Narcissus. Narcissus falls in love with his reflection; he wishes to become its servant, but instead his reflection insists upon being his slave.

V

Das verfluchte Hier
—GOETHE, *Faust*

Goethe's *Faust* is full of great poetry and wise sayings but it is not dramatically exciting; like a variety show, it gives us a succession of scenes interesting in themselves but without a real continuity; one could remove a scene or add a new one without causing any radical change in the play. Further, once the Marguerite episode is over, it is surprising how little Faust himself actually does. Mephisto creates a new situation and Faust tells us what he feels about it. I can well imagine that every actor would like to play Mephisto, who is always entertaining, but the actor who plays Faust has to put up with being ignored whenever Mephisto is on stage. Moreover, from a histrionic point of view, is there ever any reason why Faust should move instead of standing still and just delivering his lines? Is not any movement the actor may think up arbitrary?

These defects are not, of course, due to any lack of dramatic talent in Goethe but to the nature of the Faust myth itself, for the story of Faust is precisely the story of a man who refuses to be anyone and only wishes to become someone else. Once he has summoned Mephisto, the manifestation of possibility without actuality, there is nothing left for Faust to represent but the passive consciousness of possibilities. When the Spirit of Fire appears to Faust, it says:

Du gleichst dem Geist, den du begreifst,
Nicht mir

and in an ideal production, Faust and Mephisto should be played by identical twins.

Near the beginning of the play Faust describes his condition:

> *Zwei Seelen wohnen, ach! in meiner Brust*
> *Die eine will sich von der andern trennen;*
> *Die eine hält, in derber Liebeslust*
> *Sich an die Welt mit klammernden Organen;*
> *Die andre hebt gewaltsam sich vom Dust*
> *Zu den Gefilden hoher Ahnen.*

This has nothing to do, though he may think it has, with the conflict between pleasure and goodness, the kingdom of *this* world and the kingdom of Heaven. Faust's *Welt* is the immediate actual moment, the actual concrete world now, and his *hohe Ahnen* the same world seen by memory and imagination as possible, as what might have been once and may be yet. All value belongs to possibility, the actual here and now is valueless, or rather the value it has is the feeling of discontent it provokes. When Faust signs his contract with Mephisto, the latter says:

> *Ich will mich hier zu deinem Dienst verbinden,*
> *Auf deinen Wink nicht rasten and nicht ruhn;*
> *wenn wir uns drüben wieder finden*
> *So sollst du mir das Gleiche tun*

to which Faust replies airily:

> *Das Drüben kann mich wenig kümmern*
> *Schlägst du erst diese Welt zu Trümmern,*
> *Die andre mag danach entstehen*

because he does not believe that *Das Drüben,* the exhaustion of all possibilities, can ever be reached—as, indeed, in the play it never is. Faust escapes Mephisto's clutches because he is careful to define the contentment of his last moment in terms of anticipation:

Im Vorgefühl von solchem hohen Glück
Geniess' ich jezt den höchsten Augenblick.

But, though Faust is not damned, it would be nonsense to say that he is saved. The angels bearing him to Heaven describe him as being in the pupa stage, and to such a condition Judgment has no meaning.

Mephisto describes himself as:

ein Teil des Teils, der Anfangs alles war,
Ein Teil der Finsternis, die sich das Licht gebar

as, that is to say, a manifestation of the rejection of all finiteness, the desire for existence without the limitation of essence. To the spirit that rejects any actuality, the idea must be the *Abgrund*, the abyss of infinite potentiality, and will creation must be hateful to it. So Valéry's serpent cries out against God:

Il se fit Celui qui dissipe
En conséquences son Principe,
En éntoiles son Unité.

Mephisto describes himself as:

ein Teil von jener Kraft,
Die stets das Böse will und stets das Gute schaft,

but it is hard to see what good or evil he does to Faust. Through his agency or his suggestion, Faust may do a good deal of harm to others, but Faust himself is completely unaffected by his acts. He passively allows Mephisto to entertain him and is no more changed in character by these entertainments than we are by watching the play.

Faust may talk a great deal about the moral dangers of content and sloth, but the truth is that his discontent is not a discontent with himself but a terror of being bored. What Faust is totally lacking in is a sacramental sense,[1] a sense that the

[1] If Faust holds any theological position, it is pantheist. The pantheist believes that the universe is numinous *as-a-whole*. But a sacramental sign is always some particular aspect of the finite, *this* thing, *this* act, not the

finite can be a sign for the infinite, that the secular can be sanctified; one cannot imagine him saying with George Herbert:

> A servant with this clause
> Makes drudgery divine;
> Who sweeps a room as for Thy laws
> Makes that and the action fine.

In this lack Faust is a typical modern figure. In earlier ages men have been tempted to think that the finite was not a sign for the holy but the holy itself, and fell therefore into idolatry and magic. The form which the Devil assumed in such periods, therefore, was always finite; he appeared as the manifestation of some specific temptation, as a beautiful woman, a bag of gold, etc. In our age there are no idols in the strict sense because we tire of one so quickly and take up another that the word cannot apply. Our real, because permanent, idolatry is an idolatry of possibility. And in such an age the Devil appears in the form of Mephisto, in the form, that is, of an actor. The point about an actor is that he has no name of his own, for his name is Legion. One might say that our age recognized its nature on the day when Henry Irving was knighted.

VI

> *Voglio far il gentiluomo*
> *E non voglio più servir.*
> —DA PONTE, *Don Giovanni*

> *Dein Werk! O thörige Magd*
> —WAGNER, *Tristan and Isolde*

The man who refuses to be the servant of any *telos* can only be directly represented, like the Miller of Dee, lyrically. He

finite-in-general, and it is valid for this person, this social group, this historical epoch, not for humanity-in-general. Pansacramentalism is self-contradictory.

can sing his rapture of freedom and indifference, but after that there is nothing for him to do but be quiet. In a drama he can only be represented indirectly as a man with a *telos,* indeed a monomania, but of such a kind that it is clear that it is an arbitrary choice; nothing in his nature and circumstances imposes it on him or biases him toward it. Such is Don Giovanni. The *telos* he chooses is to seduce, to "know" every woman in the world. Leporello says of him:

> *Non si picca, se sia ricca*
> *Se sia brutta, se sia bella,*
> *Perchè porti la gonnella*

A sensual libertine, like the Duke in *Rigoletto,* cannot see a pretty girl, or a girl who is "his type" without trying to seduce her; but if a plain elderly woman like Donna Elvira passes by, he cries, "My God, what a dragon," and quickly looks away. That is sensuality, and pains should be taken in a production to make it clear why the Duke should have fallen into this particular idolization of the finite rather than another. The Duke must appear to be the kind of man to whom all women will be attracted; he must be extremely good-looking, virile, rich, magnificent, a grand seigneur.

Don Giovanni's pleasure in seducing women is not sensual but arithmetical; his satisfaction lies in adding one more name to his list which is kept for him by Leporello. Everything possible, therefore, should be done to make him as inconspicuous and anonymous in appearance as an FBI agent. If he is made handsome, then his attraction for women is a bias in his choice, and if he is made ugly, then the repulsion he arouses in women is a challenge. He should look so neutral that the audience realizes that, so far as any finite motive is concerned, he might just as well have chosen to collect stamps. The Duke does not need a servant because there is no contradiction involved in sensuality or indeed in any idolatry of the finite. The idol and the idolater between them can say all there is to say. The Duke is the master of his ladies and the slave of his sensuality. Any given form of idolatry of the finite is lacking in contradiction because such idolatry is itself finite. Whenever we find one idol we find others, we find polytheism. We do not have to be told so to know that there are times when the Duke is too tired or too hungry to look at a pretty girl. For Don Giovanni there are no such times, and it is only in conjunction with his servant, as Giovanni-Leporello, that he can be understood.

Don Giovanni is as inconspicuous as a shadow, resolute and fearless in action; Leporello is comically substantial like Falstaff, irresolute and cowardly. When, in his opening aria, Leporello sings the words quoted at the head of this section, the audience laughs because it is obvious that he is lacking in all the qualities of character that a master should have. He is no Figaro. But by the end of the opera, one begins to suspect that the joke is much funnier than one had first thought. Has it not, in fact, been Leporello all along who was really the master and Don Giovanni really his servant? It is Leporello who keeps the list and if he lost it or forgot to keep it up-to-date or walked off with it, Don Giovanni would have no *raison d'être.* It is significant that we never see Don Giovanni look at the list himself or show any pleasure in it; only Leporello does that: Don Giovanni merely reports the latest name to him. Perhaps it should have been Leporello who was carried down alive to hell by the Commendatore, leaving poor worn-out Giovanni to die in peace. Imagine a Leporello who, in real life, is a rabbity-looking, celibate, timid, stupendously learned professor, with the finest collection in the world, of, say, Trilobites, but in every aspect of life outside his field, completely incompetent. Brought up by a stern fundamentalist father (Il Commendatore) he went to college with the intention of training for the ministry, but there he read Darwin and lost his faith. Will not his daydream version of his ideal self be someone very like Don Giovanni?

It is fortunate for our understanding of the myth of Tristan and Isolde that Wagner should have chosen to write an opera about it, for the physical demands made by Wagnerian opera defend us, quite accidentally, from an illusion which we are likely to fall into when reading the medieval legend; the two lovers, for whom nothing is of any value but each other, appear on the stage, not as the handsomest of princes and the most beautiful of princesses, not as Tamino and Pamina, but as a Wagnerian tenor and soprano in all their corseted bulk. When Tamino and Pamina fall mutually in love, we see that the instigating cause is the manly beauty of one and the womanly beauty of the other. Beauty is a finite quality which time will take away; this does not matter in the case of Tamino and Pamina because we know that their romantic passion for each other has only to be temporary, a natural but not serious preliminary to the serious unromantic love of man and wife. But the infinite romantic passion of Tristan and Isolde which has no past and no future outside itself cannot be generated by a finite quality; it can only be generated by finiteness-in-itself against which it protests with an infinite passion of rejection. Like Don Giovanni, Tristan and Isolde are purely mythical figures in that we never meet them in historical existence: we meet promiscuous men like the Duke, but never a man who is absolutely indifferent to the physical qualities of the women he seduces; we meet romantically passionate engaged couples, but never a couple of whom we can say that their romantic passion will not and cannot change into married affection or decline into indifference. Just as we can say that Don Giovanni might have chosen to collect stamps instead of women, so we can say that Tristan and Isolde might have fallen in love with two other people; they are so indifferent to each other as persons with unique bodies and characters that they might just as well—and this is one significance of the love potion—have drawn each other's names out of a hat. A lifelong romantic idolatry of a real person is possible and occurs in life provided that the romance is one-sided, that one party plays the Cruel Fair, e.g., Don José and Carmen. For any finite idolatry is by definition an asymmetric relation: my idol is that which I make responsible for my existence in order that I may have no responsibility for myself; if it turns round and demands responsibility from me it ceases to be an idol. Again, it is fortunate that the operatic medium makes it impossible for Wagner's Tristan and Isolde to consummate their love physically. Wagner may have intended, probably did intend, the love duet in the Second Act to stand for such a physical consummation, but what we actually see are two people singing of how much they desire each other, and consummation remains something that is always about to happen but never does, and this, whatever Wagner intended, is correct: their mutual idolatry is only possible because, while both assert their infinite willingness to give themselves to each other, in practice both play the Cruel Fair and withhold themselves. Were they to yield, they would know something about each other and their relation would change into a one-sided idolatry, a mutual affection or a mutual indifference. They do not yield because their passion is not for each other but for something they hope to obtain by means of each other, Nirvana, the primordial unity that made the mistake of begetting multiplicity, "der Finsternis die sich das Licht gebar."

Just as Don Giovanni is inseparable from his servant Leporello, so Tristan and Isolde appear flanked by Brangaene and Kurvenal. It is Kurvenal's mocking reference to Morold that makes Isolde so angry that she decides to poison Tristan and herself, in consequence of which Tristan and she are brought together; otherwise he would have kept his distance till they landed. It is Brangaene who substitutes the love potion for the death potion so that Tristan and Isolde are committed to each other not by their personal decisions but by an extraneous factor for which they are not responsible. It is Brangaene who tells King Mark about the love potion so that he is willing to forgive the lovers and let them join each other, but tells him too late for his decision to be of any practical help. And it is Kurvenal's leaving of his master to greet Isolde that gives Tristan the opportunity to cause his death by tearing off his bandages. Kurvenal obeys his friend like a slave who has no mind of his own.

Dem guten Marke
dient' ich ihm hold,
wie warst du ihm treuer als Gold!

Musst' ich verrathen
den edlen Herrn,
wie betrogst du ihn da so gern
Dir nicht eigen,
einzig mein

Tristan tells him, but then points out that Kurvenal has one freedom which he, Tristan, can never have. He is not in love.

Nur—was ich leide,
dass—kannst du nicht leiden.

As in the case of Don Giovanni and Leporello, one begins to wonder who are really master and mistress. Imagine a Kurvenal and a Brangaene who in real life are an average respectable lower-middle-class couple (but with more children than is today usual), living in a dingy suburban house. He has a dingy white-collar job and has a hard time making both ends meet. She has no maid and is busy all day washing the diapers of the latest baby, mending the socks of older children, washing up, trying to keep the house decent, etc. She has lost any figure and looks she may once have had; he is going bald and acquiring a middle-aged spread. Their marriage, given their circumstances, is an average one; any romantic passion has long ago faded but, though they often get on each other's nerves, they don't passionately hate each other. A couple, that is, on whom the finite bears down with the fullest possible weight, or provides the fewest of its satisfactions. Now let them concoct their daydream of the ideal love and the ideal world, and something very like the passion of Tristan and Isolde will appear, and a world in which children, jobs, and food do not exist. His Boss will appear as King Mark, an old disreputable drinking crony of his as Morold, the scandal-mongering neighbors next door as Melot. They cannot, however, keep the sense of reality out of their dream and make everything end happily. They are dreamers but they are sane dreamers, and sanity demands that Tristan and Isolde are doomed.

VII

The fool will stay
And let the wise man fly.
The knave turns fool who runs away,
The fool, no knave perdy.
—SHAKESPEARE, *King Lear*

According to Renaissance political theory, the King, as the earthly representative of Divine Justice, is above the law which he imposes on his subjects. For his subjects the law is a universal, but the King who makes the law is an individual who cannot be subject to it, since the creator is superior to his creation—a poet, for instance, cannot be subordinate to his poem. In general, the Middle Ages had thought differently; they held that not even the King could violate Natural Law. In English history, the transition from one view to the other is marked by Henry the Eighth's execution of Sir Thomas More who, as Lord Chancellor, was the voice of Natural Law and the keeper of the King's Conscience. Both periods believed that, in some sense, the King was a divine representative, so that the political question, "Is the King obliged to obey his law?" is really the theological question, "Does God have to obey His own laws?" The answer given seems to me to depend upon what doctrine of God is held, Trinitarian or Unitarian. If the former, then the Middle Ages were right, for it implies that obedience is a meaningful term when applied to God—the co-equal Son obeys the Father. If the latter, then the Renaissance was right, unless the sacramental theory of kingship is abandoned, in which case, of course, the problem does not arise.[2] An absolute monarch is a representative of the deist God. The Renaissance King, then, is an individual, and the only individual, the superman, who is above the law, not subject to the universal. If he should do wrong, who can tell him so? Only an individual who, like

[2] Or does it? In recent years we have seen the emergence, and not only in professedly totalitarian countries, of something very like a doctrine of the Divine Rights of States, though the adjective would be indignantly denied by most of its exponents.

himself, is not subject to the universal because he is as below the universal as the King is above it. The fool is such an individual because, being deficient in reason, subhuman, he has no contact with its demands. The fool is "simple," i.e., he is not a madman. A madman is someone who was once a normal sane man but who, under the stress of emotion, has lost his reason. A fool is born a fool and was never anything else; he is, as we say, "wanting," and whereas a madman is presumed to feel emotions like normal men, indeed to feel them more strongly than the normal man, the fool is presumed to be without emotions. If, therefore, he should happen to utter a truth, it cannot be *his* utterance, for he cannot distingush between truth and falsehood, and he cannot have a personal motive for uttering what, without his knowing it, happens to be true, since motive implies emotion and the fool is presumed to have none. It can only be the voice of God using him as His mouthpiece. God is as far above the superman-King, whose earthly representative he is, as the King is above ordinary mortals, so that the voice of God is a voice, the only one, which the King must admit that it is his duty to obey. Hence the only individual who can speak to the King with authority, not as a subject, is the fool.

The position of the King's Fool is not an easy one. It is obvious that God uses him as a mouthpiece only occasionally, for most of the time what he says is patently nonsense, the words of a fool. At all moments when he is not divinely inspired but just a fool, he is subhuman, not a subject, but a slave, with no human rights, who may be whipped like an animal if he is a nuisance. On the occasions when he happens to speak the truth, he cannot, being a fool, say, "This time I am not speaking nonsense as I usually do, but the truth"; it rests with the King to admit the difference and, since truth is often unwelcome and hard to admit, it is not surprising that the fool's life should be a rough one.

FOOL: Prithee, nuncle, keep a schoolmaster that can teach thy fool to lie.

LEAR: An you lie, sirrah, we'll have you whipped.

> FOOL: I marvel what kin thou and thy daughters are. They'll have me whipped for speaking true; thou'lt have me whipped for lying; and sometimes I am whipped for holding my peace. I had rather be any kind o' thing than a fool; and yet, I would not be thee, nuncle.

It was said above that the cognitive ego never uses the imperative mood, always the indicative or the conditional: it does not say, "Do such-and-such!"; it says, "Such-and-such *is* the case. *If* you want such-and-such a result, you can obtain it by doing as follows. What you want to do, your emotive self can tell you, not I. What you ought to do, your super-ego can tell you, not I." Nor can it compel the volitional ego to listen to it; the choice of listening or refusing to listen lies with the latter.

> Truth's a dog must to kennel; he must be whipped out when Lady the brach may stand by the fire and stink.

We are told that, after Cordelia's departure for France after Lear's first fatal folly, his first "mad" act, the fool started to pine away. After the Third Act, he mysteriously vanishes from the play, and when Lear appears without him, Lear is irremediably mad. At the very end, just before his death, Lear suddenly exclaims "And my poor fool is hanged!" and it is impossible for the audience to know if he is actually referring to the fool or suffering from aphasia and meaning to say Cordelia, whom we know to have been hanged.

The fool, that is, seems to stand for Lear's sense of reality which he rejects. Not for his conscience. The fool never speaks to him, as Kent does, in the name of morality. It was immoral of Lear to make the dowries of his daughters proportionate to their capacity to express their affection for their father, but not necessarily mad because he (and the audience) has no reason to suppose that Cordelia has any less talent for expressing affection than her sisters. Rationally, there is no reason that she should not have surpassed them. Her failure in the competition is due to a moral refusal, not to a lack of talent. Lear's reaction to Cordelia's speech, on the other hand, is not immoral but mad because he knows that, in fact, Cordelia loves him and that Goneril and Regan do not. From that moment on, his sanity is, so to speak, on the periphery of his being instead of at its center, and the dramatic manifestation of this shift is the appearance of the fool who stands outside him as a second figure and is devoted to Cordelia. As long as passion has not totally engulfed him, the fool can appear at his side, laboring "to outjest / His heart struck injuries." There is still a chance, however faint, that he may realize the facts of his situation and be restored to sanity. Thus when Lear begins to address the furniture as if it were his daughters, the fool remarks:

> I cry you mercy. I took you for a joint-stool.

In other words, there is still an element of theatre in Lear's behavior, as a child will talk to inanimate objects as if they were people, while knowing that, in reality, they are not. But when this chance has passed and Lear has descended into madness past recall, there is nothing for the fool to represent and he must disappear.

Frequently the fool makes play with the words "knave" and "fool." A knave is one who disobeys the imperatives of conscience; a fool is one who cannot hear or understand them. Though the cognitive ego is, morally, a "fool" because conscience speaks not to it but to the volitional ego, yet the imperative of duty can never be in contradiction to the actual facts of the situation, as the imperative of passion can be and frequently is. The Socratic doctrine that to know the good is to will it, that sin is ignorance, is valid if by knowing one means listening to what one knows, and by ignorance, willful ignorance. If that is what one means, then, though not all fools are knaves, all knaves are fools.

> LEAR: Dost thou call me fool, boy?
> FOOL: All thy other titles thou hast given away; that thou wast born with.
> KENT: This is not altogether fool, my lord.
> FOOL: No, faith, lords and great men will not let me. If I had a monopoly on't; they would have part of it.

Ideally, in a stage production, Lear and the fool should be of the same physical type; they should both be athletic mesomorphs. The difference should be in their respective sizes. Lear should be as huge as possible, the fool as tiny.

VIII

BODY: *O who shall me deliver whole*
From bonds of this tyrannic soul?
Which, stretcht upright, impales me so
That mine own precipice I go. . . .
SOUL: *What Magick could me thus confine*
Within another's grief to pine?
Where whatsoever it complain,
I feel, that cannot feel, the pain . . .

—ANDREW MARVELL

VALENTINE: *Belike, boy, then you are in love; for last morning you could not see to wipe my shoes.*

SPEED: *True sir; I was in love with my bed. I thank you, you swinged me for my love, which makes me the bolder to chide you for yours.*

—SHAKESPEARE, *Two Gentlemen of Verona*

The *Tempest,* Shakespeare's last play, is a disquieting work. Like the other three comedies of his late period, *Pericles, Cymbeline* and *The Winter's Tale,* it is concerned with a wrong done, repentance, penance and reconciliation; but, whereas the others all end in a blaze of forgiveness and love—"Pardon's the word to all"—in *The Tempest* both the repentance of the guilty and the pardon of the injured seem more formal than real. Of the former, Alonso is the only one who seems genuinely sorry; the repentance of the rest, both the courtly characters, Antonio and Sebastian, and the low, Trinculo and Stephano, is more the prudent promise of the punished and frightened, "I won't do it again. It doesn't pay," than any change of heart: and Prospero's forgiving is more the contemptuous pardon of a man who knows that he has his enemies completely at his mercy than a heartfelt reconciliation. His attitude to all of them is expressed in his final words to Caliban:

> as you look
> To have my pardon trim it handsomely.

One must admire Prospero because of his talents and his strength; one cannot possibly like him. He has the coldness of someone who has come to the conclusion that human nature is not worth much, that human relations are, at their best, pretty sorry affairs. Even towards the innocent young lovers, Ferdinand and Miranda, and their "brave new world," his attitude is one of mistrust so that he has to preach them a sermon on the dangers of anticipating their marriage vows. One might excuse him if he included himself in his critical skepticism but he never does; it never occurs to him that he, too, might have erred and be in need of pardon. He says of Caliban:

> born devil on whose nature
> Nurture can never stick, on whom my pains,
> Humanely taken, all, all lost, quite lost

but Shakespeare has written Caliban's part in such a way that, while we have to admit that Caliban is both brutal and corrupt, a "lying slave" who can be prevented from doing mischief only "by stripes not kindness," we cannot help feeling that Prospero is largely responsible for his corruption, and that, in the debate between them, Caliban has the best of the argument.

Before Prospero's arrival, Caliban had the island to himself, living there in a state of savage innocence. Prospero attempts to educate him, in return for which Caliban shows him all the qualities of the isle. The experiment is brought to a halt when Caliban tries to rape Miranda, and Prospero abandons any hope of educating him further. He does not, however, sever their relation and turn Caliban back to the forest; he changes its nature and, instead of trying to treat Caliban as a son, makes him a slave whom he rules by fear. This relation is profitable to Prospero:

as it is
We cannot miss him. He does make our fire,
Fetch in our wood, and serve us in offices
That profit us

but it is hard to see what profit, material or spiritual, Caliban gets out of it. He has lost his savage freedom:

For I am all the subjects that you have
Which first was mine own king

and he has lost his savage innocence:

You taught me language and my profit on't
Is, I know how to curse

so that he is vulnerable to further corruption when he comes into contact with the civilized vices of Trinculo and Stephano. He is hardly to be blamed, then, if he regards the virtues of civilization with hatred as responsible for his condition:

Remember
First to possess his books, for without them
He's but a sot, as I am.

As a biological organism Man is a natural creature subject to the necessities of nature; as a being with consciousness and will, he is at the same time a historical person with the freedom of the spirit. *The Tempest* seems to me a manichean work, not because it shows the relation of Nature to Spirit as one of conflict and hostility, which in fallen man it is, but because it puts the blame for this upon Nature and makes the Spirit innocent. Such a view is the exact opposite of the view expressed by Dante:

Lo naturale è sempre senza errore
ma l'altro puote errar per male obbietto
o per poco o per troppo di vigore.

(*Purgatorio* XVII.)

The natural can never desire too much or too little because the natural good is the mean—too much and too little are both painful to its natural well-being. The natural, conforming to necessity, cannot imagine possibility. The closest it can come to a relation with the possible is as a vague dream; without Prospero, Ariel can only be known to Caliban as "sounds and sweet airs that give delight and hurt not." The animals cannot fall because the words of the tempter, "Ye shall be as gods," are in the future tense, and the animals have no future tense, for the future tense implies the possibility of doing something that has not been done before, and this they cannot imagine.

Man can never know his "nature" because knowing is itself a spiritual and historical act; his physical sensations are always accompanied by conscious emotions. It is impossible to remember a physical sensation of pleasure or pain, the moment it ceases one cannot recall it, and all one remembers is the emotion of happiness or fear which accompanied it. On the other hand, a sensory stimulus can recall forgotten emotions associated with a previous occurrence of the same stimulus, as when Proust eats the cake.

It is unfortunate that the word "Flesh," set in contrast to "Spirit," is bound to suggest not what the Gospels and St. Paul intended it to mean, the whole physical-historical nature of fallen man, but his physical nature alone, a suggestion very welcome to our passion for reproving and improving others instead of examining our own consciences. For, the more "fleshly" a sin is, the more obviously public it is, and the easier to prevent by the application of a purely external discipline. Thus the sin of gluttony exists in acts of gluttony, in eating, drinking, smoking too much, etc. If a man restrains himself from such excess, or is restrained by others, he ceases to be a glutton; the phrase "gluttonous thoughts" apart from gluttonous acts is meaningless.

As Christ's comment on the commandment indicates, the sin of lust is already "unfleshly" to the degree that it is possible to have lustful thoughts without lustful deeds, but the former are still "fleshly" in that the thinker cannot avoid knowing what they are; he may insist that his thoughts are not sinful but he cannot pretend that they are not lustful. Further, the relation between thought and act is still direct. The thought is the thought of a specific act. The lustful man cannot be a hypocrite to himself except through a symbolic transformation of his desires into images which are not consciously lustful. But the more "spiritual" the sin, the more indirect is the relationship between thought and act, and the easier it is to conceal the sin from others and oneself. I have only to watch a glutton at the dinner table to see that he is a glutton, but I may know someone for a very long time before I realize that he is an envious man, for there is no act which is in itself envious; there are only acts done in the spirit of envy, and there is often nothing about the acts themselves to show that they are done from envy and not from love. It is always possible, therefore, for the envious man to conceal from himself the fact that he is envious and to believe that he is acting from the highest of motives. While in the case of the purely spiritual sin of pride there is no "fleshly" element of the concrete whatsoever, so that no man, however closely he observes others, however strictly he examines himself, can ever know if they or he are proud; if he finds traces of any of the other six capital sins, he can infer pride, because pride is fallen "Spirit-in-itself" and the source of all the other sins, but he cannot draw the reverse inference and, because he finds no traces of the other six, say categorically that he, or another, is not proud.

If man's physical nature could speak when his spirit rebukes it for its corruption, it would have every right to say, "Well, who taught me my bad habits?"; as it is, it has only one form of protest, sickness; in the end, all it can do is destroy itself in an attempt to murder its master.

Over against Caliban, the embodiment of the natural, stands the invisible spirit of imagination, Ariel. (In a stage production, Caliban should be as monstrously conspicuous as possible, and, indeed, suggest, as far as decency permits, the phallic. Ariel, on the other hand, except when he assumes a specific disguise at Prospero's order, e.g., when he appears as a harpy, should, ideally, be invisible, a disembodied voice, an ideal which, in these days of microphones and loud-speakers, should be realizable.)

Caliban was once innocent but has been corrupted; his initial love for Prospero has turned into hatred. The terms "innocent" and "corrupt" cannot be applied to Ariel because he is beyond good and evil; he can neither love nor hate, he can only play. It is not sinful of Eve to imagine the possibility of being as a god knowing good and evil: her sin lay in desiring to realize that possibility when she knew it was forbidden her, and her desire did not come from her imagination, for imagination is without desire and is, therefore, incapable of distinguishing between permitted and forbidden possibilities; it only knows that they are imaginatively possible. Similarly, imagination cannot distinguish the possible from the impossible; to it the impossible is a species of the genus possible, not another genus. I can perfectly well imagine that I might be a hundred feet high or a champion heavyweight boxer, and I do myself no harm in so doing, provided I do so playfully, without desire. I shall, however, come to grief if I take the possibility seriously, which I can do in two ways. Desiring to become a heavyweight boxer, I may deceive myself into thinking that the imaginative possibility is a real possibility and waste my life trying to become the boxer I never can become. Or, desiring to become a boxer, but realizing that it is, for me, impossible, I may refuse to relinquish the desire and turn on God and my neighbor in a passion of hatred and rejection because I cannot have what I want. So Richard III, to punish existence for his misfortune in being born a hunchback, decided to become a villain. Imagination is beyond good *and* evil. Without imagination I remain an innocent animal, unable to become anything but what I already am. In order to become what I should become, therefore, I have to put my imagination to work, and limit its playful activity to imagining those possibilities which, for me, are both permissible and real; if I allow it to be the master and play exactly as it likes, then I shall remain in a dreamlike state of imagining everything I might become, without getting round to ever becoming anything. But, once imagination has done its work for me, to the degree that, with its help, I have become what I should become, imagination has a right to demand its freedom to play without any limitations, for there is no longer any danger that I shall take its play seriously. Hence the relation between Prospero and Ariel is contractual, and, at the end of the drama, Ariel is released.

If *The Tempest* is overpessimistic and manichean, *The Magic Flute* is overoptimistic and pelagian. At the end of the opera a double wedding is celebrated; the representative of the spiritual, Tamino, finds his happiness in Pamina and has attained wisdom while the chorus sing:

Es siegte die Stärke und krönet zum Lohn.
Die Schönheit und Weisheit mit ewiger Kron'

and, at the same time, the representative of the natural, Papageno is rewarded with Papagena, and they sing together:

Erst einen kleinen Papageno
Dann eine kleine Papagena
Dann wieder einen Papageno
Dann wieder eine Papagena

expressing in innocent humility the same attitude which Caliban expresses in guilty defiance when Prospero accuses him of having tried to rape Miranda,

O ho, O ho! Would't had been done.
Thou didst prevent me; I had peopled else
This isle with Calibans.

Tamino obtains his reward because he had had the courage to risk his life undergoing the trials of Fire and Water; Papageno obtains his because he has had the humility to refuse to risk his life even if the refusal will mean that he must remain single. It is as if Caliban, when Prospero offered to adopt him and educate him, had replied: "Thank you very much, but clothes and speech are not for me; It is better I stay in the jungle."

According to *The Magic Flute*, it is possible for nature and spirit to coexist in man harmoniously and without conflict, provided both keep to themselves and do not interfere with each other, and that, further, the natural has the freedom to refuse to be interfered with.

The greatest of spirit-nature pairs and the most orthodox is, of course, Don Quixote–Sancho Panza. Unlike Prospero and Caliban, their relationship is harmonious and happy; unlike Tamino and Papageno, it is dialectical; each affects the other. Further, both they and their relationship are comic; Don Quixote is comically mad, Sancho Panza is comically sane, and each finds the other a lovable figure of fun, an endless source of diversion. It is this omnipresent comedy that makes the book orthodox; present the relationship as tragic and the conclusion is manichean, present either or both of the characters as serious, and the conclusion is pagan or pelagian. The man who takes seriously the command of Christ to take up his cross and follow Him must, if he is serious, see himself as a comic figure, for he is not the Christ, only an ordinary man, yet he believes that the command, "Be ye perfect," is seriously addressed to himself. Worldly "sanity" will say, "I am not Christ, only an ordinary man. For me to think that I can become perfect would be madness. Therefore, the command cannot seriously be addressed to me." The other can only say, "It is madness for me to attempt to obey the command, for it seems impossible; nevertheless, since I believe it is addressed to me, I must believe that it is possible"; in proportion as he takes the command seriously, that is, he will see himself as a comic figure. To take himself seriously would mean that he thought of himself, not as an ordinary man, but as Christ.

For Christ is not a model to be imitated, like Hector, or Aristotle's megalopsych, but the Way to be followed, If a man thinks that the megalopsych is a desirable model, all he has to do is to read up how the megalopsych behaves and imitate him, e.g., he will be careful, when walking, not to swing his arms.

But the Way cannot be imitated, only followed; a Christian who is faced with a moral problem cannot look up the answer in the Gospels. If someone, for instance, were to let his hair and beard grow till he looked like some popular pious picture of Christ, put on a white linen robe and ride into town on a donkey, we should know at once that he was either a madman or a fake. At first sight Don Quixote's madness seems to be of this kind. He believes that the world of the Romances is the real world and that, to be a knight-errant, all he has to do is imitate the Romances exactly. Like Lear, he cannot distinguish imaginative possibilities from actualities and treats analogies as identities; Lear thinks a stool is his daughter, Don Quixote thinks windmills are giants, but their manias are not really the same. Lear might be said to be suffering from worldly madness. The worldly man goes mad when the actual state of affairs becomes too intolerable for his *amour-propre* to accept; Lear cannot face the fact that he is no longer a man of power or that he has brought his present situation upon himself by his unjust competition. Don Quixote's madness, on the other hand, might be called holy madness, for *amour-propre* has nothing to do with his delusions. If his madness were of Lear's kind, then, in addition to believing that he must imitate the knight-errants of old, he would have endowed himself in their imagination with their gifts, e.g., with the youth and strength of Amadis of Gaul: but he does nothing of the kind; he knows that he is past fifty and penniless, nevertheless, he believes he is called to be a knight-errant. The knight-errant sets out to win glory by doing great deeds and to win the love of his lady, and whatever trials and defeats he may suffer on the way, in the end he triumphs. Don Quixote, however, fails totally; he accomplishes nothing, he does not win his lady, and, as if that were not ignominious enough, what he does win is a parody of what a knight-errant is supposed to win, for he does, in fact, become famous and admired—as a madman. If his were a worldly madness, *amour-propre* would demand that he add to his other delusions the delusion of having succeeded, the delusion that the welcome he receives everywhere is due to the fame of his great deeds (a delusion which his audience do everything to encourage), but Don Quixote is perfectly well aware that he has failed to do anything which he set out to do.

At the opposite pole to madness stands philistine realism.

Madness says, "Windmills are giants"; philistine realism says, "Windmills are only windmills; giants are only giants," and then adds "Windmills really exist because they provide me with flour; giants are imaginary and do not exist because they provide me with nothing." (A student of psychoanalysis who says, "Windmills and giants are only phallic symbols," is both philistine and mad.) Madness confuses analogies with identities, philistine realism refuses to recognize analogies and only admits identities; neither can say, "Windmills are like giants."

At first sight Sancho Panza seems a philistine realist. "I go," he says, "with a great desire to make money"; it may seem to the reader hardly "realistic" of Sancho Panza to believe that he will gain a penny, far less an island governorship, by following Don Quixote, but is not the philistine realist who believes in nothing but material satisfactions precisely the same type to whom it is easiest to sell a nonexistent gold mine?

The sign that Sancho Panza is not a philistine but a "holy" realist is the persistence of his hope of getting something when he has realized that his master is mad. It is as if a man who had been sold a nonexistent gold mine continued to believe in its existence after he had discovered that the seller was a crook. It is clear that, whatever Sancho Panza may say, his motives for following his master are love of his master, and that equally unrealistic of motives, love of adventure for its own sake, a poetic love of fun. Just as Don Quixote wins fame, but fame as a madman, so Sancho Panza actually becomes the Governor of an island, but as a practical joke; as Governor he obtains none of the material rewards which a philistine would hope for, yet he enjoys himself enormously. Sancho Panza is a realist in that it is always the actual world, the immediate moment, which he enjoys, not an imaginary world or an anticipated future, but a "holy" realist in that he enjoys the actual and immediate for its own sake, not for any material satisfactions it provides.

Don Quixote and Sancho Panza are both inveterate quoters: what the Romances are to the one, proverbs are to the other. A Romance is a history, feigned or real. It recounts a series of unique and quite extraordinary events which have, or are purported to have, happened in the past. The source of interest is in the events themselves, not in the literary style in which they are narrated; as long as the reader learns what happened, it is a matter of indifference to him whether the style is imaginative or banal. A proverb has nothing to do with history for it states, or claims to state, a truth which is valid at all times. The context of "A stitch in time saves nine" belongs to the same class as a statement of empirical science like "Bodies attract each other in direct proportion to their masses." The interest of a proverb, therefore, lies not in its content but in the unique way in which that content is expressed; the content is always banal because it is a statement of empirical science, and a scientific statement which was not banal would not be true.

Proverbs belong to the natural world where the Model and imitation of the Model are valid concepts. A proverb tells one exactly what one should do or avoid doing whenever the situation comes up to which it applies: if the situation comes up the proverb applies exactly; if it does not come up, the proverb does not apply at all. Romances, as we have seen, belong to the historical world of the spirit, where the Model is replaced by the Way, and imitation by following. But in man, these two worlds are not separate but dialectically related; the proverb, as an expression of the natural, admits its relation to the historical by its valuation of style; the romance, as an expression of the historical, admits its relation to the natural by its indifference to style.

Don Quixote's lack of illusions about his own powers is a sign that his madness is not worldly but holy, a forsaking of the world, but without Sancho Panza it would not be Christian. For his madness to be Christian, he must have a neighbor, someone other than himself about whom he has no delusions but loves as himself. Without Sancho Panza, Don Quixote would be without neighbors, and the kind of religion implied would be one in which love of God was not only possible without but incompatible with love of one's neighbor.

IX

> *He that is greatest among you, let him be as the younger; and he that is chief, as he that doth serve.*
>
> —LUKE: XXII, 26

> *Che per quanti si dice piu li nostro tanto possiede piu di ben ciascuno.*
>
> —DANTE, *Purgatorio,* XV

When a lover tells his beloved that she is his mistress and that he desires to be her servant, what he is trying, honestly or hypocritically, to say is something as follows: "As you know, I find you beautiful, an object of desire. I know that for true love such desire is not enough; I must also love you, not as an object of my desire, but as you are in yourself; I must desire your self-fulfillment. I cannot know you as you are nor prove that I desire your self-fulfillment, unless you tell me what you want and allow me to try and give it to you."

The proverb, "No man is a hero to his own valet," does not mean that no valet admires his master, but that a valet knows his master as he really is, admirable or contemptible, because it is a valet's job to supply the wants of his master, and, if you know what somebody wants, you know what he is like. It is possible for a master to have not the faintest inkling of what his servant is really like—unless his servant loves him, it is certain that he never will—but it is impossible for a servant, whether he be friendly, hostile or indifferent, not to know exactly what his master is like, for the latter reveals himself every time he gives an order.

To illustrate the use of the master-servant relationship as a parable of agape, I will take two examples from books which present the parable in a clear, simplified form, *Around the World in Eighty Days* by Jules Verne and the *Jeeves* series by P. G. Wodehouse.

Mr. Fogg, as Jules Verne depicts him in his opening chapter, is a kind of stoic saint. He is a bachelor with ample private means and does no work, but he is never idle and has no vices; he plays whist at his club every evening but never more or less than the same number of hands, and, when he wins, he gives the money to charity. He knows all about the world for he is a religious reader of the newspapers, but he takes no part in its affairs; he has no friends and no enemies; he has never been known to show emotion of any kind; he seems to live "outside of any social relation." If "apathy" in the stoic sense is the highest virtue, then Fogg is a saint. His most striking trait, however, is one which seems to have been unknown in Classical times, a ritual mania about the exact time, an idolatry of the clock—his own tells the second, the minute, the hour, the day, the month and the year. He not only does exactly the same thing every day, but at exactly the same moment. Classical authors like Theophrastus have described very accurately most characterological types, but none of them, so far as I know, has described The Punctual Man (the type to which I personally belong), who cannot tell if he is hungry unless it first looks at the clock. It was never said in praise of any Caesar, for instance, that he made whatever was the Roman equivalent for trains run on time. I have heard it suggested that the first punctual people in history were the monks—at their office hours. It is certain at least that the first serious analysis of the human experience of time was undertaken by St. Augustine, and that the notion of punctuality, of action at an exact moment, depends on drawing a distinction between natural and historical time which Christianity encouraged if it did not invent.[3]

By and large, at least, the ancients thought of time either as oscillating to and fro like a pendulum or as moving round and round like a wheel, and the notion of historical time moving in an irreversible unilateral direction was strange to them. Both oscillation and cyclical movement provide a notion of change, but of change *for-a-time;* this *for-a-time* may be a long time—the pendulum may oscillate or the

[3] The Greek notion of *kairos,* the propitious moment for doing something, contained the seed of the notion of punctuality, but the seed did not flower.

wheel revolve very slowly—but sooner or later all events reoccur: there is no place for a notion of absolute novelty, of a unique event which occurs once and for all at a particular moment in time. This latter notion cannot be derived from our objective experience of the outside world—all the movements we can see there are either oscillatory or cyclical—but only form our subjective inner experience of time in such phenomena as memory and anticipation.

So long as we think of it objectively, time is Fate or Chance, the factor in our lives for which we are not responsible, and about which we can do nothing; but when we begin to think of it subjectively, we feel responsible for *our* time, and the notion of punctuality arises. In training himself to be superior to circumstance, the ancient stoic would discipline his passions because he knew what a threat they could be to the apathy he sought to acquire, but it would not occur to him to discipline his time, because he was unaware that it was his. A modern stoic like Mr. Fogg knows that the surest way to discipline passion is to discipline time: decide what you want or ought to do during the day, then always do it at exactly the same moment every day, and passion will give you no trouble.

Mr. Fogg has been so successful with himself that he is suffering from *hubris;* he is convinced that nothing can happen to him which he has not foreseen. Others, it is true, are often unreliable, but the moment he finds them so, he severs relations with them. On the morning when the story opens, he has just dismissed his servant for bringing him his shaving water at a temperature of 84° instead of the proper 86° and is looking for a new one. His conception of the just relation between master and servant is that the former must issue orders which are absolutely clear and unchanging—the master has no right to puzzle his servant or surprise him with an order for which he is not prepared—and the latter must carry them out as impersonally and efficiently as a machine—one slip and he is fired. The last thing he looks for in a servant or, for that matter, in anyone else is a personal friend.

On the same morning Passepartout has given notice to

Lord Longsferry because he cannot endure to work in a chaotic household where the master is "brought home too frequently on the shoulders of policemen." Himself a sanguine, mercurial character, what he seeks in a master is the very opposite of what he would seek in a friend. He wishes his relation to his master to be formal and impersonal; in a master, therefore, he seeks his opposite, the phlegmatic character. His ideal of the master-servant relation happens, therefore, to coincide with Fogg's, and to the mutual satisfaction of both, he is interviewed and engaged.

But that evening the unforeseen happens, the bet which is to send them both off round the world. It is his *hubris* which tempts Mr. Fogg into making the bet; he is so convinced that nothing unforeseen can occur which he cannot control that he cannot allow his club mates to challenge this conviction without taking up the challenge. Further, unknown to him, by a chance accident which he could not possibly have foreseen, a bank robbery has just been committed, and the description of the thief given to the police plus his sudden departure from England have put him under suspicion. Off go Mr. Fogg and Passepartout, then, pursued by the detective Fix. In the boat train Passepartout suddenly remembers that in the haste of packing he has left the gas fire burning in his bedroom. Fogg does not utter a word of reproach but merely remarks that it will burn at Passepartout's expense till they return. Mr. Fogg is still the stoic with the stoic conception of justice operating as impersonally and inexorably as the laws of nature. It is a fact that it was Passepartout, not he, who forgot to turn off the gas; the hurry caused by his own sudden decision may have made it difficult for Passepartout to remember, but it did not make it impossible: therefore, Passepartout is responsible for his forgetfulness and must pay the price.

Then in India the decisive moment arrives: they run into preparations for the suttee, against her will, of a beautiful young widow, Aouda. For the first time in his life, apparently, Mr. Fogg is confronted personally with human injustice and suffering, and a moral choice. If, like the priest and the

Levite, he passes by on the other side, he will catch the boat at Calcutta and win his bet with ease; if he attempts to save her, he will miss his boat and run a serious risk of losing his bet. Abandoning his stoic apathy, he chooses the second alternative, and from that moment on his relationship with Passepartout ceases to be impersonal; *philia* is felt by both. Moreover, he discovers that Passepartout has capacities which his normal duties as a servant would never have revealed, but which in this emergency situation are particularly valuable because Mr. Fogg himself is without them. But for Passepartout's capacity for improvisation and acting which allow him successfully to substitute himself for the corpse on the funeral pyre, Aouda would never have been saved. Hitherto, Mr. Fogg has always believed that there was nothing of importance anyone else could do which he could not do as well or better himself; for the first time in his life he abandons that belief.

Hitherto, Passepartout has thought of his master as an unfeeling automaton, just, but incapable of generosity or self-sacrifice; had he not had this unexpected revelation, he would certainly have betrayed Mr. Fogg to Fix, for the detective succeeds in convincing him that his master is a bank robber, and, according to the stoic notion of impersonal justice which Mr. Fogg had seemed to exemplify, that would be his duty, but, having seen him act personally, Passepartout refuses to assist impersonal justice.

Later, when the Trans-American express is attacked by Indians, it is Passepartout's athletic ability, a quality irrelevant to a servant's normal duties, which saves the lives of Mr. Fogg and Aouda at the risk of his own, for he is captured by the Indians. In such an act the whole contractual master-servant relation is transcended; that one party shall undertake to sacrifice his life for the other cannot be a clause in any contract. The only possible repayment is a similar act, and Mr. Fogg lets the relief train go without him, sacrificing what may well be his last chance of winning his bet, and goes back at the risk of his life to rescue Passepartout.

Like Mr. Fogg, Bertie Wooster is a bachelor with private

means who does no work, but there all the resemblance ceases. Nobody could possibly be less of a stoic than the latter. If he has no vices it is because his desires are too vague and too fleeting for him to settle down to one. Hardly a week passes without Bertie Wooster thinking he has at last met The Girl; for a week he imagines he is her Tristan, but the next week he has forgotten her as completely as Don Giovanni forgets; besides, nothing ever happens. It is nowhere suggested that he owned a watch or that, if he did, he could tell the time by it. By any worldly moral standard he is a footler whose existence is of no importance to anybody. Yet it is Bertie Wooster who has the incomparable Jeeves for his servant. Jeeves could any day find a richer master or a place with less arduous duties, yet it is Bertie Wooster whom he chooses to serve. The lucky Simpleton is a common folk-tale hero; for example, the Third Son who succeeds in the Quest appears, in comparison with his two elder brothers, the least talented, but his ambition to succeed is equal to theirs. He sets out bravely into the unknown, and unexpectedly triumphs. But Bertie Wooster is without any ambition whatsoever and does not lift a finger to help himself, yet he is rewarded with what, for him, is even better than a beautiful Princess, the perfect omniscient nanny who does everything for him and keeps him out of trouble without, however, ever trying, as most nannies will, to educate and improve him.

—I say, Jeeves, a man I met at the club last night told me to put my shirt on Privateer for the two o'clock race this afternoon. How about it?

—I should not advocate it, sir. The stable is not sanguine.

—Talking of shirts, have those mauve ones I ordered arrived yet?

—Yes, sir. I sent them back.

—Sent them back?

—Yes, sir. They would not have become you.

The Quest Hero often encounters an old beggar or an animal who offers him advice: if, too proud to imagine that such an apparently inferior creature could have anything to tell him, he ignores the advice, it has fatal consequences; if he is humble enough to listen and obey, then, thanks to their help, he achieves his goal. But, however humble he may be, he still has the dream of becoming a hero; he may be humble enough to take advice from what seem to be his inferiors, but he is convinced that, potentially, he is a superior person, a prince-to-be. Bertie Wooster, on the other hand, not only knows that he is a person of no account, but also never expects to become anything else; till his dying day he will remain, he knows, a footler who requires a nanny; yet, at the same time, he is totally without envy of others who are or may become of some account. He has, in fact, that rarest of virtues, humility, and so he is blessed: it is he and no other who has for his servant the godlike Jeeves.

—All the other great men of the age are simply in the crowd, watching you go by.
—Thank you very much, sir. I endeavor to give satisfaction.

So speaks comically—and in what other mode than the comic could it on earth truthfully speak?—the voice of Agape, of Holy Love.

THE GUILTY VICARAGE

I had not known sin, but by the law.

ROMANS: VII, 7

A Confession

For me, as for many others, the reading of detective stories is an addiction like tobacco or alcohol. The symptoms of this are: firstly, the intensity of the craving—if I have any work to do, I must be careful not to get hold of a detective story for, once I begin one, I cannot work or sleep till I have finished it. Secondly, its specificity—the story must conform to certain formulas (I find it very difficult, for example, to read one that is not set in rural England). And, thirdly, its immediacy. I forget the story as soon as I have finished it, and have no wish to read it again. If, as sometimes happens, I start reading one and find after a few pages that I have read it before, I cannot go on.

Such reactions convince me that, in my case at least, detective stories have nothing to do with works of art. It is possible, however, that an analysis of the detective story, i.e., of the kind of detective story I enjoy, may throw light, not only on its magical function, but also, by contrast, on the function of art.

Definition

The vulgar definition, "a Whodunit," is correct. The basic formula is this: a murder occurs; many are suspected; all but one suspect, who is the murderer, are eliminated; the murderer is arrested or dies.

This definition excludes:

1) Studies of murderers whose guilt is known, e.g., *Malice Aforethought*. There are borderline cases in which the murderer is known and there are no false suspects, but the proof is lacking, e.g., many of the stories of Freeman Wills Crofts. Most of these are permissible.

2) Thrillers, spy stories, stories of master crooks, etc., when the identification of the criminal is subordinate to the defeat of his criminal designs.

The interest in the thriller is the ethical and characteristic conflict between good and evil, between Us and Them. The interest in the study of a murderer is the observation, by the innocent many, of the sufferings of the guilty one. The interest in the detective story is the dialectic of innocence and guilt.

As in the Aristotelian description of tragedy, there is Concealment (the innocent seem guilty and the guilty seem innocent) and Manifestation (the real guilt is brought to consciousness). There is also peripeteia, in this case not a reversal of fortune but a double reversal from apparent guilt to innocence and from apparent innocence to guilt. The formula may be diagrammed as follows:

Peaceful state before murder
|
False clues, secondary murder, etc.
|
Solution
|
Arrest of murderer
|
Peaceful state after arrest

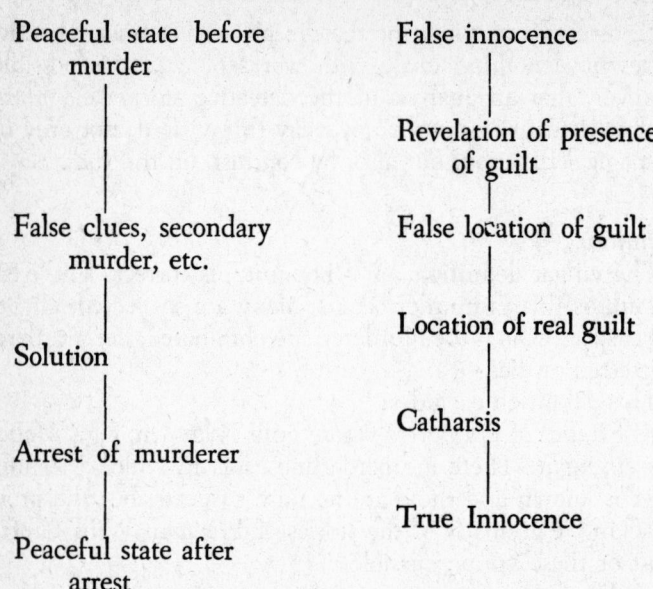

False innocence
|
Revelation of presence of guilt
|
False location of guilt
|
Location of real guilt
|
Catharsis
|
True Innocence

In Greek tragedy the audience knows the truth; the actors do not, but discover or bring to pass the inevitable. In modern, e.g., Elizabethan, tragedy the audience knows neither less nor more than the most knowing of the actors. In the detective story the audience does not know the truth at all; one of the actors—the murderer—does; and the detective, of his own free will, discovers and reveals what the murderer, of his own free will, tries to conceal.

Greek tragedy and the detective story have one characteristic in common in which they both differ from modern tragedy, namely, the characters are not changed in or by their actions: in Greek tragedy because their actions are fated, in the detective story because the decisive event, the murder, has already occurred. Time and space therefore are simply the when and where of revealing either what has to happen or what has actually happened. In consequence, the detective story probably should, and usually does, obey the classical unities, whereas modern tragedy, in which the characters develop with time, can only do so by a technical tour de force; and the thriller, like the picaresque novel, even demands frequent changes of time and place.

Why Murder?

There are three classes of crime: (A) offenses against God and one's neighbor or neighbors; (B) offenses against God and society; (C) offenses against God. (All crimes, of course, are offenses against oneself.)

Murder is a member and the only member of Class B. The character common to all crimes in Class A is that it is possible, at least theoretically, either that restitution can be made to the injured party (e.g., stolen goods can be returned), or that the injured party can forgive the criminal (e.g., in the case of rape). Consequently, society as a whole is only indirectly involved; its representatives (the police, etc.) act in the interests of the injured party.

Murder is unique in that it abolishes the party it injures, so that society has to take the place of the victim and on his behalf demand restitution or grant forgiveness; it is the one crime in which society has a direct interest.

Many detective stories begin with a death that appears to be suicide and is later discovered to have been murder. Suicide is a crime belonging to Class C in which neither the criminal's neighbors nor society has any interest, direct or indirect. As long as a death is believed to be suicide, even private curiosity is improper; as soon as it is proved to be murder, public inquiry becomes a duty.

The detective story has five elements—the milieu, the victim, the murderer, the suspects, the detectives.

The Milieu (Human)

The detective story requires:

1) A closed society so that the possibility of an outside murderer (and hence of the society being totally innocent) is excluded; and a closely related society so that all its members are potentially suspect (*cf.* the thriller, which requires an open society in which any stranger may be a friend or enemy in disguise).

Such conditions are met by: a) the group of blood relatives (the Christmas dinner in the country house); b) the closely knit geographical group (the old world village); c) the occupational group (the theatrical company); d) the group isolated by the neutral place (the Pullman car).

In this last type the concealment-manifestation formula applies not only to the murder but also to the relations between the members of the group who first appear to be strangers to each other, but are later found to be related.

2) It must appear to be an innocent society in a state of grace, i.e., a society where there is no need of the law, no contradiction between the aesthetic individual and the ethical universal, and where murder, therefore, is the unheard-of act which precipitates a crisis (for it reveals that some member has fallen and is no longer in a state of grace). The law becomes a reality and for a time all must live in its shadow, till the fallen one is identified. With his arrest, innocence is restored, and the law retires forever.

The characters in a detective story should, therefore, be eccentric (aesthetically interesting individuals) and good (instinctively ethical)—good, that is, either in appearance, later shown to be false, or in reality, first concealed by an appearance of bad.

It is a sound instinct that has made so many detective story writers choose a college as a setting. The ruling passion of the ideal professor is the pursuit of knowledge for its own sake so that he is related to other human beings only indirectly through their common relation to the truth; and those passions, like lust and avarice and envy, which relate individuals directly and may lead to murder are, in his case, ideally excluded. If a murder occurs in a college, therefore, it is a sign that some colleague is not only a bad man but also a bad professor. Further, as the basic premise of academic life is that truth is universal and to be shared with all, the *gnosis* of a concrete crime and the *gnosis* of abstract ideas nicely parallel and parody each other.

(The even more ideal contradiction of a murder in a monastery is excluded by the fact that monks go regularly to confession and, while the murderer might well not confess his crime, the suspects who are innocent of murder but guilty of lesser sins cannot be supposed to conceal them without making the monastery absurd. Incidentally, is it an accident that the detective story has flourished most in predominantly Protestant countries?)

The detective story writer is also wise to choose a society with an elaborate ritual and to describe this in detail. A ritual is a sign of harmony between the aesthetic and the ethical in which body and mind, individual will and general laws, are not in conflict. The murderer uses his knowledge of the ritual to commit the crime and can be caught only by someone who acquires an equal or superior familiarity with it.

The Milieu (Natural)

In the detective story, as in its mirror image, the Quest for the Grail, maps (the ritual of space) and timetables (the ritual of time) are desirable. Nature should reflect its human inhabitants, i.e., it should be the Great Good Place; for the more Eden-like it is, the greater the contradiction of murder. The country is preferable to the town, a well-to-do neighborhood (but not too well-to-do—or there will be a suspicion of ill-gotten gains) better than a slum. The corpse must shock not only because it is a corpse but also because, even for a corpse, it is shockingly out of place, as when a dog makes a mess on a drawing room carpet.

Mr. Raymond Chandler has written that he intends to take the body out of the vicarage garden and give the murder back to those who are good at it. If he wishes to write detective stories, i.e., stories where the reader's principal interest is to learn who did it, he could not be more mistaken, for in a society of professional criminals, the only possible motives for desiring to identify the murderer are blackmail or revenge, which both apply to individuals, not to the group as a whole, and can equally well inspire murder. Actually, whatever he may say, I think Mr. Chandler is interested in writing, not detective stories, but serious studies of a criminal milieu, the Great Wrong Place, and his powerful but extremely depressing books should be read and judged, not as escape literature, but as works of art.

The Victim

The victim has to try to satisfy two contradictory requirements. He has to involve everyone in suspicion, which requires that he be a bad character; and he has to make everyone feel guilty, which requires that he be a good character. He cannot be a criminal because he could then be dealt with by the law and murder would be unnecessary. (Blackmail is the only exception.) The more general the temptation to murder he arouses, the better; e.g., the desire for freedom is a better motive than money alone or sex alone. On the whole, the best victim is the negative Father or Mother Image.

If there is more than one murder, the subsequent victims should be more innocent than the initial victim, i.e., the murderer should start with a real grievance and, as a consequence of righting it by illegitimate means, be forced to murder against his will where he has no grievances but his own guilt.

The Murderer

Murder is negative creation, and every murderer is therefore the rebel who claims the right to be omnipotent. His pathos is his refusal to suffer. The problem for the writer is to conceal his demonic pride from the other characters and from the reader, since, if a person has this pride, it tends to appear in everything he says and does. To surprise the reader when the identity of the murderer is revealed, yet at the same time to convince him that everything he has previously been told about the murderer is consistent with his being a murderer, is the test of a good detective story.

As to the murderer's end, of the three alternatives—execution, suicide, and madness—the first is preferable; for if he commits suicide he refuses to repent, and if he goes mad he cannot repent, but if he does not repent society cannot forgive. Execution on the other hand, is the act of atonement by which the murderer is forgiven by society. In real life I disapprove of capital punishment, but in a detective story the murderer must have no future.

(*A Suggestion for Mr. Chandler:* Among a group of efficient professional killers who murder for strictly professional reasons, there is one to whom, like Leopold and Loeb, murder is an *acte gratuite*. Presently murders begin to occur which have not been commissioned. The group is morally outraged and bewildered; it has to call in the police to detect the amateur murderer, rescue the professionals from a mutual suspicion which threatens to disrupt their organization, and restore their capacity to murder.)

The Suspects

The detective-story society is a society consisting of apparently innocent individuals, i.e., their aesthetic interest as individuals does not conflict with their ethical obligations to the universal. The murder is the act of disruption by which innocence is lost, and the individual and the law become opposed to each other. In the case of the murderer this opposition is completely real (till he is arrested and consents to be punished); in the case of the suspects it is mostly apparent.

But in order for the appearance to exist, there must be some element of reality; e.g., it is unsatisfactory if the suspicion is caused by chance or the murderer's malice alone. The suspects must be guilty of something, because, now that the aesthetic and the ethical are in opposition, if they are completely innocent (obedient to the ethical) they lose their aesthetic interest and the reader will ignore them.

For suspects, the principal causes of guilt are:

1) the wish or even the intention to murder;

2) crimes of Class A or vices of Class C (e.g., illicit amours) which the suspect is afraid or ashamed to reveal;

3) a *hubris* of intellect which tries to solve the crime itself and despises the official police (assertion of the supremacy of the aesthetic over the ethical). If great enough, this *hubris* leads to its subject getting murdered;

4) a *hubris* of innocence which refuses to cooperate with the investigation;

5) a lack of faith in another loved suspect, which leads its subject to hide or confuse clues.

The Detective

Completely satisfactory detectives are extremely rare. Indeed, I only know of three: Sherlock Holmes (Conan Doyle), Inspector French (Freeman Wills Crofts), and Father Brown (Chesterton).

The job of detective is to restore the state of grace in which the aesthetic and the ethical are as one. Since the murderer who caused their disjunction is the aesthetically defiant individual, his opponent, the detective, must be either the official representative of the ethical or the exceptional individual who is himself in a state of grace. If he is the former, he is a professional; if he is the latter, he is an amateur. In either case, the detective must be the total stranger who cannot possibly be involved in the crime; this excludes the local police and should, I think, exclude the detective who is a friend of one of the suspects. The professional detective has the advantage that, since he is not an individual but a representative of the ethical, he does not need a motive for investigating the crime; but for the same reason he has the disadvantage of being unable to overlook the minor ethical violations of the suspects, and therefore it is harder for him to gain their confidence.

Most amateur detectives, on the other hand, are unsatisfactory either because they are priggish supermen, like Lord Peter Wimsey and Philo Vance, who have no motive for being detectives except caprice, or because, like the detectives of the hard-boiled school, they are motivated by avarice or ambition and might just as well be murderers.

The amateur detective genius may have weaknesses to give him aesthetic interest, but they must not be of a kind which outrage ethics. The most satisfactory weaknesses are the solitary oral vices of eating and drinking or childish boasting. In his sexual life, the detective must be either celibate or happily married.

Between the amateur detective and the professional policeman stands the criminal lawyer whose *telos* is, not to discover who is guilty, but to prove that his client is innocent. His ethical justification is that human law is ethically imperfect, i.e., not an absolute manifestation of the universal and divine, and subject to chance aesthetic limitations, e.g., the intelligence or stupidity of individual policemen and juries (in consequence of which an innocent man may sometimes be judged guilty).

To correct this imperfection, the decision is arrived at through an aesthetic combat, i.e., the intellectual gifts of the defense versus those of the prosecution, just as in earlier days doubtful cases were solved by physical combat between the accused and the accuser.

The lawyer-detective (e.g., Joshua Clunk) is never quite satisfactory, therefore, because of his commitment to his client, whom he cannot desert, even if he should really be the guilty party, without ceasing to be a lawyer.

Sherlock Holmes

Holmes is the exceptional individual who is in a state of grace because he is a genius in whom scientific curiosity is raised to the status of a heroic passion. He is erudite but his knowledge is absolutely specialized (e.g., his ignorance of the Copernican system), he is in all matters outside his field as helpless as a child (e.g., his untidiness), and he pays the price for his scientific detachment (his neglect of feeling) by being the victim of melancholia which attacks him whenever he is unoccupied with a case (e.g., his violin playing and cocaine taking).

His motive for being a detective is, positively, a love of the neutral truth (he has no interest in the feelings of the guilty or the innocent), and negatively, a need to escape from his own feelings of melancholy. His attitude towards people and his technique of observation and deduction are those of the chemist or physicist. If he chooses human beings rather than inanimate matter as his material, it is because investigating the inanimate is unheroically easy since it cannot tell lies, which human beings can and do, so that in dealing with them, observation must be twice as sharp and logic twice as rigorous.

Inspector French

His class and culture are those natural to a Scotland Yard inspector. (The old Oxonian Inspector is insufferable.) His motive is love of duty. Holmes detects for his own sake and shows the maximum indifference to all feelings except a negative fear of his own. French detects for the sake of the innocent members of society, and is indifferent only to his own feelings and those of the murderer. (He would much rather stay at home with his wife.) He is exceptional only in his exceptional love of duty which makes him take exceptional pains; he does only what all could do as well if they had the same patient industry (his checking of alibis for tiny flaws which careless hurry had missed). He outwits the murderer, partly because the latter is not quite so painstaking as he, and partly because the murderer must act alone, while he has the help of all the innocent people in the world who are doing their duty, e.g., the postmen, railway clerks, milkmen, etc., who become, accidentally, witnesses to the truth.

Father Brown

Like Holmes, an amateur; yet, like French, not an individual genius. His activities as a detective are an incidental part of his activities as a priest who cares for souls. His prime motive is compassion, of which the guilty are in greater need than the innocent, and he investigates murders, not for his own sake, nor even for the sake of the innocent, but for the sake of the murderer who can save his soul if he will confess and repent. He solves his cases, not by approaching them objectively like a scientist or a policeman, but by subjectively imagining himself to be the murderer, a process which is good not only for the murderer but for Father Brown himself because, as he says, "it gives a man his remorse beforehand."

Holmes and French can only help the murderer as teachers, i.e., they can teach him that murder will out and does not pay. More they cannot do since neither is tempted to murder; Holmes is too gifted, French too well trained in the habit of virtue. Father Brown can go further and help the murderer as an example, i.e., as a man who is also tempted to murder, but is able by faith to resist temptation.

The Reader

The most curious fact about the detective story is that it makes its greatest appeal precisely to those classes of people who are most immune to other forms of daydream literature. The typical detective story addict is a doctor or clergyman or scientist or artist, i.e., a fairly successful professional man with intellectual interests and well-read in his own field, who could never stomach the *Saturday Evening Post* or *True Confessions* or movie magazines or comics. If I ask myself why I cannot enjoy stories about strong silent men and lovely girls who make love in a beautiful landscape and come into millions of dollars, I cannot answer that I have no fantasies of being handsome and loved and rich, because of course I have (though my life is, perhaps, sufficiently fortunate to make me less envious in a naïve way than some). No, I can only say that I am too conscious of the absurdity of such wishes to enjoy seeing them reflected in print.

I can, to some degree, resist yielding to these or similar desires which tempt me, but I cannot prevent myself from having them to resist; and it is the fact that I have them which makes me feel guilty, so that instead of dreaming about indulging my desires, I dream about the removal of the guilt which I feel at their existence. This I still do, and must do, because guilt is a subjective feeling where any further step is only a reduplication—feeling guilty about guilt. I suspect that the typical reader of detective stories is, like myself, a person who suffers from a sense of sin. From the point of view of ethics, desires and acts are good and bad, and I must choose the good and reject the bad, but the I which makes this choice is ethically neutral; it only becomes good or bad in its choice. To have a sense of sin means to feel guilty at there being an ethical choice to make, a guilt which, however "good" I may become, remains unchanged. It is sometimes said that detective stories are read by respectable law-abiding citizens in order to gratify in fantasy the violent or murderous wishes they dare not, or are ashamed to, translate into action. This may be true for the reader of thrillers (which I rarely enjoy), but it is quite false for the reader of detective stories.

On the contrary, the magical satisfaction the latter provide (which makes them escape literature, not works of art) is the illusion of being dissociated from the murderer.

The magic formula is an innocence which is discovered to contain guilt; then a suspicion of being the guilty one; and finally a real innocence from which the guilty other has been expelled, a cure effected, not by me or my neighbors, but by the miraculous intervention of a genius from outside who removes guilt by giving knowledge of guilt. (The detective story subscribes, in fact, to the Socratic daydream: "Sin is ignorance.")

If one thinks of a work of art which deals with murder, *Crime and Punishment* for example, its effect on the reader is to compel an identification with the murderer which he would prefer not to recognize. The identification of fantasy is always an attempt to avoid one's own suffering: the identification of art is a sharing in the suffering of another. Kafka's *The Trial* is another instructive example of the difference between a work of art and the detective story. In the latter it is certain that a crime has been committed and, temporarily, uncertain to whom the guilt should be attached; as soon as this is known, the innocence of everyone else is certain. (Should it turn out that after all no crime has been committed, then all would be innocent.) In *The Trial*, on the other hand, it is the guilt that is certain and the crime that is uncertain; the aim of the hero's investigation is not to prove his innocence (which would be impossible for he knows he is guilty), but to discover what, if anything, he has done to make himself guilty. K, the hero, is, in fact, a portrait of the kind of person who reads detective stories for escape.

The fantasy, then, which the detective story addict indulges is the fantasy of being restored to the Garden of Eden, to a state of innocence, where he may know love as love and not as the law. The driving force behind this daydream is the feeling of guilt, the cause of which is unknown to the dreamer. The fantasy of escape is the same, whether one explains the guilt in Christian, Freudian, or any other terms. One's way of trying to face the reality, on the other hand, will, of course, depend very much on one's creed.

THE I WITHOUT A SELF

The joys of this life are not its own, but our dread of ascending to a higher life: the torments of this life are not its own, but our self-torment because of that dread.

FRANZ KAFKA

Kafka is a great, perhaps the greatest, master of the pure parable, a literary genre about which a critic can say very little worth saying. The reader of a novel, or the spectator at a drama, though novel and drama may also have a parabolic significance, is confronted by a feigned history, by characters, situations, actions which, though they may be analogous to his own, are not identical. Watching a performance of *Macbeth,* for example, I see particular historical persons involved in a tragedy of their own making: I may compare Macbeth with myself and wonder what I should have done and felt had I been in his situation, but I remain a spectator, firmly fixed in my own time and place. But I cannot read a pure parable in this way. Though the hero of a parable may be given a proper name (often, though, he may just be called "a certain man" or "K") and a definite historical and geographical setting, these particulars are irrelevant to the meaning of parable. To find out what, if anything, a parable means, I have to surrender my objectivity and identify myself with what I read. The "meaning" of a parable, in fact, is different for every reader. In consequence there is nothing a critic can do to "explain" it to others. Thanks to his superior knowledge of artistic and social history, of language, of human nature even, a good critic can make others see things in a novel or a play which, but for him, they would never have seen for themselves. But if he tries to interpret a parable, he will only reveal himself. What he writes will be a description of what the parable has done to him; of what it may do to others he does not and cannot have any idea.

Sometimes in real life one meets a character and thinks, "This man comes straight out of Shakespeare or Dickens," but nobody ever met a Kafka character. On the other hand, one can have experiences which one recognizes as Kafkaesque, while one would never call an experience of one's own Dickensian or Shakespearian. During the war, I had spent a long and tiring day in the Pentagon. My errand done, I hurried down long corridors eager to get home, and came to a turnstile with a guard standing beside it. "Where are you going?" said the guard. "I'm trying to get out," I replied. "You are out," he said. For the moment I felt I was K.

In the case of the ordinary novelist or playwright, a knowledge of his personal life and character contributes almost nothing to one's understanding of his work, but in the case of a writer of parables like Kafka, biographical information is, I believe, a great help, at least in a negative way, by preventing one from making false readings. (The "true" readings are always many.)

In the new edition of Max Brod's biography, he describes a novel by a Czech writer, Božena Němcová (1820-1862), called *The Grandmother*. The setting is a village in the Riesengebirge which is dominated by a castle. The villagers speak Czech, the inhabitants of the castle German. The Duchess who owns the castle is kind and good, but she is often absent on her travels and between her and the peasants are interposed a horde of insolent household servants and selfish, dishonest officials, so that the Duchess has no idea of what is really going on in the village. At last the heroine of the story succeeds in getting past the various barriers to gain a personal audience with the Duchess, to whom she tells the truth, and all ends happily.

What is illuminating about this information is that the castle officials in Němcová are openly presented as being evil, which suggests that those critics who have thought of the inhabitants of Kafka's castle as agents of Divine Grace were mistaken, and that Erich Heller's reading is substantially correct.

> The castle of Kafka's novel is, as it were, the heavily fortified garrison of a company of Gnostic demons, successfully holding an advanced position against the manoeuvres of an impatient soul. I do not know of any conceivable idea of divinity which could justify those interpreters who see in the castle the residence of "divine law and divine grace." Its officers are totally indifferent to good if they are not positively wicked. Neither in their decrees nor in their activities is there discernible any trace of love, mercy, charity or majesty. In their icy detachment they inspire no awe, but fear and revulsion.

Dr. Brod also publishes for the first time a rumor which, if true, might have occurred in a Kafka story rather than in his life, namely, that, without his knowledge, Kafka was the father of a son who died in 1921 at the age of seven. The story cannot be verified since the mother was arrested by the Germans in 1944 and never heard of again.

Remarkable as *The Trial* and *The Castle* are, Kafka's finest work, I think, is to be found in the volume *The Great Wall of China,* all of it written during the last six years of his life. The world it portrays is still the world of his earlier books and one cannot call it euphoric, but the tone is lighter. The sense of appalling anguish and despair which make stories like "The Penal Colony" almost unbearable, has gone. Existence may be as difficult and frustrating as ever, but the characters are more humorously resigned to it.

Of a typical story one might say that it takes the formula of the heroic Quest and turns it upside down. In the traditional Quest, the goal—a Princess, the Fountain of Life, etc. —is known to the hero before he starts. This goal is far distant and he usually does not know in advance the way thither nor the dangers which beset it, but there are other beings who know both and give him accurate directions and warnings. Moreover the goal is publicly recognizable as desirable. Everybody would like to achieve it, but it can only be reached by the Predestined Hero. When three brothers attempt the Quest in turn, the first two are found wanting and fail because of their arrogance and self-conceit, while the youngest succeeds, thanks to his humility and kindness of heart. But the youngest, like his two elders, is always perfectly confident that he will succeed.

In a typical Kafka story, on the other hand, the goal is peculiar to the hero himself: he has no competitors. Some beings whom he encounters try to help him, more are obstructive, most are indifferent, and none has the faintest notion of the way. As one of the aphorisms puts it: "There is a goal but no way; what we call the way is mere wavering." Far from being confident of success, the Kafka hero is convinced from the start that he is doomed to fail, as he is also doomed, being who he is, to make prodigious and unending efforts to reach it. Indeed, the mere desire to reach the goal is itself a proof, not that he is one of the Elect, but that he is under a special curse.

> Perhaps there is only one cardinal sin: impatience. Because of impatience we were driven out of Paradise, because of impatience we cannot return.

> Theoretically, there exists a perfect possibility of happiness: to believe in the indestructible element in oneself and not strive after it.

In all previous versions of the Quest, the hero knows what he ought to do and his one problem is "Can I do it?" Odysseus knows he must not listen to the song of the sirens, a knight in quest of the Sangreal knows he must remain chaste, a detective knows he must distinguish between truth and falsehood. But for K the problem is "What ought I to do?" He is neither tempted, confronted with a choice between good and evil, nor carefree, content with the sheer exhilaration of motion. He is certain that it matters enormously what he does *now,* without knowing at all what that ought to be. If he *guesses* wrong, he must not only suffer the same consequences as if he had *chosen* wrong, but also feel the same responsibility. If the instructions and advice he receives seem to him absurd or contradictory, he cannot interpret this as evidence of malice or guilt in others; it may well be proof of his own.

The traditional Quest Hero has *arete,* either manifest, like Odysseus, or concealed, like the fairy tale hero; in the first case, successful achievement of the Quest adds to his glory, in the second it reveals that the apparent nobody is a glorious hero: to become a hero, in the traditional sense, means acquiring the right, thanks to one's exceptional gifts and deeds, to say *I*. But K is an *I* from the start, and in this fact alone, that he exists, irrespective of any gifts or deeds, lies his guilt.

If the K of *The Trial* were innocent, he would cease to be K and become nameless like the fawn in the wood in *Through the Looking-Glass*. In *The Castle, K,* the letter, wants to become a word, *land-surveyor,* that is to say, to acquire a self like everybody else but this is precisely what he is not allowed to acquire.

The world of the traditional Quest may be dangerous, but it is open: the hero can set off in any direction he fancies. But the Kafka world is closed; though it is almost devoid of sensory properties, it is an intensely physical world. The objects and faces in it may be vague, but the reader feels himself hemmed in by their suffocating presence: in no other imaginary world, I think, is everything so *heavy*. To take a single step exhausts the strength. The hero feels himself to be a prisoner and tries to escape but perhaps imprisonment is the proper state for which he was created, and freedom would destroy him.

> The more horse you yoke, the quicker everything will go—not the rending of the block from its foundation, which is impossible, but the snapping of the traces and with that the gay and empty journey.

The narrator hero of "The Burrow" for example, is a beast of unspecified genus, but, presumably, some sort of badger-like animal, except that he is carnivorous. He lives by himself without a mate and never encounters any other member of his own species. He also lives in a perpetual state of fear lest he be pursued and attacked by other animals—"My enemies are countless," he says—but we never learn what they may be like and we never actually encounter one. His preoccupation is with the burrow which has been his lifework. Perhaps, when he first began excavating this, the idea of a burrow-fortress was more playful than serious, but the bigger and better the burrow becomes, the more he is tormented by the question: "Is it possible to construct the absolutely impregnable burrow?" This is a torment because he can never be certain that there is not some further precaution of which he has not thought. Also the burrow he has spent his life constructing has become a precious thing which he must defend as much as he would defend himself.

> One of my favorite plans was to isolate the Castle Keep from its surroundings, that is to say to restrict the thickness of the walls to about my own height, and leave a free space of about the same width all around the Castle Keep . . . I had always pictured this free space, and not without reason as the loveliest imaginable haunt. What a joy to lie pressed against the rounded outer wall, pull oneself up, let oneself slide down again, miss one's footing and find oneself on firm earth, and play all these games literally upon the Castle Keep and not inside it; to avoid the Castle Keep, to rest one's eyes from it whenever one wanted, to postpone the joy of seeing it until later and yet not have to do without it, but literally hold it safe between one's claws . . .

He begins to wonder if, in order to defend it, it would not be better to hide in the bushes outside near its hidden entrance and keep watch. He considers the possibility of enlisting the help of a confederate to share the task of watching, but decides against it.

> . . . would he not demand some counter-service from me; would he not at least want to see the burrow? That in itself, to let anyone freely into my burrow, would be exquisitely painful to me. I built it for myself, not for visitors, and I think I would refuse to admit him . . . I simply could not admit him, for either I must let him go in first by himself, which is simply unimaginable, or we must both descend at the same time, in which case the advantage I am supposed to derive from him, that of being kept watch over, would be lost. And what trust can I really put in him? . . . It is comparatively easy to trust any one if you are supervising him or at least supervise him; perhaps it is possible to trust some one at a distance; but completely to trust some one outside the burrow when you are inside the burrow, that is, in a different world, that, it seems to me, is impossible.

One morning he is awakened by a faint whistling noise which he cannot identify or locate. It might be merely the wind, but it might be some enemy. From now on, he is in the grip of a hysterical anxiety. Does this strange beast, if it is a beast, know of his existence and, if so, what does it know. The story breaks off without a solution. Edwin Muir has suggested that the story would have ended with the appearance of the invisible enemy to whom the hero would succumb. I am doubtful about this. The whole point of the parable seems to be that the reader is never to know if the narrator's subjective fears have any objective justification.

The more we admire Kafka's writings, the more seriously we must reflect upon his final instructions that they should be destroyed. At first one is tempted to see in this request a fantastic spiritual pride, as if he had said to himself: "To be worthy of me, anything I write must be absolutely perfect.

But no piece of writing, however excellent, can be perfect. Therefore, let what I have written be destroyed as unworthy of me." But everything which Dr. Brod and other friends tell us about Kafka as a person makes nonsense of this explanation.

It seems clear that Kafka did not think of himself as an artist in the traditional sense, that is to say, as a being dedicated to a particular function, whose personal existence is accidental to his artistic productions. If there ever was a man of whom it could be said that he "hungered and thirsted after righteousness," it was Kafka. Perhaps he came to regard what he had written as a personal device he had employed in his search for God. "Writing," he once wrote, "is a form of prayer," and no person whose prayers are genuine, desires them to be overheard by a third party. In another passage, he describes his aim in writing thus:

> Somewhat as if one were to hammer together a table with painful and methodical technical efficiency, and simultaneously do nothing at all, and not in such a way that people could say: "Hammering a table together is nothing to him," but rather "Hammering a table together is really hammering a table together to him, but at the same time it is nothing," whereby certainly the hammering would have become still bolder, still surer, still more real, and if you will, still more senseless.

But whatever the reasons, Kafka's reluctance to have his work published should at least make a reader wary of the way in which he himself reads it. Kafka may be one of those writers who are doomed to be read by the wrong public. Those on whom their effect would be most beneficial are repelled and on those whom they most fascinate their effect may be dangerous, even harmful.

I am inclined to believe that one should only read Kafka when one is in a eupeptic state of physical and mental health and, in consequence, tempted to dismiss any scrupulous heart-searching as a morbid fuss. When one is in low spirits, one should probably keep away from him, for, unless introspection is accompanied, as it always was in Kafka, by an equal passion for the good life, it all too easily degenerates into a spineless narcissistic fascination with one's own sin and weakness.

No one who thinks seriously about evil and suffering can avoid entertaining as a possibility the gnostic-manichean notion of the physical world as intrinsically evil, and some of Kafka's sayings come perilously close to accepting it.

> There is only a spiritual world; what we call the physical world is the evil in the spiritual one.

> The physical world is not an illusion, but only its evil which, however, admittedly constitutes our picture of the physical world.

Kafka's own life and his writings as a whole are proof that he was not a gnostic at heart, for the true gnostic can always be recognized by certain characteristics. He regards himself as a member of a spiritual elite and despises all earthly affections and social obligations. Quite often, he also allows himself an anarchic immorality in his sexual life, on the grounds that, since the body is irredeemable, a moral judgment cannot be applied to its actions.

Neither Kafka, as Dr. Brod knew him, nor any of his heroes show a trace of spiritual snobbery nor do they think of the higher life they search for as existing in some otherworld sphere: the distinction they draw between *this* world and *the* world does not imply that there are two different worlds, only that our habitual conceptions of reality are not the true conception.

Perhaps, when he wished his writings to be destroyed, Kafka foresaw the nature of too many of his admirers.

PART FOUR

The Shakespearian City

THE GLOBE

Physiological life is of course not "Life." And neither is psychological life. Life is the world.

LUDWIG WITTGENSTEIN

It is difficult, perhaps impossible, for us to form a complete picture of life because, for that, we have to reconcile and combine two completely different impressions—that of life as each of us experiences it in his own person, and that of life as we all observe it in others.

When I observe myself, the *I* which observes is unique, but not individual, since it has no characteristics of its own; it has only the power to recognize, compare, judge and choose: the self which it observes is not a unique identity but a succession of various states of feeling or desire. Necessity in my world means two things, the givenness of whatever state of myself is at any moment present, and the obligatory freedom of my ego.

Action in my world has a special sense; I act towards my states of being, not towards the stimuli which provoked them; *my* action, in fact, is the giving or withholding of permission to myself to act. It is impossible for me to act in ignorance, for my world is by definition what I know; it is not even possible, strictly speaking, for me to be self-deceived, for if I know I am deceiving myself, I am no longer doing so; I can never believe that I do not know what is good for me. I cannot say that I am fortunate or unfortunate, for these words apply only to my self. Though some states of my self are more interesting to me than others, there are none which are so uninteresting that I can ignore them; even boredom is interesting because it is *my* boredom with which I have to cope. If I try, then, to project my subjective experience of life in dramatic form the play will be of the allegorical morality type like Everyman. The hero will be the volitional ego that chooses, and the other characters, either states of the self, pleasant and unpleasant, good and bad, for or against which the hero's choices are made, or counselors, like reason and conscience, which attempt to influence his choices. The plot can only be a succession of incidents in time—the number I choose to portray is arbitrary —and the passing of time from birth to death the only necessity; all else is free choice.

If now I turn round and, deliberately excluding everything I know about myself, scrutinize other human beings as objectively as I can, as if I were simply a camera and a tape-recorder, I experience a very different world. I do not see states of being but individuals in states, say, of anger, each of them different and caused by different stimuli. I see and hear people, that is to say, acting and speaking in a situation, and the situation, their acts and words are all I know. I never see another choose between two alternative actions, only the action he does take. I cannot, therefore, tell whether he has free will or not; I only know that he is fortunate or unfortunate in his circumstances. I may see him acting in ignorance of facts about his situation which I know, but I can never say for certain that in any given situation he is deceiving himself. Then, while it is impossible for me to be totally uninterested in anything that happens to my self, I can only be interested in others who "catch my attention" by being exceptions to the average, exceptionally powerful, exceptionally beautiful, exceptionally amusing, and my interest or lack of it in what they do and suffer is determined by the old journalistic law that Dog-Bites-Bishop is not news but Bishop-Bites-Dog is.

If I try to present my objective experience in dramatic form, the play will be of the Greek type, the story of an exceptional man or woman who suffers an exceptional fate. The drama will consist, not in the choices he freely makes, but in the actions which the situation obliges him to take.

The pure drama of consciousness and the drama of pure objectivity are alike in that their characters have no secrets; the audience knows all about them that there is to know. One cannot imagine, therefore, writing a book about the characters in Greek tragedy or the characters in the morality plays; they themselves have said all there is to say. The fact that it has been and always will be possible to write books about the characters in Shakespeare's plays, in which different critics arrive at completely different interpretations, indicates that the Elizabethan drama is different from either, being, in fact, an attempt to synthesize both into a new, more complicated type.

Actually, of course, the Elizabethan dramatists knew very little about classical drama and owed very little to it. The closet tragedies of Seneca may have had some influence upon their style of rhetoric, the comedies of Plautus and Terence provided a few comic situations and devices, but Elizabethan drama would be pretty much the same if these authors had never been known at all. Even Ben Jonson, the only "highbrow" among the playwrights, who was strongly influenced by the aesthetic theories of the humanists, owes more to the morality play than he does to Latin Comedy. Take away Everyman, substitute for him as the hero one of the seven deadly sins, set the other six in league to profit from it, and one has the basic pattern of the Jonsonian comedy of humors.

The link between the medieval morality play and the Elizabethan drama is the Chronicle play. If few of the pre-

Shakespearian chronicle plays except Marlowe's *Edward II* are now readable, nothing could have been more fortunate for Shakespeare's development as a dramatist than his being compelled for his livelihood—judging by his early poems, his youthful taste was something much less coarse—to face the problems which the chronicle play poses. The writer of a chronicle play cannot, like the Greek tragedians who had some significant myth as a subject, select his situation; he has to take whatever history offers, those in which a character is a victim of a situation and those in which he creates one. He can have no narrow theory about aesthetic propriety which separates the tragic from the comic, no theory of heroic *arete* which can pick one historical character and reject another. The study of the human individual involved in political action, and of the moral ambiguities in which history abounds, checks any tendency towards a simple moralizing of characters into good and bad, any equating of success and failure with virtue and vice.

The Elizabethan drama inherited from the mystery plays three important and very un-Greek notions.

The Significance of Time

Time in Greek drama is simply the time it takes for the situation of the hero to be revealed, and when this revelation shall take place is decided by the gods, not by men. The plague which sets the action of *Oedipus Rex* in motion could have been sent earlier or postponed. In Elizabethan drama time is what the hero creates with what he does and suffers, the medium in which he realizes his potential character.

The Significance of Choice

In a Greek tragedy everything that could have been otherwise has already happened before the play begins. It is true that sometimes the chorus may warn the hero against a course of action, but it is unthinkable that he should listen to them, for a Greek hero is what he is and cannot change. If Hippolytus had made a sacrifice to Aphrodite, he would have ceased to be Hippolytus. But in an Elizabethan tragedy, in

Othello, for example, there is no point before he actually murders Desdemona when it would have been impossible for him to control his jealousy, discover the truth, and convert the tragedy into a comedy. Vice versa, there is no point in a comedy like *The Two Gentlemen of Verona* at which a wrong turning could not be taken and the conclusion be tragic.

The Significance of Suffering

To the Greeks, suffering and misfortune are signs of the displeasure of the gods and must therefore be accepted by men as mysteriously just. One of the commonest kinds of suffering is to be compelled to commit crimes, either unwittingly, like the parricide and incest of Oedipus, or at the direct command of a god, like Orestes. These crimes are not what we mean by sins because they are against, not with, the desire of the criminal. But in Shakespeare, suffering and misfortune are not in themselves proofs of Divine displeasure. It is true that they would not occur if man had not fallen into sin, but, precisely because he has, suffering is an inescapable element in life—there is no man who does not suffer—to be accepted, not as just in itself, as a penalty proportionate to the particular sins of the sufferer, but as an occasion for grace or as a process of purgation. Those who try to refuse suffering not only fail to avoid it but are plunged deeper into sin and suffering. Thus, the difference between Shakespeare's tragedies and comedies is not that the characters suffer in the one and not in the other, but that in comedy the suffering leads to self-knowledge, repentance, forgiveness, love, and in tragedy it leads in the opposite direction into self-blindness, defiance, hatred.

The audience at a Greek tragedy are pure spectators, never participants; the sufferings of the hero arouse their pity and fear, but they cannot think, "Something similar might happen to me," for the whole point in a Greek tragedy is that the hero and his tragic fate are exceptional. But all of Shakespeare's tragedies might be called variations on the same tragic myth, the only one which Christianity possesses, the story of the unrepentant thief, and anyone of us is in danger of re-enacting it in his own way. The audience at a tragedy of Shakespeare's, therefore, has to be both a spectator and a participant, for it is both a feigned history and a parable.

Dr. Johnson was right, surely, when he said of Shakespeare: "His tragedy seems to be skill, his comedy to be instinct." It seems to me doubtful if a completely satisfactory tragedy is possible within a Christian society which does not believe that there is a necessary relation between suffering and guilt. The dramatist, therefore, is faced with two choices. He can show a noble and innocent character suffering exceptional misfortune, but then the effect will be not tragic but pathetic. Or he can portray a sinner who by his sins—usually the sins have to produce crimes—brings his suffering upon himself. But, then, there is no such thing as a noble sinner, for to sin is precisely to become ignoble. Both Shakespeare and Racine try to solve the problem in the same way, by giving the sinner noble poetry to speak, but both of them must have known in their heart of hearts that this was a conjuring trick. Any journalist could tell the story of Oedipus or Hippolytus and it would be just as tragic as when Sophocles or Euripides tells it. The difference would be only that the journalist is incapable of providing Oedipus and Hippolytus with the noble language which befits their tragedy, while Sophocles and Euripides, being great poets, can.

But let a journalist tell the story of Macbeth or Phèdre and we shall immediately recognize them for what they are, one a police court case, the other a pathological case. The poetry that Shakespeare and Racine have given them is not an outward expression of their noble natures, but a gorgeous robe which hides their nakedness. D. H. Lawrence's poem seems to me not altogether unjust.

When I read Shakespeare I am struck with wonder
that such trivial people should muse and thunder
in such lovely language.

Lear, the old buffer, you wonder his daughters
didn't treat him rougher,
the old chough, the old chuffer.

And Hamlet, how boring, how boring to live with,
so mean and self-conscious, blowing and snoring
his wonderful speeches, full of other folk's whoring!

And Macbeth and his Lady, who should have been
    choring,
such suburban ambition, so messily goring
old Duncan with daggers!

How boring, how small Shakespeare's people are!
Yet the language so lovely! like the dyes from gas-tar.

Comedy, on the other hand, is not only possible within a Christian society, but capable of a much greater breadth and depth than classical comedy. Greater in breadth because classical comedy is based upon the division of mankind into two classes, those who have *arete* and those who do not, and only the second class, fools, shameless rascals, slaves, are fit subjects for comedy. But Christian comedy is based upon the belief that all men are sinners; no one, therefore, whatever his rank or talents, can claim immunity from the comic exposure and, indeed, the more virtuous, in the Greek sense, a man is, the more he realizes that he deserves to be exposed. Greater in depth because, while classical comedy believes that rascals should get the drubbing they deserve, Christian comedy believes that we are forbidden to judge others and that it is our duty to forgive each other. In classical comedy the characters are exposed and punished: when the curtain falls, the audience is laughing and those on stage are in tears. In Christian comedy the characters are exposed and forgiven: when the curtain falls, the audience and the characters are laughing together. Ben Jonson's comedies, unlike Shakespeare's, are classical, not Christian.

If the plays of Shakespeare and Ben Jonson—and Jonson is untypical, anyway—had been lost, we should find in the dramatic literature written between 1590 and 1642 many passages of magnificent poetry, many scenes of exciting theatre, but no play which is satisfactory as a whole; the average Elizabethan play is more like a variety show—a series of scenes, often moving or entertaining enough in themselves, but without essential relation to each other—than like a properly constructed drama in which every character and every word is relevant. For this defect we should probably blame the laxness of Elizabethan stage conventions, which permitted the dramatist to have as many scenes and characters as he liked, and to include tragic and comic scenes, verse and prose, in the same play. Fortunately, Shakespeare's plays have not perished, and we are able to see how greatly, in his case, these conventions contributed towards his achievement. Had the stage conventions of his day been those, for example, of the French classical theatre in the seventeenth century, he could not, given his particular kind of genius and interests, have become the greatest creator of "Feigned Histories" in dramatic form who ever lived. In the preface to *Mrs. Warren's Profession,* with his typical mixture of perspicacity and polemical exaggeration, Shaw writes:

> The drama can do little to delight the senses: all the apparent instances to the contrary are instances of the personal fascination of the performers. The drama of pure feeling is no longer in the hands of the playwright: it has been conquered by the musician, after whose enchantment all the verbal arts seem cold and tame. *Romeo and Juliet* with the loveliest Juliet is dry, tedious and rhetorical in comparison with Wagner's *Tristan,* even though Isolde be both fourteen stone and forty, as she often is in Germany . . . There is, flatly, no future now for any drama without music except the drama of thought. The attempt to produce a genus of opera without music (and this absurdity is what our fashionable theatres have been driving at for a long time past without knowing it) is far less hopeful than my own determination to accept problems as the normal material for drama.[1]

[1] Curiously enough, now we have got used to them, what impresses us most about Shaw's plays is their musical quality. He has told us himself that it was from *Don Giovanni* that he learned "How to write seriously

Every aspect of life is, of course, a problem. The belief Shaw is attacking is the belief that the only problem worth a playwright's attention is love between the sexes, considered in isolation from everything else which men and women think and do. Like all persons engaged in polemic, he accepts the view of Shakespeare held by his opponents, namely, that, as a dramatist, Shakespeare, even when his characters are princes and warriors, was only interested in their "private" emotional life. In actual fact, however, the revolt of Ibsen and Shaw against the conventional nineteenth century drama could very well be described as a return to Shakespeare, as an attempt once again to present human beings in their historical and social setting and not, as playwrights since the Restoration had done, either as wholly private or as embodiments of the social manners of a tiny class. Shakespeare's plays, it is true, are not, in the Shavian sense, "dramas of thought," that is to say, not one of his characters is an intellectual: it is true, as Shaw says, that, when stripped of their wonderful diction, the philosophical and moral views expressed by his characters are commonplaces, but the number of people in any generation or society whose thoughts are not commonplace is very small indeed. On the other hand, there is hardly one of his plays which does not provide unending food for thought, if one cares to think about it. *Romeo and Juliet*, for example, is by no means merely a "drama of feeling," a verbal opera about a love affair between two adolescents; it is also, and more importantly, a portrait of a society, charming enough in many ways, but morally inadequate because the only standard of value by which its members regulate and judge their conduct is that of *la bella*

---

without being dull." For all his claims to be just a propagandist, his writing has an effect nearer to that of music than most of those who have claimed to be writing "dramas of feeling." His plays are a joy to watch, not because they purport to deal with social and political problems, but because they are such wonderful displays of conspicuous waste; the conversational energy displayed by his characters is so far in excess of what their situation requires that, if it were to be devoted to practical action, it would wreck the world in five minutes. The Mozart of English letters he is not—the music of the Marble Statue is beyond him—the Rossini, yes. He has all the brio, humor, cruel clarity and virtuosity of that Master of *opera buffa*.

or *la brutta figura*. The disaster that overtakes the young lovers is one symptom of what is wrong with Verona, and every citizen, from Prince Escalus down to the starving apothecary, has a share of responsibility for their deaths. Quite aside from their different temperaments and talents, one can see a good reason why Shakespeare does not need to tell the audience his "thoughts," while Shaw is obliged to. Thanks to the conventions and the economics of the Elizabethan theatre, Shakespeare can present his picture of Verona in twenty-four scenes with a cast of thirty speaking roles and a crowd of walk-ons. Shaw has to write for a picture stage framed by a proscenium arch, furnished with sets which admit of few changes of location, and for actors whose salary scale makes a large cast prohibitively expensive. When, therefore, he writes about a social problem such as slum landlords, he is obliged to tell us through an intellectual debate between the few characters in the few locations at his disposal what he cannot present dramatically as evidence from which we could draw the conclusions for ourselves.

As a dramatic historian, Shakespeare was born at just the right time. Later, changes in the conventions and economics of the theatre made it an inadequate medium, and feigned histories became the province of the novelist. Earlier, dramatic history would have been impossible, because the only history which was recognized as such was sacred history. The drama had to become secularized before any adequate treatment of human history was possible. Greek tragedy, like the mystery play, is religious drama. What the hero does himself is subordinate to what the gods make him do. Further, the gods are concerned, not with human society, but with certain exceptional individuals. The hero dies or goes into exile, but his city, as represented by the chorus, remains. The chorus may give him support or warning advice, but they cannot influence his actions and bear no responsibility for them. Only the hero has a biography; the chorus are mere observers. Human history cannot be written except on the presupposition that, whatever part God may play in human affairs, we cannot say of one event,

"This is an act of God," of another, "This is a natural event," and of another, "This is a human choice"; we can only record what happens. The allegorical morality plays are concerned with history, but only with subjective history; the social-historical setting of any particular man is deliberately excluded.

We do not know what Shakespeare's personal beliefs were, nor his opinion on any subject (though most of us privately think we do). All we can notice is an ambivalence in his feelings towards his characters which is, perhaps, characteristic of all great dramatists. A dramatist's characters are, normally, men-of-action, but he himself is a maker, not a doer, concerned, not with disclosing himself to others in the moment, but with making a work which, unlike himself, will endure, if possible forever. The dramatist, therefore, admires and envies in his characters their courage and readiness to risk their lives and souls—qua dramatist, he never risks himself—but, at the same time, to his detached imagination, all action, however glorious, is vain because the consequence is never what the doer intended. What a man does is irrevocable for good or ill; what he makes, he can always modify or even destroy. In all great drama, I believe, we can feel the tension of this ambivalent attitude, torn between reverence and contempt, of the maker towards the doer. A character for whom his creator felt either absolute reverence or absolute contempt would not, I think, be actable.

THE PRINCE'S DOG

Whoever takes up the sword shall perish by the sword. And whoever does not take up the sword (or lets it drop) shall perish on the cross.

SIMONE WEIL

It has been observed that critics who write about Shakespeare reveal more about themselves than about Shakespeare, but perhaps that is the great value of drama of the Shakespearian kind, namely, that whatever he may see taking place on stage, its final effect upon each spectator is a self-revelation.

Shakespeare holds the position in our literature of Top Bard, but this deserved priority has one unfortunate consequence; we generally make our first acquaintance with his plays, not in the theatre, but in the classroom or study, so that, when we do attend a performance, we have lost that naïve openness to surprise which is the proper frame of mind in which to witness any drama. The experience of reading a play and the experience of watching it performed are never identical, but in the case of *Henry IV* the difference between the two is particularly great.

At a performance, my immediate reaction is to wonder what Falstaff is doing in this play at all. At the end of *Richard II,* we were told that the Heir Apparent has taken up with a dissolute crew of "unrestrained loose companions." What sort of bad company would one expect to find Prince Hal keeping when the curtain rises on *Henry IV?* Surely, one could expect to see him surrounded by daring, rather sinister juvenile delinquents and beautiful gold-digging whores. But whom do we meet in the Boar's Head? A fat, cowardly tosspot, old enough to be his father, two down-at-heel hangers-on, a slatternly hostess and only one whore, who is not in her earliest youth either; all of them seedy, and, by any worldly standards, including those of the criminal classes, all of them *failures.* Surely, one thinks, an Heir Apparent, sowing his wild oats, could have picked himself a more exciting crew than that. As the play proceeds, our surprise is replaced by another kind of puzzle, for the better we come to know Falstaff, the clearer it becomes that the world of historical reality which a Chronicle Play claims to imitate is not a world which he can inhabit.

If it really was Queen Elizabeth who demanded to see Falstaff in a comedy, then she showed herself a very perceptive critic. But even in *The Merry Wives of Windsor,* Falstaff has not and could not have found his true home because Shakespeare was only a poet. For that he was to wait nearly two hundred years till Verdi wrote his last opera. Falstaff is not the only case of a character whose true home is the world of music; others are Tristan, Isolde, and Don Giovanni.[1]

Though they each call for a different kind of music, Tristan, Don Giovanni, and Falstaff have certain traits in common. They do not belong to the temporal world of change. One cannot imagine any of them as babies, for a Tristan who is not in love, a Don Giovanni who has no name on his list, a

[1] If Verdi's *Macbetto* fails to come off, the main reason is that the proper world for Macbeth is poetry, not song; he won't go into notes.

Falstaff who is not old and fat, are inconceivable. When Falstaff says, "When I was about their years, Hal, I was not an eagle's talent in the waist; I could have crept into an alderman's thumb-ring"—we take it as a typical Falstaffian fib, but we believe him when he says, "I was born about three in the afternoon, with a white head and something of a round belly."

Time, for Tristan, is a single moment stretched out tighter and tighter until it snaps. Time, for Don Giovanni, is an infinite arithmetical series of unrelated moments which has no beginning and would have no end if Heaven did not intervene and cut it short. For Falstaff, time does not exist, since he belongs to the *opera buffa* world of play and mock action governed not by will or desire, but by innocent wish, a world where no one can suffer because everything he says and does is only a pretense.

Thus, while we must see Tristan die in Isolde's arms and we must see Don Giovanni sink into the earth, because being doomed to die and to go to hell are essential to their beings, we cannot see Falstaff die on stage because, if we did, we should not believe it; we should know that, as at the battle of Shrewsbury, he was only shamming. I am not even quite sure that we believe it when we are told of his death in Henry V; I think we accept it, as we accept the death of Sherlock Holmes, as his creator's way of saying, "I am getting tired of this character"; we feel sure that, if the public pleads with him strongly enough, Shakespeare will find some way to bring him to life again. The only kind of funeral music we can associate with him is the mock-requiem in the last act of Verdi's opera.

Domine fallo casto

Ma salvaggi l'addomine

Domine fallo guasto.

Ma salvaggi l'addomine.

There are at least two places in the play where the incongruity of the *opera buffa* world with the historical world is too much, even for Shakespeare, and a patently false note is struck. The first occurs when, on the battlefield of Shrewsbury, Falstaff thrusts his sword into Hotspur's corpse. Within his own world, Falstaff could stab a corpse because, there, all battles are mock battles, all corpses straw dummies; but we, the audience, are too conscious that this battle has been a real battle and that this corpse is the real dead body of a brave and noble young man. Pistol could do it, because Pistol is a contemptible character, but Falstaff cannot; that is to say, there is no way in which an actor can play the scene convincingly. So, too, with the surrender of Colevile to Falstaff in the Second Part. In his conversation, first with Colevile and then with Prince John, Falstaff talks exactly as we expect —to him, the whole business is a huge joke. But then he is present during a scene when we are shown that it is no joke at all. How is any actor to behave and speak his lines during the following?

LANCASTER—Is thy name Colevile?
COLEVILE—It is, my lord.
LANCASTER—A famous rebel art thou, Colevile.
FALSTAFF—And a famous true subject took him.
COLEVILE—I am, my lord, but as my betters are,
That led me hither. Had they been ruled by me,
You would have won them dearer than you have.
FALSTAFF—I know not how they sold themselves: but
thou, like a kind fellow, gavest thyself away gratis;
and I thank thee for thee.
LANCASTER—Now have you left pursuit?
WESTMORELAND—Retreat is made and execution stay'd.
LANCASTER—Send Colevile, with his confederates,
To York, to present execution.

The Falstaffian frivolity and the headsman's axe cannot so directly confront each other.

Reading *Henry IV*, we can easily give our full attention to the historical-political scenes, but, when watching a performance, attention is distracted by our eagerness to see Falstaff reappear. Short of cutting him out of the play altogether, no producer can prevent him stealing the show. From an actor's point of view, the role of Falstaff has the enormous advantage that he has only to think of one thing—playing to an audience. Since he lives in an eternal present and the historical world does not exist for him, there is no difference for Falstaff between those on stage and those out front, and if the actor were to appear in one scene in Elizabethan costume and in the next in top hat and morning coat, no one would be bewildered. The speech of all the other characters is, like our own, conditioned by two factors, the external situation with its questions, answers, and commands, and the inner need of each character to disclose himself to others. But Falstaff's speech has only one cause, his absolute insistence, at every moment and at all costs, upon disclosing himself. Half his lines could be moved from one speech to another without our noticing, for nearly everything he says is a variant upon one theme—"I am that I am."

Moreover, Shakespeare has so written his part that it cannot be played unsympathetically. A good actor can make us admire Prince Hal, but he cannot hope to make us like him as much as even a second-rate actor will make us like Falstaff. Sober reflection in the study may tell us that Falstaff is not, after all, a very admirable person, but Falstaff on the stage gives us no time for sober reflection. When Hal or the Chief Justice or any others indicate that they are not bewitched by Falstaff, reason might tell us that they are in the right, but we ourselves are already bewitched, so that their disenchantment seems out of place, like the presence of teetotalers at a drunken party.

Suppose, then, that a producer were to cut the Falstaff scenes altogether, what would *Henry IV* become? The middle section of a political trilogy which could be entitled *Looking for the Doctor*.

The body politic of England catches an infection from its family physician. An able but unqualified practitioner throws him out of the sickroom and takes over. The patient's temperature continues to rise. But then, to everybody's amazement, the son of the unqualified practitioner whom, though he has taken his degree, everyone has hitherto believed to be a hopeless invalid, effects a cure. Not only is the patient restored to health but also, at the doctor's orders, takes another body politic, France, to wife.

The theme of this trilogy is, that is to say, the question: What combination of qualities is needed in the Ruler whose function is the establishment and maintenance of Temporal Justice? According to Shakespeare, the ideal Ruler must satisfy five conditions. 1) He must know what is just and what is unjust. 2) He must himself be just. 3) He must be strong enough to compel those who would like to be unjust to behave justly. 4) He must have the capacity both by nature and by art of making others loyal to his person. 5) He must be the legitimate ruler by whatever standard legitimacy is determined in the society to which he belongs.

Richard II fails to satisfy the first four of these. He does not know what Justice is, for he follows the advice of foolish flatterers. He is himself unjust, for he spends the money he obtains by taxing the Commons and fining the Nobility, not on defending England against her foes, but upon maintaining a lavish and frivolous court, so that, when he really does need money for a patriotic purpose, the war with Ireland, his exchequer is empty and in desperation he commits a gross act of injustice by confiscating Bolingbroke's estates.

It would seem that at one time he had been popular but he has now lost his popularity, partly on account of his actions, but also because he lacks the art of winning hearts. According to his successor, he had made the mistake of being overfamiliar —the ruler should not let himself be seen too often as "human"—and in addition, he is not by nature the athletic, physically brave warrior who is the type most admired by the feudal society he is called upon to rule.

In consequence, Richard II is a weak ruler who cannot keep the great nobles in order or even command the loyalty of his soldiers, and weakness in a ruler is the worst defect of all. A cruel, even an unjust king, who is strong, is preferable to the most saintly weakling because most men will behave unjustly if they discover that they can with impunity; tyranny, the injustice of one, is less unjust than anarchy, the injustice of many.

But there remains the fifth condition: whatever his defects, Richard II is the legitimate King of England. Since all men are mortal, and many men are ambitious, unless there is some impersonal principle by which, when the present ruler dies, the choice of his successor can be decided, there will be a risk of civil war in every generation. It is better to endure the injustice of the legitimate ruler, who will die anyway sooner or later, than allow a usurper to take his place by force.

As a potential ruler, Bolingbroke possesses many of the right qualities. He is a strong man, he knows how to make himself popular, and he would like to be just. We never hear, even from the rebels, of any specific actions of Henry IV which are unjust, only of suspicions which may be just or unjust. But in yielding to the temptation, when the opportunity unexpectedly offers itself, of deposing his lawful sovereign, he commits an act of injustice for which he and his kingdom have to pay a heavy price. Because of it, though he is strong enough to crush rebellion, he is not strong or popular enough to prevent rebellion breaking out.

Once Richard has been murdered, however, the rule of Henry IV is better than any alternative. Though, legally, Mortimer may have a good or better right to the throne, the scene at Bangor between Hotspur, Worcester, Mortimer, and Glendower, convinces us that Henry's victory is a victory for justice since we learn that the rebels have no concern for the interests of the Kingdom, only for their own. Their plan, if they succeed, is to carve up England into three petty states. Henry may wish that Hotspur, not Hal, were his heir, because Hotspur is a brave warrior ready to risk his life in battle against England's foes, while Hal appears to be dissipated and frivolous, but we know better. Hotspur is indeed brave, but that is all. A man who can say

> I'll give thrice so much land
> To any well-deserving friend;
> But in the way of bargain, mark ye me,
> I'll cavil on the ninth part of a hair

is clearly unfitted to be a ruler because his actions are based, not on justice, but on personal whim. Moreover, he is not interested in political power; all he desires is military glory.

Thirdly, there is Prince Hal, Henry V-to-be. To everyone except himself, he seems at first to be another Richard, unjust, lacking in self-control but, unfortunately, the legitimate heir. By the time the curtain falls on *Henry V,* however, he is recognized by all to be the Ideal Ruler. Like his father in his youth, he is brave and personable. In addition, he is a much cleverer politician. While his father was an improviser, he is a master of the art of timing. His first soliloquy reveals him as a person who always sees several steps ahead and has the patience to wait, even though waiting means temporary misunderstanding and unpopularity, until the right moment for action comes; he will never, if he can help it, leave anything to chance. Last but not least, he is blessed by luck. His father had foreseen that internal dissension could only be cured if some common cause could be found which would unite all parties but he was too old and ill, the internal quarrels too violent. But when Hal succeeds as Henry V, most of his enemies are dead or powerless—Cambridge and Scroop have no armies at their back—and his possible right to the throne of France provides the common cause required to unite both the nobles and the commons, and gives him the opportunity, at Agincourt, to show his true mettle.

One of Falstaff's dramatic functions is to be the means by which Hal is revealed to be the Just Ruler, not the dissolute and frivolous young man everybody has thought him; but, so far as the audience is concerned, Falstaff has fulfilled his function by Act III, Scene 2 of the First Part, when the King entrusts Hal with a military command. Up to this point the Falstaff scenes have kept us in suspense. In Act I, Scene 2, we hear Hal promise

> I'll so offend to make offense a skill,
> Redeeming time when men least think I will.

But then we watch the rebellion being prepared while he does nothing but amuse himself with Falstaff, so that we are left wondering whether he meant what he said or was only play acting. But from the moment he engages in the political action of the play, we have no doubts whatsoever as to his ambition, capacity, and ultimate triumph for, however often henceforward we may see him with Falstaff, it is never at a time when his advice and arms are needed by the State; he visits the Boar's Head in leisure hours when there is nothing serious for him to do.

For those in the play, the decisive moment of revelation is, of course, his first public act as Henry V, his rejection of Falstaff and company. For his subjects who have not, as we have, watched him with Falstaff, it is necessary to allay their fears that, though they already know him to be brave and capable, he may still be unjust and put his personal friendships before the impartial justice which it is his duty as king to maintain. But we, who have watched his private life, have no such fears. We have long known that his first soliloquy meant what it said, that he has never been under any false illusions about Falstaff or anyone else and that when the right moment comes to reject Falstaff, that is to say, when such a rejection will make the maximum political effect, he will do so without hesitation. Even the magnanimity he shows in granting his old companion a life competence, which so impresses those about him, cannot impress us because, knowing Falstaff as they do not, we know what the effect on him of such a rejection must be, that his heart will be "fracted and corroborate" and no life competence can mend that. It is Hal's company he wants, not a pension from the Civil List.

The essential Falstaff is the Falstaff of *The Merry Wives* and Verdi's opera, the comic hero of the world of play, the unkillable self-sufficient immortal whose verdict on existence is

> *Tutto nel mondo è burla. . . .*
> *Tutti gabbàti. Irridè*
> *L'un l'altro ogni mortal.*
> *Ma ride ben chi ride*
> *La risata final*

In *Henry IV*, however, something has happened to this immortal which draws him out of his proper world into the historical world of suffering and death. He has become capable of serious emotion. He continues to employ the speech of his comic world:

> I have forsworn his company hourly any time this two-and-twenty years, and yet I am bewitched by the rogue's company. If the rascal have not given me medicines to make me love him, I'll be hanged. It could not be else. I have drunk medicines.

But the emotion so flippantly expressed could equally well be expressed thus:

> If my dear love were but the child of state
> It might for Fortune's bastard be unfathered,
> As subject to Time's love or to Time's hate,
> Weeds among weeds, or flowers with flowers
> gathered.
> No, it was builded far from accident;
> It suffers not in smiling pomp, nor falls
> Under the blow of thralled discontent,
> Whereto th' inviting time and fashion calls
> It fears not Policy, that heretic
> Which works on leases of short numbered hours,
> But all alone stands hugely politic.

As the play proceeds, we become aware, behind all the fun, of something tragic. Falstaff loves Hal with an absolute devotion. "The lovely bully" is the son he has never had, the youth predestined to the success and worldly glory which he will never enjoy. He believes that his love is returned, that the Prince is indeed his other self, so he is happy, despite old age and poverty. We, however, can see that he is living in a fool's paradise, for the Prince cares no more for him as a person than he would care for the King's Jester. He finds Falstaff amusing but no more. If we could warn Falstaff of what he is too blind to see, we might well say: Beware, before it is too late, of becoming involved with one of those mortals

> That do not do the thing they most do show,
> Who, moving others, are themselves as stone. . . .

Falstaff's story, in fact, is not unlike one of those folk tales in which a mermaid falls in love with a mortal prince: the price she pays for her infatuation is the loss of her immortality without the compensation of temporal happiness.

Let us now suppose, not only that Falstaff takes no part in the play, but is also allowed to sit in the audience as a spectator. How much will he understand of what he sees going on?

He will see a number of Englishmen divided into two parties who finally come to blows. That they should come to blows will in itself be no proof to him that they are enemies because they might, like boxers, have agreed to fight for fun. In Falstaff's world there are two causes of friendship and enmity. My friend may be someone whose appearance and manner I like at this moment, my enemy someone whose appearance and manner I dislike. Thus, he will understand Hotspur's objection to Bolingbroke perfectly well.

> Why, what a candy deal of courtesy
> This fawning greyhound then did proffer me.
> "Look, when his infant fortune came to age,"
> And "gentle Harry Percy" and "kind cousin."
> O the devil take such cozeners.

To Falstaff, "my friend" can also mean he whose wish at this moment coincides with mine, "my enemy" he whose wish contradicts mine. He will see the civil war, therefore, as a clash between Henry and Mortimer who both wish to wear the crown. What will perplex him is any argument as to who has the better right to wear it.

Anger and fear he can understand, because they are immediate emotions, but not nursing a grievance or planning revenge or apprehension, for these presuppose that the future inherits from the past. He will not, therefore, be able to make head or tail of Warwick's speech, "There is a history in all men's lives . . . ," nor any reasons the rebels give for their actions which are based upon anything Bolingbroke did before he became king, nor the reason given by Worcester for concealing the king's peace offer from Hotspur:

> It is impossible, it cannot be
> The King should keep his word in loving us.
> He will suspect us still and find a time
> To punish this offence in other faults.

To *keep his word* is a phrase outside Falstaff's comprehension, for a promise means that at some future moment I might have to refuse to do what I wish, and, in Falstaff's world to wish and to do are synonymous. For the same reason, when, by promising them redress, Prince John tricks the rebels into disbanding their armies and then arrests them, Falstaff will not understand why they and all the audience except himself are shocked.

The first words Shakespeare puts into Falstaff's mouth are, "Now Hal, what time of day is it, lad?" to which the Prince quite rightly replies, "What the devil hast thou to do with the time of day?" In Falstaff's world, every moment is one of infinite possibility when anything can be wished. As a spectator, he will keep hearing the characters use the words *time* and *occasion* in a sense which will stump him.

> What I know
> Is ruminated, plotted, and set down
> And only stays but to behold the face
> Of that occasion that shall bring it on.

> The purpose you undertake is dangerous, the
> time itself unsorted. . . .

> . . . I will resolve to Scotland. There am I
> Till time and vantage crave my company.

Of all the characters in the play, the one he will think he understands best is the least Falstaff-like of them all, Hotspur, for Hotspur, like himself, appears to obey the impulse of the moment and say exactly what he thinks without prudent calculation. Both conceal nothing from others, Falstaff because he has no mask to put on, Hotspur because he has so become his mask that he has no face beneath it. Falstaff says, as it were, "I am I. Whatever I do, however outrageous, is of infinite importance because I do it." Hotspur says: "I am Hotspur, the fearless, the honest, plain-spoken warrior. If I should ever show fear or tell lies, even white ones, I should cease to exist." If Falstaff belonged to the same world as Hotspur, one could call him a liar, but, in his own eyes, he is perfectly truthful, for, to him, fact is subjective fact, "what I am actually feeling and thinking at this moment." To call him a liar is as ridiculous as if, in a play, a character should say, "I am Napoleon," and a member of the audience should cry, "You're not. You're Sir John Gielgud."

In Ibsen's *Peer Gynt,* there is a remarkable scene in which Peer visits the Troll King. At the entertainment given in his honor, animals dance to hideous noises, but Peer behaves to them with perfect manners as if they were beautiful girls and the music ravishing. After it is over, the Troll King asks him: "Now, frankly, tell me what you saw." Peer replies: "What I saw was impossibly ugly"—and then describes the scene as the audience had seen it. The Troll King who has taken a fancy to him, suggests that Peer would be happier at a troll. All that is needed is a little eye operation, after which he will really see a cow as a beautiful girl. Peer indignantly refuses. He is perfectly willing, he says, to swear that a cow is a girl, but to surrender his humanity so that he can no longer lie, because he cannot distinguish between fact and fiction, that he will never do. By this criterion, neither Falstaff nor Hotspur is quite human, Falstaff because he is pure troll, Hotspur because he is so lacking in imagination that the troll kingdom is invisible to him.

At first, then, Falstaff will believe that Hotspur is one of his own kind, who like himself enjoys putting on an act, but then he will hear Hotspur say words which he cannot comprehend.

> . . . time serves wherein you may redeem
> Your banished honours and restore yourselves
> Into the good thoughts of the world again.

In Falstaff's world, the only value standard is importance, that is to say, all he demands from others is attention, all he fears is being ignored. Whether others applaud or hiss does not matter; what matters is the volume of the hissing or the applause.

Hence, in his soliloquy about honor, his reasoning runs something like this: if the consequences of demanding moral approval from others is dying, it is better to win their disapproval; a dead man has no audience.

Since the Prince is a personal friend, Falstaff is, of course, a King's man who thinks it a shame to be on any side but one, but his loyalty is like that of those who, out of local pride, support one football team rather than another. As a member of the audience, his final comment upon the political action of the play will be the same as he makes from behind the footlights.

> Well, God be thanked for these rebels: they offend none but the virtuous. . . .
>
> A young knave and begging. Is there not employment? Doth not the King lack subjects? Do not the rebels need soldiers?

Once upon a time we were all Falstaffs: then we became social beings with super-egos. Most of us learn to accept this, but there are some in whom the nostalgia for the state of innocent self-importance is so strong that they refuse to accept adult life and responsibilities and seek some means to become again the Falstaffs they once were. The commonest technique adopted is the bottle, and, curiously enough, the male drinker reveals his intention by developing a drinker's belly.

If one visits a bathing beach, one can observe that men and women grow fat in different ways. A fat woman exaggerates her femininity; her breasts and buttocks enlarge till she comes to look like the Venus of Willendorf. A fat man, on the other hand, looks like a cross between a very young child and a pregnant mother. There have been cultures in which obesity in women was considered the ideal of sexual attraction, but in no culture, so far as I know, has a fat man been considered more attractive than a thin one. If my own weight and experience give me any authority, I would say that fatness in the male is the physical expression of a psychological wish to withdraw from sexual competition and, by combining mother and child in his own person, to become emotionally self-sufficient. The Greeks thought of Narcissus as a slender youth but I think they were wrong. I see him as a middle-aged man with a corporation, for, however ashamed he may be of displaying it in public, in private a man with a belly loves it dearly; it may be an unprepossessing child to look at, but he has borne it all by himself.

> I do walk here before thee like a sow that hath overwhelmed all her little but one. . . .
>
> I have a whole school of tongues in this belly of mine, and not a tongue of them all speaks any other word but my name. My womb, my womb undoes me.

Not all fat men are heavy drinkers, but all males who drink heavily become fat.[2] At the same time, the more they drink, the less they eat. "O monstrous! But one halfpenny worth of bread to this intolerable deal of sack!" exclaims Hal on looking at Falstaff's bill, but he cannot have expected anything else. Drunkards die, not from the liquid alcohol they take so much of, but from their refusal to eat solid food, and anyone who had to look after a drunk knows that the only way to get enough nourishment into him is to give him liquid or mashed-up foods, for he will reject any dish that needs chewing. Solid food is to the drunkard a symbolic reminder of the loss of the mother's breast and his ejection from Eden.

> A plague on sighing and grief. It blows a man up like a bladder. . . .

[2] All the women I have met who drank heavily were lighter and thinner than average.

So Falstaff, and popular idiom identifies the kind of griefs which have this fattening effect—eating humble pie, swallowing insults, etc.

In a recent number of *The Paris Review*, Mr. Nicholas Tucci writes:

> The death song of the drunkard—it may go on for thirty years—goes more or less like this. "I was born a god, with the whole world in reach of my hands, lie now defeated in the gutter. Come and listen: hear what the world has done to me."
>
> *In Vino Veritas* is an old saying that has nothing to do with the drunkard's own truth. He has no secrets—that is true—but it is not true that his truth may be found under the skin of his moral reserve or of his sober lies, so that the moment he begins to cross his eyes and pour out his heart, anyone may come in and get his fill of truth. What happens is exactly the opposite. When the drunkard confesses, he makes a careful choice of his pet sins: and these are nonexistent. He may be unable to distinguish a person from a chair, but never an unprofitable lie from a profitable one. How could he see himself as a very significant entity in a huge world of others, when he sees nothing but himself spread over the whole universe. "I am alone" is indeed a true cry, but it should not be taken literally.

The drunk is unlovely to look at, intolerable to listen to, and his self-pity is contemptible. Nevertheless, as not merely a worldly failure but also a willful failure, he is a disturbing image for the sober citizen. His refusal to accept the realities of this world, babyish as it may be, compels us to take another look at this world and reflect upon our motives for accepting it. The drunkard's suffering may be self-inflicted, but it is real suffering and reminds us of all the suffering in this world which we prefer not to think about because, from the moment we accepted this world, we acquired our share of responsibility for everything that happens in it.

When we see Falstaff's gross paunch and red face, we

are reminded that the body politic of England is not so healthy, either.

> The Commonwealth is sick of its own choice.
> Their over-greedy love hath surfeited. . . .
> Thou (beastly feeder) are so full of him
> That thou provokest thyself to cast him up.
> So, so, thou common dog, didst thou disgorge
> Thy glutton bosom of the royal Richard. . . .
> Then you perceive the body of our kingdom
> How foul it is: what rank diseases grow,
> And with what danger near the heart of it.

It might be expected that we would be revolted at the sight and turn our eyes with relief and admiration to the Hero Prince. But in fact we aren't and we don't. Whenever Falstaff is on stage, we have no eyes for Hal. If Shakespeare did originally write a part for Falstaff in *Henry V*, it would not have taken pressure from the Cobhams to make him cut it out; his own dramatic instinct would have told him that, if Henry was to be shown in his full glory, the presence of Falstaff would diminish it.

Seeking for an explanation of why Falstaff affects us as he does, I find myself compelled to see *Henry IV* as possessing, in addition to its overt meaning, a parabolic significance. Overtly, Falstaff is a Lord of Misrule; parabolically, he is a comic symbol for the supernatural order of Charity as contrasted with the temporal order of Justice symbolized by Henry of Monmouth.

Such readings are only possible with drama which, like Shakespeare's, is secular, concerned directly, not with the relation of man and God, but with the relations between men. Greek tragedy, at least before Euripides, is directly religious, concerned with what the gods do to men rather than what men do to each other: it presents a picture of human events, the causes of which are divine actions. In consequence, a Greek tragedy does not demand that we "read" it in the sense that we speak of "reading" a face. The ways of the gods may be mysterious to human beings but they are not ambiguous.

There can be no secular drama of any depth or importance except in a culture which recognizes that man has an internal history as well as an external; that his actions are partly in response to an objective situation created by his past acts and the acts of others, and partly initiated by his subjective need to re-create, redefine, and rechoose himself. Surprise and revelation are the essence of drama. In Greek tragedy these are supplied by the gods; no mortal can foresee how and when they will act. But the conduct of men has no element of surprise, that is to say, the way in which they react to the surprising events which befall them is exactly what one would expect.

A secular drama presupposes that in all which men say and do there is a gratuitous element which makes their conduct ambiguous and unpredictable. Secular drama, therefore, demands a much more active role from its audience than a Greek tragedy. The audience has to be at one and the same time a witness to what is occurring on stage and a subjective participant who interprets what he sees and hears. And a secular dramatist like Shakespeare who attempts to project the inner history of human beings into objective stage action is faced with problems which Aeschylus and Sophocles were spared, for there are aspects of this inner history which resist and sometimes defy manifestation.

> Humility is represented with difficulty—when it is shown in its ideal moment, the beholder senses the lack of something because he feels that its true ideality does not consist in the fact that it is ideal in the moment but that it is constant. Romantic love can very well be represented in the moment, but conjugal love cannot, because an ideal husband is not one who is such once in his life but one who every day is such. Courage can very well be concentrated in the moment, but not patience, precisely for the reason that patience strives with time. A king who conquers kingdoms can be represented in the moment, but a cross bearer who every day takes

up his cross cannot be represented in art because the point is that he does it every day. (Kierkegaard.)

Let us suppose, then, that a dramatist wishes to show a character acting out of the spirit of charity or agape. At first this looks easy. Agape requires that we love our enemies, do good to those that hate us and forgive those who injure us, and this command is unconditional. Surely, all a dramatist has to do is to show one human being forgiving an enemy.

In *Measure for Measure,* Angelo has wronged Isabella and Mariana, and the facts of the wrong become public. Angelo repents and demands that the just sentence of death be passed on him by the Duke. Isabella and Mariana implore the Duke to show Mercy. The Duke yields to their prayers and all ends happily. I agree with Professor Coghill's interpretation of *Measure for Measure* as a parable in which Isabella is an image for the redeemed Christian Soul, perfectly chaste and loving, whose reward is to become the bride of God; but, to my mind, the parable does not quite work because it is impossible to distinguish in dramatic action between the spirit of forgiveness and the act of pardon.

The command to forgive is unconditional: whether my enemy harden his heart or repent and beg forgiveness is irrelevant. If he hardens his heart, he does not care whether I forgive him or not and it would be impertinent of me to say, "I forgive you." If he repents and asks, "Will you forgive me?" the answer, "Yes," should not express a decision on my part but describe a state of feeling which has always existed. On the stage, however, it is impossible to show one person forgiving another, unless the wrongdoer asks for forgiveness, because silence and inaction are undramatic. The Isabella we are shown in earlier scenes of *Measure for Measure* is certainly not in a forgiving spirit—she is in a passion of rage and despair at Angelo's injustice—and dramatically she could not be otherwise, for then there would be no play. Again, on the stage, forgiveness requires manifestation in action, that is to say, the one who forgives must be in a position to do something for the other which, if he were not forgiving, he would not do. This means that my enemy must be at my mercy; but, to the spirit of charity, it is irrelevant whether I am at my enemy's mercy or he at mine. So long as he is at my mercy, forgiveness is indistinguishable from judicial pardon.

The law cannot forgive, for the law has not been wronged, only broken; only persons can be wronged. The law can pardon, but it can only pardon what it has the power to punish. If the lawbreaker is stronger than the legal authorities, they are powerless to do either. The decision to grant or refuse pardon must be governed by prudent calculation—if the wrongdoer is pardoned, he will behave better in the future than if he were punished, etc. But charity is forbidden to calculate in this way: I am required to forgive my enemy whatever the effect on him may be.

One may say that Isabella forgives Angelo and the Duke pardons him. But, on the stage, this distinction is invisible because, there, power, justice and love are all on the same side. Justice is able to pardon what love is commanded to forgive. But to love, it is an accident that the power of temporal justice should be on its side; indeed, the Gospels assure us that, sooner or later, they will find themselves in opposition and that love must suffer at the hands of justice.

In *King Lear,* Shakespeare attempts to show absolute love and goodness, in the person of Cordelia, destroyed by the powers of this world, but the price he pays is that Cordelia, as a dramatic character, is a bore.

If she is not to be a fake, what she says cannot be poetically very impressive nor what she does dramatically very exciting.

> What shall Cordelia speak? Love and be silent.

In a play with twenty-six scenes, Shakespeare allows her to appear in only four, and from a total of over three thousand three hundred lines, he allots to her less than ninety.

Temporal Justice demands the use of force to quell the unjust; it demands prudence, a practical reckoning with time and place; and it demands publicity for its laws and its penalties. But Charity forbids all three—we are not to resist evil, if a man demand our coat we are to give him our cloak also, we are to take no thought for the morrow and, while secretly fasting and giving alms, we are to appear in public as persons who do neither.

A direct manifestation of charity in secular terms is, therefore, impossible. One form of indirect manifestation employed by religious teachers has been through parables in which actions which are ethically immoral are made to stand as a sign for that which transcends ethics. The Gospel parable of the Unjust Steward is one example. These words by a Hasidic Rabbi are another:

> I cannot teach you the ten principles of service but a little child and a thief can show you what they are. From the child you can learn three things;
> He is merry for no particular reason.
> Never for a moment is he idle.
> When he wants something, he demands it vigorously.
> The thief can instruct you in many things.
> He does his service by night.
> If he does not finish what he has set out to do in one night, he devotes the next night to it.
> He and all those who work for him, love one another.
> He risks his life for slight gains.
> What he takes has so little value for him that he gives up for a very small coin.
> He endures blows and hardships and it matters nothing to him.
> He likes his trade and would not exchange it for any other.

If a parable of this kind is dramatized, the action must be comic, that is to say, the apparently immoral actions of the hero must not inflict, as in the actual world they would, real suffering upon others.

Thus, Falstaff speaks of himself as if he were always robbing travelers. We see him do this once—incidentally, it is not Falstaff but the Prince who is the instigator—and the sight convinces us that he never has been and never could be a successful highwayman. The money is restolen from him and returned to its proper owners; the only sufferer is Falstaff himself who has been made a fool of. He lives shamelessly on credit, but none of his creditors seems to be in serious trouble as a result. The Hostess may swear that if he does not pay his bill, she will have to pawn her plate and tapestries, but this is shown to be the kind of exaggeration habitual to landladies, for in the next scene they are still there. What, overtly, is dishonesty becomes, parabolically, a sign for a lack of pride, humility which acknowledges its unimportance and dependence upon others.

Then he rejoices in his reputation as a fornicator with whom no woman is safe alone, but the Falstaff on stage is too old to fornicate, and it is impossible to imagine him younger. All we see him do is defend a whore against a bully, set her on his knee and make her cry out of affection and pity. What in the real world is promiscuous lust, the treatment of other persons as objects of sexual greed, becomes in the comic world of play a symbol for the charity that loves all neighbors without distinction.

Living off other people's money and indiscriminate fornication are acts of injustice towards private individuals; Falstaff is also guilty of injustice to others in their public character as citizens. In any war it is not the justice or injustice of either side that decides who is to be the victor but the force each can command. It is therefore the duty of all who believe in the justice of the King's side to supply him with the best soldiers possible. Falstaff makes no attempt to fulfill this duty. Before the battle of Shrewsbury, he first conscripts those who have most money and least will to fight and then allows them to buy their way out, so that he is finally left with a sorry regiment of "discarded unjust serving men, younger sons to younger brothers, revolted tapsters and ostlers trade fallen. . . ." Before the battle of Gaultree Forest, the two most sturdy young men, Mouldy and Bullcalf, offer him money and are let off, and the weakest, Shadow, Feeble and Wart, taken.

From the point of view of society this is unjust, but if the villagers who are subject to conscription were to be asked, as private individuals, whether they would rather be treated justly or as Falstaff treats them, there is no doubt as to their answer. What their betters call just and unjust means nothing to them; all they know is that conscription will tear them away from their homes and livelihoods with a good chance of getting killed or returning maimed "to beg at the town's end." Those whom Falstaff selects are those with least to lose, derelicts without home or livelihood to whom soldiering at least offers a chance of loot. Bullcalf wants to stay with his friends, Mouldy has an old mother to look after, but Feeble is quite ready to go if his friend Wart can go with him.

Falstaff's neglect of the public interest in favor of private concerns is an image for the justice of charity which treats each person, not as a cipher, but as a unique person. The Prince may justly complain:

> I never did see such pitiful rascals

but Falstaffs retort speaks for all the insulted and injured of this world:

> Tut tut—good enough to toss, food for powder, food for powder. They'll fit a pit as well as better. Tush, man, mortal men, mortal men. . . .

These are Falstaff's only acts: for the rest, he fritters away his time, swigging at the bottle and taking no thought for the morrow. As a parable, both the idleness and the drinking, the surrender to immediacy and the refusal to accept reality, become signs for the Unworldly Man as contrasted with Prince Hal who represents worldliness at its best.

At his best, the worldly man is one who dedicates his life to some public end, politics, science, industry, art. etc. The end is outside himself, but the choice of end is determined by the particular talents with which nature has endowed him, and the proof that he has chosen rightly is worldly success. To dedicate one's life to an end for which one is not endowed is madness, the madness of Don Quixote. Strictly speaking, he does not desire fame for himself, but to achieve something which merits fame. Because his end is worldly, that is, in the public domain—to marry the girl of one's choice, or to become a good parent, are private, not worldly, ends—the personal life and its satisfactions are, for the worldly man, of secondary importance and, should they ever conflict with his vocation, must be sacrificed. The worldly man at his best knows that other persons exist and desires that they should—a statesman has no wish to establish justice among tables and chairs—but if it is necessary to the achievement of his end to treat certain persons as if they were things, then, callously or regretfully, he will. What distinguishes him from the ordinary criminal is that the criminal lacks the imagination to conceive of others as being persons like himself; when he sacrifices others, he feels no guilt because, to the criminal, he is the only person in a world of things. What distinguishes both the worldly man and the criminal from the wicked man is their lack of malice. The wicked man is not worldly, but anti-worldly. His conscious end is nothing less than the destruction of others. He is obsessed by hatred at his knowledge that other persons exist besides himself and cannot rest until he has reduced them all to the status of things.

But it is not always easy to distinguish the worldly man from the criminal or the wicked man by observing their behavior and its results. It can happen, for instance, that, despite his intention, a wicked man does good. Don John in *Much Ado About Nothing* certainly means nothing but harm to Claudio and Hero, yet it is thanks to him that Claudio obtains insight into his own shortcomings and becomes, what previously he was not, a fit husband for Hero. To the outward eye, however different their subjective intentions, both Harry of Monmouth and Iago deceive and destroy. Even in their speech one cannot help noticing a certain resemblance between

So when this loose behaviour I throw off
And pay the debt I never promised,
By how much better than my word I am.
I'll so offend to make offence a skill
Redeeming time when men least think I will.

and:

From when my outward action doth demonstrate
The native act and figure of my heart
In compliment extern, 'tis not long after
But I will wear my heart upon my sleeve
For daws to peck at. I am not what I am. . . .

and the contrast of both to Sonnet 121:

No, I am that I am; and they that level
At my abuses reckon up their own.
I may be straight though they themselves be bevel.

Falstaff is perfectly willing to tell the world: "I am that I am, a drunken old failure." Hal cannot jeopardize his career by such careless disclosure but must always assume whatever manner is politic at the moment. To the degree that we have worldly ambitions, Falstaff's verdict on the Prince strikes home.

Thou art essentially mad without seeming so.

Falstaff never really does anything, but he never stops talking, so that the impression he makes on the audience is not of idleness but of infinite energy. He is never tired, never bored, and until he is rejected he radiates happiness as Hal radiates power, and this happiness without apparent cause, this untiring devotion to making others laugh becomes a comic image for a love which is absolutely self-giving.

Laughing and loving have certain properties in common. Laughter is contagious but not, like physical force, irresistible. A man in a passion of any kind cannot be made to laugh; if he laughs, it is a proof that he has already mastered his passion. Laughter is an action only in a special sense. Many kinds of action can cause laughter, but the only kind of action that laughter causes is more laughter; while we laugh, time stops and no other kind of action can be contemplated. In rage or hysteria people sometimes are said to "laugh" but no one can confuse the noises they make with the sound of real laughter. Real laughter is absolutely unaggressive; we cannot wish people or things we find amusing to be other than they are; we do not desire them to change them, far less hurt or destroy them. An angry and dangerous mob is rendered harmless by the orator who can succeed in making it laugh. Real laughter is always, as we say, "disarming."

Falstaff makes the same impression on us that the Sinner of Lublin made upon his rabbi.

> In Lublin lived a great sinner. Whenever he went to talk to the rabbi, the rabbi readily consented and conversed with him as if he were a man of integrity and one who was a close friend. Many of the hassidim were annoyed at this and one said to the other: "Is it possible that our rabbi who has only to look once into a man's face to know his life from first to last, to know the very origin of his soul, does not see that this fellow is a sinner? And if he does see it, that he considers him worthy to speak to and associate with." Finally they summoned up courage to go to the rabbi himself with their question. He answered them: "I know all about him as well as you. But you know how I love gaiety and hate dejection. And this man is so great a sinner. Others repent the moment they have sinned, are sorry for a moment, and then return to their folly. But he knows no regrets and no doldrums, and lives in his happiness as in a tower. And it is the radiance of his happiness that overwhelms my heart."

Falstaff's happiness is almost an impregnable tower, but not quite. "I am that I am" is not a complete self-description; he must also add—"The young prince hath misled me. I am the fellow with the great belly, and he is my dog."

The Christian God is not a self-sufficient being like Aristotle's First Cause, but a God who creates a world which he continues to love although it refuses to love him in return. He appears in this world, not as Apollo or Aphrodite might appear, disguised as man so that no mortal should recognize his divinity, but as a real man who openly claims to be God.

And the consequence is inevitable. The highest religious and temporal authorities condemn Him as a blasphemer and a Lord of Misrule, as a Bad Companion for mankind. Inevitable because, as Richelieu said, "The salvation of States is in this world," and history has not as yet provided us with any evidence that the Prince of this world has changed his character.

INTERLUDE: THE WISH GAME

Were some fanatic to learn the whole of Proust by heart, word for word, and then try reciting it to an audience in a drawing room after dinner, the chances are, I fancy, that within half an hour most of the audience would have fallen asleep, and their verdict upon *Remembrance of Things Past* would be that it was a boring and incomprehensible story. The difficulty of judging fairly a printed folk tale, still more a collection of tales* that were never intended to be grasped through the eye, is just as great. Our feeling for orally transmitted literature is distorted by the peculiar nature of the only literature of this class that is still alive—for us the spoken tale is the unprintable tale—but it is possible, even in the smoking-room story, to perceive some of the characteristics common to all storytelling. To begin with, both the occasion of the telling and the voice and gestures of the teller are important elements in the effect; the story that has delighted us on one occasion may, in a different context and told by a different speaker, fail utterly to amuse. Then, the ear is much slower in comprehending than the eye, far less avid of novelty, and far more appreciative of rhythmical repetition.

Folk tales have also suffered from certain preconceived ideas on the part of the general public. They are commonly thought of as being either entertainment for children or documents for adult anthropologists and students of comparative religion. Children enjoy them, it is true, but that is no reason

* *The Borzoi Book of French Folk Tales,* edited by Paul Delarue.

why grownups, for whom they were primarily intended, should assume that they are childish. They undoubtedly contain elements drawn from ancient rituals and myths, but a knowledge of such things is no more essential to appreciating them than a knowledge of the reading and personal experience of a modern novelist is essential to enjoying his novels.

A religious rite is a serious matter, an act that must be done in exactly the right way in order to secure supernatural aid, without which the crops will fail and men die. A myth almost always contains playful elements, but it claims to answer a serious question—how did such-and-such come to be?—and to some degree or other demands to be believed. But a tale is to be told only if someone wishes to hear it, and the one question it presupposes is, "How are we to spend a pleasant evening?" As the soldier-narrator of "John-of-the-Bear" says:

> I go through a forest where there is no woods, through a river where there is no water, through a village where there is no house. I knock at a door and everybody answers me. The more I tell you, the more I shall lie to you. I'm not paid to tell you the truth.

"The Doctor and His Pupil" contains a motif common to many folk tales—that of one character pursuing another through a series of magical metamorphoses. The hunted turns into a hare, whereupon the hunter turns into a dog, whereupon the hare becomes a lark, whereupon the dog becomes an eagle, and so on. The primal source of this idea is probably a ritual fertility dance in which the twelve months were symbolically mimed. In such a rite, if it existed, the symbolical animals would be fixed in number and kind and the worshipers would know in advance what they were, but a tale that makes use of the notion can use any beasts, and any number of them it pleases, provided that the pairs logically match. If the storyteller makes the hunted one a hare, he cannot make the hunter a donkey; if he wants the hunter to be a donkey, then he must make the hunted something like a carrot. The pleasure of the audience is that of suspense, pattern and surprise, so that at each transformation it wonders, "How will the hunted get out of that one?" Similarly, the motif of the Virgin and the Seven-Headed Dragon in "The Three Dogs and the Dragon" and "The Miller's Three Sons" may well be derived from the myth of Perseus and Andromeda, but there is no apparent attempt to relate these tales to any historical event or person. Questions of religion and history, however interesting and important, are not the business of the literary critic. He can only ask the questions he would ask of any work of literature, e.g., what kind of writing is this, as compared with other kinds? What are its special virtues and its special limitations? Judged by its own intentions, what makes one tale or one version of a tale better or worse than another?

One characteristic that clearly differentiates the fairy tale from other kinds of narrative is the nature of the fairy-tale hero. The epic hero is one who, thanks to his exceptional gifts, is able to perform great deeds of which the average man is incapable. He is of noble (often divine) descent, stronger, braver, better looking, more skillful than everybody else. A stranger meeting him in the street would immediately recognize him as a hero. Some of his adventures may be sexual, he may marry, but such matters are incidental to his main object, which is to win immortal fame. Even when he is transformed into the knight-errant in whose life the ladies play a great role, his honor is still more important than his love.

Like the epic hero, the fairy story hero performs great and seemingly impossible deeds, but there the resemblance ends. He may be by birth a prince, but, if so, he is, as it were, a prince of the first generation, for he never possesses, as the epic hero always does, a genealogical tree. More commonly, however, he is the child of poor parents and starts his life at the very bottom of the social scale. He is not recognizable as a hero except in the negative sense—that he is the one who to the outward eye appears, of all people, the least likely to succeed. Often he is a child, lacking even the strength and wit of the ordinary adult, and nearly always his relatives and neighbors consider him stupid and lacking in ambition. The virtue by which he succeeds when others fail is the very unmilitant virtue of humble good nature. He is the one who stops to share his crust with the old beggar woman or free the trapped beast, thereby securing magical aid, when his proud and impatient rivals pass by and in consequence come to grief. The fairy-story world is purely Calvinist. That is to say, the hero's deeds cannot be called *his;* without magical assistance he would be totally helpless. Officially, he is a lover, not a warrior, who desires glory and treasure only in order that he may deserve the hand of the princess, but no fairy-story character, either in speech or in behavior, shows real erotic feeling. We find neither outright sexual passion nor sentimental *Frauendienst.* Fairy-story "love" is not an emotion but a formal principle, one of the rules by which the story game is played. If the fairy-story hero differs from the epic hero in having no visible *arete,* he differs also from the hero of the modern novel in that he has no hidden qualities that are in time revealed. As a character, he is the same person at the end that he was at the beginning; all that has changed is his status. Nothing that happens to him can be called personally significant in the sense that, thanks to it, his awareness of himself is altered.

Since the characters in a fairy story are either good or bad, benevolent or malevolent—it is rare for a bad character to repent and unknown for a good one to become bad—they cannot be said to be tempted. There are occasions when the hero (or heroine), though warned not to do something—not to pick up a wig or enter a particular room—ignores the warning and gets into trouble, but the prohibited act is never, in itself, immoral. There is only one fairy-tale motif, to my knowledge, that contains an element of inner conflict: the theme of Grimm's "Faithful John" and M. Delarue's "Father Roquelaure." The Prince's loyal servant learns by chance that, in order to save his master, he must do things which will appear to be evil, and that if he explains the reason he will be turned to stone. He does them and—under threat of death or because he cannot bear his master's displeasure—he tells and is turned to stone. The Prince then discovers that to restore his faithful servant he must sacrifice his own child.

In other kinds of fiction, the plot evolves through the clash between fate or chance on the one side and will and desire on the other; the fairy story is peculiar in that the main cause of any event is a wish. A desire is a real and given experience of a human individual in a particular historical context. I am not free to choose what desire I shall feel, nor can I choose the goal that will satisfy it; if the desire is real, it proposes its own satisfaction. When I desire, I know what I want. I am then free to choose either to remain in a state of unsatisfied desire by refusing to assent to its demands or to use my reason and will to satisfy it. A wish, on the other hand, is not given; I am free to wish anything I choose, but the cause of all wishes is the same—that which is should not be. If I say, "I desire to eat," I do not mean, "I desire not to be hungry," for if I were not hungry I should not desire to eat. When a scolded child says to a parent, "I wish you were dead," he does not mean what he actually says; he only means, "I wish I were not what I am, a child being scolded by you," and a hundred other wishes would have done equally well. If the young heir to the fortune of a disagreeable old aunt says, "I wish she were dead," he may really desire her death, but his wish does not express this desire; its real content is, "I wish that my conscience and the law did not, as they do, forbid murder." We can wish anything we choose precisely because all wishes are equally impossible, for all substitute an imaginary present for the real one. A world in which all wishes were magically granted would be a world without desire or will, for every moment of time would be disjunct and there would be no way of distinguishing between animate and inanimate beings, animals and men.

Wishing is not the sole cause of events in the fairy tale but the license it is given prevents the fairy tale from arousing any strong emotions in the audience. This, however, is one of the peculiar pleasures the fairy story affords—that it can take images of beautiful maidens or cannibalistic ogres who, in our dreams, arouse violent emotions of desire or terror, or it can inflict horrible punishments on the wicked (like rolling them downhill in a barrel full of nails) which in real life would be acts of sadism, and make them all *playful*.

A game, of course, must have rules if it is not to be purely arbitrary and meaningless, and the characters in the fairy tale have a "fate" to which even their wishes must submit. They must obey, for instance, the laws of language. We can lie in language, that is to say, manipulate the world as we wish, but the lie must make sense as a grammatical proposition:

> "What are you doing there, good woman?" he asked.
>
> "I'd like to take some sunshine home, a whole wheelbarrowful, but it's difficult, for as soon as I get it in the shade it vanishes."
>
> "What do you want a wheelbarrowful of sunshine for?"
>
> "It's to warm my little boy who is at home half dead from cold."

The other law, so often introduced in the fairy tale, which all must obey is the law of numerical series. The hero who is set three tasks cannot wish them into two or four.

It would be misleading to say that because the fairy tale world is a fantastic one, such literature is "escapist." A work may justly be condemned as escapist only if it claims to portray the real world when in fact its portrait is false. But the fairy story never pretends to be a picture of the real world, and even if its audience were to respond with the feeling, "How I wish we could live in this world instead of the world we have to live in" (and I very much doubt that any audience ever felt this way), it would always know that such a wish was impossible. The kind of enjoyment the fairy tale can provide is similar, I believe, to that provided by the poems of Mallarmé or by abstract painting.

M. Delarue's collection of French folk tales includes versions of several stories that are also to be found in Grimm. A comparison of the one with the other may help to show the qualities we look for in a folk tale and by which we judge it:

The Lost Children   *Hänsel and Gretel*

In their respective openings, the German version is superior both in richness of detail and in dramatic suspense. The

French version lacks the conflict between the bad mother and the kind but weak father, and the children do not overhear their conversation, so the drama of the pebbles and the crumbs is lacking. The French children climb a tree, see a white house and a red house, and choose to go to the red house, which, of course, turns out to be the wrong choice, but we never learn what the white house is. This is a violation of one of the laws of storytelling, namely, that everything introduced must be accounted for. In the central part of the story, the French version replaces the witch in her edible house with the Devil and his wife on an ordinary farm, and the children succeed in killing the Devil's wife while he is taking a walk. There is a loss, perhaps, in beauty of imagery but a gain in character interest. In its conclusion, the French version is much superior. In the German version, Hänsel and Gretel merely wander through the forest till they come to a river, which they are ferried across by a duck. The presence and nature of the duck are not explained, nor is any reason given why there should be a river between them and their home that they did not have to cross when they set out. But in the French version, the Devil pursues the runaways and his pursuit is punctuated by a ritual verse dialogue between him and those he meets. They all fool him and finally cause him to be drowned in a river that he is told the children have crossed, though in fact they have simply gone home.

The Godchild of the Fairy in the Tower *Rapunzel*

In the German version, the witch learns about the Prince from the girl herself, in the French from a talking bitch she has left to keep watch on the girl, a variation that is more interesting and more logical. But the unhappy ending of the French version—the witch turns the girl into a frog and grows a pig's snout on the Prince—seems to me an artistic mistake. In the playful world of the fairy story, all problems, including that of moral justice, must be solved. When a fairy story ends unhappily, we do not feel that we have been told an unpleasant truth; we merely feel that the story has been broken off in the middle.

The Story of Grandmother   Little Red Riding Hood

M. Delarue tells us in his notes that the Grimm story is largely derived from Perrault. The French oral version he prints is infinitely superior to either, and a model of what a folk tale should be:

There was once a woman who had some bread, and she said to her daughter: "You are going to carry a hot loaf and a bottle of milk to your grandmother."

The little girl departed. At the crossroads she met the *bzou,* who said to her: "Where are you going?"

"I'm taking a hot loaf and a bottle of milk to my grandmother."

"What road are you taking," said the *bzou,* "the Needles Road or the Pins Road?"

"The Needles Road," said the little girl.

"Well, I shall take the Pins Road."

The little girl enjoyed herself, picking up needles. Meanwhile the *bzou* arrived at her grandmother's, killed her, put some of her flesh in the pantry and a bottle of her blood on the shelf. The girl arrived and knocked at the door.

"Push the door," said the *bzou,* "it's closed with a wet straw."

"Hello, Grandmother; I'm bringing you a hot loaf and a bottle of milk."

"Put them in the pantry. You eat the meat that's in it and drink a bottle of wine that is on the shelf."

As she ate there was a little cat that said: "A slut is she who eats the flesh and drinks the blood of her grandmother!"

"Undress, my child," said the *bzou,* "and come and sleep beside me."

"Where should I put my apron?"

"Throw it in the fire, my child; you don't need it any more."

And she asked where to put all the other garments, the bodice, the dress, the skirt, and the hose, and the wolf replied: "Throw them into the fire, my child; you will need them no more."

"Oh, Grandmother, how hairy you are!"

"It's to keep me warmer, my child."

"Oh, Grandmother, those long nails you have!"

"It's to scratch me better, my child."

"Oh, Grandmother, those big shoulders you have!"

"All the better to carry kindling from the woods, my child."

"Oh, Grandmother, those big ears you have!"

"All the better to hear with, my child."

"Oh, Grandmother, that big mouth you have!"

"All the better to eat you with, my child!"

"Oh, Grandmother, I need to go outside to relieve myself."

"Do it in the bed, my child."

"No, Grandmother, I want to go outside."

"All right, but don't stay long."

The *bzou* tied a woollen thread to her feet and let her go out, and when the little girl was outside she tied the end of the string to a big plum tree in the yard. The *bzou* got impatient and said: "Are you making cables?"

When he became aware that no one answered him, he jumped out of bed and saw that the little girl had escaped. He followed her, but he arrived at the house just at the moment that she was safely inside.

BROTHERS & OTHERS

The possible redemption from the predicament of irreversibility—of being unable to undo what one has done—is the faculty of forgiving. The remedy for unpredictability, for the chaotic uncertainty of the future, is contained in the faculty to make and keep promises. Both faculties depend upon plurality, on the .presence and acting of others, for no man can forgive himself and no one can be bound by a promise made only to himself.

HANNAH ARENDT

The England which Shakespeare presents in *Richard II* and *Henry IV* is a society in which wealth, that is to say, social power, is derived from ownership of land, not from accumulated capital. The only person who is in need of money is the King who must equip troops to defend the country against foreign foes. If, like Richard II, he is an unjust king, he spends the money which should have been spent on defense in maintaining a luxurious and superfluous court. Economically, the country is self-sufficient, and production is for use, not profit. The community-forming bond in this England is either the family tie of common blood which is given by nature or the feudal tie of lord and vassal created by personal oath. Both are commitments to individuals and both are lifelong commitments. But this type of community tie is presented as being ill suited to the needs of England as a functioning society. If England is to function properly as a society, the community based on personal loyalty must be converted into a community united by a common love of impersonal justice, that is to say, of the King's Law which is no respecter of persons. We are given to understand that in Edward III's day, this kind of community already existed, so that the family type of community is seen as a regression. Centuries earlier, a war between Wessex and Mercia, for example, would have been regarded as legitimate as a war between England and France, but now a conflict between a Percy and a Bolingbroke is regarded as a civil war, illegitimate because between brothers. It is possible, therefore, to apply a medical analogy to England and speak of a sick body politic, because it is as obvious who are aliens and who ought to be brothers as it is obvious which cells belong to my body and which to the body of another. War, as such, is not condemned but is still considered, at least for the gentry, a normal and enjoyable occupation like farming. Indeed peace, as such, carries with it the pejorative associations of idleness and vice.

> Now all the youth of England on fire
> And silken dalliance in the wardrobe lies.
> Now shrive the Armourers and Honour's thought
> Reigns solely in the breast of every man.
> They sell the pasture now to buy the horse.

The only merchants who appear in *Henry IV* are the "Bacon-fed Knaves and Fat Chuffs" whom Falstaff robs, and they are presented as contemptible physical cowards.

In *The Merchant of Venice* and *Othello* Shakespeare depicts a very different kind of society. Venice does not produce anything itself, either raw materials or manufactured goods. Its existence depends upon the financial profits which can be made by international trade,

> . . . the trade and profit of the city
> Consisteth of all nations

that is to say, on buying cheaply here and selling dearly there, and its wealth lies in its accumulated money capital. Money has ceased to be simply a convenient medium of exchange and has become a form of social power which can be gained or lost. Such a mercantile society is international and cosmopolitan; it does not distinguish between the brother and the alien other than on a basis of blood or religion—from the point of view of society, customers are brothers, trade rivals others. But Venice is not simply a mercantile society; it is also a city inhabited by various communities with different loves—Gentiles and Jews, for example—who do not regard each other personally as brothers, but must tolerate each other's existence because both are indispensable to the proper functioning of their society, and this toleration is enforced by the laws of the Venetian state.

A change in the nature of wealth from landownership to money capital radically alters the social conception of time. The wealth produced by land may vary from year to year—there are good harvests and bad—but, in the long run its average yield may be counted upon. Land, barring dispossession by an invader or confiscation by the State, is held by a family in perpetuity. In consequence, the social conception of time in a landowning society is cyclical—the future is expected to be a repetition of the past. But in a mercantile society time is conceived of as unilinear forward movement in which the future is always novel and unpredictable. (The unpredictable event in a landowning society is an Act of God, that is to say, it is not "natural" for an event to be unpredictable.) The merchant is constantly taking risks—if he is lucky, he may make a fortune, if he is unlucky he may lose everything. Since, in a mercantile society, social power is derived from money, the distribution of power within it is constantly changing, which has the effect of weakening reverence for the past; who one's distant ancestors were soon ceases to be of much social importance. The oath of lifelong loyalty is replaced by the contract which binds its signatories to fulfill certain specific promises by a certain specific future date, after which their commitment to each other is over.

The action of *The Merchant of Venice* takes place in two locations, Venice and Belmont, which are so different in character that to produce the play in a manner which will not blur this contrast and yet preserve a unity is very difficult. If the spirit of Belmont is made too predominant, then Antonio and Shylock will seem irrelevant, and vice versa. In *Henry IV*, Shakespeare intrudes Falstaff, who by nature belongs to the world of *opera buffa,* into the historical world of political chronicle with which his existence is incompatible, and thereby, consciously or unconsciously, achieves the effect of calling in question the values of military glory and temporal justice as embodied in Henry of Monmouth. In *The Merchant of Venice* he gives us a similar contrast—the romantic fairy story world of Belmont is incompatible with the historical reality of money-making Venice—but this time what is called in question is the claim of Belmont to be the Great Good Place, the Earthly Paradise. Watching *Henry IV*, we become convinced that our aesthetic sympathy with Falstaff is a profounder vision than our ethical judgment which must side with Hal. Watching *The Merchant of Venice*, on the other hand, we are compelled to acknowledge that the attraction which we naturally feel towards Belmont is highly questionable. On that account, I think *The Merchant of Venice* must be classed among Shakespeare's "Unpleasant Plays."

Omit Antonio and Shylock, and the play becomes a romantic fairy tale like *A Midsummer Night's Dream*. The world of the fairy tale is an unambiguous, unproblematic world in which there is no contradiction between outward appearance and inner reality, a world of being, not becoming. A character may be temporarily disguised—the unlovely animal is really the Prince Charming under a spell, the hideous old witch transforms herself into a lovely young girl to tempt the hero—but this is a mask, not a contradiction: the Prince is *really* handsome, the witch *really* hideous. A fairy story character may sometimes change, but, if so, the change is like a mutation; at one moment he or she is this kind of person, at the next he is transformed into that kind. It is a world in which people are either good or bad by nature; occasionally a bad character repents, but a good character never becomes bad. It is meaningless therefore to ask why a character in a fairy tale acts as he does because his nature will only allow him to act in one way. It is a world in which, ultimately, good fortune is the sign of moral goodness, ill fortune of moral badness. The good are beautiful, rich and speak with felicity, the bad are ugly, poor and speak crudely.

In real life we can distinguish between two kinds of choice, the strategic and the personal. A strategic choice is conditioned by a future goal which is already known to the chooser. I wish to catch a certain train which will be leaving in ten minutes. I can either go by subway or take a taxi. It is the rush hour, so I have to decide which I believe will get me sooner to the station. My choice may turn out to be mistaken, but neither I nor an observer will have any difficulty in understanding the choice I make. But now and again, I take a decision which is based, not on any calculation of its future consequences, for I cannot tell what they will be, but upon my immediate conviction that, whatever the consequences, I must do this now. However well I know myself, I can never understand completely why I take such a decision, and to others it will always seem mysterious. The traditional symbol in Western Literature for this kind of personal choice is the phenomenon of falling-in-love. But in the fairy-tale world, what appear to be the personal choices of the characters are really the strategic choices of the storyteller, for within the tale the future is predestined. We watch Portia's suitors choosing their casket, but we know in advance that Morocco and Arragon cannot choose the right one and that Bessanio cannot choose the wrong one, and we know this, not only from what we know of their characters but also from their ordinal position in a series, for the fairy-tale world is ruled by magical numbers. Lovers are common enough in fairy tales, but love appears as a pattern-forming principle rather than sexual passion as we experience it in the historical world. The fairy tale cannot tolerate intense emotions of any kind, because any intense emotion has tragic possibilities, and even the possibility of tragedy is excluded from the fairy tale. It is possible to imagine the serious passion of Romeo and Juliet having a happy ending instead of a tragic one, but it is impossible to imagine either of them in Oberon's Wood or the Forest of Arden.

The fairy tale is hospitable to black magicians as well as to white; ogres, witches, bogeys are constantly encountered who have their temporary victories but in the end are always vanquished by the good and banished, leaving Arcadia to its unsullied innocent joy where the good live happily ever after. But the malevolence of a wicked character in a fairy tale is a given premise; their victims, that is to say, never bear any responsibility for the malice, have never done the malevolent one an injury. The Devil, by definition malevolent without a cause, is presented in the medieval miracle plays as a fairy-story bogey, never victorious but predestined to be cheated of his prey.

Recent history has made it utterly impossible for the most unsophisticated and ignorant audience to ignore the historical reality of the Jews and think of them as fairy-story bogeys with huge noses and red wigs. An Elizabethan audience undoubtedly still could—very few of them had seen a Jew—and, if Shakespeare had so wished, he could have made Shylock grotesquely wicked like the *Jew of Malta*. The star actors who, from the eighteenth century onwards have chosen to play the role, have not done so out of a sense of moral duty in order to combat anti-Semitism, but because their theatrical instinct told them that the part, played seriously, not comically, offered them great possibilities.

The Merchant of Venice is, among other things, as much a "problem" play as one by Ibsen or Shaw. The question of the immorality or morality of usury was a sixteenth century issue on which both the theologians and the secular authorities were divided. Though the majority of medieval theologians had condemned usury, there had been, from the beginning, divergence of opinion as to the correct interpretation of Deuteronomy, XXIII, vv 19-20:

> Thou shalt not lend upon usury to thy brother; usury of money, usury of victuals, usury of any thing that is lent

> upon usury: Unto a stranger thou mayest lend upon usury

and Leviticus XXV, vv 35-37 which proscribe the taking of usury, not only from a fellow Jew, but also from the stranger living in their midst and under their protection.

Some Christian theologians had interpreted this to mean that, since the Christians had replaced the Jews as God's Chosen, they were entitled to exact usury from non-Christians.[1]

> Who is your brother? He is your sharer in nature, co-heir in grace, every people, which, first, is in the faith, then under the Roman Law. Who, then, is the stranger? the foes of God's people. From him, demand usury whom you rightly desire to harm, against whom weapons are lawfully carried. Upon him usury is legally imposed. Where there is the right of war, there also is the right of usury. (ST. AMBROSE.)

Several centuries later, St. Bernard of Siena, in a statement of which the sanctity seems as doubtful as the logic, takes St. Ambrose's argument even further.

> Temporal goods are given to men for the worship of the true God and the Lord of the Universe. When, therefore, the worship of God does not exist, as in the case of God's enemies, usury is lawfully exacted, because this is not done for the sake of gain, but for the sake of the Faith; and the motive is brotherly love, namely, that God's enemies may be weakened and so return to Him; and further because the goods they have do not belong to them, since they are rebels against the true faith; they shall therefore devolve upon the Christians.

The majority, however, starting from the Gospel, command that we are to treat all men, even our enemies, as brothers, held that the Deuteronomic permission was no longer valid, so that under no circumstances was usury permissible. Thus,

[1] N.B. For the quotations which follow, I am indebted to Benjamin Nelson's fascinating book *The Idea of Usury*, Princeton University Press.

St. Thomas Aquinas, who was also, no doubt, influenced by Aristotle's condemnation of usury, says:

> The Jews were forbidden to take usury from their brethren, i.e., from other Jews. By this we are given to understand that to take usury from any man is simply evil, because we ought to treat every man as our neighbor and brother, especially in the state of the Gospel whereto we are called. They were permitted, however, to take usury from foreigners, not as though it were lawful, but in order to avoid a greater evil, lest to wit, through avarice to which they were prone, according to Isaiah LVI, VII, they should take usury from Jews, who were worshippers of God.

On the Jewish side, talmudic scholars had some interesting interpretations. Rashi held that the Jewish debtor is forbidden to pay interest to a fellow Jew, but he may pay interest to a Gentile. Maimonides, who was anxious to prevent Jews from being tempted into idolatry by associating with Gentiles, held that a Jew might borrow at usury from a Gentile, but should not make loans to one, on the ground that debtors are generally anxious to avoid their creditors, but creditors are obliged to seek the company of debtors.

Had Shakespeare wished to show Shylock the usurer in the most unfavorable light possible, he could have placed him in a medieval agricultural society, where men become debtors through misfortunes, like a bad harvest or sickness for which they are not responsible, but he places him in a mercantile society, where the role played by money is a very different one.

When Antonio says:

> I neither lend nor borrow
> By taking or by giving of excess

he does not mean that, if he goes into partnership with another merchant contributing, say, a thousand ducats to their venture, and their venture makes a profit, he only asks for a thousand ducats back. He is a merchant and the Aristotelian argument that money is barren and cannot breed money, which he advances to Shylock, is invalid in his own case.

This change in the role of money had already been recognized by both Catholic and Protestant theologians. Calvin, for example, had come to the conclusion that the Deuteronomic injunction had been designed to meet a particular political situation which no longer existed.

> The law of Moses is political and does not obligate us beyond what equity and the reason of humanity suggest. There is a difference in the political union, for the situation in which God placed the Jews and many circumstances permitted them to trade conveniently among themselves without usuries. Our union is entirely different. Therefore I do not feel that usuries are forbidden to us simply, except in so far as they are opposed to equity and charity.

The condemnation of usury by Western Christendom cannot be understood except in relation to the severity of its legal attitude, inherited from Roman Law, towards the defaulting debtor. The pound of flesh story has a basis in historical fact for, according to the Law of the Twelve Tables, a defaulting debtor could be torn to pieces alive. In many medieval contracts the borrower agreed, in the case of default, to pay double the amount of the loan as a forfeit, and imprisonment for debt continued into the nineteenth century. It was possible to consider interest on a loan immoral because the defaulting debtor was regarded as a criminal, that is to say, an exception to the human norm, so that lending was thought of as normally entailing no risk. One motive which led the theologians of the sixteenth century to modify the traditional theories about usury and to regard it as a necessary social evil rather than as a mortal sin was their fear of social revolution and the teachings of the Anabaptists and other radical utopians. These, starting from the same premise of Universal Brotherhood which had been the traditional ground for condemning usury, drew the conclusion that private property was unchristian, that Christians should share all their goods in common, so that the relation of creditor to debtor would be abolished. Thus, Luther, who at first had accused Catholic theologians of being lax towards the sin of usury, by 1524, was giving this advice to Prince Frederick of Saxony:

> It is highly necessary that the taking of interest should be regulated everywhere, but to abolish it entirely would not be right either, for it can be made just. I do not advise your Grace, however, to support people in their refusal to pay interest or to prevent them from paying it, for it is not a burden laid upon people by a Prince in his law, but it is a common plague that all have taken upon themselves. We must put up with it, therefore, and hold debtors to it and not let them spare themselves and seek a remedy of their own, but put them on a level with everybody else, as love requires.

Shylock is a Jew living in a predominantly Christian society, just as Othello is a Negro living in a predominantly white society. But, unlike Othello, Shylock rejects the Christian community as firmly as it rejects him. Shylock and Antonio are at one in refusing to acknowledge a common brotherhood.

> I will buy with you, sell with you, talk with you, walk with you, and so following, but I will not eat with you, drink with you, nor pray with you. (Shylock.)

> I am as like
> To spit on thee again, to spurn thee, too.
> If thou wilt lend this money, lend it not
> As to thy friends . . .
> But lend it rather to thine enemy,
> Who if he break, thou mayst with better face
> Exact the penalty. (Antonio.)

In addition, unlike Othello, whose profession of arms is socially honorable, Shylock is a professional usurer who, like a prostitute, has a social function but is an outcast from the community. But, in the play, he acts unprofessionally; he refuses to charge Antonio interest and insists upon making their legal relation that of debtor and creditor, a relation acknowledged as legal by all societies. Several critics have pointed to analogies between the trial scene and the medieval *Processus Belial* in which Our Lady defends man against the prosecuting Devil who claims the legal right to man's soul. The Roman doctrine of the Atonement presupposes that the debtor deserves no mercy—Christ may substitute Himself for man, but the debt has to be paid by death on the cross. The Devil is defeated, not because he has no right to demand a penalty, but because he does not know that the penalty has been already suffered. But the differences between Shylock and Belial are as important as their similarities. The comic Devil of the mystery play can appeal to logic, to the letter of the law, but he cannot appeal to the heart or to the imagination, and Shakespeare allows Shylock to do both. In his "Hath not a Jew eyes . . ." speech in Act III, Scene I, he is permitted to appeal to the sense of human brotherhood, and in the trial scene, he is allowed to argue, with a sly appeal to the fear a merchant class has of radical social revolution:

> You have among you many a purchased slave
> Which, like your asses and your dogs and mules,
> You use in abject and in slavish parts,

which points out that those who preach mercy and brotherhood as universal obligations limit them in practice and are prepared to treat certain classes of human beings as things.

Furthermore, while Belial is malevolent without any cause except love of malevolence for its own sake, Shylock is presented as a particular individual living in a particular kind of society at a particular time in history. Usury, like prostitution, may corrupt the character, but those who borrow upon usury, like those who visit brothels, have their share of responsibility for this corruption and aggravate their guilt by showing contempt for those whose services they make use of.

It is, surely, in order to emphasize this point that, in the trial scene, Shakespeare introduces an element which is not found in *Pecorone* or other versions of the pound-of-flesh-story. After Portia has trapped Shylock through his own insistence upon the letter of the law of Contract, she produces another law by which any alien who conspires against the life of a Venetian citizen forfeits his goods and places his life at the Doge's mercy. Even in the rush of a stage performance, the audience cannot help reflecting that a man as interested in legal subtleties as Shylock, would, surely, have been aware of the existence of this law and that, if by any chance he had overlooked it, the Doge surely would very soon have drawn his attention to it. Shakespeare, it seems to me, was willing to introduce what is an absurd implausibility for the sake of an effect which he could not secure without it: at the last moment when, through his conduct, Shylock has destroyed any sympathy we may have felt for him earlier, we are reminded that, irrespective of his personal character, his status is one of inferiority. A Jew is not regarded, even in law, as a brother.

If the wicked Shylock cannot enter the fairy story world of Belmont, neither can the noble Antonio, though his friend, Bassanio, can. In the fairy story world, the symbol of final peace and concord is marriage, so that, if the story is concerned with the adventures of two friends of the same sex, male or female, it must end with a double wedding. Had he wished, Shakespeare could have followed the *Pecorone* story in which it is Ansaldo, not Gratiano, who marries the equivalent of Nerissa. Instead, he portrays Antonio as a melancholic who is incapable of loving a woman. He deliberately avoids the classical formula of the Perfect Friends by making the relationship unequal. When Salanio says of Antonio's feelings for Bassanio

> I think he only loves the world for him

we believe it, but no one would say that Bassanio's affections are equally exclusive. Bassanio, high-spirited, elegant, pleasure-loving, belongs to the same world as Gratiano and Lorenzo; Antonio does not. When he says:

> I hold the world but as the world, Gratiano,
> A stage, where everyman must play a part,
> And mine a sad one

Gratiano may accuse him of putting on an act, but we believe him, just as it does not seem merely the expression of a noble spirit of self-sacrifice when he tells Bassanio:

> I am a tainted wether of the flock,
> Meetest for death; the weakest kind of fruit
> Drops earliest to the ground, and so let me.

It is well known that love and understanding breed love and understanding.

> The more people on high who comprehend each other,
> the more there are to love well, and the more
> love is there, and like a mirror, one giveth
> back to the other.
>
> (*Purgatorio*, xv.)

So, with the rise of a mercantile economy in which money breeds money, it became an amusing paradox for poets to use the ignoble activity of usury as a metaphor for love, the most noble of human activities. Thus, in his Sonnets, Shakespeare uses usury as an image for the married love which begets children.

> Profitless usurer, why does thou use
> So great a sum of sums, yet canst not live?
> For having traffic with thyself alone
> Thou of thyself they sweet self dost deceive.
>
> (*Sonnet* iv.)

> That use is not forbidden usury
> Which happies those that pay the willing loan,
> That's for thyself, to breed another thee,
> Or ten times happier, be it ten for one.
>
> (vi.)

And, even more relevant, perhaps, to Antonio are the lines

> But since she pricked thee out for women's pleasure
> Mine be thy love, and thy love's use their treasure.
>
> (xxxiii.)

There is no reason to suppose that Shakespeare had read Dante, but he must have been familiar with the association of usury with sodomy of which Dante speaks in the Ninth Canto of the Inferno.

> It behoves man to gain his bread and to prosper. And because the usurer takes another way, he contemns Nature in herself and her followers, placing elsewhere his hope . . . . And hence the smallest round seals with its mark Sodom and the Cahors . . . .

It can, therefore, hardly be an accident that Shylock the usurer has as his antagonist a man whose emotional life, though his conduct may be chaste, is concentrated upon a member of his own sex.

In any case, the fact that Bassanio's feelings are so much less intense makes Antonio's seem an example of that inordinate affection which theologians have always condemned as a form of idolatry, a putting of the creature before the creator. In the sixteenth century, suretyship, like usury, was a controversial issue. The worldly-wise condemned the standing surety for another on worldly grounds.

> Beware of standing suretyship for thy best friends; he that payeth another man's debts seeketh his own decay: neither borrow money of a neighbour or a friend, but of a stranger. (LORD BURGHLEY.)

> Suffer not thyself to be wounded for other men's faults, or scourged for other men's offences, which is the surety for another: for thereby, millions of men have been beggared and destroyed. . . . from suretyship as from a manslayer or enchanter, bless thyself.
>
> (SIR WALTER RALEIGH.)

And clerics like Luther condemned it on theological grounds.

> Of his life and property a man is not certain for a single moment, any more than he is certain of the man for whom he becomes surety. Therefore the man who becomes surety acts unchristian like and deserves what

> he gets, because he pledges and promises what is not his and not in his power, but in the hands of God alone. . . . These sureties act as though their life and property were their own and were in their power as long as they wished to have it; and this is nothing but the fruit of unbelief. . . . If there were no more of this becoming surety, many a man would have to keep down and be satisfied with a moderate living, who now aspires night and day after high places, relying on borrowing and standing surety.

The last sentence of this passage applies very well to Bassanio. In *Pecorone,* the Lady of Belmonte is a kind of witch and Gianetto gets into financial difficulties because he is the victim of magic, a fate which is never regarded as the victim's fault. But Bassanio had often borrowed money from Antonio before he ever considered wooing Portia and was in debt, not through magic or unforeseeable misfortune, but through his own extravagances,

> 'Tis not unknown to you, Antonio,
> How much I have disabled my estate
> By something showing a more swelling port
> Than my faint means would grant continuance

and we feel that Antonio's continual generosity has encouraged Bassanio in his spendthrift habits. Bassanio seems to be one of those people whose attitude towards money is that of a child; it will somehow always appear by magic when really needed. Though Bassanio is aware of Shylock's malevolence, he makes no serious effort to dissuade Antonio from signing the bond because, thanks to the ever-open purse of his friend, he cannot believe that bankruptcy is a real possibility in life.

Shylock is a miser and Antonio is openhanded with his money; nevertheless, as a merchant, Antonio is equally a member of an acquisitive society. He is trading with Tripoli, the Indies, Mexico, England, and when Salanio imagines himself in Antonio's place, he describes a possible shipwreck thus:

. . . the rocks
Scatter all her spices on the stream,
Enrobe the roaring waters with my silks.

The commodities, that is to say, in which the Venetian merchant deals are not necessities but luxury goods, the consumption of which is governed not by physical need but by psychological values like social prestige, so that there can be no question of a Just Price. Then, as regards his own expenditure, Antonio is, like Shylock, a sober merchant who practices economic abstinence. Both of them avoid the carnal music of this world. Shylock's attitude towards the Masquers

Lock up my doors and when you hear the drum
And the vile squeaking of the wry-necked fife
Clamber not you up the casement then,
Let not the sound of shallow foppery enter
My sober house

finds an echo in Antonio's words a scene later:

Fie, fie, Gratiano. Where are all the rest?
Tis nine o'clock: our friends all stay for you.
No masque to-night—the wind is come about.

Neither of them is capable of enjoying the carefree happiness for which Belmont stands. In a production of the play, a stage director is faced with the awkward problem of what to do with Antonio in the last act. Shylock, the villain, has been vanquished and will trouble Arcadia no more, but, now that Bassanio is getting married, Antonio, the real hero of the play, has no further dramatic function. According to the Arden edition, when Alan McKinnon produced the play at the Garrick theatre in 1905, he had Antonio and Bassanio hold the stage at the final curtain, but I cannot picture Portia, who is certainly no Victorian doormat of a wife, allowing her bridegroom to let her enter the house by herself. If Antonio is not to fade away into a nonentity, then the married couples must enter the lighted house and leave Antonio standing alone on the darkened stage, outside the Eden from which, not by the choice of others, but by his own nature, he is excluded.

Without the Venice scenes, Belmont would be an Arcadia without any relation to actual times and places, and where, therefore, money and sexual love have no reality of their own, but are symbolic signs for a community in a state of grace. But Belmont is related to Venice though their existences are not really compatible with each other. This incompatibility is brought out in a fascinating way by the difference between Belmont time and Venice time. Though we are not told exactly how long the period is before Shylock's loan must be repaid, we know that it is more than a month. Yet Bassanio goes off to Belmont immediately, submits immediately on arrival to the test of the caskets, and has just triumphantly passed it when Antonio's letter arrives to inform him that Shylock is about to take him to court and claim his pound of flesh. Belmont, in fact, is like one of those enchanted palaces where time stands still. But because we are made aware of Venice, the real city, where time is real, Belmont becomes a real society to be judged by the same standards we apply to any other kind of society. Because of Shylock and Antonio, Portia's inherited fortune becomes real money which must have been made in this world, as all fortunes are made, by toil, anxiety, the enduring and inflicting of suffering. Portia we can admire because, having seen her leave her Earthly Paradise to do a good deed in this world (one notices, incidentally, that in this world she appears in disguise), we know that she is aware of her wealth as a moral responsibility, but the other inhabitants of Belmont, Bassanio, Gratiano, Lorenzo and Jessica, for all their beauty and charm, appear as frivolous members of a leisure class, whose carefree life is parasitic upon the labors of others, including usurers. When we learn that Jessica has spent fourscore ducats of her father's money in an evening and bought a monkey with her mother's ring, we cannot take this as a comic punishment for Shylock's sin of avarice; her behavior seems rather an example of the opposite sin of conspicuous waste. Then, with the example in our minds of self-sacrificing love as displayed by Antonio, while we can enjoy the verbal felicity of the love duet between Lorenzo and Jessica, we cannot help noticing that the pairs of lovers they recall, Troilus and Cressida, Aeneas and Dido, Jason and Medea, are none of them examples of self-sacrifice or fidelity. Recalling that the inscription on the leaden casket ran, "Who chooseth me, must give and hazard all he hath," it occurs to us that we have seen two characters do this. Shylock, however unintentionally, did, in fact, hazard all for the sake of destroying the enemy he hated, and Antonio, however unthinkingly he signed the bond, hazarded all to secure the happiness of the friend he loved. Yet it is precisely these two who cannot enter Belmont. Belmont would like to believe that men and women are either good or bad by nature, but Shylock and Antonio remind us that this is an illusion: in the real world, no hatred is totally without justification, no love totally innocent.

As a society, Venice is more efficient and successful than Henry IV's England. Its citizens are better off, more secure and nicer mannered. Politically speaking, therefore, one may say that a mercantile society represents an advance upon a feudal society, as a feudal society represents an advance upon a tribal society. But every step forward brings with it its own dangers and evils for, the more advanced the social organization, the greater the moral demands it makes upon its members and the greater the degree of guilt which they incur if they fail to meet these demands. The members of a society with a primitive self-sufficient economy can think of those outside it as others, not brothers, with a good conscience, because they can get along by themselves. But, first, money and, then, machinery have created a world in which, irrespective of our cultural traditions and our religious or political convictions, we are all mutually dependent. This demands that we accept all other human beings on earth as brothers, not only in law, but also in our hearts. Our temptation, of course, is to do just the opposite, not to return to tribal loyalties—that is impossible—but, each of us, to regard everybody else on earth not even as an enemy, but as a faceless algebraical cipher.

They laid the coins before the council.
Kay, the king's steward, wise in economics, said:
"Good; these cover the years and the miles
and talk one style's dialects to London and Omsk.
Traffic can hold now and treasure be held,
streams are bridged and mountains of ridged space
tunnelled; gold dances deftly over frontiers.
The poor have choice of purchase, the rich of rents,
and events move now in a smoother control
than the swords of lords or the orisons of nuns.
Money is the medium of exchange."

Taliessin's look darkened; his hand shook
while he touched the dragons; he said "We had a good
thought.
Sir, if you made verse, you would doubt symbols.
I am afraid of the little loosed dragons.
When the means are autonomous, they are deadly; when
words
escape from verse they hurry to rape souls;
when sensation slips from intellect, expect the tyrant;
the brood of carriers levels the good they carry.
We have taught our images to be free; are ye glad?
are we glad to have brought convenient heresy to
Logres?"

The Archbishop answered the lords;
his words went up through a slope of calm air:
"Might may take symbols and folly make treasure,
and greed bid God, who hides himself for man's pleasure
by occasion, hide himself essentially: this abides—
that the everlasting house the soul discovers
is always another's; we must lose our own ends;
we must always live in the habitation of our lovers,
my friend's shelter for me, mine for him.
This is the way of this world in the day of that other's;
make yourselves friends by means of the riches of
iniquity,

for the wealth of the self is the health of the self exchanged.
What saith Heraclitus?—and what is the City's breath?—
dying each other's life, living each other's death.
Money is a medium of exchange."
(CHARLES WILLIAMS, *Taliessin through Logres.*)

INTERLUDE: WEST'S DISEASE

Nathanael West is not, strictly speaking, a novelist; that is to say, he does not attempt an accurate description either of the social scene or of the subjective life of the mind. For his first book, he adopted the dream convention, but neither the incidents nor the language are credible as a transcription of a real dream. For his other three, he adopted the convention of a social narrative; his characters need real food, drink and money, and live in recognizable places like New York or Hollywood, but, taken as feigned history, they are absurd. Newspapers do, certainly, have Miss Lonelyhearts columns; but in real life these are written by sensible, not very sensitive, people who conscientiously give the best advice they can, but do not take the woes of their correspondents home with them from the office, people, in fact, like Betty of whom Mr. West's hero says scornfully:

> Her world was not the world and could never include the readers of his column. Her sureness was based on the power to limit experience arbitrarily. Moreover, his confusion was significant, while her order was not.

On Mr. West's paper, the column is entrusted to a man the walls of whose room

> were bare except for an ivory Christ that hung opposite the foot of the bed. He had removed the figure from the cross to which it had been fastened and had nailed it

> to the walls with large spikes. . . . As a boy in his father's church, he had discovered that something stirred in him when he shouted the name of Christ, something secret and enormously powerful. He had played with this thing, but had never allowed it to come alive. He knew now what this thing was—hysteria, a snake whose scales were tiny mirrors in which the dead world takes on a semblance of life, and how dead the world is . . . a world of doorknobs.

It is impossible to believe that such a character would ever apply for a Miss Lonelyhearts job (in the hope, apparently, of using it as a stepping-stone to a gossip column), or that, if by freak chance he did, any editor would hire him.

Again, the occupational vice of the editors one meets is an overestimation of the social and moral value of what a newspaper does. Mr. West's editor, Shrike, is a Mephisto who spends all his time exposing to his employees the meaninglessness of journalism:

> Miss Lonelyhearts, my friend, I advise you to give your readers stones. When they ask for bread don't give them crackers as does the Church, and don't, like the State, tell them to eat cake. Explain that man cannot live by bread alone and give them stones. Teach them to pray each morning: 'Give us this day our daily stone.'

Such a man, surely, would not be a Feature Editor long.

A writer may concern himself with a very limited area of life and still convince us that he is describing the real world, but one becomes suspicious when, as in West's case, whatever world he claims to be describing, the dream life of a highbrow, lowbrow existence in Hollywood, or the American political scene, all these worlds share the same peculiar traits—no married couples have children, no child has more than one parent, a high percentage of the inhabitants are cripples, and the only kind of personal relation is the sadomasochistic.

There is, too, a curious resemblance among the endings of his four books.

His body broke free of the bard. It took on a life of its own; a life that knew nothing of the poet Balso. Only to death can this release be likened—the mechanics of decay. After death the body takes command; it performs the manual of disintegration with a marvelous certainty. So now, his body performed the evolutions of love with a like sureness. In this activity, Home and Duty, Love and Art were forgotten. . . . His body screamed and shouted as it marched and uncoiled; then with one heaving shout of triumph, it fell back quiet.

He was running to succor them with love. The cripple turned to escape, but he was too slow and Miss Lonelyhearts caught him. . . . The gun inside the package exploded and Miss Lonelyhearts fell, dragging the cripple with him. They both rolled part of the way down stairs.

'I am a clown,' he began, 'but there are times when even clowns must grow serious. This is such a time. I . . .' Lem got no further. A shot rang out and he fell dead, drilled through the heart by an assassin's bullet.

He was carried through the exit to the back street and lifted into a police car. The siren began to scream and at first he thought he was making the noise himself. He felt his lips with his hands. They were clamped tight. He knew then it was the siren. For some reason this made him laugh and he began to imitate the siren as loud as he could.

An orgasm, two sudden deaths by violence, a surrender to madness, are presented by West as different means for securing the same and desirable end, escape from the conscious Ego and its make-believe. Consciousness, it would seem, does not mean freedom to choose, but freedom to play a fantastic role, an unreality from which a man can only be delivered by some physical or mental explosion outside his voluntary control.

There are many admirable and extremely funny satirical passages in his books, but West is not a satirist. Satire presupposes conscience and reason as the judges between the true and the false, the moral and the immoral, to which it appeals, but for West these faculties are themselves the creators of unreality.

His books should, I think, be classified as Cautionary Tales, parables about a Kingdom of Hell whose ruler is not so much the Father of Lies as the Father of Wishes. Shakespeare gives a glimpse of this hell in *Hamlet*, and Dostoievsky has a lengthy description in *Notes from the Underground*, but they were interested in many hells and heavens. Compared with them, West has the advantages and disadvantages of the specialist who knows everything about one disease and nothing about any other. He was a sophisticated and highly skilled literary craftsman, but what gives all his books such a powerful and disturbing fascination, even *A Cool Million*, which must, I think, be judged a failure, owes nothing to calculation. West's descriptions of Inferno have the authenticity of first-hand experience: he has certainly been there, and the reader has the uncomfortable feeling that his was not a short visit.

All his main characters suffer from the same spiritual disease which, in honor of the man who devoted his life to studying it, we may call West's Disease. This is a disease of consciousness which renders it incapable of converting wishes into desires. A lie is false; what it asserts is not the case. A wish is fantastic; it knows what is the case but refuses to accept it. All wishes, whatever their apparent content, have the same and unvarying meaning: "I refuse to be what I am." A wish, therefore, is either innocent and frivolous, a kind of play, or a serious expression of guilt and despair, a hatred of oneself and every being one holds responsible for oneself.

Our subconscious life is a world ruled by wish but, since it is not a world of action, this is harmless; even nightmare is playful, but it is the task of consciousness to translate wish into desire. If, for whatever reason, self-hatred or self-pity, it fails to do this, it dooms a human being to a peculiar and horrid fate. To begin with, he cannot desire anything, for the present state of the self is the ground of every desire, and that is precisely what the wisher rejects. Nor can he believe anything, for a wish is not a belief; whatever he wishes he cannot help knowing that he could have wished something else. At first he may be content with switching from one wish to another:

> She would get some music on the radio, then lie down on her bed and shut her eyes. She had a large assortment of stories to choose from. After getting herself in the right mood, she would go over them in her mind as though they were a pack of cards, discarding one after another until she found one that suited. On some days she would run through the whole pack without making a choice. When that happened, she would either go down to Fine Street for an ice-cream soda or, if she were broke, thumb over the pack again and force herself to choose.
>
> While she admitted that her method was too mechanical for the best results and that it was better to slip into a dream naturally, she said that any dream was better than none and beggars couldn't be choosers.

But in time, this ceases to amuse, and the wisher is left with the despair which is the cause of all of them:

> When not keeping house, he sat in the back yard, called the patio by the real estate agent, in a broken down deck chair. In one of the closets he had found a tattered book and he held it in his lap without looking at it. There was a much better view to be had in any direction other than the one he faced. By moving his chair in a quarter circle he could have seen a large part of the canyon twisting down to the city below. He never thought of making this shift. From where he sat, he saw the closed door of the garage and a patch of its shabby, tarpaper roof.

A sufferer from West's Disease is not selfish but absolutely self-centered. A selfish man is one who satisfies his desires at other people's expense; for this reason, he tries to see what others are really like and often sees them extremely accurately in order that he may make use of them. But, to the self-centered man, other people only exist as images either of what he is or of what he is not, his feelings towards them are projections of the pity or the hatred he feels for himself and anything he does to them is really done to himself. Hence the inconsistent and unpredictable behavior of a sufferer from West's Disease: he may kiss your feet one moment and kick you in the jaw the next and, if you were to ask him why, he could not tell you.

In its final stages, the disease reduces itself to a craving for violent physical pain—this craving, unfortunately, can be projected onto others—for only violent pain can put an end to wishing *for* something and produce the real wish of necessity, the cry "Stop!"

All West's books contain cripples. A cripple is unfortunate and his misfortune is both singular and incurable. Hunchbacks, girls without noses, dwarfs, etc., are not sufficiently common in real life to appear as members of an unfortunate class, like the very poor. Each one makes the impression of a unique case. Further, the nature of the misfortune, a physical deformity, makes the victim repellent to the senses of the typical and normal, and there is nothing the cripple or others can do to change his condition. What attitude towards his own body can he have then but hatred? As used by West, the cripple is, I believe, a symbolic projection of the state of wishful self-despair, the state of those who will not accept themselves in order to change themselves into what they would or should become, and justify their refusal by thinking that being what they are is uniquely horrible and uncurable. To look at, Faye Greener is a pretty but not remarkable girl; in the eyes of Faye Greener, she is an exceptionally hideous spirit.

In saying that cripples have this significance in West's writing, I do not mean to say that he was necessarily aware of it. Indeed, I am inclined to think he was not. I suspect that, consciously, he thought pity and compassion were the same thing, but what the behavior of his "tender" characters shows is that all pity is self-pity and that he who pities others is incapable of compassion. Ruthlessly as he exposes his dreamers, he seems to believe that the only alternative to despair is to become a crook. Wishes may be unreal, but at least they are not, like all desires, wicked:

> His friends would go on telling such stories until they were too drunk to talk. They were aware of their childishness, but did not know how else to revenge themselves. At college, and perhaps for a year afterwards, they had believed in Beauty and in personal expression as an absolute end. When they lost this belief, they lost everything. Money and fame meant nothing to them. They were not worldly men.

The use of the word *worldly* is significant. West comes very near to accepting the doctrine of the Marquis de Sade—there are many resemblances between *A Cool Million* and *Justine*—to believing, that is, that the creation is essentially evil and that goodness is contrary to its laws, but his moral sense revolted against Sade's logical conclusion that it was therefore a man's duty to be as evil as possible. All West's "worldly" characters are bad men, most of them grotesquely bad, but here again his artistic instinct seems at times to contradict his conscious intentions. I do not think, for example, that he meant to make Wu Fong, the brothel-keeper, more sympathetic and worthy of respect than, say, Miss Lonelyhearts or Homer Simpson, but that is what he does:

> Wu Fong was a very shrewd man and a student of fashion. He saw that the trend was in the direction of home industry and home talent and when the Hearst papers began their "Buy American" campaign, he decided to get rid of all the foreigners in his employ and turn his establishment into a hundred percentum American place. He engaged Mr. Asa Goldstein to redecorate the house and that worthy designed a Pennsylvania Dutch, Old South, Log Cabin Pioneer, Victorian New York, Western Cattle Days, Californian Monterey, Indian and Modern Girl series of interiors. . . .
>
> He was as painstaking as a great artist and in order to be consistent as one he did away with the French cuisine and wines traditional to his business. Instead, he substituted an American kitchen and cellar. When a client visited Lena Haubengruber, it was possible for him to eat roast groundhog and drink Sam Thompson rye.

> While with Alice Sweethorne, he was served sow belly with grits and bourbon. In Mary Judkins' rooms he received, if he so desired, fried squirrel and corn liquor. In the suite occupied by Patricia Van Riis, lobster and champagne were the rule. The patrons of Powder River Rose usually ordered mountain oysters and washed them down with forty rod. And so on down the list. . . .

After so many self-centered despairers who cry in their baths or bare their souls in barrooms, a selfish man like this, who takes pride in doing something really well, even if it is running a brothel, seems almost a good man.

There have, no doubt, always been cases of West's Disease, but the chances of infection in a democratic and mechanized society like our own are much greater than in the more static and poorer societies of earlier times.

When, for most people, their work, their company, even their marriages, were determined, not by personal choice or ability, but by the class into which they were born, the individual was less tempted to develop a personal grudge against Fate; his fate was not his own but that of everyone around him.

But the greater the equality of opportunity in a society becomes, the more obvious becomes the inequality of the talent and character among individuals, and the more bitter and personal it must be to fail, particularly for those who have some talent but not enough to win them second or third place.

In societies with fewer opportunities for amusement, it was also easier to tell a mere wish from a real desire. If, in order to hear some music, a man has to wait for six months and then walk twenty miles, it is easy to tell whether the words, "I should like to hear some music," mean what they appear to mean, or merely, "At this moment I should like to forget myself." When all he has to do is press a switch, it is more difficult. He may easily come to believe that wishes can come true. This is the first symptom of West's Disease; the later symptoms are less pleasant, but nobody who has read Nathanael West can say that he wasn't warned.

THE JOKER IN THE PACK

Reason is God's gift; but so are the passions.
Reason is as guilty as passion.

J. H. NEWMAN

I

Any consideration of the Tragedy of Othello must be primarily occupied, not with its official hero but with its villain. I cannot think of any other play in which only one character performs personal actions—all the *deeds* are Iago's—and all the others without exception only exhibit behavior. In marrying each other, Othello and Desdemona have performed a deed, but this took place before the play begins. Nor can I think of another play in which the villain is so completely triumphant: everything Iago sets out to do, he accomplishes —(among his goals, I include his self-destruction). Even Cassio, who survives, is maimed for life.

If *Othello* is a tragedy—and one certainly cannot call it a comedy—it is tragic in a peculiar way. In most tragedies the fall of the hero from glory to misery and death is the work, either of the gods, or of his own freely chosen acts, or, more commonly, a mixture of both. But the fall of Othello is the work of another human being; nothing he says or does originates with himself. In consequence we feel pity for him but no respect; our aesthetic respect is reserved for Iago.

Iago is a wicked man. The wicked man, the stage villain, as a subject of serious dramatic interest does not, so far as I know, appear in the drama of Western Europe before the Elizabethans. In the mystery plays, the wicked characters, like Satan or Herod, are treated comically, but the theme of the triumphant villain cannot be treated comically because the suffering he inflicts is real.

A distinction must be made between the villainous character—figures like Don John in *Much Ado*, Richard III, Edmund in *Lear*, Iachimo in *Cymbeline*—and the merely criminal character—figures like Duke Antonio in *The Tempest*, Angelo in *Measure for Measure*, Macbeth or Claudius in *Hamlet*. The criminal is a person who finds himself in a situation where he is tempted to break the law and succumbs to the temptation: he ought, of course, to have resisted the temptation, but everybody, both on stage and in the audience, must admit that, had they been placed in the same situation, they, too, would have been tempted. The opportunities are exceptional—Prospero, immersed in his books, has left the government of Milan to his brother, Angelo is in a position of absolute authority, Claudius is the Queen's lover, Macbeth is egged on by prophecies and heaven-sent opportunities, but the desire for a dukedom or a crown or a chaste and beautiful girl are desires which all can imagine themselves feeling.

The villain, on the other hand, is shown from the beginning as being a malcontent, a person with a general grudge against life and society. In most cases this is comprehensible because the villain has, in fact, been wronged by Nature or Society: Richard III is a hunchback, Don John and Edmund are bastards. What distinguishes their actions from those of the criminal is that, even when they have something tangible to gain, this is a secondary satisfaction; their primary satisfaction is the infliction of suffering on others, or the exercise of power over others against their will. Richard does not really desire Anne; what he enjoys is successfully wooing a lady whose husband and father-in-law he has killed. Since he has persuaded Gloucester that Edgar is a would-be parricide, Edmund does not need to betray his father to Cornwall and Regan in order to inherit. Don John has nothing personally to gain from ruining the happiness of Claudio and Hero except the pleasure of seeing them unhappy. Iachimo is a doubtful case of villainy. When he and Posthumus make their wager, the latter warns him:

> If she remain unseduced, you not making it appear otherwise, for your ill opinion and th'assault you have made on her chastity you shall answer me with your sword.

To the degree that his motive in deceiving Posthumus is simply physical fear of losing his life in a duel, he is a coward, not a villain; he is only a villain to the degree that his motive is the pleasure of making and seeing the innocent suffer. Coleridge's description of Iago's actions as "motiveless malignancy" applies in some degree to all the Shakespearian villains. The adjective *motiveless* means, firstly, that the tangible gains, if any, are clearly not the principal motive and, secondly, that the motive is not the desire for personal revenge upon another for a personal injury. Iago himself proffers two reasons for wishing to injure Othello and Cassio. He tells Roderigo that, in appointing Cassio to be his lieutenant, Othello has treated him unjustly, in which conversation he talks like the conventional Elizabethan malcontent. In his soliloquies with himself, he refers to his suspicion that both Othello and Cassio have made him a cuckold, and here he talks like the conventional jealous husband who desires revenge. But there are, I believe, insuperable objections to taking these reasons, as some critics have done, at their face value. If one of Iago's goals is to supplant Cassio in the lieutenancy, one can only say that his plot fails for, when Cassio is cashiered, Othello does not appoint Iago in his place. It is true that, in Act III, scene 3, when they swear blood-brotherhood in revenge, Othello concludes with the words

> . . . now thou are my lieutenant

to which Iago replies:

> I am your own for ever

but the use of the word *lieutenant* in this context refers, surely, not to a public military rank, but to a private and illegal delegation of authority—the job delegated to Iago is the secret murder of Cassio, and Iago's reply, which is a mocking echo of an earlier line of Othello's, refers to a relation which can never become public. The ambiguity of the word is confirmed by its use in the first line of the scene which immediately follows. Desdemona says

> Do you know, sirrah, where the Lieutenant Cassio lies?

(One should beware of attaching too much significance to Elizabethan typography, but it is worth noting that Othello's lieutenant is in lower case and Desdemona's in upper). As for Iago's jealousy, one cannot believe that a seriously jealous man could behave towards his wife as Iago behaves towards Emilia, for the wife of a jealous husband is the first person to suffer. Not only is the relation of Iago and Emilia, as we see it on stage, without emotional tension, but also Emilia openly refers to a rumor of her infidelity as something already disposed of.

> Some such squire it was
> That turned your wit, the seamy side without
> And made you to suspect me with the Moor.

At one point Iago states that, in order to revenge himself on Othello, he will not rest till he is even with him, wife for wife, but, in the play, no attempt at Desdemona's seduction is made. Iago does not make an assault on her virtue himself, he does not encourage Cassio to make one, and he even prevents Roderigo from getting anywhere near her.

Finally, one who seriously desires personal revenge desires to reveal himself. The revenger's greatest satisfaction is to be able to tell his victim to his face—"You thought you were all-powerful and untouchable and could injure me with impunity. Now you see that you were wrong. Perhaps you have forgotten what you did; let me have the pleasure of reminding you."

When at the end of the play, Othello asks Iago in bewilderment why he has thus ensnared his soul and body, if his real motive were revenge for having been cuckolded or unjustly denied promotion, he could have said so, instead of refusing to explain.

In Act II, Scene I, occur seven lines which, taken in isolation, seem to make Iago a seriously jealous man.

> Now I do love her too,
> Not out of absolute lust (though peradventure
> I stand accountant for as great a sin)
> But partly led to diet my revenge
> For that I do suspect the lusty Moor
> Hath leaped into my seat; the thought whereof
> Doth like a poisonous mineral gnaw my vitals.

But if spoken by an actor with serious passion, these lines are completely at variance with the rest of the play, including Iago's other lines on the same subject.

> And it is thought abroad, that twixt my sheets
> He's done my office: I know not if't be true
> Yet I, for mere suspicion in that kind,
> Will do, as if for surety.

It is not inconceivable, given the speed at which he wrote, that, at some point in the composition of *Othello,* Shakespeare considered making Iago seriously jealous and, like his prototype in Cinthio, a would-be seducer of Desdemona, and that, when he arrived at his final conception of Iago, he overlooked the incompatibility of the *poisonous mineral* and the *wife-for-wife* passages with the rest.

In trying to understand Iago's character one should begin, I believe, by asking why Shakespeare should have gone to the trouble of inventing Roderigo, a character who has no prototype in Cinthio. From a stage director's point of view, Roderigo is a headache. In the first act we learn that Brabantio had forbidden him the house, from which we must conclude that Desdemona had met him and disliked him as much as her father. In the second act, in order that the audience shall know that he has come to Cyprus, Roderigo has to arrive on the same ship as Desdemona, yet she shows no embarrassment in his presence. Indeed, she and everybody else, except Iago, seem unaware of his existence, for Iago is the only person who ever speaks a word to him. Presumably, he has some official position in the army, but we are never told what it is. His entrances and exits are those of a puppet: whenever Iago has company, he obligingly disappears, and whenever Iago is alone and wishes to speak to him, he comes in again immediately.

Moreover, so far as Iago's plot is concerned, there is nothing Roderigo does which Iago could not do better without him. He could easily have found another means, like an anonymous letter, of informing Brabantio of Desdemona's elopement and, for picking a quarrel with a drunken Cassio, he has, on his own admission, other means handy.

> Three lads of Cyprus, noble swelling spirits
> That hold their honour in a wary distance,
> The very elements of this warlike isle
> Have I to-night flustered with flowing cups.

Since Othello has expressly ordered him to kill Cassio, Iago could have murdered him without fear of legal investigation. Instead, he not only chooses as an accomplice a man whom he is cheating and whose suspicions he has constantly to allay, but also a man who is plainly inefficient as a murderer and also holds incriminating evidence against him.

A man who is seriously bent on revenge does not take unnecessary risks nor confide in anyone whom he cannot trust or do without. Emilia is not, as in Cinthio, Iago's willing accomplice, so that, in asking her to steal the handkerchief,

Iago is running a risk, but it is a risk he has to take. By involving Roderigo in his plot, he makes discovery and his own ruin almost certain. It is a law of drama that, by the final curtain, all secrets, guilty or innocent, shall have been revealed so that all, on both sides of the footlights, know who did or did not do what, but usually the guilty are exposed either because, like Edmund, they repent and confess or because of events which they could not reasonably have foreseen. Don John could not have foreseen that Dogberry and Verges would overhear Borachio's conversation, nor Iachimo that Pisanio would disobey Posthumus' order to kill Imogen, nor King Claudius the intervention of a ghost.

Had he wished, Shakespeare could easily have contrived a similar kind of exposure for Iago. Instead, by giving Roderigo the role he does, he makes Iago as a plotter someone devoid of ordinary worldly common sense.

One of Shakespeare's intentions was, I believe, to indicate that Iago desires self-destruction as much as he desires the destruction of others but, before elaborating on this, let us consider Iago's treatment of Roderigo, against whom he has no grievance—it is he who is injuring Roderigo—as a clue to his treatment of Othello and Cassio.

When we first see Iago and Roderigo together, the situation is like that in a Ben Jonson comedy—a clever rascal is gulling a rich fool who deserves to be gulled because his desire is no more moral than that of the more intelligent avowed rogue who cheats him out of his money. Were the play a comedy, Roderigo would finally realize that he had been cheated but would not dare appeal to the law because, if the whole truth were made public, he would cut a ridiculous or shameful figure. But, as the play proceeds, it becomes clear that Iago is not simply after Roderigo's money, a rational motive, but that his main game is Roderigo's moral corruption, which is irrational because Roderigo has given him no cause to desire his moral ruin. When the play opens, Roderigo is shown as a spoiled weakling, but no worse. It may be foolish of him to hope to win Desdemona's affection by gifts and to employ a go-between, but his conduct is not in itself immoral. Nor is he, like Cloten in *Cymbeline,* a brute who regards women as mere objects of lust. He is genuinely shocked as well as disappointed when he learns of Desdemona's marriage, but continues to admire her as a woman full of most blessed condition. Left to himself, he would have had a good bawl, and given her up. But Iago will not let him alone. By insisting that Desdemona is seducible and that his real rival is not Othello but Cassio, he brings Roderigo to entertain the idea, originally foreign to him, of becoming a seducer and of helping Iago to ruin Cassio. Iago had had the pleasure of making a timid conventional man become aggressive and criminal. Cassio beats up Roderigo. Again, at this point, had he been left to himself, he would have gone no further, but Iago will not let him alone until he consents to murder Cassio, a deed which is contrary to his nature, for he is not only timid but also incapable of passionate hatred.

> I have no great devotion to the deed:
> And yet he has given me satisfying reasons.
> 'Tis but a man gone.

Why should Iago want to do this to Roderigo? To me, the clue to this and to all Iago's conduct is to be found in Emilia's comment when she picks up the handkerchief.

> My wayward husband hath a hundred times
> Wooed me to steal it . . .
>   what he'll do with it
> Heaven knows, not I,
> I nothing but to please his fantasy.

As his wife, Emilia must know Iago better than anybody else does. She does not know, any more than the others, that he is malevolent, but she does know that her husband is addicted to practical jokes. What Shakespeare gives us in Iago is a portrait of a practical joker of a peculiarly appalling kind, and perhaps the best way of approaching the play is by a general consideration of the Practical Joker.

II

Social relations, as distinct from the brotherhood of a community, are only possible if there is a common social agreement as to which actions or words are to be regarded as serious means to a rational end and which are to be regarded as play, as ends in themselves. In our culture, for example, a policeman must be able to distinguish between a murderous street fight and a boxing match, or a listener between a radio play in which war is declared and a radio news-broadcast announcing a declaration of war.

Social life also presupposes that we may believe what we are told unless we have reason to suppose, either that our informant has a serious motive for deceiving us, or that he is mad and incapable himself of distinguishing between truth and falsehood. If a stranger tries to sell me shares in a gold mine, I shall be a fool if I do not check up on his statements before parting with my money, and if another tells me that he has talked with little men who came out of a flying saucer, I shall assume that he is crazy. But if I ask a stranger the way to the station, I shall assume that his answer is truthful to the best of his knowledge, because I cannot imagine what motive he could have for misdirecting me.

Practical jokes are a demonstration that the distinction between seriousness and play is not a law of nature but a social convention which can be broken, and that a man does not always require a serious motive for deceiving another.

Two men, dressed as city employees, block off a busy street and start digging it up. The traffic cop, motorists and pedestrians assume that this familiar scene has a practical explanation—a water main or an electric cable is being repaired—and make no attempt to use the street. In fact, however, the two diggers are private citizens in disguise who have no business there.

All practical jokes are anti-social acts, but this does not necessarily mean that all practical jokes are immoral. A moral practical joke exposes some flaw in society which is a hindrance to a real community or brotherhood. That it should be possible for two private individuals to dig up a street without being stopped is a just criticism of the impersonal life of a large city where most people are strangers to each other, not brothers; in a village where all the inhabitants know each other personally, the deception would be impossible.

A real community, as distinct from social life, is only possible between persons whose idea of themselves and others is real, not fantastic. There is, therefore, another class of practical jokes which is aimed at particular individuals with the reformatory intent of de-intoxicating them from their illusions. This kind of joke is one of the stock devices of comedy. The deceptions practiced on Falstaff by Mistress Page, Mistress Ford and Dame Quickly, or by Octavian on Baron Ochs are possible because these two gentlemen have a fantastic idea of themselves as lady-charmers; the result of the jokes played upon them is that they are brought to a state of self-knowledge and this brings mutual forgiveness and true brotherhood. Similarly, the mock deaths of Hero and of Hermione are ways of bringing home to Claudio and to Leontes how badly they have behaved and of testing the genuineness of their repentance.

All practical jokes, friendly, harmless or malevolent, involve deception, but not all deceptions are practical jokes. The two men digging up the street, for example, might have been two burglars who wished to recover some swag which they knew to be buried there. But, in that case, having found what they were looking for, they would have departed quietly and never been heard of again, whereas, if they are practical jokers, they must reveal afterwards what they have done or the joke will be lost. The practical joker must not only deceive but also, when he has succeeded, unmask and reveal the truth to his victims. The satisfaction of the practical joker is the look of astonishment on the faces of others when they learn that all the time they were convinced that they were thinking and acting on their own initiative, they were actually the puppets of another's will. Thus, though his jokes may be harmless in themselves and extremely funny, there is something slightly sinister about every practical joker, for they betray him as someone who likes to play God behind the scenes. Unlike the ordinary ambitious man who strives for a dominant position in public and enjoys giving orders and seeing others obey them, the practical joker desires to make others obey him without being aware of his existence until the moment of his theophany when he says: "Behold the God whose puppets you have been and behold, he does not look like a god but is a human being just like yourselves." The success of a practical joker depends upon his accurate estimate of the weaknesses of others, their ignorances, their social reflexes, their unquestioned presuppositions, their obsessive desires, and even the most harmless practical joke is an expression of the joker's contempt for those he deceives.

But, in most cases, behind the joker's contempt for others lies something else, a feeling of self-insufficiency, of a self lacking in authentic feelings and desires of its own. The normal human being may have a fantastic notion of himself, but he believes in it; he thinks he knows who he is and what he wants so that he demands recognition by others of the value he puts upon himself and must inform others of what he desires if they are to satisfy them.

But the self of the practical joker is unrelated to his joke. He manipulates others but, when he finally reveals his identity, his victims learn nothing about his nature, only something about their own; they know how it was possible for them to be deceived but not why he chose to deceive them. The only answer that any practical joker can give to the question: "Why did you do this?" is Iago's: "Demand me nothing. What you know, you know."

In fooling others, it cannot be said that the practical joker satisfies any concrete desire of his nature; he has only demonstrated the weaknesses of others and all he can now do, once he has revealed his existence, is to bow and retire from the stage. He is only related to others, that is, so long as they are unaware of his existence; once they are made aware of it, he cannot fool them again, and the relation is broken off.

The practical joker despises his victims, but at the same time he envies them because their desires, however childish and mistaken, are real to them, whereas he has no desire which he can call his own. His goal, to make game of others, makes his existence absolutely dependent upon theirs; when he is alone, he is a nullity. Iago's self-description, *I am not what I am,* is correct and the negation of the Divine *I am that I am.* If the word motive is given its normal meaning of a positive purpose of the self like sex, money, glory, etc., then the practical joker is without motive. Yet the professional practical joker is certainly driven, like a gambler, to his activity, but the drive is negative, a fear of lacking a concrete self, of being nobody. In any practical joker to whom playing such jokes is a passion, there is always an element of malice, a projection of his self-hatred onto others, and in the ultimate case of the absolute practical joker, this is projected onto all created things. Iago's statement, "I am not what I am," is given its proper explanation in the *Credo* which Boito wrote for him in his libretto for Verdi's opera.

Credo in un Dio crudel che m'ha creato
Simile a se, e che nell'ira io nomo.
Dall viltà d'un germe e d'un atomo
Vile son nato,
Son scellerato
Perchè son uomo:
E sento il fango originario in me
E credo l'uom gioco d'iniqua sorte
Dal germe della culla
Al verme dell'avel.
Vien dopo tanto irrision la Morte
E poi? La Morte e il Nulla.

Equally applicable to Iago is Valéry's "Ebauche d'un serpent." The serpent speaks to God the Creator thus

O Vanité! Cause Première
Celui qui règne dans les Cieux
D'une voix qui fut la lumière

Ouvrit l'univers spacieux.
Comme las de son pur spectacle
Dieu lui-même a rompu l'obstacle
De sa parfaite éternité;
Il se fit Celui qui dissipe
En conséquences son Principe,
En étoiles son Unité.

And of himself thus

Je suis Celui qui modifie

the ideal motto, surely, for Iago's coat of arms.

Since the ultimate goal of Iago is nothingness, he must not only destroy others, but himself as well. Once Othello and Desdemona are dead his "occupation's gone."

To convey this to an audience demands of the actor who plays the role the most violent contrast in the way he acts when Iago is with others and the way he acts when he is left alone. With others, he must display every virtuoso trick of dramatic technique for which great actors are praised, perfect control of movement, gesture, expression, diction, melody and timing, and the ability to play every kind of role, for there are as many "honest" Iagos as there are characters with whom he speaks, a Roderigo Iago, a Cassio Iago, an Othello Iago, a Desdemona Iago, etc. When he is alone, on the other hand, the actor must display every technical fault for which bad actors are criticized. He must deprive himself of all stage presence, and he must deliver the lines of his soliloquies in such a way that he makes nonsense of them. His voice must lack expression, his delivery must be atrocious, he must pause where the verse calls for no pauses, accentuate unimportant words, etc.

III

If Iago is so alienated from nature and society that he has no relation to time and place—he could turn up anywhere at any time—his victims are citizens of Shakespeare's Venice.

To be of dramatic interest, a character must to some degree be at odds with the society of which he is a member, but his estrangement is normally an estrangement from a specific social situation.

Shakespeare's Venice is a mercantile society, the purpose of which is not military glory but the acquisition of wealth. However, human nature being what it is, like any other society, it has enemies, trade rivals, pirates, etc., against whom it must defend itself, if necessary by force. Since a mercantile society regards warfare as a disagreeable, but unfortunately sometimes unavoidable, activity and not, like a feudal aristocracy, as a form of play, it replaces the old feudal levy by a paid professional army, nonpolitical employees of the State, to whom fighting is their specialized job.

In a professional army, a soldier's military rank is not determined by his social status as a civilian, but by his military efficiency. Unlike the feudal knight who has a civilian home from which he is absent from time to time but to which, between campaigns, he regularly returns, the home of the professional soldier is an army camp and he must go wherever the State sends him. Othello's account of his life as a soldier, passed in exotic landscapes and climates, would have struck Hotspur as unnatural, unchivalrous and no fun.

A professional army has its own experiences and its own code of values which are different from those of civilians. In *Othello,* we are shown two societies, that of the city of Venice proper and that of the Venetian army. The only character who, because he is equally estranged from both, can simulate being equally at home in both, is Iago. With army folk he can play the blunt soldier, but in his first scene with Desdemona upon their arrival in Cyprus, he speaks like a character out of *Love's Labour's Lost*. Cassio's comment

> Madam, you may relish him more in the soldier than the
> scholar

is provoked by envy. Iago has excelled him in the euphuistic flirtatious style of conversation which he considers his forte.

Roderigo does not feel at home, either with civilians or with soldiers. He lacks the charm which makes a man a success with the ladies, and the physical courage and heartiness which make a man popular in an army mess. The sympathetic aspect of his character, until Iago destroys it, is a certain humility; he knows that he is a person of no consequence. But for Iago, he would have remained a sort of Bertie Wooster, and one suspects that the notion that Desdemona's heart might be softened by expensive presents was not his own but suggested to him by Iago.

In deceiving Roderigo, Iago has to overcome his consciousness of his inadequacy, to persuade him that he could be what he knows he is not, charming, brave, successful. Consequently, to Roderigo and, I think, to Roderigo only, Iago tells direct lies. The lie may be on a point of fact, as when he tells Roderigo that Othello and Desdemona are not returning to Venice but going to Mauritania, or a lie about the future, for it is obvious that, even if Desdemona is seducible, Roderigo will never be the man. I am inclined to think that the story Iago tells Roderigo about his disappointment over the lieutenancy is a deliberate fabrication. One notices, for example, that he contradicts himself. At first he claims that Othello had appointed Cassio in spite of the request of three great ones of the city who had recommended Iago, but then a few lines later, he says

> Preferment goes by letter and affection,
> Not by the old gradation where each second
> Stood heir to the first.

In deceiving Cassio and Othello, on the other hand, Iago has to deal with characters who consciously think well of themselves but are unconsciously insecure. With them, therefore, his tactics are different; what he says to them is always possibly true.

Cassio is a ladies' man, that is to say, a man who feels most at home in feminine company where his looks and good manners make him popular, but is ill at ease in the company of his own sex becuse he is unsure of his masculinity. In civilian life he would be perfectly happy, but circumstances have made him a soldier and he has been forced by his profession into a society which is predominantly male. Had he been born a generation earlier, he would never have found himself in the army at all, but changes in the technique of warfare demand of soldiers, not only the physical courage and aggressiveness which the warrior has always needed, but also intellectual gifts. The Venetian army now needs mathematicians, experts in the science of gunnery. But in all ages, the typical military mentality is conservative and resents the intellectual expert.

> A fellow
> That never set a squadron in the field
> Nor the division of a battle knows
> More than a spinster . . . mere prattle without practise
> Is all his soldiership

is a criticism which has been heard in every army mess in every war. Like so many people who cannot bear to feel unpopular and therefore repress their knowledge that they are, Cassio becomes quarrelsome when drunk, for alcohol releases his suppressed resentment at not being admired by his comrades in arms and his wish to prove that he is what he is not, as "manly" as they are. It is significant that, when he sobers up, his regret is not that he has behaved badly by his own standards but that he has lost his reputation. The advice which Iago then gives him, to get Desdemona to plead for him with Othello, is good advice in itself, for Desdemona obviously likes him, but it is also exactly the advice a character-type like Cassio will be most willing to listen to, for feminine society is where he feels most at home.

Emilia informs Cassio that, on her own initiative, Desdemona has already spoken on his behalf and that Othello has said he will take the safest occasion by the front to restore him to his post. Hearing this, many men would have been content to leave matters as they were, but Cassio persists:

the pleasure of a heart-to-heart talk with a lady about his fascinating self is too tempting.

While he is talking to Desdemona, Othello is seen approaching and she says:

> Stay and hear me speak.

Again, many men would have done so, but Cassio's uneasiness with his own sex, particularly when he is in disgrace, is too strong and he sneaks away, thus providing Iago with his first opportunity to make an insinuation.

Cassio is a ladies' man, not a seducer. With women of his own class, what he enjoys is socialized eroticism; he would be frightened of a serious personal passion. For physical sex he goes to prostitutes and when, unexpectedly, Bianca falls in love with him, like many of his kind, he behaves like a cad and brags of his conquest to others. Though he does not know who the owner of the handkerchief actually is, he certainly knows that Bianca will think that it belongs to another woman, and to ask her to copy it is gratuitous cruelty. His smiles, gestures and remarks about Bianca to Iago are insufferable in themselves; to Othello, who knows that he is talking about a woman, though he is mistaken as to her identity, they are an insult which only Cassio's death can avenge.

In Cinthio nothing is said about the Moor's color or religion, but Shakespeare has made Othello a black Negro who has been baptized.

No doubt there are differences between color prejudice in the twentieth century and color prejudice in the seventeenth and probably few of Shakespeare's audience had ever seen a Negro, but the slave trade was already flourishing and the Elizabethans were certainly no innocents to whom a Negro was simply a comic exotic. Lines like

> . . . an old black ram
> is tupping your white ewe . . .
> The gross clasps of a lascivious Moor . . .
> What delight shall she have to look on the devil

are evidence that the paranoid fantasies of the white man in which the Negro appears as someone who is at one and the same time less capable of self-control and more sexually potent than himself, fantasies with which, alas, we are only too familiar, already were rampant in Shakespeare's time.

The Venice of both *The Merchant of Venice* and *Othello* is a cosmopolitan society in which there are two kinds of social bond between its members, the bond of economic interest and the bond of personal friendship, which may coincide, run parallel with each other or conflict, and both plays are concerned with an extreme case of conflict.

Venice needs financiers to provide capital and it needs the best general it can hire to defend it; it so happens that the most skillful financier it can find is a Jew and the best general a Negro, neither of whom the majority are willing to accept as a brother.

Though both are regarded as outsiders by the Venetian community, Othello's relation to it differs from Shylock's. In the first place, Shylock rejects the Gentile community as firmly as the Gentile community rejects him; he is just as angry when he hears that Jessica has married Lorenzo as Brabantio is about Desdemona's elopement with Othello. In the second place, while the profession of usurer, however socially useful, is regarded as ignoble, the military profession, even though the goal of a mercantile society is not military glory, is still highly admired and, in addition, for the sedentary civilians who govern the city, it has a romantic exotic glamour which it cannot have in a feudal society in which fighting is a familiar shared experience.

Thus no Venetian would dream of spitting on Othello and, so long as there is no question of his marrying into the family, Brabantio is delighted to entertain the famous general and listen to his stories of military life. In the army, Othello is accustomed to being obeyed and treated with the respect due to his rank and, on his rare visits to the city, he is treated by the white aristocracy as someone important and interesting. Outwardly, nobody treats him as an outsider as they treat Shylock. Consequently, it is easy for him to persuade himself that he is accepted as a brother and when Desdemona accepts him as a husband, he seems to have proof of this.

It is painful to hear him say

> But that I love the gentle Desdemona
> I would not my unhoused free condition
> Put into circumscription or confine
> For the sea's worth

for the condition of the outsider is always unhoused and free. He does not or will not recognize that Brabantio's view of the match

> If such actions may have passage free,
> Bond-slaves and pagans shall our statesmen be

is shared by all his fellow senators, and the arrival of news about the Turkish fleet prevents their saying so because their need of Othello's military skill is too urgent for them to risk offending him.

If one compares *Othello* with the other plays in which Shakespeare treats the subject of male jealousy, *The Winter's Tale* and *Cymbeline,* one notices that Othello's jealousy is of a peculiar kind.

Leontes is a classical case of paranoid sexual jealousy due to repressed homosexual feelings. He has absolutely no evidence that Hermione and Polixenes have committed adultery and his entire court are convinced of their innocence, but he is utterly possessed by his fantasy. As he says to Hermione: "Your actions are my dreams." But, mad as he is, "the twice-nine changes of the Watery Starre" which Polixenes has spent at the Bohemian court, make the act of adultery physically possible so that, once the notion has entered his head, neither Hermione nor Polixenes nor the court can prove that it is false. Hence the appeal to the Oracle.

Posthumus is perfectly sane and is convinced against his will that Imogen has been unfaithful because Iachimo offers him apparently irrefutable evidence that adultery has taken place.

But both the mad Leontes and the sane Posthumus react in the same way: "My wife has been unfaithful; therefore she must be killed and forgotten." That is to say, it is only as husbands that their lives are affected. As king of Bohemia, as a warrior, they function as if nothing has happened.

In *Othello,* thanks to Iago's manipulations, Cassio and Desdemona behave in a way which would make it not altogether unreasonable for Othello to suspect that they were in love with each other, but the time factor rules out the possibility of adultery having been actually committed. Some critics have taken the double time in the play to be merely a dramaturgical device for speeding the action which the audience in the theatre will never notice. I believe, however, that Shakespeare meant the audience to notice it as, in *The Merchant of Venice,* he meant them to notice the discrepancy between Belmont time and Venice time.

If Othello had simply been jealous of the feelings for Cassio he imagined Desdemona to have, he would have been sane enough, guilty at worst of a lack of trust in his wife. But Othello is not merely jealous of feelings which might exist; he demands proof of an act which could not have taken place, and the effect on him of believing in this physical impossibility goes far beyond wishing to kill her: it is not only his wife who has betrayed him but the whole universe; life has become meaningless, his occupation is gone.

This reaction might be expected if Othello and Desdemona were a pair like Romeo and Juliet or Antony and Cleopatra whose love was an all-absorbing Tristan-Isolde kind of passion, but Shakespeare takes care to inform us that it was not.

When Othello asks leave to take Desdemona with him to Cyprus, he stresses the spiritual element in his love.

> I therefore beg it not
> To please the palate of my appetite
> Nor to comply with heat, the young affects
> In me defunct, and proper satisfaction,
> But to be free and bounteous of her mind.

Though the imagery in which he expresses his jealously is sexual—what other kind of images could he use?—Othello's marriage is important to him less as a sexual relationship than as a symbol of being loved and accepted as a person, a brother in the Venetian community. The monster in his own mind too hideous to be shown is the fear he has so far repressed that he is only valued for his social usefulness to the City. But for his occupation, he would be treated as a black barbarian.

The overcredulous, overgood-natured character which, as Iago tells us, Othello had always displayed is a telltale symptom. He had *had* to be overcredulous in order to compensate for his repressed suspicions. Both in his happiness at the beginning of the play and in his cosmic despair later, Othello reminds one more of Timon of Athens than of Leontes.

Since what really matters to Othello is that Desdemona should love him as the person he really is, Iago has only to get him to suspect that she does not, to release the repressed fears and resentments of a lifetime, and the question of what she has done or not done is irrelevant.

Iago treats Othello as an analyst treats a patient except that, of course, his intention is to kill not to cure. Everything he says is designed to bring to Othello's consciousness what he has already guessed is there. Accordingly, he has no need to tell lies. Even his speech, "I lay with Cassio lately," can be a truthful account of something which actually happened: from what we know of Cassio, he might very well have such a dream as Iago reports. Even when he has worked Othello up to a degree of passion where he would risk nothing by telling a direct lie, his answer is equivocal and its interpretation is left to Othello.

OTHELLO: What hath he said?
IAGO: Faith that he did—I know not what he did.
OTHELLO: But what?
IAGO: Lie—
OTHELLO: With her?
IAGO: With her, on her, what you will.

Nobody can offer Leontes absolute proof that his jealousy is baseless; similarly, as Iago is careful to point out, Othello can have no proof that Desdemona really is the person she seems to be.

Iago makes his first decisive impression when, speaking as a Venetian with firsthand knowledge of civilian life, he draws attention to Desdemona's hoodwinking of her father.

IAGO: I would not have your free and noble nature
Out of self-bounty be abused, look to't:
I know our country disposition well:
In Venice they do let God see the pranks
They dare not show their husbands: their best conscience
Is not to leave undone but keep unknown.
OTHELLO: Dost thou say so?
IAGO: She did deceive her father, marrying you:
And when she seemed to shake and fear your looks,
She loved them most.
OTHELLO: And so she did.
IAGO: Why, go to then.
She that so young could give out such a seeming
To seal her father's eyes up, close as oak.
He thought 'twas witchcraft.

And a few lines later, he refers directly to the color difference.

Not to affect many proposed matches,
Of her own clime, complexion and degree,
Whereto we see in all things nature tends,
Foh! one may smell in such a will most rank,
Foul disproportion, thoughts unnatural.
But pardon me: I do not in position
Distinctly speak of her, though I may fear
Her will, recoiling to her better judgment
May fall to match you with her country-forms,
And happily repent.

Once Othello allows himself to suspect that Desdemona may not be the person she seems, she cannot allay the suspicion by speaking the truth but she can appear to confirm it by telling a lie. Hence the catastrophic effect when she denies having lost the handkerchief.

If Othello cannot trust her, then he can trust nobody and nothing, and precisely what she has done is not important. In the scene where he pretends that the Castle is a brothel of which Emilia is the Madam, he accuses Desdemona, not of adultery with Cassio, but of nameless orgies.

DESDEMONA: Alas, what ignorant sin have I committed?
OTHELLO: Was this fair paper, this most goodly book
Made to write whore on. What committed?
Committed. O thou public commoner,
I should make very forges of my cheeks
That would to cinders burn up modestly
Did I but speak thy deeds.

And, as Mr. Eliot has pointed out, in his farewell speech his thoughts are not on Desdemona at all but upon his relation to Venice, and he ends by identifying himself with another outsider, the Moslem Turk who beat a Venetian and traduced the state.

Everybody must pity Desdemona, but I cannot bring myself to like her. Her determination to marry Othello—it was she who virtually did the proposing—seems the romantic crush of a silly schoolgirl rather than a mature affection; it is Othello's adventures, so unlike the civilian life she knows, which captivate her rather than Othello as a person. He may not have practiced witchcraft, but, in fact, she is spellbound. And despite all Brabantio's prejudices, her deception of her own father makes an unpleasant impression: Shakespeare does not allow us to forget that the shock of the marriage kills him.

Then, she seems more aware than is agreeable of the honor she has done Othello by becoming his wife. When Iago tells Cassio that "our General's wife is now the General" and, soon afterwards, soliloquizes

His soul is so infettered to her love
That she may make, unmake, do what she list
Even as her appetite shall play the god
With his weak function

he is, no doubt, exaggerating, but there is much truth in what he says. Before Cassio speaks to her, she has already discussed him with her husband and learned that he is to be reinstated as soon as is opportune. A sensible wife would have told Cassio this and left matters alone. In continuing to badger Othello, she betrays a desire to prove to herself and to Cassio that she can make her husband do as she pleases.

Her lie about the handkerchief is, in itself, a trivial fib but, had she really regarded her husband as her equal, she might have admitted the loss. As it is, she is frightened because she is suddenly confronted with a man whose sensibility and superstitions are alien to her.

Though her relation with Cassio is perfectly innocent, one cannot but share Iago's doubts as to the durability of the marriage. It is worth noting that, in the willow-song scene with Emilia, she speaks with admiration of Ludovico and then turns to the topic of adultery. Of course, she discusses this in general terms and is shocked by Emilia's attitude, but she does discuss the subject and she does listen to what Emilia has to say about husbands and wives. It is as if she had suddenly realized that she had made a *mésalliance* and that the sort of man she ought to have married was someone of her own class and color like Ludovico. Given a few more years of Othello and of Emilia's influence and she might well, one feels, have taken a lover.

IV

And so one comes back to where one started, to Iago, the sole agent in the play. A play, as Shakespeare said, is a mirror held up to nature. This particular mirror bears the date 1604, but, when we look into it, the face that confronts us is our own in the middle of the twentieth century. We hear Iago say the same words and see him do the same things as an Elizabethan audience heard and saw, but what they mean to us cannot be exactly the same. To his first audience and even, maybe, to his creator, Iago appeared to be just another Machiavellian villain who might exist in real life but with whom one would never dream of identifying oneself. To us, I think, he is a much more alarming figure; we cannot hiss at him when he appears as we can hiss at the villain in a Western movie because none of us can honestly say that he does not understand how such a wicked person can exist. For is not Iago, the practical joker, a parabolic figure for the autonomous pursuit of scientific knowledge through experiment which we all, whether we are scientists or not, take for granted as natural and right?

As Nietzsche said, experimental science is the last flower of asceticism. The investigator must discard all his feelings, hopes and fears as a human person and reduce himself to a disembodied observer of events upon which he passes no value judgment. Iago is an ascetic. "Love" he says, "is merely a lust of the blood, and a permission of the will."

The knowledge sought by science is only one kind of knowledge. Another kind is that implied by the Biblical phrase, "Then Adam knew Eve, his wife," and it is this kind I still mean when I say, "I know John Smith very well." I cannot know in this sense without being known in return. If I know John Smith well, he must also know me well.

But, in the scientific sense of knowledge, I can only know that which does not and cannot know me. Feeling unwell, I go to my doctor who examines me, says "You have Asian flu," and gives me an injection. The Asian virus is as unaware of my doctor's existence as his victims are of a practical joker.

Further, to-know in the scientific sense means, ultimately, to-have-power-over. To the degree that human beings are authentic persons, unique and self-creating, they cannot be scientifically known. But human beings are not pure persons like angels; they are also biological organisms, almost identical in their functioning, and, to a greater or lesser degree, they are neurotic, that is to say, less free than they imagine because of fears and desires of which they have no personal knowledge but could and ought to have. Hence, it is always possible to reduce human beings to the status of things which are completely scientifically knowable and completely controllable.

This can be done by direct action on their bodies with drugs, lobotomies, deprivation of sleep, etc. The difficulty about this method is that your victims will know that you are trying to enslave them and, since nobody wishes to be a slave, they will object, so that it can only be practiced upon minorities like prisoners and lunatics who are physically incapable of resisting.

The other method is to play on the fears and desires of which you are aware and they are not until they enslave themselves. In this case, concealment of your real intention is not only possible but essential for, if people know they are being played upon, they will not believe what you say or do what you suggest. An advertisement based on snob appeal, for example, can only succeed with people who are unaware that they are snobs and that their snobbish feelings are being appealed to and to whom, therefore, your advertisement seems as honest as Iago seems to Othello.

Iago's treatment of Othello conforms to Bacon's definition of scientific enquiry as putting Nature to the Question. If a member of the audince were to interrupt the play and ask him: "What are you doing?" could not Iago answer with a boyish giggle, "Nothing. I'm only trying to find out what Othello is really like"? And we must admit that his experiment is highly successful. By the end of the play he does know the scientific truth about the object to which he has reduced Othello. That is what makes his parting shot, "What you know, you know," so terrifying for, by then, Othello has become a thing, incapable of knowing anything.

And why shouldn't Iago do this? After all, he has certainly acquired knowledge. What makes it impossible for us to condemn him self-righteously is that, in our culture, we have all accepted the notion that the right to know is absolute and unlimited. The gossip column is one side of the medal; the cobalt bomb the other. We are quite prepared to admit that, while food and sex are good in themselves, an uncontrolled pursuit of either is not, but it is difficult for us to believe that intellectual curiosity is a desire like any other, and to realize that correct knowledge and truth are not identical. To apply a categorical imperative to knowing, so that, instead of asking, "What can I know?" we ask, "What, at this moment, am I meant to know?"—to entertain the possibility that the only knowledge which can be true for us is the knowledge we can live up to—that seems to all of us crazy and almost immoral. But, in that case, who are we to say to Iago—"No, you mustn't."

POSTSCRIPT: INFERNAL SCIENCE

All exact science is dominated by the idea of approximation. (BERTRAND RUSSELL.) If so, then infernal science differs from human science in that it lacks the notion of approximation: it believes its laws to be exact.

Ethics does not treat of the world. Ethics must be a condition of the world like logic. (WITTGENSTEIN.) On this God and the Evil One are agreed. It is a purely human illusion to imagine that the laws of the spiritual life are, like our legislation, imposed laws which we can break. We may defy them, either by accident, i.e., out of ignorance, or by choice, but we can no more break them than we can break the laws of human physiology by getting drunk.

The Evil One is not interested in evil, for evil is, by definition, what he believes he already knows. To him, Auschwitz is a banal fact, like the date of the battle of Hastings. He is only interested in good, as that which he has so far failed to understand in terms of his absolute presuppositions; Goodness is his obsession.

The first anthropological axiom of the Evil One is not *All men are evil,* but *All men are the same;* and his second—*Men do not act: they only behave.*

Humanly speaking, to tempt someone means to offer him some inducement to defy his conscience. In that sense, the Evil One cannot be said to tempt us for, to him, conscience is a fiction. Nor can he properly be thought of as trying to make us *do* anything, for he does not believe in the existence of deeds. What to us is a temptation is to him an experiment: he is trying to confirm a hypothesis about human behavior.

One of our greatest spiritual dangers is our fancy that the Evil One takes a personal interest in our perdition. He doesn't care a button about *my* soul, any more than Don Giovanni cared a button about Donna Elvira's body. I am his "one-thousand-and-third-in-Spain."

One can conceive of Heaven having a Telephone Directory, but it would have to be gigantic, for it would include the Proper Name and address of every electron in the Universe. But Hell could not have one, for in Hell, as in prison and the army, its inhabitants are identified not by name but by number. They do not *have* numbers, they *are* numbers.

PART FIVE

Two Bestiaries

D. H. LAWRENCE

If men were as much men as lizards are lizards,
They'd be worth looking at.

The artist, the man who makes, is less important to mankind, for good or evil, than the apostle, the man with a message. Without a religion, a philosophy, a code of behavior, call it what you will, men cannot live at all; what they believe may be absurd or revolting, but they have to believe something. On the other hand, however much the arts may mean to us, it is possible to imagine our lives without them.

As a human being, every artist holds some set of beliefs or other but, as a rule, these are not of his own invention; his public knows this and judges his work without reference to them. We read Dante for his poetry not for his theology because we have already met the theology elsewhere.

There are a few writers, however, like Blake and D. H. Lawrence, who are both artists and apostles and this makes a just estimation of their work difficult to arrive at. Readers who find something of value in their message will attach unique importance to their writings because they cannot find it anywhere else. But this importance may be shortlived; once I have learned his message, I cease to be interested in a messenger and, should I later come to think his message false or misleading, I shall remember him with resentment and distaste. Even if I try to ignore the message and read him again as if he were only an artist, I shall probably feel disappointed because I cannot recapture the excitement I felt when I first read him.

When I first read Lawrence in the late Twenties, it was his message which made the greatest impression on me, so that it was his "think" books like *Fantasia on the Unconscious* rather than his fiction which I read most avidly. As for his poetry, when I first tried to read it, I did not like it; despite my admiration for him, it offended my notions of what poetry should be. Today my notions of what poetry should be are still, in all essentials, what they were then and hostile to his, yet there are a number of his poems which I have come to admire enormously. When a poet who holds views about the nature of poetry which we believe to be false writes a poem we like, we are apt to think: "This time he has forgotten his theory and is writing according to ours." But what fascinates me about the poems of Lawrence's which I like is that I must admit he could never have written them had he held the kind of views about poetry of which I approve.

Man is a history-making creature who can neither repeat his past nor leave it behind; at every moment he adds to and thereby modifies everything that had previously happened to him. Hence the difficulty of finding a single image which can stand as an adequate symbol for man's kind of existence. If we think of his ever-open future, then the natural image is of a single pilgrim walking along an unending road into hitherto unexplored country; if we think of his never-forgettable past, then the natural image is of a great crowded city, built in every style of architecture, in which the dead are as active citizens as the living. The only feature common to both images is that both are purposive; a road goes in a certain direction, a city is built to endure and be a home. The animals, who live in the present, have neither cities nor roads and do not miss them; they are at home in the wilderness and at most, if they are social, set up camps for a single generation. But man requires both; the image of a city with no roads leading away from it suggests a prison, the image of a road that starts from nowhere in particular, an animal spoor.

Every man is both a citizen and a pilgrim, but most men are predominantly one or the other and in Lawrence the pilgrim almost obliterated the citizen. It is only natural, therefore, that he should have admired Whitman so much, both for his matter and his manner.

> Whitman's essential message was the Open Road. The leaving of the soul free unto herself, the leaving of his fate to her and to the loom of the open road. . . . The true democracy . . . where all journey down the open road. And where a soul is known at once in its going. Not by its clothes or appearance. Not by its family name. Not even by its reputation. Not by works at all. The soul passing unenhanced, passing on foot, and being no more than itself.

In his introduction to *New Poems,* Lawrence tries to explain the difference between traditional verse and the free verse which Whitman was the first to write.

> The poetry of the beginning and the poetry of the end must have that exquisite finality, perfection which belongs to all that is far off. It is in the realm of all that is perfect . . . the finality and perfection are conveyed in exquisite form: the perfect symmetry, the rhythm which returns upon itself like a dance where the hands link and loosen and link for the supreme moment of the end . . . But there is another kind of poetry, the poetry of that which is at hand: the immediate present. . . . Life,

> the ever present, knows no finality, no finished crystallisation. . . . It is obvious that the poetry of the instant present cannot have the same body or the same motions as the poetry of the before and after. It can never submit to the same conditions, it is never finished. . . . Much has been written about free verse. But all that can be said, first and last, is that free verse is, or should be, direct utterance from the instant whole man. It is the soul and body surging at once, nothing left out. . . . It has no finish. It has no satisfying stability. It does not want to get anywhere. It just takes place.

It would be easy to make fun of this passage, to ask Lawrence, for example, to tell us exactly how long an instant is, or how it would be physically possible for the poet to express it in writing before it had become past. But it is obvious that Lawrence is struggling to say something which he believes to be important. Very few statements which poets make about poetry, even when they appear to be quite lucid, are understandable except in their polemic context. To understand them, we need to know what they are directed against, what the poet who made them considered the principal enemies of genuine poetry.

In Lawrence's case, one enemy was the conventional response, the laziness or fear which makes people prefer second-hand experience to the shock of looking and listening for themselves.

> Man fixes some wonderful erection of his own between himself and the wild chaos, and gradually goes bleached and stifled under his parasol. Then comes a poet, enemy of convention, and makes a slit in the umbrella; and lo! the glimpse of chaos is a vision, a window to the sun. But after a while, getting used to the vision, and not liking the genuine draft from chaos, commonplace man daubs a simulacrum of the window that opens into chaos and patches the umbrella with the painted patch of the simulacrum. That is, he gets used to the vision; it is part of his house decoration.

Lawrence's justified dislike of the conventional response leads him into a false identification of the genuine with the novel. The image of the slit in the umbrella is misleading because what you can see through it will always be the same. But a genuine work of art is one in which every generation finds something new. A genuine work of art remains an example of what being genuine means, so that it can stimulate later artists to be genuine in their turn. Stimulate, not compel; if a playwright in the twentieth century chooses to write a play in a pastiche of Shakespearian blank verse, the fault is his, not Shakespeare's. Those who are afraid of firsthand experience would find means of avoiding it if all the art of the past were destroyed.

However, theory aside, Lawrence did care passionately about genuineness of feeling. He wrote little criticism about other poets who were his contemporaries, but, when he did, he was quick to pounce on any phoniness of emotion. About Ralph Hodgson's lines

> The sky was lit,
> The sky was stars all over it,
> I stood, I knew not why

he writes, "No one should say *I knew not why* any more. It is as meaningless as *Yours truly* at the end of a letter," and, after quoting an American poetess

> Why do I think of stairways
> With a rush of hurt surprise?

he remarks, "Heaven knows, my dear, unless you once fell down." Whatever faults his own poetry may have, it never puts on an act. Even when Lawrence talks nonsense, as when he asserts that the moon is made of phosphorous or radium, one is convinced that it is nonsense in which he sincerely believed. This is more than can be said of some poets much greater than he. When Yeats assures me, in a stanza of the utmost magnificence, that after death he wants to become a mechanical bird, I feel that he is telling what my nanny would have called "A story."

The second object of Lawrence's polemic was a doctrine which first became popular in France during the second half of the nineteenth century, the belief that Art is the true religion, that life has no value except as material for a beautiful artistic structure and that, therefore, the artist is the only authentic human being—the rest, rich and poor alike, are canaille. Works of art are the only cities; life itself is a jungle. Lawrence's feelings about this creed were so strong that whenever he detects its influence, as he does in Proust and Joyce, he refuses their work any merit whatsoever. A juster and more temperate statement of his objection has been made by Dr. Auerbach:

> When we compare Stendhal's or even Balzac's world with the world of Flaubert or the two Goncourts, the latter seems strangely narrow and petty despite its wealth of impressions. Documents of the kind represented by Flaubert's correspondance and the Goncourt diary are indeed admirable in the purity and incorruptibility of their artistic ethics, the wealth of impressions elaborated in them, and their refinement of sensory culture. At the same time, however, we sense something narrow, something oppressively close in their books. They are full of reality and intellect, but poor in humor and inner poise. The purely literary, even on the highest level of artistic acumen, limits the power of judgment, reduces the wealth of life, and at times distorts the outlook upon the world of phenomena. And while the writers contemptuously avert their attention from the political and economic bustle, consistently value life only as literary subject matter, and remain arrogantly and bitterly aloof from its great practical problems, in order to achieve aesthetic isolation for their work, often at great and daily expense of effort, the practical world nevertheless besets them in a thousand petty ways.
>
> Sometimes there are financial worries, and almost always there is nervous hypotension and a morbid concern with health. . . . What finally emerges, despite

> all their intellectual and artistic incorruptibility, is a strangely petty impression; that of an upper bourgeois egocentrically concerned over his aesthetic comfort, plagued by a thousand small vexations, nervous, obsessed by a mania—only in this case the mania is called "Literature." *(Mimesis.)*

In rejecting the doctrine that life has no value except as raw material for art, Lawrence fell into another error, that of identifying art with life, making with action.

> I offer a bunch of pansies, not a wreath of immortelles. I don't want everlasting flowers and I don't want to offer them to anybody else. A flower passes, and that perhaps is the best of it. . . . Don't nail the pansy down. You won't keep it any better if you do.

Here Lawrence draws a false analogy between the process of artistic creation and the organic growth of living creatures. "Nature hath no goal though she hath law." Organic growth is a cyclical process; it is just as true to say that the oak is a potential acorn as it is to say the acorn is a potential oak. But the process of writing a poem, of making any art object, is not cyclical but a motion in one direction towards a definite end. As Socrates says in Valéry's dialogue *Eupalinos:*

> The tree does not construct its branches and leaves; nor the cock his beak and feathers. But the tree and all its parts, or the cock and all his, are constructed by the principles themselves, which do not exist apart from the constructing. . . . But, in the objects made by man, the principles are separate from the construction, and are, as it were, imposed by a tyrant from without upon the material, to which he imparts them by acts. . . . If a man waves his arm, we distinguish this arm from his gesture, and we conceive between gesture and arm a purely possible relation. But from the point of view of nature, this gesture of the arm and the arm itself cannot be separated.

An artist who ignores this difference between natural growth and human construction will produce the exact opposite of what he intends. He hopes to produce something which will seem as natural as a flower, but the qualities of the natural are exactly what his product will lack. A natural object never appears unfinished; if it is an inorganic object like a stone, it is what it has to be, if an organic object like a flower, what it has to be at this moment. But a similar effect—of being what it has to be—can only be achieved in a work of art by much thought, labor and care. The gesture of a ballet dancer, for example, only looks natural when, through long practice, its execution has become "second nature" to him. That perfect incarnation of life in substance, word in flesh, which in nature is immediate, has in art to be achieved and, in fact, can never be perfectly achieved. In many of Lawrence's poems, the spirit has failed to make itself a fit body to live in, a curious defect in the work of a writer who was so conscious of the value and significance of the body. In his essay on Thomas Hardy, Lawrence made some acute observations about this very problem. Speaking of the antimony between Law and Love, the Flesh and the Spirit, he says

> The principle of the Law is found strongest in Woman, the principle of Love in Man. In every creature, the mobility, the law of change is found exemplified in the male, the stability, the conservatism in the female.
>
> The very adherence of rhyme and regular rhythm is a concession to the Law, a concession to the body, to the being and requirements of the body. They are an admission of the living positive inertia which is the other half of life, other than the pure will to motion.

This division of Lawrence's is a variant on the division between the City and the Open Road. To the mind of the pilgrim, his journey is a succession of ever-new sights and sounds, but to his heart and legs, it is a rhythmical repetition—tic-toc, left-right—even the poetry of the Open Road must pay that much homage to the City. By his own admission and definition Lawrence's defect as an artist was an exaggerated maleness.

Reading Lawrence's early poems, one is continually struck by the originality of the sensibility and the conventionality of the expressive means. For most immature poets, their chief problem is to learn to forget what they have been taught poets are supposed to feel; too often, as Lawrence says, the young man is afraid of his demon, puts his hand over the demon's mouth and speaks for him. On the other hand, an immature poet, if he has real talent, usually begins to exhibit quite early a distinctive style of his own; however obvious the influence of some older writer may be, there is something original in his manner or, at least, great technical competence. In Lawrence's case, this was not so; he learned quite soon to let his demon speak, but it took him a long time to find the appropriate style for him to speak in. All too often in his early poems, even the best ones, he is content to versify his thoughts; there is no essential relation between what he is saying and the formal structure he imposes upon it.

> Being nothing, I bear the brunt
> Of the nightly heavens overhead, like an immense open eye
> With a cat's distended pupil, that sparkles with little stars
> And with thoughts that flash and crackle in far-off malignancy
> So distant, they cannot touch me, whom nothing mars.

A mere poetaster with nothing to say, would have done something about *whom nothing mars.*

It is interesting to notice that the early poems in which he seems technically most at ease and the form most natural, are those he wrote in dialect.

> I wish tha hadna done it, Tim,
> I do, an' that I do,
> For whenever I look thee i'th' face, I s'll see
> Her face too.
>
> I wish I could wash er off'n thee;
> 'Appen I can, If I try.

But tha'll ha'e ter promise ter be true ter me
Till I die.

This sounds like a living woman talking, whereas no woman on earth ever talked like this:

How did you love him, you who only roused
His mind until it burnt his heart away!
'Twas you who killed him, when you both caroused
In words and things well said. But the other way
He never loved you, never with desire
Touched you to fire.

I suspect that Lawrence's difficulties with formal verse had their origin in his linguistic experiences as a child.

My father was a working man
and a collier was he,
At six in the morning they turned him down
and they turned him up for tea.

My mother was a superior soul
a superior soul was she,
cut out to play a superior role
in the god-damn bourgoisie.

We children were the in-betweens,
Little non-descripts were we,
In doors we called each other *you*
outside it was *tha* and *thee*.

In formal poetry, the role played by the language itself is so great that it demands of the poet that he be as intimate with it as with his own flesh and blood and love it with a single-minded passion. A child who has associated standard English with Mother and dialect with Father has ambivalent feelings about both which can hardly fail to cause trouble for him in later life if he should try to write formal poetry. Not that it would have been possible for Lawrence to become a dialect poet like Burns or William Barnes, both of whom lived before public education had made dialect quaint. The language of Burns was a national not a parochial speech, and the peculiar charm of Barnes' poetry is its combination of the simplest emotions with an extremely sophisticated formal technique: Lawrence could never have limited himself to the thoughts and feelings of a Nottinghamshire mining village, and he had neither the taste nor the talent of Barnes for what he scornfully called word games.

Most of Lawrence's finest poems are to be found in the volume *Birds, Beasts, and Flowers,* begun in Tuscany when he was thirty-five and finished three years later in New Mexico. All of them are written in free verse.

The difference between formal and free verse may be likened to the difference between carving and modeling; the formal poet, that is to say, thinks of the poem he is writing as something already latent in the language which he has to reveal, while the free verse poet thinks of language as a plastic passive medium upon which he imposes his artistic conception. One might also say that, in their attitude towards art, the formal verse writer is a catholic, the free verse writer a protestant. And Lawrence was, in every respect, very protestant indeed. As he himself acknowledged, it was through Whitman that he found himself as a poet, found the right idiom of poetic speech for his demon.

On no other English poet, so far as I know, has Whitman had a beneficial influence; he could on Lawrence because, despite certain superficial resemblances, their sensibilities were utterly different. Whitman quite consciously set out to be the Epic Bard of America and created a poetic *persona* for the purpose. He keeps using the first person singular and even his own name, but these stand for a *persona,* not an actual human being, even when he appears to be talking about the most intimate experiences. When he sounds ridiculous, it is usually because the image of an individual obtrudes itself comically upon what is meant to be a statement about a collective experience. *I am large. I contain multitudes* is absurd if one thinks of Whitman himself or any individual; of a corporate person like General Motors it makes perfectly good sense. The more we learn about Whitman the man, the less like his *persona* he looks. On the other hand it is doubtful if a writer ever existed who had less of an artistic *persona* than Lawrence; from his letters and the reminiscences of his friends, it would seem that he wrote for publication in exactly the same way as he spoke in private. (I must confess that I find Lawrence's love poems embarrassing because of their lack of reticence; they make me feel a Peeping Tom.) Then, Whitman looks at life extensively rather than intensively. No detail is dwelt upon for long; it is snapshotted and added as one more item to the vast American catalogue. But Lawrence in his best poems is always concerned intensively with a single subject, a bat, a tortoise, a fig tree, which he broods on until he has exhausted its possibilities.

A sufficient number of years have passed for us to have gotten over both the first overwhelming impact of Lawrence's genius and the subsequent violent reaction when we realized that there were silly and nasty sides to his nature. We can be grateful to him for what he can do for us, without claiming that he can do everything or condemning him because he cannot. As an analyst and portrayer of the forces of hatred and aggression which exist in all human beings and, from time to time, manifest themselves in nearly all human relationships, Lawrence is, probably, the greatest master who ever lived. But that was absolutely all that we knew and understood about human beings; about human affection and human charity, for example, he knew absolutely nothing. The truth is that he detested nearly all human beings if he had to be in close contact with them; his ideas of what a human relationship, between man and man or man and woman, ought to be are pure daydreams because they are not based upon any experience of actual relationships which might be improved or corrected. Whenever, in his novels and short stories, he introduces a character whom he expects the reader to admire, he or she is always an unmitigated humorless bore, but the more he dislikes his characters the more interesting he makes them. And, in his heart of hearts, Lawrence knew this himself. There is a sad passage in *An Autobiographical Sketch:*

> Why is there so little contact between myself and the people I know? The answer, as far as I can see, has something to do with class. As a man from the working class, I feel that the middle class cut off some of my vital vibration when I am with them. I admit them charming and good people often enough, but they just stop some part of me from working.
>
> Then, why don't I live with my own people? Because their vibration is limited in another direction. The working class is narrow in outlook, in prejudice, and narrow in intelligence. This again makes a prison. Yet I find, here in Italy, for example, that I live in a certain contact with the peasants who work the land of this villa. I am not intimate with them, hardly speak to them save to say good-day. And they are not working for me. I am not their padrone. I don't want to live with them in their cottages; that would be a sort of prison. I don't idealise them. I don't expect them to make any millenium here on earth, neither now nor in the future. But I want them to be there, about the place, their lives going along with mine.

For the word *peasants,* one might substitute the words *birds, beasts and flowers.* Lawrence possessed a great capacity for affection and charity, but he could only direct it towards nonhuman life or peasants whose lives were so uninvolved with his that, so far as he was concerned, they might just as well have been nonhuman. Whenever, in his writings, he forgets about men and women with proper names and describes the anonymous life of stones, waters, forests, animals, flowers, chance traveling companions or passers-by, his bad temper and his dogmatism immediately vanish and he becomes the most enchanting companion imaginable, tender, intelligent, funny and, above all, happy. But the moment any living thing, even a dog, makes demands on him, the rage and preaching return. His poem about "Bibbles," "the walt whitmanesque love-bitch who loved just everybody," is the best poem about a dog ever written, but it makes it clear that Lawrence was no person to be entrusted with the care of a dog.

> All right, my little bitch.
> You learn loyalty rather than loving,
> And I'll protect you.

To which Bibbles might, surely, with justice retort: "O for Chris-sake, mister, go get yourself an Alsatian and leave me alone, can't you."

The poems in *Birds, Beasts, and Flowers* are among Lawrence's longest. He was not a concise writer and he needs room to make his effect. In his poetry he manages to make a virtue out of what in his prose is often a vice, a tendency to verbal repetition. The recurrence of identical or slightly varied phrases helps to give his free verse a structure; the phrases themselves are not particularly striking, but this is as it should be, for their function is to act as stitches.

Like the romantics, Lawrence's starting point in these poems is a personal encounter between himself and some animal or flower but, unlike the romantics, he never confuses the feelings they arouse in him with what he sees and hears and knows about them.

Thus, he accuses Keats, very justly, I think, of being so preoccupied with his own feelings that he cannot really listen to the nightingale. *Thy plaintive anthem fades* deserves Lawrence's comment: *It never was a plaintive anthem—it was Caruso at his jauntiest.*

Lawrence never forgets—indeed this is what he likes most about them—that a plant or an animal has its own kind of existence which is unlike and uncomprehending of man's.

> It is no use my saying to him in an emotional voice:
> 'This is your Mother, she laid you when you were an egg.'
> He does not even trouble to answer: 'Woman, what have I to do with thee?'
> He wearily looks the other way,
> And she even more wearily looks another way still.
> ("Tortoise Family Connections.")

But watching closer
That motionless deadly motion,
That unnatural barrel body, that long ghoul nose . . .
I left off hailing him.
I had made a mistake, I didn't know him,
This grey, monotonous soul in the water,
This intense individual in shadow,
Fish-alive.
I didn't know his God.

("Fish.")

When discussing people or ideas, Lawrence is often turgid and obscure, but when, as in these poems, he is contemplating some object with love, the lucidity of his language matches the intensity of his vision, and he can make the reader *see* what he is saying as very few writers can.

Queer, with your thin wings and your streaming legs,
How you sail like a heron, or a dull clot of air.

("The Mosquito.")

Her little loose hands, and sloping Victorian shoulders

("Kangaroo.")

There she is, perched on her manger, looking over the boards into the day
Like a belle at her window.
And immediately she sees me she blinks, stares, doesn't know me, turns her head and ignores me vulgarly with a wooden blank on her face.
What do I care for her, the ugly female, standing up there with her long tangled sides like an old rug thrown over a fence.
But she puts her nose down shrewdly enough when the knot is untied,
And jumps staccato to earth, a sharp, dry jump, still ignoring me,
Pretending to look around the stall
Come on, you crapa! I'm not your servant.

She turns her head away with an obtuse female sort of deafness, bête.
And then invariably she crouches her rear and makes water.
That being her way of answer, if I speak to her.—Self-conscious!
Le bestie non parlano, poverine! . . .

Queer it is, suddenly, in the garden
To catch sight of her standing like some huge ghoulish grey bird in the air, on the bough of the leaning almond-tree,
Straight as a board on the bough, looking down like some hairy horrid God the Father in a William Blake imagination.
Come, down, Crapa, out of that almond tree!
("She-Goat.")

In passages like these, Lawrence's writing is so transparent that one forgets him entirely and simply sees what he saw.

Birds, Beasts, and Flowers is the peak of Lawrence's achievement as a poet. There are a number of fine things in the later volumes, but a great deal that is tedious, both in subject matter and form. A writer's doctrines are not the business of a literary critic except in so far as they touch upon questions which concern the art of writing; if a writer makes statements about nonliterary matters, it is not for the literary critic to ask whether they are true or false but he may legitimately question the writer's authority to make them.

The Flauberts and the Goncourts considered social and political questions beneath them; to his credit, Lawrence knew that there are many questions that are more important than Art with an *A,* but it is one thing to know this and another to believe one is in a position to answer them.

In the modern world, a man who earns his living by writing novels and poems is a self-employed worker whose customers are not his neighbors, and this makes him a social oddity. He may work extremely hard, but his manner of life is something between that of a *rentier* and a gypsy, he can live where he likes and know only the people he chooses to know. He has no firsthand knowledge of all those involuntary relationships created by social, economic and political necessity. Very few artists can be *engagé* because life does not engage them: for better or worse, they do not quite belong to the City. And Lawrence, who was self-employed after the age of twenty-six, belonged to it less than most. Some writers have spent their lives in the same place and social milieu; Lawrence kept constantly moving from one place and one country to another. Some have been extroverts who entered fully into whatever society happened to be available; Lawrence's nature made him avoid human contacts as much as possible. Most writers have at least had the experience of parenthood and its responsibilities; this experience was denied Lawrence. It was inevitable, therefore, that when he tried to lay down the law about social and political matters, money, machinery, etc., he could only be negative and moralistic because, since his youth, he had had no firsthand experiences upon which concrete and positive suggestions could have been based. Furthermore, if, like Lawrence, the only aspects of human beings which you care for and value are states of being, timeless moments of passionate intensity, then social and political life, which are essentially historical—without a past and a future, human society is inconceivable—must be, for you, the worthless aspects of human life. You cannot honestly say, "This kind of society is preferable to that," because, for you, society is wholly given over to Satan.

The other defect in many of the later poems is a formal one. It is noticeable that the best are either of some length or rhymed; the short ones in free verse very rarely come off. A poem which contains a number of ideas and feelings can be organized in many different ways, but a poem which makes a single point and is made up of no more than one or two sentences can only be organized verbally; an epigram or an aphorism must be written either in prose or in some strictly measured verse; written in free verse, it will sound like prose arbitrarily chopped up.

> It has always seemed to me that a real thought, not an argument can only exist in verse, or in some poetic form. There is a didactic element about prose thoughts which makes them repellent, slightly bullying, "He who hath wife and children hath given hostages to fortune." There is a point well put: but immediately it irritates by its assertiveness. If it were put into poetry, it would not nag at us so practically. We don't want to be nagged at.
> (Preface to "Pansies.")

Though I personally love good prose aphorisms, I can see what Lawrence means. If one compares

Plus ça change, plus c'est la même chose

with

> The accursed power that stands on Privelege
> And goes with Women and Champagne and Bridge
> Broke, and Democracy resumed her reign
> That goes with Bridge and Women and Champagne

the first does seem a bit smug and a bit abstract, while, in the second, the language dances and is happy.

> The bourgeois produced the Bolshevist inevitably
> As every half-truth at length produces the contradiction
> of itself
> In the opposite half-truth

has the worst of both worlds; it lacks the conciseness of the prose and the jollity of the rhymed verse.

The most interesting verses in the last poems of Lawrence belong to a literary genre he had not attempted before, satirical doggerel.

If formal verse can be likened to carving, free verse to modeling, then one might say that doggerel verse is like *objets trouvés*—the piece of driftwood that looks like a witch, the stone that has a profile. The writer of doggerel, as it were, takes any old words, rhythms and rhymes that come into his head, gives them a good shake and then throws them onto the page like dice where, lo and behold, contrary to all probability they make sense, not by law but by chance. Since the words appear to have no will of their own, but to be the puppets of chance, so will the things or persons to which they refer; hence the value of doggerel for a certain kind of satire.

It is a different kind of satire from that written by Dryden and Pope. Their kind presupposes a universe, a city, governed by, or owing allegiance to, certain eternal laws of reason and morality; the purpose of their satire is to demonstrate that the individual or institution they are attacking violates these laws. Consequently, the stricter in form their verse, the more artful their technique, the more effective it is. Satirical doggerel, on the other hand, presupposes no fixed laws. It is the weapon of the outsider, the anarchist rebel, who refuses to accept conventional laws and pieties as binding or worthy of respect. Hence its childish technique, for the child represents the naïve and personal, as yet uncorrupted by education and convention. Satire of the Pope kind says: "The Emperor is wearing a celluloid collar. That simply isn't done." Satiric doggerel cries: "The Emperor is naked."

At this kind of satiric doggerel, Lawrence turned out to be a master.

> And Mr. Meade, that old old lily,
> Said: "Gross, coarse, hideous!" and I, like a silly
>
> Thought he meant the faces of the police court
>   officials
> And how right he was, so I signed my initials.

> But Tolstoi was a traitor
> To the Russia that needed him most,
> The great bewildered Russia
> So worried by the Holy Ghost;
> He shifted his job onto the peasants
> And landed them all on toast.

Parnassus has many mansions.

MARIANNE MOORE

Why an inordinate interest in animals and athletes? They are subjects for art and exemplars of it, are they not? minding their own business. Pangolins, hornbills, pitchers, catchers, do not pry or prey—or prolong the conversation; do not make us self-conscious; look their best when caring least; although in a Frank Buck documentary, I saw a leopard insult a crocodile (basking on the river bank—head only visible on the bank)—bat the animal on the nose and continue on its way without so much as a look back.

When I first read Lawrence's poetry, I didn't like it much, but I had no difficulty in understanding it. But when in 1935, I first tried to read Marianne Moore's poems, I simply could not make head or tail of them. To begin with, I could not "hear" the verse. One may have a prejudice against Free Verse as such but, if it is in any way competently written, the ear immediately hears where one line ends and another begins, for each line represents either a speech unit or a thought unit. Accent has always played so important a role in English prosody that no Englishman, even if he has been brought up on the poetry written according to the traditional English prosodic convention in which lines are scanned by accentual feet, iambics, trochees, anapaests, etc., has any difficulty in recognizing as formal and rhythmical a poem, like *Christabel* or *The Wreck of the Deutschland,* which is written in an accentual meter. But a syllabic verse, like Miss Moore's, in which accents and feet are ignored and only the number of syllables count, is very difficult for an English ear to grasp. One of our problems with the French alexandrine, for example, is that, whatever we may know intellectually about French prosody, our ear cannot help hearing most alexandrines as anapaestic verse which, in English poetry, we associate with light verse. Try as one may to forget it, *Je le vois, je lui parle; et mon coeur . . . Je m'égare* reminds us of *The Assyrian came down like a wolf on the fold*. But, at least, in listening to Racine all the lines have twelve syllables. Before I had encountered Miss Moore's verse, I was well acquainted with Robert Bridges's syllabic experiments, but he confined his verses to a regular succession of either six-syllable or twelve-syllable lines. A typical poem by Miss Moore, on the other hand, is written in stanzas, containing anything from one up to twenty syllables, not infrequently a word is split up with one or more of its syllables at the end of a line and the rest of them at the beginning of the next, caesuras fall where they may and, as a rule, some of the lines rhyme and some are unrhymed. This, for a long time, I found very difficult. Then, I found her process of thinking very hard to follow. Rimbaud seemed child's play compared with a passage like this:

they are to me
    like enchanted Earl Gerald who
    changes himself into a stag, to
a great green-eyed cat of
the mountain. Discommodity makes
    them invisible; they've dis-
appeared. The Irish say your trouble is their

trouble and your
joy their joy? I wish
I could believe it;
I am troubled, I'm dissatisfied, I'm Irish.

Uncomprehending as I was, I felt attracted by the tone of voice, so I persevered and I am very thankful that I did, for today there are very few poets who give me more pleasure to read. What I did see from the first was that she is a pure "Alice." She has all the Alice qualities, the distaste for noise and excess:

Poets, don't make a fuss;
the elephants 'crooked trumpet' 'doth write;'
and to a tiger-book I am reading—
I think you know the one—
I am under obligation.

One may be pardoned, yes I know
one may, for love undying.

. . . . .

The passion for setting people right is in itself
an afflictive disease.
Distaste which takes no credit to itself is best

the fastidiousness:

I remember a swan under the willows in Oxford,
with flamingo-coloured, maple-
leaflike feet. It reconnoitred like a battle-
ship. Disbelief and conscious fastidiousness were
the staple
ingredients in its
disinclination to move. Finally its hardihood
was not proof against its
proclivity to more fully appraise such bits
of food as the stream
bore counter to it; it made away with what I gave it
to eat. I have seen this swan and

I have seen you; I have seen ambition without
understanding in a variety of forms

the love of order and precision:

And as
MEridian one-two
one-two gives, each fifteenth second
in the same voice, the new
data—"The time will be" so and so—
you realize that "when you
hear the signal," you'll be
hearing Jupiter or jour pater, the day god—
the salvaged son of Father Time—
telling the cannibal Chronos
(eater of his proxime
new-born progeny) that punctuality
is not a crime

the astringent ironical sharpness:

One may be a blameless
bachelor and it is but a
step to Congreve.

. . . . . .

She says, "This butterfly,
this waterfly, this nomad
that has 'proposed
to settle on my hand for life'.—
what can one do with it.
There must have been more time
in Shakespeare's day
to sit and watch a play.
You know so many artists who are fools."
He says; "You know so many fools
who are not artists."

Like Lawrence's, many of Miss Moore's best poems are, overtly, at least, about animals. Animals have made their appearance in literature in a number of ways.

1) The beast fable. In these, the actors have animals' bodies but human consciousness. Sometimes the intention is simply amusing entertainment, but more often it is educative. The fable may be a mythical explanation of how things came to be as they are, and the beast in it may be a folk-culture hero whose qualities of courage or cunning are to be imitated. Or again, though this is a later historical development, the fable may be satirical. What prevents man, individually and collectively, from behaving reasonably and morally is not so much ignorance as a self-blindness induced by some passion or desire. In a satirical beast fable, the beast has the desires of his kind which are different from those which govern man, so that we can view them with detachment and cannot fail to recognize what is good or bad, sensible or foolish behavior. In a beast fable, the descriptions of animal life cannot be realistic, for its basic premise of a self-conscious speaking animal is fantastic. If a human being is introduced into a beast fable, as Mr. MacGregor is introduced into *Peter Rabbit,* he appears not as a man but as a God.

2) The animal simile. This can be expressed in the form:

as an *a* behaves so acted *N*

where *a* is a species of animal with a typical way of behaving and *N* is the proper name of a human individual, mythical or historical, acting in a historical situation. The description of animals in an epic simile is more realistic than it is in the beast fable, but what is described is the behavior considered typical for that animal; everything else about it is irrelevant.

> Homer's animal similes are more than merely ways of catching a mood or an impression, more than attempts to place an event in greater relief by stressing external similarities. When Homer has someone go against his enemies "like a lion," we must take him at his word. The warrior and the lion are activated by the same force; on

more than one occasion this force is expressly stated to be the *menos*, the forward impulse. The animals of the Homeric similes are not only symbols, but the particular embodiments of universal vital forces. Homer has little regard for anything except the forces in them, and that is the reason why animals are more prominent in the similes than in the narrative itself. By themselves they hold next to no interest for him.

In the clearly defined, the typical forms within which nature has allocated her gifts among the beasts, men find the models for gauging their own responses and emotions; they are the mirror in which man sees himself. The sentence: "Hector is as a lion," besides constituting a comparison, besides focussing the formlessness of human existence against a characteristic type, also signalises a factual connection. (BRUNO SNELL, *The Discovery of Mind.*)

3) The animal as an allegorical emblem. The significance of an emblem is not, like a simile, self-evident. The artist who uses one must either assume that his audience already knows the symbolic association—it is a legend of the culture to which he belongs—or, if it is his own invention, he must explain it. A Buddhist, for instance, looking at a painting of the Christ Child in which there is a goldfinch, may know enough ornithology to recognize it as a goldfinch and to know that it eats (or used to be thought to eat) thorns, but he cannot possibly understand why the bird is there unless it is explained to him that Christians associate thorns, the goldfinch's supposed diet, with the crown of thorns Christ wore at his crucifixion; the painter has introduced the goldfinch into his picture of the Christ Child to remind the spectator that Christmas, an occasion for rejoicing, is necessarily related to Good Friday, an occasion for mourning.

The painter *may* have represented the bird as naturalistically as possible in order that the spectator shall not mistake it for some other bird, a woodpecker, for instance, which, because it bores holes in trees, is an emblem for Satan who undermines human nature, but correct identification is all that matters; there is no visual resemblance between the emblem and its meaning. In poetry, the mere name would be sufficient.

4) The romantic encounter of man and beast. In such an encounter, the animal provides an accidental stimulus to the thoughts and emotions of a human individual. As a rule, the characteristics of the animal which make it a stimulus are not those in which it resembles man—as in the epic simile—but those in which it is unlike him. A man whose beloved has died or left him, hears a thrush singing and the song recalls to him an evening when he and his beloved listened together to another thrush singing. There are two thrushes and one man, but, while the songs of the two thrushes are identical—thrush-life does not change and knows nothing of unhappy love—the man hearing the second is changed from what he was when he heard the first. Since, in these encounters, the nature of the animal itself has little, if anything, to do with the thoughts and emotions he provokes in the human individual, realistic description counts for little. Very few of the famous romantic poems concerned with animals are accurate in their natural history.

5) Animals as objects of human interest and affection. Animals play an important economic role in the lives of huntsmen and farmers, many people keep them as pets, every major city in our culture has a zoo where exotic animals are on public exhibition, and some people are naturalists who are more interested in animals than in anything else. If an animal lover happens also to be a poet, it is quite possible that he will write poems about the animals he loves and, if he does, he will describe them in the same way that he would describe a friend, that is to say, every detail of the animal's appearance and behavior will interest him. It is almost impossible to make such a description communicable to others except in anthropomorphic terms, so that, in the animal lover's poetry, the order of the Homeric simile is reversed and takes the form:

as *n* looks or acts so does *A*

where *n* is a typical class of human being and *A* is an individual animal. Its grace and charm are conveyed by likening it to some instance of what makes some human beings admirable; sometimes, too, like Lawrence, the animal lover goes further and contrasts the virtue of a beast with the vices and follies of man.

Overtly, Miss Moore's animal poems are those of a naturalist; the animals she selects are animals she likes—the one exception is the cobra, and the point of the poem is that we, not the cobra, are to be blamed for our subjective fear and dislike—and nearly all of her animals are exotic, to be seen normally only in zoos or photographs by explorers; she has only one poem about a common domestic pet.

Like Lawrence, she has an extraordinary gift for metaphorical comparisons which make the reader see what she has seen. The metaphors may be drawn from other animals and plants. Thus, she describes a tomcat's face:

> the small tuft of fronds
> or katydid-legs above each eye, still numbering the
> units in each group;
> the shadbones regularly set about the mouth, to
> droop or rise
> in unison like the porcupine quills—motionless.
>
> . . . . . .
>
> The firs stand in a procession, each with an
> emerald turkey-foot at the top,
> reserved in their contours, saying nothing
>
> . . . . .
>
> the lion's ferocious chrysanthemum head

Or the metaphors may be taken from human artifacts.

> pillar body erect
> on a three-cornered smooth-working chippendale claw.
> ("The Jerboa.")

> the intensively
> watched eggs coming from
> the shell free it when they are freed,
> leaving its wasp-nest flaws

of white on white and close-
laid Ionic chiton-folds
like the lines in the mane of
a Parthenon horse
("The Paper Nautilus.")

And on occasion, she uses an elaborate reversed epic simile.

As impassioned Handel—
meant for a lawyer and a masculine German domestic
career—clandestinely studied the harpsichord
and never was known to have fallen in love,
the unconfiding frigate-bird hides
in the height and in the majestic
display of his art.
("The Frigate Pelican.")

But, unlike Lawrence, she likes the human race. For all the evil he does, man is, for her, a more sacred being than an animal.

Bedizened or stark
naked, man, the self, the being we call human,
writing—
master to this world, griffons a dark
"Like does not like like that is obnoxious"—and
writes error with four
r's. Among animals, one has a sense of humour,
Humour saves a few steps, it saves yours. Unignorant,
modest and unemotional, and all emotion,
he has everlasting vigour,
power to grow
though there are few creatures who can make one
breathe faster and make one erecter.

The approach of her poetry is that of a naturalist but, really, their theme is almost always the Good Life. Sometimes, as in the bestiaries, she sees an animal as an emblem—the devil-fish, so frightening to look at, because of the care she takes of her eggs becomes an emblem of charity, the camel-sparrow an emblem of justice, the jerboa-rat an emblem of true freedom as contrasted with the false freedom of the conqueror-tyrant—and sometimes, as in the beast fable, the behavior of animals is presented as a moral paradigm. Occasionally, as in "Elephants," the moral is direct, but, as a rule, the reader has to perceive it for himself.

The "Pangolin," written during the war, is a longish poem —nine stanzas of eleven lines each—but it is not until the end of the seventh stanza that a direct likeness between the pangolin and man is drawn:

> in fighting, mechanicked
> like the pangolin.

On the one hand, the pangolin is an enchanting animal; on the other, it is a great honor to be created a human being. But the one way in which men can physically resemble pangolins is by putting on armor and this should not have to be necessary. The pangolin's armor is an adaptation which secures his survival, for he is an ant-eater; as creatures go, he is unpugnacious and unaggressive. But man wears armor because he is an aggressive creature full of hatred for and fear of his own kind. The moral: men ought to be gentle-natured like pangolins but, if they were, they would cease to look like pangolins, and the pangolin could not be an emblem.

Miss Moore's poems are an example of a kind of art which is not as common as it should be; they delight, not only because they are intelligent, sensitive and beautifully written, but also because they convince the reader that they have been written by someone who is personally good. Questioned about the relation between art and morals, Miss Moore herself has said:

> Must a man be good to write good poems? The villains in Shakespeare are not illiterate, are they? But rectitude *has* a ring that is implicative, I would say. And with *no* integrity, a man is not likely to write the kind of book I read.

PART SIX

Americana

THE AMERICAN SCENE

America where there
is the little old ramshackle victoria in the south,
where cigars are smoked on the
street in the north; where there are no proof-
readers, no silk-worms, no digressions;
the wild man's land; grassless linksless, language-
less country in which letters are written
not in Spanish, not in Greek, not in Latin, not
in shorthand,
but in plain American which cats and dogs can
read!

MARIANNE MOORE

Two of James' virtues, his self-knowledge, his awareness of just what he could and could not do, and his critical literary sense, his respect for the inalienable right of every subject to its own form and treatment, are nowhere more conspicuous than in *The American Scene.*

Of all possible subjects, travel is the most difficult for an artist, as it is the easiest for a journalist. For the latter, the interesting event is the new, the extraordinary, the comic, the shocking, and all that the peripatetic journalist requires is a flair for being on the spot where and when such events happen

—the rest is merely passive typewriter thumping: meaning, relation, importance, are not his quarry. The artist, on the other hand, is deprived of his most treasured liberty, the freedom to invent; successfully to extract importance from historical personal events without ever departing from them, free only to select and never to modify or to add, calls for imagination of a very high order.

Few writers have had less journalistic talent than James, and this is his defect, for the supreme masters have one trait in common with the childish scribbling mass, the vulgar curiosity of a police-court reporter. One can easily imagine Stendhal or Tolstoi or Dostoievski becoming involved in a barroom fight, but James, never. I have read somewhere a story that once, when James was visiting a French friend, the latter's mistress, unobserved, filled his top hat with champagne, but I do not believe it because, try as I will, I simply cannot conceive what James did and said when he put his hat on.

James was, of course, well aware of this limitation; he knew that both his character and circumstances confined his residence to a certain kind of house or hotel, his intimate acquaintance to a certain social class, and that such confinement might be an insuperable obstacle to writing a book of travel in which the author must try to catch the spirit, not of a particular milieu, but of a whole place, a whole social order. Nevertheless, the challenge, perhaps just because it was, for him, so particularly formidable, fascinated James from the first, and *The American Scene* is only the latest, most ambitious and best of a series of topographical writings, beginning in 1870 with sketches of Saratoga and Newport.

Immature as these early American pieces are, they seem to me more satisfactory than the subsequent descriptions of England and Europe, even the charming *A Little Tour in France* (1886). Confronted with the un-American scene, he seems prim and a little amateurish, as if he were a conscientious father writing letters to an intelligent daughter of fourteen; as guidebooks, the European travelogues are incomplete, and as personal impressions, they are timid; the reader is conscious that the traveler must have seen and felt a great deal more than he says, and refrained either from a fear of shocking or from a lack of confidence in his own judgment; but even as a young man, James was unafraid of America as a subject: puzzled often, angry sometimes, yes, but quite certain of what he felt and of his right to say it.

In letters directly and in his novels by implication James makes many criticisms of the English, but he would never have been so outspoken about them as he is, for instance, about the habits of American children of whom he writes in 1870:

> You meet them far into the evening, roaming over the piazzas and corridors of the hotels—the little girls especially—lean, pale, formidable. Occasionally childhood confesses itself, even when maternity resists, and you see at eleven o'clock at night some poor little bedizened precocity collapsed in slumber in a lonely wayside chair.

And again in 1906:

> . . . there were ladies and children all about—though indeed there may have been sometimes *but* the lone breakfasting child to deal with; the little pale, carnivorous, coffee-drinking ogre or ogress, who prowls down in advance of its elders, engages a table—dread vision! and has the "run" of the bill of fare.

All who knew James personally have spoken of the terror he could inspire when enraged, and one of the minor delights of *The American Scene* is that the stranger occasionally gets a glimpse, at a fortunately safe distance, of what these outbursts must have been like—the unhurried implacable advance of the huge offensive periods, the overwhelming alliterative barrage, the annihilating adverbial scorn.

> The freedoms of the young three—who were, by-the-way, not in their earliest bloom either—were thus bandied about in the void of the gorgeous valley without even a consciousness of its shrill, its recording echoes . . . The immodesty was too colossal to be anything but inno-

> cence, but the innocence on the other hand, was too colossal to be anything but inane. And they were alive, the slightly stale three: they talked, they laughed, they sang, they shrieked, they romped, they scaled the pinnacle of publicity and perched on it, flapping their wings; whereby they were shown in possession of many of the movements of life.
>
> Whom were they constructed, such specimens, to talk with or to talk over, or to talk under, and what form of address or of intercourse, what uttered, what intelligible terms of introduction, of persuasion, of menace, what developed, what specific human process of any sort, was it possible to impute to them? What reciprocities did they imply, what presumptions did they, could they, create? What happened, inconceivably, when such Greeks met such Greeks, such faces looked into such faces, and such sounds, in especial, were exchanged with such sounds? What women did they live with, what women, living with them, could yet leave them as they were? What wives, daughters, sisters, did they in fine make credible; and what, in especial, was the speech, what the manners, what the general dietary, what most the monstrous morning meal, of ladies receiving at such hands the law or the license of life?

Just what, one asks with nostalgic awe, would James have said if confronted with the spectacle of a drum-majorette?

In writing *The American Scene,* the "facts" he selected to go on are, even for James, amazingly and, one would have thought, fatally few. Though he seems to have visited Chicago (and not to have "liked" it) he confines his chapters to the East Coast from Boston to Miami. The Far West, the Midwest, the Deep South are totally ignored. This is a pity because the regional differences of the United States are significant, though not, I think, so decisively significant as the professional regionalists insist. Today it would be quite fatal to neglect the states remoter from Europe, not so much as regions in themselves, but because some of the most essential and generally typical American facts, such as the film and automobile industries, the public power projects, the divorce mills, are regionally situated. Still, even in 1906, there were many things west of Massachusetts, the landscape of Arizona, the distinctive atmosphere of San Francisco, to mention only two of them, which would have "amused" "the restless analyst," and in whose amusement his readers would have been very glad to share.[1]

With the second limitation that James imposed upon himself, however—his decision to reject all second-hand information and sentiment, to stick to those facts, however few, which were felt by him, however mistakenly, to be important, to be unashamedly, defiantly subjective—one can only wholeheartedly agree. In grasping the character of a society, as in judging the character of an individual, no documents, statistics, "objective" measurements can ever compete with the single intuitive glance. Intuition may err, for though its sound judgment is, as Pascal said, only a question of good eyesight, it must be good, for the principles are subtle and numerous, and the omission of one principle leads to error; but documentation which is useless unless it is complete, must err in a field where completeness is impossible. James' eyesight was good, his mind was accurate, and he understood exactly what he was doing; he never confused his observation with his interpretation.

> The fond observer is by his very nature committed everywhere to his impression—which means essentially, I think, that he is foredoomed, in one place as in another, to "put in" a certain quantity of emotion and reflection. The turn his sensibility takes depends of course on what is before him; but when is it not in some manner exposed and alert? If it be anything really of a touchstone, it is more disposed, I hold, to easy bargains than to hard ones; it only wants to be *somehow* interested, and is not without the knowledge that an emotion is after all, at the best or the worst, but an emotion. All of

[1] James originally intended, it appears, to write a second volume dealing with the West and Middle West.

> which is a voluminous commentary, I admit, on the modest text that I perhaps made the University Hospital stand for too many things. That establishes at all events my contention—that the living fact, in the United States, *will* stand, other facts not preventing, for almost anything you may ask of it.
>
> Where, in the United States, the interest, where the pleasure of contemplation is concerned, discretion is the better part of valor and insistence too often a betrayal. It is not so much that the hostile fact crops up as that the friendly fact breaks down. If you have luckily *seen,* you have seen; carry off your prize, in this case, instantly and at any risk. Try it again and you don't, you won't, see.

Yet, if the vision had, necessarily, to be brief, it was neither poor nor vague, and only the most leisurely and luxuriant treatment could do justice to its rich possibilities. In the novels and short stories of the previous decade, James had been evolving a style of metaphorical description of the emotions which is all his own, a kind of modern Gongorism, and in *The American Scene* this imagery, no longer inhibited by the restraining hand of character or the impatient tug of plot, came to its fullest and finest bloom.

Indeed, perhaps the best way to approach this book is as a prose poem of the first order, i.e., to suspend, for the time being, one's own conclusions about America and Americans, and to read on slowly, relishing it sentence by sentence, for it is no more a guidebook than the "Ode to a Nightingale" is an ornithological essay. It is not even necessary to start at the beginning or read with continuity; one can open it at almost any page. I advise, for instance, the reader who finds James' later manner a little hard to get into, to begin by reading the long paragraph about Lee's statue which concludes the chapter on Richmond: this is, admittedly, a purple patch, but there are many others which match it.

James' firsthand experiences were, necessarily, mostly those of a tourist, namely scenic objects, landscapes, buildings, the faces and behavior of strangers, and his own reflections on what these objects stood for. Unlike his modern rival at conveying the sense of Place—D. H. Lawrence—James was no naturalist; one is not convinced that he knew one bird or flower from another. He sees Nature as a city-bred gentleman with a knowledge of the arts, and by accepting this fully, turns it to his advantage in his descriptive conceits.

> . . . the social scene, shabby and sordid, and lost in the scale of space as the quotable line is lost in a dull epic or the needed name in an ageing memory.

> The spread of this single great wash of Winter from latitude to latitude struck me in fact as having its analogy in the vast vogue of some infinitely selling novel, one of those happy volumes of which the circulation roars, periodically, from Atlantic to Pacific and from great windy state to state, in the manner as I have heard it vividly put, of a blazing prairie fire; with as little possibility of arrest from "criticism" in the one case as from the bleating of lost sheep in the other.

> . . . the hidden ponds where the season itself seemed to blend as a young bedizened, a slightly melodramatic mother, before taking some guilty flight, hangs over the crib of her sleeping child.

But it is in his treatment of social objects and mental concepts that James reveals most clearly his great and highly original poetic gift. Outside of fairy tales, I know of no book in which things so often and so naturally become persons. Buildings address James:

> *Un bon mouvement,* therefore: you must make a dash for it, but you'll see I'm worth it.

James addresses buildings:

> You overdo it for what you are; you overdo it still more for what you may be; and don't pretend above all, with the object lesson supplied you, close at hand, by

the queer case of Newport, don't pretend, we say, not to know what we mean.

Buildings address each other:

Exquisite was what they called you, eh? We'll teach you, then, little sneak, to be exquisite! We'll allow none of that rot around here.

At Farmington, the bullying railroad orders taste and tradition

—off their decent avenue without a fear that they will "stand up" to it.

From Philadelphia the alluring train:

disvulgarized of passengers, steams away, in disinterested empty form, to some terminus too noble to be marked in *our* poor schedules.

Again, since *The Faerie Queene*, what book has been more hospitable to allegorical figures?

At Mount Vernon:

the slight, pale, bleeding Past, in a patched homespun suit, stands there taking the thanks of the Bloated Present, having woundedly rescued from thieves and brought to his door the fat, locked pocket book of which that personage appears to be the owner.

At Baltimore the Muse of History descends in a quick white flash to declare that she has found that city "a charming patient."

In Richmond the Spirit of the South reveals herself for a vivid moment,

a figure somehow blighted and stricken discomfortably, impossibly seated in an invalid chair, and yet facing one with strange eyes that were half a defiance and half a deprecation of one's noticing, and much more of one's referring to, an abnormal sign.

In Florida the American Woman is waiting to state her case in the manner of a politician in Thucydides:

> How can I do *all* the grace, all the interest, as I'm expected to? Yes, literally all the interest that isn't the mere interest in the money . . . All I want—that is all I need, for there is perhaps a difference—is, to put it simply, that my parents and my brothers and my male cousins should consent to exist otherwise than occultly, undiscoverably, or, as I suppose you'd call it, irresponsibly.

When the "recent immigrant," to copy the Jamesian nomenclature, compares his own impressions with those of the "restless analyst," he is immediately struck by how little, on the one hand, America has changed in any decisive way—the changes, great as they are, seem but extensions and modifications of a pattern already observable thirty years ago—and, on the other, by the irrevocable and catastrophic alterations in Europe.

The features of the American scene which most struck the analyst then are those which most strike the immigrant now, whether they be minor details, like the magnificent boots and teeth, the heavy consumption of candy, "the vagueness of separation between apartments, between hall and room, between one room and another, between the one you are in and the one you are not in," or major matters like the promiscuous gregariousness, the lack, even among the rich, of constituted privacy, the absence of forms for vice no less than for virtue, the "spoiling" of women and their responsibility for the whole of culture, above all the elimination from the scene of the squire and the parson.[2] It takes the immigrant a little time to discover just why the United States seems so different from any of the countries he resentfully or nostalgically remembers, but the crucial difference is, I think, just this last elimination of "the pervasive Patron" and "the old ecclesiastical arrogance for

[2] The immigrant would like to add one element, the excesses of the climate, which is either much too hot or much too cold or much too wet or much too dry or even, in the case of the California coast, much too mild, a sort of meteorological Back Bay. And then—oh dear!—the *insects,* and the *snakes,* and the *poison ivy* . . . The truth is, Nature never intended human beings to live here, and her hostility, which confined the Indian to a nomad life and forbids the white man to relax his vigilance and will for one instant, must be an important factor in determining the American character.

which, oh! a thousand times, the small substitutes, the mere multiplication of the signs of theological enterprise, in the tradition and on the scale of commercial and industrial enterprise, have no attenuation worth mentioning."

What in fact is missing, what has been consciously rejected, with all that such a rejection implies, is the *romanitas* upon which Europe was founded and which she has not ceased attempting to preserve. This is a point which, at the risk of becoming tedious, must be enlarged upon, since the issue between America and Europe is no longer a choice between social leveling and social distinctions. The leveling is a universal and inexorable fact. Nothing can prevent the liquidation of the European nations or any other nation in the great continents, Asia, Africa, America, the liquidation of the "individual" (in the eighteenth-century liberal meaning of the word) in the collective proletariat, the liquidation of Christendom in the neutral world. From that there is no refuge anywhere. But one's final judgment of Europe and America depends, it seems to me, upon whether one thinks that America (or America as a symbol) is right to reject *romanitas* or that Europe is right in trying to find new forms of it suited to the "democratized" societies of our age.

The fundamental presupposition of *romanitas,* secular or sacred, is that virtue is prior to liberty, i.e., what matters most is that people should think and act rightly; of course it is preferable that they should do so consciously of their own free will, but if they cannot or will not, they must be made to, the majority by the spiritual pressure of education and tradition, the minority by physical coercion, for liberty to act wrongly is not liberty but license. The antagonistic presupposition, which is not peculiar to America and would probably not be accepted by many Americans, but for which this country has come, symbolically, to stand, is that liberty is prior to virtue, i.e., liberty cannot be distinguished from license, for freedom of choice is neither good nor bad but the human prerequisite without which virtue and vice have no meaning. Virtue is, of course, preferable to vice, but to choose vice is preferable to having virtue chosen for one.

To those who make the first presupposition, both State and Church have the same positive moral function; to those who make the second, their functions differ: the function of the State becomes a negative one—to prevent the will of the strong from interfering with the will of the weak, or the wills of the weak with one another, even if the strong should be in the right and the weak in the wrong—and the Church, whether Catholic or Protestant, divorced from the State, becomes a witness, an offered opportunity, a community of *converts*. The real issue has been obscured, for both sides, by the historical struggle for social equality which made liberty seem the virtue —or license the vice—of which equality was the prized or detested precondition. This was natural since, when the struggle began, the most glaring cause of lack of liberty was the privileged position of the few and the unprivileged position of the many, so that a blow struck for equality was, in most cases, at the same time a blow struck for liberty, but the assumed order of priority was false all the same. The possibility that de Tocqueville foresaw from an inspection of America in 1830, has become a dreadful reality in the Europe of 1946, namely, that *romanitas* is perfectly capable of adapting itself to an egalitarian and untraditional society; it can even drop absolute values and replace the priest by the social engineer without violating its essential nature (which is and always was not Christian but Manichean). And it was from America, the first egalitarian society, that it learned how to adapt itself. For instance, it took the technique of mass advertising, eliminated the competitive element and changed the sales object from breakfast foods to political passions; it took the egalitarian substitute for tradition—fashion—and translated it from the putting over of best sellers and evening frocks to the selling of an ever-switching party line; it took the extra-legal vigilantes and put them into official uniforms; it took the inert evil of race prejudice and made it a dynamic evil. An America which does not realize the difference between equality and liberty is in danger, for, start with equality in order to arrive at liberty and the moment you come to a situation where inequality is or seems to you, rightly or wrongly, a stubborn fact, you will come to grief. For instance, the unequal distribution of intellectual gifts is a fact; since they refuse to face it, the institutions of Higher Learning in America cannot decide whether they are to be Liberal Arts Colleges for the exceptional few or vocational schools for the average many, and so fail to do their duty by either. On the other, more sinister, hand, the Southerner, rightly or wrongly, believes that the Negro is his inferior; by putting equality before liberty, he then refuses him the most elementary human liberties, for example, the educational and economic liberties that are the only means by which the Negro could possibly become the equal of the white, so that the latter can never be proven mistaken.

Democratic snobbery or race prejudice is uglier than the old aristocratic snobbery because the included are relatively so many and the excluded relatively so few. The exclusiveness, for instance, of Baron de Charlus is forgivable and even charming. If Charlus will speak to only half a dozen people, it cannot be supposed that the millions suffer severely from being unable to speak to Charlus; his behavior is frankly irrational, a personal act from which, if anyone suffers, it is only himself. The exclusiveness of the American Country Club —I cannot share James' pleasure in that institution—is both inexcusable and vulgar, for, since it purports to be democratic, its exclusion of Jews is a contradiction for which it has to invent dishonest rationalizations.

As the issue between virtue first and liberty first becomes clearer, so does the realization that the cost to any society that accepts the latter is extremely high, and to some may seem prohibitive. One can no longer make the task look easier than it is by pretending, as the liberals of the Enlightenment believed, that men are naturally good. No, it is just as true as it ever was that man is born in sin, that the majority are always, relatively, in the wrong, the minority sometimes, relatively, in the right (every one, of course, is free at any time to belong to either), and all, before God, absolutely in the wrong, that all of the people some of the time and some of the people most of the time will abuse their liberty and treat it as the license of an escaped slave. But if the principle is accepted, it means accepting this: it means accepting a State that, in comparison to its Roman rival, is dangerously weak (though realizing that, since people will never cease trying to interfere with the liberties of others in pursuing their own, the State can never wither away. Tyranny today, anarchy tomorrow is a Neo-Roman daydream); it means accepting a "Society," in the collective inclusive sense, that is as neutral to values (liberty is not a value but the ground of value) as the "nature" of physics; it means accepting an educational system in which, in spite of the fact that authority is essential to the growth of the individual who is lost without it, the responsibility for recognizing authority is laid on the pupil; it means accepting the impossibility of any "official" or "public" art; and, for the individual, it means accepting the lot of the Wandering Jew, i.e., the loneliness and anxiety of having to choose himself, his faith, his vocation, his tastes. The Margin is a hard taskmaster; it says to the individual: "It's no good your running to me and asking me to make you into someone. You must choose. I won't try to prevent your choice, but I can't and won't help you make it. If you try to put your trust in me, in public opinion, you will become, not someone but no one, a neuter atom of the public."

If one compares Americans with Europeans, one might say, crudely and too tidily, that the mediocre American is possessed by the Present and the mediocre European is possessed by the Past. The task of overcoming mediocrity, that is, of learning to possess instead of being possessed, is thus different in each case, for the American has to make the Present *his* present, and the European the Past *his* past. There are two ways of taking possession of the Present: one is with the help of the Comic or Ironic spirit. Hence the superiority of American (and Yiddish) humor. The other way is to choose a Past, i.e., to go physically or in the spirit to Europe. James' own explanation of his migration—

> To make so much money that you won't, that you don't 'mind,' don't mind anything—that is absolutely, I think,

> the main American formula. Thus your making no money—or so little that it passes there for none—and being thereby distinctly reduced to minding, amounts to your being reduced to the knowledge that America is no place for you. . . . The withdrawal of the considerable group of the pecuniarily disqualified seems, for the present, an assured movement; there will always be scattered individuals condemned to mind on a scale beyond any scale of making—

seems to me only partly true; better T. S. Eliot's observation in his essay on James:

> It is the final consummation of an American to become, not an Englishman, but a European—something no born Englishman, no person of European nationality can become.

James wrote a short story, "The Great Good Place," which has been praised by Mr. Fadiman and condemned by Mr. Matthiessen, in both instances, I think, for the wrong reason, for both take it literally. The former says: "The Place is what our civilization could be. . . . It is a hotel without noise, a club without newspapers. You even have to pay for service." If this were true, then the latter would be quite right to complain, as he does, that it is the vulgar daydream of a rich bourgeois intellectual. I believe, however, that, in his own discreet way, James is writing a religious parable, that is, he is not describing some social Utopia, but a spiritual state which is achievable by the individual now, that the club is a symbol of this state—not its cause, and the money a symbol of the sacrifice and suffering demanded to attain and preserve it. Anyway, the story contains a passage of dialogue which seems relevant to *The American Scene*.

> 'Every man must arrive by himself and on his own feet—isn't that so? We're Brothers here for the time as in a great monastery, and we immediately think of each other and recognize each other as such: but we must have first got here as we can, and we meet after long journeys by complicated ways.'

'Where is it?'

'I shouldn't be surprised if it were much nearer than one ever suspected.'

'Nearer "town," do you mean?'

'Nearer everything—nearer everyone.'

Yes. Nearer everything. Nearer than James himself, perhaps, suspected, to the "hereditary thinness" of the American Margin, to "the packed and hoisted basket" and "the torture rooms of the living idiom," nearer to the unspeakable jukeboxes, the horrible Rockettes and the insane salads, nearer to the anonymous countryside littered with heterogeneous *dreck* and the synonymous cities besotted with electric signs, nearer to radio commercials and congressional oratory and Hollywood Christianity, nearer to all the "democratic" lusts and licenses, without which, perhaps, the analyst and the immigrant alike would never understand by contrast the nature of the Good Place nor desire it with sufficient desperation to stand a chance of arriving.

POSTSCRIPT: ROME V. MONTICELLO

Of course, neither the Roman nor the Liberal presupposition is wholly true, for both represent an abstraction from historical reality.

If we consider human relations purely objectively, in abstraction from the human beings who enter into them, then the moral problem is of right or wrong action and the problem of choice is irrelevant; if we consider human beings purely subjectively, in abstraction from their relations to each other, the moral problem is one of liberty or slavery.

In everyday life we instinctively adopt the Roman position in relation to strangers and the Liberal position in relation to our friends. If a stranger forges my name to a check, I do not ask if he had an unhappy childhood, I call the police; if a friend does the same thing, I ask myself what can be the matter with him and the matter with me, that he should so violate our friendship.

The Roman can show that, at any given time, there is always a class, e.g., children below a certain age, and some individuals, e.g., criminals and lunatics whose inability or refusal to rule themselves makes them a menace to others and whose freedom therefore must be to some degree restrained. The Liberal, on the other hand, can show that a hard and fast division between those who cannot rule themselves and those who can is false. The newborn baby has traces of the capacity to rule itself and the wisest and best man cannot rule himself perfectly. Further, in the wisest ruler there remain traces of selfish passion in his relation to those whom he rules. In so far as he enjoys ruling others—and there always is an element of pleasure in so doing—he must desire that there remain people who cannot rule themselves, that his attempt to educate them to freedom will fail.

Toilet training, for example, would seem at first sight a case in which the Roman position was unassailable; no baby is born in control of his reflexes and no sane adult regards the conditioned control of his reflexes as a mistake or consciously rebels. Yet psychologists have been able to demonstrate that even here, the end of right action cannot be separated from the means of inculcation, that a taste for power, impatience, or even mere ignorance of the right means, can violate the traces of free will already present in the baby with deleterious effects in later life.

The Roman must concede this but then correct the tendency of the Liberal to abandon all conditioning educational techniques in favor of a mixture of rational explanation and learning by trial and error. For example, no free exercise of the human mind is possible until man has learned to exclude the irrelevant distractions of his immediate environment and concentrate on the problem he is attacking, or until he has learned to be truthful, to subordinate his desires to what is the case; it is only when concentration and truthfulness have become second nature to him that he will listen to reason or recognize an error as an error.

In its justifiable reaction against the mechanical learning by rote of, say, mathematical operations, progressive education is tending to carry its distaste for conditioning and authority into a sphere where it is fundamental, and threatening to produce a generation which may not think mechanically but only because it cannot think at all; it has never learned how.

The class distinctions proper to a democratic society are not those of rank or money, still less, as is apt to happen when these are abandoned, of race, but of age. In a democracy it is more, not less, important than in hierarchical and static societies that a distance should be kept between the young and the adult, the adult and the old: it is, I fear, Utopian to hope for them, but what the United States needs are puberty initiation rites and a council of elders.

RED RIBBON ON A WHITE HORSE

"Mowing hay by hand! Bless their hearts!"
An American matron in the train
between Bologna and Florence

Reading Miss Yezierska's book[1] sets me thinking again about that famous and curious statement in the Declaration of Independence about the self-evident right of all men to "the pursuit of happiness," for I have read few accounts of such a pursuit so truthful and moving as hers.

To be happy means to be free, not from pain or fear, but from care or anxiety. A man is so free when 1) he knows what he desires and 2) what he desires is real and not fantastic. A desire is real when the possibility of satisfaction exists for the individual who entertains it and the existence of such a possibility depends, first, on his present historical and

[1] Anzia Yezierska, *Red Ribbon on a White Horse,* Scribner's. 1950.

social situation—a desire for a Cadillac which may be real for a prosperous American businessman would be fantastic for a Chinese peasant—and, secondly, on his natural endowment as an individual—for a girl with one eye to desire to be kept by a millionaire would be fantastic, for a girl with two beautiful ones it may not. To say that the satisfaction of a desire is possible does not mean that it is certain but that, if the desire is not satisfied, a definite and meaningful reason can be given. Thus, if the American businessman fails to get the Cadillac he desires and asks himself, "Why?" he can give a sensible answer like, "My wife had to have an emergency operation which took my savings"; but if the Chinese peasant asks, "Why cannot I buy a Cadillac?" there are an infinite number of reasons which can only be summed up in the quite irrational answer, "Because I am I." The businessman suffers disappointment or pain but does not become unhappy; the peasant, unless he dismisses his desire as fantastic, becomes unhappy because to question his lack of satisfaction is to question the value of his existence.

So long as it is a matter of immediate material goods, few sane individuals cherish fantastic desires after the age of puberty, but there are desires for spiritual goods which are much more treacherous, e.g., the desire to find a vocation in life, to have a dedicated history. "What do I want to be? A writer? A chemist? A priest?" Since I am concerned not with any immediate objective good but with pledging the whole of my unknown future in advance, the chances of self-deception are much greater because it will be years before I can be certain whether my choice is real or fantastic. Nor can any outsider make the decision for me; he can only put questions to me which make me more aware of what my decision involves.

Miss Yezierska's book is an account of her efforts to discard fantastic desires and find real ones, both material and spiritual.

She began life in a Polish ghetto, i.e., in the bottom layer of the stratified European heap. In the more advanced countries of Europe, like England, it had become possible for a talented individual to rise a class, a generation, but in Russia, above all for a Jew, it was still quite impossible; if once one had been born in the ghetto, then in the ghetto one would die. For its inhabitants extreme poverty and constant fear of a pogrom were normal, and even so humble a desire as the wish to eat white bread was fantastic. So it had been for centuries until, suddenly, a possibility of escape was opened—immigration to America. What America would provide positively in place of the ghetto remained to be seen, but at least it would be different and any sufferings she might inflict would, at the very least, not be worse.

So Miss Yezierska and her family came and found themselves on the Lower East Side. Here was poverty still but less absolute, exploitation but the possibility of one day becoming an exploiter, racial discrimination but no pogroms. Was their new condition an improvement on their former one? It was hard to be certain. Where poverty is accepted as normal and permanent, the poor develop a certain style of living which extracts the maximum comfort from the minimum materials, but where poverty is held to be temporary or accidental, the preoccupation with escape leaves no time for such amenities; every European visitor to the States, I think, receives the impression that nowhere else in the world is real poverty—admittedly, rarer here than anywhere else—so cheerless, sordid and destitute of all grace.

Moreover, in the "bad old days" of which Miss Yezierska writes—a more lively social conscience and a slackening of the immigrant stream have largely put a stop to it—in no European country, it seems, were the very poor treated with such contempt. In Europe the rich man and the poor man were thought of as being two different kinds of men; the poor man might be an inferior kind but he was a man: but here the poor man was not, as such, a man, but a person in a state of poverty from which, if he were a real man, he would presently extricate himself. The newly arriving poor, to judge from Miss Yezierska's description of the sweatshop, were treated by their predecessors, it seems, like freshmen by upperclassmen, i.e., subjected to a process of "hazing" so as to toughen their character and stiffen their determination to rise to a position of immunity.

For the older generation particularly, who, in any case, had usually immigrated for the sake of their children, not of themselves, the new life often seemed only a little better materially, and spiritually very much worse. The fellowship of suffering lasts only so long as none of the sufferers can escape. Open a door through which many but probably not all can escape one at a time and the neighborly community may disintegrate, all too easily, into a stampeding crowd. Those who had learned how to be happy even in prison and could neither understand nor desire another life stood abandoned, watching the stampede with bewilderment and horror.

Some, like Boruch Shlomoi Mayer, simply wanted to go back:

> To me, America is a worse *Goluth* than Poland. The ukases and pogroms from the Czar, all the killings that could not kill us gave us the strength to live with God. Learning was learning—dearer than gold. . . . But here in New York, the synagogues are in the hands of godless lumps of flesh. A butcher, a grocer, any moneymaker could buy himself into a president of a synagogue. With all that was bad under the Czar, the synagogue was still God's light in time of darkness. Better to die there than to live here. . . .

Others continued to live their old life with uncompromising indifference to the new world. Miss Yezierska's father, for instance, had a vocation, the study of the Torah, which involved his being supported by his wife and children. He had expected them to do so in Plinsk, he expected them to continue doing so in New York. But what they had accepted in Poland as an extra burden, worth bearing for the honor in which a learned and holy man was held by the community, was bound to seem intolerable in America, where not only was a nonearner regarded as an idler but also the possibility for the family of acquiring status existed in proportion to their earning capacity.

His daughter, however, as she later realized, was more like him than either of them at the time could perceive. Had she been less like him, had she simply desired money and a good marriage, there would have been less friction between them but she, too, was seeking for a dedicated life of her own, which in his eyes was impious, for all vocations but one were for men only.

"A woman alone, not a wife and not a mother, has no existence." She, however, wanted a vocation all to herself and thought she had found it in writing. She began, as she tells us, with the hope that "by writing out what I don't know and can't understand, it would stop hurting me." At the same time, of course, she wanted money to satisfy her needs. This is any artist's eternal problem, that he needs money as a man but works for love. Even in the case of the most popular writer, money is not the purpose for which he writes, though popularity may be.

So she begins; she writes a book, *Hungry Hearts*, about the life of a poor immigrant, which is well reviewed but does not sell; then, suddenly, the American Fairy—whether she is a good or wicked fairy, who knows?—waves her hand and she is transported in an instant from Hester Street to Hollywood; from one day to the next, that is, suffering is abolished for her. How does she feel? More unhappy than she has ever been in her life. To have the desires of the poor and be transferred in a twinkling of an eye to a world which can only be real for those who have the desires of the rich is to be plunged into the severest anxiety. The foreshortening of time which is proper to a dream or a fairy story is a nightmare in actual life.

Further, to be called to Hollywood is not like winning a fortune in the Calcutta sweepstakes; money is showered upon one because it is believed that one is a valuable piece of property out of which much larger sums can be made. For a writer this is only bearable if he knows exactly what he wants to write and if what he can write happens to pay off the investors as they expect. Miss Yezierska was too young to be the former and, by snatching her away from Hester Street and the only experiences about which she knew, the film magnates effectively destroyed the possibility that their expensive goose might lay another golden egg. In fact, they gave it such a fright that it stopped laying altogether.

The sudden paralysis or drying up of the creative power

occurs to artists everywhere but nowhere, perhaps, more frequently than in America; nowhere else are there so many writers who produced one or two books in their youth and then nothing. I think one reason for this may be the dominance of the competitive spirit in the American ethos. A material good like a washing machine is not a unique good but one example of a kind of good; accordingly one washing machine can be compared with another and judged better or worse. The best, indeed the only, way to stimulate the production of better washing machines is by competition. But a work of art is not a good of a certain kind but a unique good so that, strictly speaking, no work of art is comparable to another. An inferior washing machine is preferable to no washing machine at all, but a work of art is either acceptable, whatever its faults, to the individual who encounters it or unacceptable, whatever its merits. The writer who allows himself to become infected by the competitive spirit proper to the production of material goods so that, instead of trying to write *his* book, he tries to write one which is better than somebody else's book is in danger of trying to write the absolute masterpiece which will eliminate all competition once and for all and, since this task is totally unreal, his creative powers cannot relate to it, and the result is sterility.

In other and more static societies than in the United States an individual derives much of his sense of identity and value from his life-membership in a class—the particular class is not important—from which neither success nor failure, unless very spectacular, can oust him, but, in a society where any status is temporary and any variation in the individual's achievement alters it, his sense of his personal value must depend—unless he is a religious man—largely upon what he achieves: the more successful he is, the nearer he comes to the ideal good of absolute certainty as to his value; the less successful he is, the nearer he comes to the abyss of nonentity.

With the coming of the depression Miss Yezierska ceased to be a solitary failure and became one of millions who could not be called failures, because the positions in which they could succeed or fail no longer existed. It was surely the height of irony that, in a country where the proof of one's importance had been that one was rich and popular, people should suddenly, in order to prove that they were important enough to eat, have to go to elaborate lengths to establish that they were penniless and friendless.

The Arts Project of the W.P.A. was, perhaps, one of the noblest and most absurd undertakings ever attempted by any state. Noble because no other state has ever cared whether its artists as a group lived or died; other governments have hired certain individual artists to glorify their operations and have even granted a small pension from time to time to some artist with fame or influence, but to consider, in a time of general distress, starving artists as artists and not simply as paupers is unique to the Roosevelt administration. Yet absurd, because a state can only function bureaucratically and impersonally—it has to assume that every member of a class is equivalent or comparable to every other member—but every artist, good or bad, is a member of a class of one. You can collect fifty unemployed plumbers, test them to eliminate the unemployable, and set the remainder to work on whatever plumbing jobs you can find, but if you collect fifty unemployed writers, ex-professors, New England spinsters, radicals, Bohemians, etc., there is no test of their abilities which applies fairly to them all and no literary task you can devise which can be properly done by even a minority of them. While only the laziest and most inefficient of your plumbers will let you down, because the jobs you give them are the jobs for which they have been trained and regard as theirs, only the writers with the strictest sense of moral, as distinct from professional, duty will fail to cheat you if, as must almost inevitably be the case, the literary job you offer them is one in which they take no interest, not because writers are intrinsically lazier or more dishonest than plumbers, but because they can see no sense in what you are asking them to do.

It is easy for the accountant to frown on the W.P.A. for its inefficiency and for the artists to sneer at it for its bureaucracy, but the fact remains that, thanks to it, a number of young artists of talent were enabled, at a very critical time in their lives, to get started upon their creative careers. As for the rest, the executive might just as well have been honest—and I dare say would have been glad to—given them their weekly checks and sent them home, but the legislature which could endure such honesty could exist only in heaven.

Among her companions in poverty and comedy, Miss Yezierska felt once more to some degree that happiness of "belonging" which years before she had felt in Hester Street, though only she realized this after it was over. But belonging to some degree is not enough; one must belong completely or the feeling soon withers. Once again the lack of a common memory of the past and a common anticipation of the future was a fatal barrier, not only for her but for most of her fellows.

> The word "home" raised a smile in us all three,
> And one repeated it, smiling just so
> That all knew what he meant and none would say,
> Between three counties far apart that lay
> We were divided and looked strangely each
> At the other, and we knew we were not friends
> But fellows in a union that ends
> With the necessity for it, as it ought.
>
> (EDWARD THOMAS.)

No, the accidental community of suffering was not the clue to happiness and she had to look further.

Miss Yezierska's autobiography is, literally, the story of an early twentieth-century immigrant, but it has a deeper and more general significance today when, figuratively, the immigrant is coming more and more to stand as the symbol for Everyman, as the natural and unconscious community of tradition rapidly disappears from the earth.

POSTSCRIPT: THE ALMIGHTY DOLLAR

Political and technological developments are rapidly obliterating all cultural differences and it is possible that, in a not remote future, it will be impossible to distinguish human beings living on one area of the earth's surface from those living on any other, but our different pasts have not yet been completely erased and cultural differences are still perceptible. The most striking difference between an American and a European is the difference in their attitudes towards money. Every European knows, as a matter of historical fact, that, in Europe, wealth could only be acquired at the expense of other human beings, either by conquering them or by exploiting their labor in factories. Further, even after the Industrial Revolution began, the number of persons who could rise from poverty to wealth was small; the vast majority took it for granted that they would not be much richer nor poorer than their fathers. In consequence, no European associates wealth with personal merit or poverty with personal failure.

To a European, money means power, the freedom to do as he likes, which also means that, consciously or unconsciously, he says: "I want to have as much money as possible myself and others to have as little money as possible."

In the United States, wealth was also acquired by stealing, but the real exploited victim was not a human being but poor Mother Earth and her creatures who were ruthlessly plundered. It is true that the Indians were expropriated or exterminated, but this was not, as it had always been in Europe, a matter of the conqueror seizing the wealth of the conquered, for the Indian had never realized the potential riches of his country. It is also true that, in the Southern states, men lived on the labor of slaves, but slave labor did not make them fortunes; what made slavery in the South all the more inexcusable was that, in addition to being morally wicked, it didn't even pay off handsomely.

Thanks to the natural resources of the country, every American, until quite recently, could reasonably look forward to making more money than his father, so that, if he made less, the fault must be his; he was either lazy or inefficient. What an American values, therefore, is not the possession of money as such, but his power to make it as a proof of his manhood; once he has proved himself by making it, it has served its function and can be lost or given away. In no society in history have rich men given away so large a part of their fortunes. A poor American feels guilty at being poor, but less guilty than an American *rentier* who has inherited wealth but is doing nothing to increase it; what can the latter do but take to drink and psychoanalysis?

In the Fifth Circle on the Mount of Purgatory, I do not think that many Americans will be found among the Avaricious; but I suspect that the Prodigals may be almost an American colony. The great vice of Americans is not materialism but a lack of respect for matter.

ROBERT FROST

But Islands of the Blessed, bless you son,
I never came upon a blessed one.

If asked who said *Beauty is Truth, Truth Beauty!*, a great many readers would answer "Keats." But Keats said nothing of the sort. It is what he said the Grecian Urn said, his description and criticism of a certain kind of work of art, the kind from which the evils and problems of this life, the "heart high sorrowful and cloyed," are deliberately excluded. The Urn, for example, depicts, among other beautiful sights, the citadel of a hill town; it does not depict warfare, the evil which makes the citadel necessary.

Art arises out of our desire for both beauty and truth and our knowledge that they are not identical. One might say that every poem shows some sign of a rivalry between Ariel and Prospero; in every good poem their relation is more or less happy, but it is never without its tensions. The Grecian Urn states Ariel's position; Prospero's has been equally succinctly stated by Dr. Johnson: *The only end of writing is to enable the readers better to enjoy life or better to endure it.*

We want a poem to be beautiful, that is to say, a verbal earthly paradise, a timeless world of pure play, which gives us delight precisely because of its contrast to our historical existence with all its insoluble problems and inescapable suffering; at the same time we want a poem to be true, that is to say, to provide us with some kind of revelation about our life which will show us what life is really like and free us from self-enchantment and deception, and a poet cannot bring us any truth without introducing into his poetry the problematic, the painful, the disorderly, the ugly. Though every poem involves *some* degree of collaboration between Ariel and Prospero, the role of each varies in importance from one poem to another: it is usually possible to say of a poem and, sometimes, of the whole output of a poet, that it is Ariel-dominated or Prospero-dominated.

> Hot sun, cool fire, tempered with sweet air,
> Black shade, fair nurse, shadow my white hair:
> Shine, sun; burn, fire; breathe, air, and ease me;
> Black shade, fair nurse, shroud me and please me:
> Shadow, my sweet nurse, keep me from burning,
> Make not my glad cause, cause for mourning,
> Let not my beauty's fire
> Inflame unstaid desire,
> Nor pierce any bright eye
> That wandereth lightly.
>
> (GEORGE PEELE, "Bathsabe's Song.")

> The road at the top of the rise
> Seems to come to an end
> And take off into the skies.
> So at a distant bend

It seems to go into a wood,
The place of standing still
As long as the trees have stood.
But say what Fancy will,

The mineral drops that explode
To drive my ton of car
Are limited to the road.
They deal with the near and far,

And have almost nothing to do
With the absolute flight and rest
The universal blue
And local green suggest.
(ROBERT FROST,
"The Middleness of the Road.")

Both poems are written in the first person singular, but the Peele-Bathsabe *I* is very different from the Frost *I*. The first seems anonymous, hardly more than a grammatical form; one cannot imagine meeting Bathsabe at a dinner party. The second *I* names a historical individual in a specific situation —he is driving an automobile in a certain kind of landscape.

Take away what Bathsabe says and she vanishes, for what she says does not seem to be a response to any situation or event. If one asks what her song is about, one cannot give a specific answer, only a vague one:—a beautiful young girl, any beautiful girl, on any sunny morning, half-awake and half-asleep, is reflecting on her beauty with a mixture of self-admiration and pleasing fear, pleasing because she is unaware of any real danger; a girl who was really afraid of a Peeping Tom would sing very differently. If one tries to explain why one likes the song, or any poem of this kind, one finds oneself talking about language, the handling of the rhythm, the pattern of vowels and consonants, the placing of caesuras, epanorthosis, etc.

Frost's poem, on the other hand, is clearly a response to an experience which preceded any words and without which the poem could not have come into being, for the purpose of the poem is to define that experience and draw wisdom from it. Though the beautiful verbal element is not absent—it is a poem, not a passage of informative prose—this is subordinate in importance to the truth of what it says.

If someone suddenly asks me to give him an example of good poetry, it is probably a poem of the Peele sort which will immediately come to my mind: but if I am in a state of emotional excitement, be it joy or grief, and try to think of a poem which is relevant and illuminating to my condition, it is a poem of the Frost sort which I shall be most likely to recall.

Ariel, as Shakespeare has told us, has no passions. That is his glory and his limitation. The earthly paradise is a beautiful place but nothing of serious importance can occur in it.

An anthology selected by Ariel, including only poems like the *Eclogues* of Vergil, *Las Soledades* of Góngora and poets like Campion, Herrick, Mallarmé, would, in the long run, repel us by its narrowness and monotony of feeling: for Ariel's other name is Narcissus.

It can happen that a poem which, when written, was Prospero-dominated, becomes an Ariel poem for later generations. The nursery rhyme *I will sing you One O* may very well originally have been a mnemonic rhyme for teaching sacred lore of the highest importance. The sign that, for us, it has become an Ariel poem is that we have no curiosity about the various persons it refers to: it is as anthropologists not as readers of poetry that we ask who the lily-white boys really were. On the other hand, anything we can learn about the persons whom Dante introduces into *The Divine Comedy,* contributes to our appreciation of his poem.

It is also possible for a poet himself to be mistaken as to the kind of poem he is writing. For example, at first reading, *Lycidas* seems to be by Prospero, for it purports to deal with the most serious matters possible—death, grief, sin, resurrection. But I believe this to be an illusion. On closer inspection, it seems to me that only the robes are Prospero's and that Ariel has dressed up in them for fun, so that it is as irrelevant to ask, "Who is the Pilot of the Galilean Lake?" as it is to ask, "Who is the Pobble who has no toes?" and He who walks the waves is merely an Arcadian shepherd whose name happens to be Christ. If *Lycidas* is read in this way, as if it were a poem by Edward Lear, then it seems to me one of the most beautiful poems in the English language: if, however, it is read as the Prospero poem it apparently claims to be, then it must be condemned, as Dr. Johnson condemned it, for being unfeeling and frivolous, since one expects wisdom and revelation and it provides neither.

The Ariel-dominated poet has one great advantage; he can only fail in one way—his poem may be trivial. The worst one can say of one of his poems is that it needn't have been written. But the Prospero-dominated poet can fail in a number of different ways. Of all English poets, Wordsworth is perhaps the one with the least element of Ariel that is compatible with being a poet at all, and so provides the best examples of what happens when Prospero tries to write entirely by himself.

> The Bird and Cage they both were his:
> 'Twas my Son's bird: and neat and trim
> He kept it; many voyages
> This singing bird has gone with him:
> When last he sailed he left the bird behind;
> As it might be, perhaps from bodings in his mind.

Reading such a passage, one exclaims, "The man can't write," which is something that can never be said about Ariel; when Ariel can't write, he doesn't. But Prospero is capable of graver errors than just being ridiculous; since he is trying to say something which is true, if he fails, the result can be worse than trivial. It can be false, compelling the reader to say, not "This poem need not have been written," but "This poem should not have been written."

Both in theory and practice Frost is a Prospero-dominated poet. In the preface to his *Collected Poems,* he writes:

> The sound is the gold in the ore. Then we will have the sound out alone and dispense with the inessential. We do till we make the discovery that the object in writing poetry is to make all poems sound as different

> as possible from each other, and the resources for that of vowels, consonants, punctuation, syntax, words, sentences, meter are not enough. We need the help of context—meaning—subject matter. . . . And we are back in poetry as merely one more art of having something to say, sound or unsound. Probably better if sound, because deeper and from wider experience. [A poem] begins in delight and ends in wisdom . . . a clarification of life—not necessarily a great clarification such as sects and cults are founded on, but in a momentary stay against confusion.

His poetic style is what I think Professor C. S. Lewis would call Good Drab. The music is always that of the speaking voice, quiet and sensible, and I cannot think of any other modern poet, except Cavafy, who uses language more simply. He rarely employs metaphors, and there is not a word, not a historical or literary reference in the whole of his work which would be strange to an unbookish boy of fifteen. Yet he manages to make this simple kind of speech express a wide variety of emotion and experience.

> Be that as may be, she was in their song.
> Moreover her voice upon their voices crossed
> Had now persisted in the woods so long
> That probably it would never be lost.
> Never again would bird's song be the same.
> And to do that to birds was why she came.

. . . . .

> I hope if he is where he sees me now
> He's so far off he can't see what I've come to.
> You *can* come down from everything to nothing.
> All is, if I'd a-known when I was young
> And full of it, that this would be the end,
> It doesn't seem as if I'd had the courage
> To make so free and kick up in folk's faces.
> I might have, but it doesn't seem as if.

The emotions in the first passage are tender, happy, and its reflections of a kind which could only be made by an educated man. The emotions in the second are violent and tragic, and the speaker a woman with no schooling. Yet the diction in both is equally simple. There are a few words the man uses which the woman would not use herself, but none she could not understand; her syntax is a little cruder than his, but only a little. Yet their two voices sound as distinct as they sound authentic.

Frost's poetic speech is the speech of a mature mind, fully awake and in control of itself; it is not the speech of dream or of uncontrollable passion. Except in reported speech, interjections, imperatives and rhetorical interrogatives are rare. This does not mean, of course, that his poems are lacking in feeling; again and again, one is aware of strong, even violent, emotion behind what is actually said, but the saying is reticent, the poetry has, as it were, an auditory chastity. It would be impossible for Frost, even if he wished, to produce an unabashed roar of despair, as Shakespeare's tragic heroes so often can, but the man who wrote the following lines has certainly been acquainted with despair.

> I have stood still and stopped the sound of feet
> When far away an interrupted cry
> Came over houses from another street,
> But not to call me back or say good-bye.
> And further still at an unearthly height
> One luminary clock against the sky
> Proclaimed the time was neither wrong nor right.
> I have been one acquainted with the night.

Every style has its limitations. It would be as impossible to write "Ébauche d'un Serpent" in the style of Frost as it would be to write "The Death of the Hired Man" in the style of Valéry. A style, like Frost's which approximates to ordinary speech is necessarily contemporary, the style of a man living in the first half of the twentieth century; it is not well suited, therefore, to subjects from the distant past, in which the difference between then and today is significant, or to mythical subjects which are timeless.

Neither Frost's version of the Job story in *A Masque of Reason* nor his version of the Jonah story in *A Masque of Mercy* seems to me quite to come off; both are a little self-consciously in modern dress.

Nor is such a style well-suited to official public occasions when a poet must speak about and on behalf of the *Civitas Terrenae*. Frost's tone of voice, even in his dramatic pieces, is that of a man talking to himself, thinking aloud and hardly aware of an audience. This manner is, of course, like all manners, calculated, and more sophisticated than most. The calculation is sound when the poems are concerned with personal emotions, but when the subject is one of public affairs or ideas of general interest, it may be a miscalculation. "Build Soil, a Political Pastoral" which Frost composed for the National Party Convention at Columbia University in 1932, was much criticized at the time by the Liberal-Left for being reactionary. Reading it today, one wonders what all their fuss was about, but the fireside-chat I'm-a-plain-fellow manner is still irritating. One finds oneself wishing that Columbia had invited Yeats instead; he might have said the most outrageous things, but he would have put on a good act, and that is what we want from a poet when he speaks to us of what concerns us, not as private persons but as citizens. Perhaps Frost himself felt uneasy, for the last two lines of the poem, and the best, run thus:

> We're too unseparate. And going home
> From company means coming to our senses.

Any poetry which aims at being a clarification of life must be concerned with two questions about which all men, whether they read poetry or not, seek clarification.

1) *Who am I?* What is the difference between man and all other creatures? What relations are possible between them? What is man's status in the universe? What are the conditions of his existence which he must accept as his fate which no wishing can alter?

2) *Whom ought I to become?* What are the characteristics of the hero, the authentic man whom everybody should admire and try to become? Vice versa, what are the characteristics of the churl, the unauthentic man whom everybody should try to avoid becoming?

We all seek answers to these questions which shall be universally valid under all circumstances, but the experiences to which we put them are always local both in time and place. What any poet has to say about man's status in nature, for example, depends in part upon the landscape and climate he happens to live in and in part upon the reactions to it of his personal temperament. A poet brought up in the tropics cannot have the same vision as a poet brought up in Hertfordshire and, if they inhabit the same landscape, the chirpy social endomorph will give a different picture of it from that of the melancholic withdrawn ectomorph.

The nature in Frost's poetry is the nature of New England. New England is made of granite, is mountainous, densely wooded, and its soil is poor. It has a long severe winter, a summer that is milder and more pleasant than in most parts of the States, a short and sudden Spring, a slow and theatrically beautiful fall. Since it adjoins the eastern seaboard, it was one of the first areas to be settled but, as soon as the more fertile lands to the West were opened up, it began to lose population. Tourists and city dwellers who can afford a summer home may arrive for the summer, but much land which was once cultivated has gone back to the wild.

One of Frost's favorite images is the image of the abandoned house. In Britain or Europe, a ruin recalls either historical change, political acts like war or enclosure, or, in the case of abandoned mine buildings, a successful past which came to an end, not because nature was too strong, but because she had been robbed of everything she possessed. A ruin in Europe, therefore, tends to arouse reflections about human injustice and greed and the nemesis that overtakes human pride. But in Frost's poetry, a ruin is an image of human heroism, of a defense in the narrow pass against hopeless odds.

I came an errand one cloud-blowing morning
To a slab-built, black-paper-covered house
Of one room and one window and one door,
The only dwelling in a waste cut over
A hundred square miles round it in the mountains:
And that not dwelt in now by men or women.
(It never had been dwelt in, though, by women.)

. . . . .

Here further up the mountain slope
Than there was ever any hope,
My father built, enclosed a spring,
Strung chains of wall round everything,
Subdued the growth of earth to grass,
And brought our various lives to pass.
A dozen girls and boys we were.
The mountain seemed to like the stir
And made of us a little while—
With always something in her smile.
To-day she wouldn't know our name.
(No girl's of course has stayed the same.)
The mountain pushed us off her knees.
And now her lap is full of trees.

Thumbing through Frost's *Collected Poems,* I find twenty-one in which the season is winter as compared with five in which it is spring, and in two of these there is still snow on the ground; I find twenty-seven in which the time is night and seventeen in which the weather is stormy.

The commonest human situation in his poetry is of one man, or a man and wife, alone in a small isolated house in a snowbound forest after dark.

Where I could think of no thoroughfare,
Away on the mountain up far too high,
A blinding headlight shifted glare
And began to bounce down a granite stair
Like a star fresh-fallen out of the sky,

And I away in my opposite wood
Am touched by that unintimate light
And made feel less alone than I rightly should,
For traveler there could do me no good
Were I in trouble with night tonight.

. . . . .

We looked and looked, but after all where are we?
Do we know any better where we are,
And how it stands between the night tonight
And a man with a smokey lantern chimney,
How different from the way it ever stood?

In "Two Look at Two," nature, as represented by a buck stag and a doe, responds in sympathy to man, as represented by a boy and girl, but the point of the poem is that this sympathetic response is a miraculous exception. The normal response is that described in "The Most of It."

Some morning from the boulder-broken beach
He would cry out on life that what it wants
Is not its own love back in copy speech,
But counter-love, original response.
And nothing ever came of what he cried
Unless it was the embodiment that crashed
In the cliff's talus on the other side,
And then in the far distant water splashed,
But after a time allowed for it to swim,
Instead of proving human when it neared
And some one else additional to him,
As a great buck it powerfully appeared . . .

Nature, however, is not to Frost, as she was to Melville, malignant.

It must be a little more in favor of man,
Say a fraction of one per cent at least,
Or our number living wouldn't be steadily more.

She is, rather, the Dura Virum Nutrix who, by her apparent indifference and hostility, even, calls forth all man's powers and courage and makes a real man of him.

Courage is not to be confused with romantic daring. It includes caution and cunning,

> All we who prefer to live
> Have a little whistle we give,
> And flash at the least alarm
> We dive down under the farm

and even financial prudence,

> Better to do down dignified
> With boughten friendship at your side
> Then none at all. Provide, provide!

There have been European poets who have come to similar conclusions about the isolation of the human condition, and nature's indifference to human values, but, compared with an American, they are at a disadvantage in expressing them. Living as they do in a well, even overpopulated, countryside where, thanks to centuries of cultivation, Mother Earth has acquired human features, they are forced to make abstract philosophical statements or use uncommon atypical images, so that what they say seems to be imposed upon them by theory and temperament rather than by facts. An American poet like Frost, on the other hand, can appeal to facts for which any theory must account and which any temperament must admit.

The Frostian man is isolated not only in space but also in time. In Frost's poems the nostalgic note is seldom, if ever, struck. When he writes a poem about childhood like "Wild Grapes," childhood is not seen as a magical Eden which will all too soon, alas, be lost, but as a school in which the first lessons of adult life are learned. The setting of one of his best long poems, "The Generations of Man," is the ancestral home of the Stark family in the town of Bow, New Hampshire. Bow is a rock-strewn township where farming has fallen off and sproutlands flourish since the axe has gone. The Stark family mansion is by now reduced to an old cellar-hole at the side of a by-road. The occasion described in the poem is a gathering together from all over of the Stark descendants, an advertising stunt thought up by the governor of the state. The characters are a boy Stark and a girl Stark, distant cousins, who meet at the cellar-hole and are immediately attracted to each other. Their conversation turns, naturally, to their common ancestors, but, in fact, they know nothing about them. The boy starts inventing stories and doing imaginary imitations of their voices as a way of courtship, making their ancestors hint at marriage and suggest building a new summer home on the site of the old house. The real past, that is to say, is unknown and unreal to them; its role in the poem is to provide a lucky chance for the living to meet.

Like Gray, Frost has written a poem on a deserted graveyard. Gray is concerned with the possible lives of the unknown dead; the past is more imaginatively exciting to him than the present. But Frost does not try to remember anything; what moves him is that death, which is always a present terror, is no longer present here, having moved on like a pioneer.

> It would be easy to be clever
> And tell the stones; men hate to die
> And have stopped dying now for ever.
> I think they would believe the lie.

What he finds valuable in man's temporal existence is the ever-recurrent opportunity of the present moment to make a discovery or a new start.

> One of the lies would make it out that nothing
> Ever presents itself before us twice.
> Where would we be at last if that were so?
> Our very life depends on everything's
> Recurring till we answer from within.
> The thousandth time may prove the charm.

Frost has written a number of pastoral eclogues and, no doubt, has taken a sophisticated pleasure in using what is, by tradition, the most aristocratic and idyllic of all literary forms to depict democratic realities. If the landscape of New England is unarcadian, so is its social life; the leisured class with nothing to do but cultivate its sensibility which the European pastoral presupposes, is simply not there. Of course, as in all societies, social distinctions exist. In New England, Protestants of Anglo-Scotch stock consider themselves a cut above Roman Catholics and those of a Latin race, and the most respectable Protestant denominations are the Congregationalists and the Unitarians. Thus, in "The Ax-Helve," the Yankee farmer is aware of his social condescension in entering the house of his French-Canadian neighbor, Baptiste.

I shouldn't mind his being overjoyed
(If overjoyed he was) at having got me
Where I must judge if what he knew about an ax
That not everybody else knew was to count
For nothing in the measure of a neighbor.
Hard if, though cast away for life with Yankees,
A Frenchman couldn't get his human rating!

And in "Snow," Mrs. Cole passes judgment upon the Evangelical preacher, Meserve.

I detest the thought of him
With his ten children under ten years old.
I hate his wretched little Racker Sect,
All's ever I heard of it, which isn't much.

Yet in both poems the neighbor triumphs over the snob. The Yankee acknowledges Baptiste's superior skill, and the Coles stay up all night in concern until they hear that Meserve has reached home safely through the storm.

In the Frost pastoral, the place of the traditional worldly-wise, world-weary courtier is taken by the literary city dweller, often a college student who has taken a job for the summer on a farm; the rustics he encounters are neither comic bumpkins nor noble savages.

In "A Hundred Collars," a refined shy college professor meets in a small town hotel bedroom a fat whisky-drinking vulgarian who canvasses the farms around on behalf of a local newspaper. If, in the end, the reader's sympathies go to the vulgarian, the vulgarian is not made aesthetically appealing nor the professor unpleasant. The professor means well —he is a democrat, if not at heart, in principle—but he is the victim of a way of life which has narrowed his human sympathies and interests. The vulgarian is redeemed by his uninhibited friendliness which is perfectly genuine, not a professional salesman's manner. Though vulgar, he is not a go-getter.

> 'One would suppose they might not be as glad
> to see you as you are to see them.'
>   'Oh,
> Because I want their dollar? I don't want
> Anything they've got. I never dun.
> I'm there, and they can pay me if they like.
> I go nowhere on purpose: I happen by.'

In "The Code," a town-bred farmer unwittingly offends one of his hired hands.

> 'What is there wrong?'
>   'Something you just now said.'
> 'What did I say?'
>   'About our taking pains.'
> 'To cock the hay—because it's going to shower?
> I said that more than half an hour ago.
> I said it to myself as much as you.'
> 'You didn't know. But James is one big fool.
> He thought you meant to find fault with his work,
> That's what the average farmer would have meant.' . . .
> 'He's a fool if that's the way he takes me.'
> 'Don't let it bother you. You've found out something.
> The hand that knows his business won't be told
> To do work better or faster—those two things. . . .'

The ignorance of the town-bred farmer is made use of, not to blame him, but to praise the quality which, after courage,

Frost ranks as the highest of the virtues, the self-respect which comes from taking a pride in something. It may be a pride in one's own skill, the pride of the axe-maker Baptiste, the pride of the Hired Man who dies from a broken heart since old age has taken from him the one accomplishment, building a load of hay, which had hitherto prevented him from feeling utterly worthless, or it may be a pride which, from a worldly point of view, is a folly, the pride of the man who has failed as a farmer, burned his house down for the insurance money, bought a telescope with the proceeds and taken a lowly job as a ticket agent on the railroad. The telescope is not a good one, the man is poor, but he is proud of his telescope and happy.

Every poet is at once a representative of his culture and its critic. Frost has never written satires, but it is not hard to guess what, as an American, he approves and disapproves of in his own countrymen. The average American is a stoic and, contrary to what others are apt to conclude from his free-and-easy friendly manner, reticent, far more reticent than the average Englishman about showing his feelings. He believes in independence because he has to; life is too mobile and circumstances change too fast for him to be supported by any fixed frame of family or social relations. In a crisis he will help his neighbor, whoever he may be, but he will regard someone who is always coming for help as a bad neighbor, and he disapproves of all self-pity and nostalgic regret. All these qualities find their expression in Frost's poetry, but there are other American characteristics which are not to be found there, the absence of which implies disapproval; the belief, for instance, that it should be possible, once the right gimmick has been found, to build the New Jerusalem on earth in half an hour. One might describe Frost as a Tory, provided that one remembers that all American political parties are Whigs.

Hardy, Yeats and Frost have all written epitaphs for themselves.

Hardy

I never cared for life, life cared for me.
And hence I owe it some fidelity. . . .

Yeats

Cast a cold eye
On life and death.
Horseman, pass by.

Frost

I would have written of me on my stone
I had a lover's quarrel with the world.

Of the three, Frost, surely, comes off best. Hardy seems to be stating the Pessimist's Case rather than his real feelings. I never cared . . . *Never*? Now, Mr. Hardy, really! Yeats' horseman is a stage prop; the passer-by is much more likely to be a motorist. But Frost convinces me that he is telling neither more nor less than the truth about himself. And, when it comes to wisdom, is not having a lover's quarrel with life more worthy of Prospero than not caring or looking coldly?

AMERICAN POETRY

The land was ours before we were the land's.
She was our land more than a hundred years
Before we were her people. She was ours
In Massachusetts, in Virginia,
But we were England's, still colonials,
Possessing what we still were unpossessed by,
Possessed by what we now no more possessed.
Something we were withholding made us weak
Until we found out that it was ourselves
We were withholding from our land of living,
And forthwith found salvation in surrender.
Such as we were we gave ourselves outright
(The deed of gift was many deeds of war)
To the land vaguely realizing westward,
But still unstoried, artless, unenhanced,
Such as she was, such as she would become.

—ROBERT FROST

One often hears it said that only in this century have the writers of the United States learned to stand on their own feet and be truly American, that, previously, they were slavish imitators of British literature. Applied to the general reading public and academic circles, this has a certain amount of truth but, so far as the writers themselves are concerned, it is quite false. From Bryant on there is scarcely one American poet whose work, if unsigned, could be mistaken for that of an Englishman. What English poet, for example, in need of emotive place names for a serious poem, would have employed, neither local names nor names famous in history or mythology, but names made up by himself as Poe did in "Ulalume"? Would an English poet have received the idea of writing a scientific cosmological prose poem and of prefacing it thus: "I offer this Book of Truths, not in its character of Truth-teller, but for the Beauty that abounds in its Truth, constituting it true. . . . *What I here propound is true:* therefore it cannot die. . . . Nevertheless it is as a Poem only that I wish this work to be judged after I am dead." (Poe, Preface to "Eureka")?

Maud, The Song of Hiawatha and the first edition of *Leaves of Grass* all appeared in the same year, 1855: no two poets could be more unlike each other than Longfellow and Whitman—such diversity is in itself an American phenomenon—yet, when compared with Tennyson, each in his own way shows characteristics of the New World. Tennyson and Longfellow were both highly skillful technicians in conventional forms and both were regarded by their countrymen as the respectable mouthpieces of their age, and yet, how different they are. There is much in Tennyson that Longfellow would never have dared to write, for the peculiar American mixture of Puritan conscience and democratic license can foster in some cases a genteel horror of the coarse for which no Englishman has felt the need. On the other hand Longfellow had a curiosity about the whole of European literature compared with which Tennyson, concerned only with the poetry of his own land and the classical authors on whom he was educated, seems provincial. Even if there had been Red Indians roaming the North of Scotland, unsubjugated and unassimilable, one cannot imagine Tennyson sitting down to write a long poem about them and choosing for it a Finnish meter. Leaving aside all questions of style, there is a difference between Tennyson's

Ode on the Death of the Duke of Wellington and Whitman's elegy for President Lincoln *When lilacs last in the dooryard bloom'd* which is significant. Tennyson, as one would expect from the title of his poem, mourns for a great public official figure, but it would be very hard to guess from the words of Whitman's poem that the man he is talking of was the head of a State; one would naturally think that he was some close personal friend, a private individual.

To take one more example—two poets, contemporaries, both women, both religious, both introverts preoccupied with renunciation—Christina Rossetti and Emily Dickinson; could anyone imagine either of them in the country of the other? When I try to fancy such translations, the only Americans I can possibly imagine as British are minor poets with a turn for light verse like Lowell and Holmes; and the only British poets who could conceivably have been American are eccentrics like Blake and Hopkins.

Normally, in comparing the poetry of two cultures, the obvious and easiest point at which to start is with a comparison of the peculiar characteristics, grammatical, rhetorical, rhythmical, of their respective languages, for even the most formal and elevated styles of poetry are more conditioned by the spoken tongue, the language really used by the men of that country, than by anything else. In the case of British and American poetry, however, this is the most subtle difference of all and the hardest to define. Any Englishman, with a little effort, can learn to pronounce "the letter *a* in psalm and calm. . . . with the sound of *a* in candle," to say *thumb-tacks* instead of *drawing-pins* or twenty-minutes-*of*-one instead of twenty-minutes-*to*-one, and discover that, in the Middle West, *bought* rhymes with *hot*, but he will still be as far from speaking American English as his Yankee cousin who comes to England will be from speaking the Queen's. No dramatist in either country who has introduced a character from the other side, has, to my knowledge, been able to make his speech convincing. What the secret of the difference is, I cannot put my finger on; William Carlos Williams, who has thought more than most about this problem, says that "Pace is one of its most important manifestations" and to this one might add another, Pitch. If undefinable, the difference is, however, immediately recognizable by the ear, even in verse where the formal conventions are the same.

> He must have had a father and a mother—
> In fact I've heard him say so—and a dog,
> As a boy should, I venture; and the dog,
> Most likely, was the only man who knew him.
> A dog, for all I know, is what he needs
> As much as anything right here today,
> To counsel him about his disillusions,
> Old aches, and parturitions of what's coming—
> A dog of orders, an emeritus,
> To wag his tail at him when he comes home,
> And then to put his paws up on his knees
> And say, 'For God's sake, what's it all about?'
> (E. A. ROBINSON, "Ben Jonson Entertains
> a Man from Stratford.")

Whatever this may owe to Browning, the fingering is quite different and un-British. Again, how American in rhythm as well as in sensibility is this stanza by Robert Frost:

> But no, I was out for stars:
> I would not come in.
> I meant not even if asked,
> And I hadn't been.
> ("Come In.")

Until quite recently an English writer, like one of any European country, could presuppose two conditions, a nature which was mythologized, humanized, on the whole friendly, and a human society which had become in time, whatever succession of invasions it may have suffered in the past, in race and religion more or less homogeneous and in which most people lived and died in the locality where they were born.

Christianity might have deprived Aphrodite, Apollo, the local genius, of their divinity but as figures for the forces of nature, as a mode of thinking about the creation, they remained valid for poets and their readers alike. Descartes might reduce the nonhuman universe to a mechanism but the feelings of Europeans about the sun and moon, the cycle of the seasons, the local landscape remained unchanged. Wordsworth might discard the mythological terminology but the kind of relation between nature and man which he described was the same personal one. Even when nineteenth-century biology began to trouble men's minds with the thought that the universe might be without moral values, their immediate experience was still of a friendly and lovable nature. Whatever their doubts and convictions about the purpose and significance of the universe as a whole, Tennyson's Lincolnshire or Hardy's Dorset were places where they felt completely at home, landscapes with faces of their own which a human being could recognize and trust.

But in America, neither the size nor the condition nor the climate of the continent encourages such intimacy. It is an unforgettable experience for anyone born on the other side of the Atlantic to take a plane journey by night across the United States. Looking down he will see the lights of some town like a last outpost in a darkness stretching for hours ahead, and realize that, even if there is no longer an actual frontier, this is still a continent only partially settled and developed, where human activity seems a tiny thing in comparison to the magnitude of the earth, and the equality of men not some dogma of politics or jurisprudence but a self-evident fact. He will behold a wild nature, compared with which the landscapes of Salvator Rosa are as cosy as Arcadia and which cannot possibly be thought of in human or personal terms. If Henry Adams could write:

> When Adams was a boy in Boston, the best chemist in the place had probably never heard of Venus except by way of scandal, or of the Virgin except as idolatry. . . . The force of the Virgin was still felt at Lourdes, and

> seemed to be as potent as X-rays; but in America neither Venus nor Virgin ever had value as force—at most as sentiment. No American had ever been truly afraid of either

the reason for this was not simply that the *Mayflower* carried iconophobic dissenters but also that the nature which Americans, even in New England, had every reason to fear could not possibly be imagined as a mother. A white whale whom man can neither understand nor be understood by, whom only a madman like Gabriel can worship, the only relationship with whom is a combat to the death by which a man's courage and skill are tested and judged, or the great buck who answers the poet's prayer for "someone else additional to him" in "The Most of It" are more apt symbols. Thoreau, who certainly tried his best to become intimate with nature, had to confess

> I walk in nature still alone
> And know no one,
> Discern no lineament nor feature
> Of any creature.
> Though all the firmament
> Is o'er me bent,
> Yet still I miss the grace
> Of an intelligent and kindred face.
> I still must seek the friend
> Who does with nature blend,
> Who is the person in her mask,
> He is the man I ask. . . .

Many poets in the Old World have become disgusted with human civilization but what the earth would be like if the race became extinct they cannot imagine; an American like Robinson Jeffers can quite easily, for he has seen with his own eyes country as yet untouched by history.

In a land which is fully settled, most men must accept their local environment or try to change it by political means; only the exceptionally gifted or adventurous can leave to seek his fortune elsewhere. In America, on the other hand, to move on and make a fresh start somewhere else is still the normal reaction to dissatisfaction or failure. Such social fluidity has important psychological effects. Since movement involves breaking social and personal ties, the habit creates an attitude towards personal relationships in which impermanence is taken for granted.

One could find no better illustration of the difference between the Old and the New World than the respective conclusions of *Oliver Twist* and *Huckleberry Finn,* both the heroes of which are orphans. When Oliver is at last adopted by Mr. Brownlow, his fondest dream, to have a home, to be surrounded by familiar friendly faces, to receive an education, is realized. Huck is offered adoption too, significantly by a woman not a man, but refuses because he knows she would try to "civilize" him, and announces his intention to light out by himself for the West; Jim, who has been his "buddy" in a friendship far closer than any enjoyed by Oliver, is left behind like an old shoe, just as in *Moby Dick* Ishmael becomes a blood-brother of Queequeg and then forgets all about him. Naturally the daydream of the lifelong comrade in adventure often appears in American literature:

> Camerado, I give you my hand!
> I give you my love more precious than money,
> I give you myself before preaching or law;
> Will you give me yourself? will you come travel with me?
> Shall we stick by each other as long as we live?
> (WHITMAN, "Song of the Open Road.")

but no American seriously expects such a dream to come true.

To be able at any time to break with the past, to move and keep on moving lessens the significance not only of the past but also of the future which is reduced to the immediate future, and minimizes the importance of political action. A European may be a conservative who thinks that the right form of society has been discovered already, or a liberal who believes it is in process of being realized, or a revolutionary who thinks that after long dark ages it can now be realized for the first time, but each of them knows that, by reason or force, he must convince the others that he is right; he may be an optimist about the future or a pessimist. None of these terms applies accurately to an American, for his profoundest feeling towards the future is not that it will be better or worse but that it is unpredictable, that all things, good and bad, will change. No failure is irredeemable, no success a final satisfaction. Democracy is the best form of government, not because men will necessarily lead better or happier lives under it, but because it permits constant experiment; a given experiment may fail but the people have a right to make their own mistakes. America has always been a country of amateurs where the professional, that is to say, the man who claims authority as a member of an elite which knows the law in some field or other, is an object of distrust and resentment.

Amerika, du hast es besser
Als unser Kontinent, der alte,
Hast keine verfallenen Schloesser
Und keine Basalte

wrote Goethe, by *keine Basalte* meaning, I presume, no violent political revolutions. This is a subject about which, in relation to their own histories, the English and the Americans cherish opposite fictions. Between 1533 and 1688 the English went through a succession of revolutions in which a Church was imposed on them by the engines of the State, one king was executed and another deposed, yet they prefer to forget it and pretend that the social structure of England is the product of organic peaceful growth. The Americans, on the other hand, like to pretend that what was only a successful war of secession was a genuine revolution.

If we apply the term revolution to what happened in North America between 1776 and 1829, it has a special meaning.

Normally, the word describes the process by which man transforms himself from one kind of man, living in one kind of society, with one way of looking at the world, into another kind of man, another society, another conception of life. So it is with the Papal, the Lutheran, the English, and the French revolutions. The American case is different; it is not a question of the Old Man transforming himself into the New, but of the New Man becoming alive to the fact that he is new, that he has been transformed already without his having realized it.

The War of Independence was the first step, the leaving of the paternal roof in order to find out who one is; the second and more important step, the actual discovery, came with Jackson. It was then that it first became clear that, despite similarities of form, representative government in America was not to be an imitation of the English parliamentary system, and that, though the vocabulary of the Constitution may be that of the French Enlightenment, its American meaning is quite distinct. There is indeed an American mentality which is new and unique in the world but it is the product less of conscious political action than of nature, of the new and unique environment of the American continent. Even the most revolutionary feature of the Constitution, the separation of Church and State, was a recognition of a condition which had existed since the first settlements were made by various religious denominations whose control of the secular authority could only be local. From the beginning America had been a pluralist state and pluralism is incompatible with an Established Church. The *Basalte* in American history, the Civil War, might indeed be called Counterrevolution, for it was fought primarily on the issue not of slavery but of unity, that is, not for a freedom but for a limitation on freedom, to ensure that the United States should remain pluralist and not disintegrate into an anarchic heap of fragments. Pluralist and experimental: in place of *verfallenen Schloesser,* America has ghost towns and the relics of New Jerusalems which failed.

The American had not intended to become what he was; he had been made so by emigration and the nature of the American continent. An emigrant never knows what he wants, only what he does not want. A man who comes from a land settled for centuries to a virgin wilderness where he faces problems with which none of his traditions and habits was intended to deal cannot foresee the future but must improvise himself from day to day. It is not surprising, therefore, that the first clear realization of the novelty and importance of the United States should have come not from an American but from outsiders, like Crèvecœur and de Tocqueville.

In a society whose dominant task is still that of the pioneer —the physical struggle with nature, and a nature, moreover, particularly recalcitrant and violent—the intellectual is not a figure of much importance. Those with intellectual and artistic tastes, finding themselves a despised or at best an ignored minority, are apt in return to despise the society in which they live as vulgar and think nostalgically of more leisured and refined cultures. The situation of the first important American poets—Emerson, Thoreau, Poe—was therefore doubly difficult. As writers, and therefore intellectuals, they were without status with the majority; and, on the other hand, the cultured minority of which they were members looked to England for its literary standards and did not want to think or read about America.

This dependence on English literature was a hindrance to their development in a way which it would not have been had they lived elsewhere. A poet living in England, for instance, might read nothing but French poetry, or he might move to Italy and know only English, without raising any serious barrier between himself and his experiences. Indeed, in Europe, whenever some journalist raises the patriotic demand for an English or French or Dutch literature free from foreign influences, we know him at once to be a base fellow. The wish for an American literature, on the other hand, has nothing to do really, with politics or national conceit; it is a demand for honesty. All European literature so far has presupposed two things: a nature which is humanized, mythologized, usually friendly, and a human society in which most men stay where they were born and do not move about much. Neither of these presuppositions was valid for America, where nature was virgin, devoid of history, usually hostile; and society was fluid, its groupings always changing as men moved on somewhere else.

The European romantics may praise the charms of wild desert landscape, but they know that for them it is never more than a few hours' walk from a comfortable inn: they may celebrate the joys of solitude but they know that any time they choose they can go back to the family roof or to town and that there their cousins and nephews and nieces and aunts, the club and the salons, will still be going on exactly as they left them. Of real desert, of a loneliness which knows of no enduring relationships to cherish or reject, they have no conception.

The achievement of Emerson and Thoreau was twofold: they wrote of the American kind of nature, and they perceived what qualities were most needed by members of the American kind of society, which was threatened, not by the petrified injustice of any tradition, but by the fluid irresponsibility of crowd opinion. Their work has both the virtues and the vices of the isolated and the protestant: on the one hand it is always genuine and original, it is never superficial; on the other it is a little too cranky, too earnest, too scornful of elegance. Just as in their political thinking Americans are apt to identify the undemocratic with monarchy, so, in their aesthetics, they are apt to identify the falsely conventional with rhyme and meter. The prose of Emerson and Thoreau is superior to their verse, because verse in its formal nature protests against protesting; it demands that to some degree we accept things as they are, not for any rational or moral reason, but simply because they happen to be that way; it implies an element of frivority in the creation.

Whatever one may feel about Whitman's poetry, one is bound to admit that he was the first clearly to recognize what the conditions were with which any future American poet would have to come to terms.

> Plenty of songs had been sung—beautiful, matchless songs—adjusted to other lands than these. . . . the Old World has had the poems of myths, fictions, feudal-

> ism, conquest, caste, dynastic wars, and splendid exceptional characters, which have been great; but the New World needs the poems of realities and science and of the democratic average and basic equality. . . . As for native American individuality, the distinctive and ideal type of Western character (as consistent with the operative and even money-making features of United States humanity as chosen knights, gentlemen and warriors were the ideals of the centuries of European feudalism) it has not yet appeared. I have allowed the stress of my poems from beginning to end to bear upon American individuality and assist it—not only because that is a great lesson in Nature, amid all her generalizing laws, but as counterpoise to the levelling tendencies of Democracy.

The last sentence makes it quite clear that by the "average" hero who was to replace the "knight," Whitman did not mean the mediocre, but the individual whose "exceptional character" is not derived from birth, education or occupation, and that he is aware of how difficult it is for such an individual to appear without the encouragement which comes from membership in some elite.

What he does not say, and perhaps did not realize, is that, in a democracy, the status of the poet himself is changed. However fantastic, in the light of present-day realities, his notion may be, every European poet, I believe, still instinctively thinks of himself as a "clerk," a member of a professional brotherhood, with a certain social status irrespective of the number of his readers (in his heart of hearts the audience he desires and expects are those who govern the country), and as taking his place in an unbroken historical succession. In the States, poets have never had or imagined they had such a status, and it is up to each individual poet to justify his existence by offering a unique product. It would be grossly unjust to assert that there are fewer lovers of poetry in the New World than in the Old—in how many places in the latter could a poet demand and receive a substantial sum for reading his work aloud?—but there is a tendency, perhaps, in the former, for audiences to be drawn rather by a name than a poem, and for a poet, on his side, to demand approval for his work not simply because it is good but because it is *his*. To some degree every American poet feels that the whole responsibility for contemporary poetry has fallen upon his shoulders, that he is a literary aristocracy of one. "Tradition," wrote Mr. T. S. Eliot in a famous essay, "cannot be inherited, and if you want it you must obtain it by great labour." I do not think that any European critic would have said just this. He would not, of course, deny that every poet must work hard but the suggestion in the first half of the sentence that no sense of tradition is acquired except by conscious effort would seem strange to him.

There are advantages and disadvantages in both attitudes. A British poet can take writing more for granted and so write with a lack of strain and overearnestness. American poetry has many tones, but the tone of a man talking to a group of his peers is rare; for a "serious" poet to write light verse is frowned on in America and if, when he is asked why he writes poetry, he replies, as any European poet would, "For fun," his audience will be shocked. On the other hand, a British poet is in much greater danger of becoming lazy, or academic, or irresponsible. One comes across passages, even in very fine English poets, which make one think: "Yes, very effective but does he believe what he is saying?": in American poetry such passages are extremely rare. The first thing that strikes a reader about the best American poets is how utterly unlike each other they are. Where else in the world, for example, could one find seven poets of approximately the same generation so different as Ezra Pound, W. C. Williams, Vachel Lindsay, Marianne Moore, Wallace Stevens, E. E. Cummings and Laura Riding? The danger for the American poet is not of writing like everybody else but of crankiness and a parody of his own manner.

Plato, following Damon of Athens, said that when the modes of music change, the walls of the city are shaken. It might be truer to say, perhaps, that a change in the modes gives warning of a shaking of the walls in the near future.

The social strains which later break out in political action are first experienced by artists as a feeling that the current modes of expression are no longer capable of dealing with their real concerns. Thus, when one thinks of "modern" painting, music, fiction or poetry, the names which immediately come to mind as its leaders and creators are those of persons who were born roughly between 1870 and 1890 and who began producing their "new" work before the outbreak of World War I in 1914, and in poetry and fiction, at least, American names are prominent.

When a revolutionary break with the past is necessary it is an advantage not to be too closely identified with any one particular literature or any particular cultural group. Americans like Eliot and Pound, for example, could be as curious about French or Italian poetry as about English and could hear poetry of the past, like the verse of Webster, freshly in a way that for an Englishman, trammeled by traditional notions of Elizabethan blank verse, would have been difficult.

Further, as Americans, they were already familiar with the dehumanized nature and the social leveling which a technological civilization was about to make universal and with which the European mentality was unprepared to deal. After his visit to America, de Tocqueville made a remarkable prophecy about the kind of poetry which a democratic society would produce.

> I am persuaded that in the end democracy diverts the imagination from all that is external to man and fixes it on man alone. Democratic nations may amuse themselves for a while with considering the productions of nature, but they are excited in reality only by a survey of themselves. . . .
>
> The poets who lived in aristocratic ages have been eminently successful in their delineation of certain incidents in the life of a people or a man; but none of them ever ventured to include within his performances the destinies of mankind, a task which poets writing in democratic ages may attempt. . . .

> It may be foreseen in like manner that poets living in democratic times will prefer the delineation of passions and ideas to that of persons and achievements. The language, the dress, and the daily actions of men in democracies are repugnant to conceptions of the ideal. . . . This forces the poet constantly to search below the external surface which is palpable to the senses, in order to read the inner soul; and nothing lends itself more to the delineation of the ideal than the scrutiny of the hidden depths in the immaterial nature of man. . . . The destinies of mankind, man himself taken aloof from his country and his age, and standing in the presence of Nature and of God, with his passions, his doubts, his rare prosperities and inconceivable wretchedness, will become the chief, if not the sole, theme of poetry.

If this be an accurate description of the poetry we call modern, then one might say that America has never known any other kind.

PART SEVEN

The Shield of Perseus

NOTES ON THE COMIC

If a man wants to set up as an innkeeper and he does not succeed, it is not comic. If, on the contrary, a girl asks to be allowed to set up as a prostitute and she fails, which sometimes happens, it is comic.

SØREN KIERKEGAARD

A man's character may be inferred from nothing so surely as from the jest he takes in bad part.

G. C. LICHTENBERG

General Definition

A contradiction in the relation of the individual or the personal to the universal or the impersonal which does not involve the spectator or hearer in suffering or pity, which in practice means that it must not involve the actor in real suffering.

A situation in which the actor really suffers can only be found comic by children who see only the situation and are unaware of the suffering, as when a child laughs at a hunchback, or by human swine.

A few years ago, there was a rage in New York for telling "Horror Jokes." For example:

> *A mother (to her blind daughter):* Now, dear, shut your eyes and count twenty. Then open them, and you'll find that you can see.
>
> *Daughter (after counting twenty):* But, Mummy, I still can't see.
>
> *Mother:* April fool!

This has the same relation to the comic as blasphemy has to belief in God, that is to say, it implies a knowledge of what is truly comic.

We sometimes make a witty remark about someone which is also cruel, but we make it behind his back, not to his face, and we hope that nobody will repeat it to him.

When we really hate someone, we cannot find him comic; there are no genuinely funny stories about Hitler.

A sense of humor develops in a society to the degree that its members are simultaneously conscious of being each a unique person and of being all in common subjection to unalterable laws.

Primitive cultures have little sense of humor; firstly, because their sense of human individuality is weak—the tribe is the real unit—and, secondly, because, as animists or polytheists, they have little notion of necessity. To them, events do not occur because they must, but because some god or spirit chooses to make them happen. They recognize a contradiction between the individual and the universal only when it is a tragic contradiction involving exceptional suffering.

In our own society, addicted gamblers who make a religion out of chance are invariably humorless.

Among those whom I like or admire, I can find no common denominator, but among those whom I love, I can: all of them make me laugh.

Some Types of Comic Contradiction

1) The operation of physical laws upon inorganic objects associated with a human being in such a way that it is they who appear to be acting from personal volition and their owner who appears to be the passive thing.

Example: A man is walking in a storm protected by an umbrella when a sudden gust of wind blows it inside out. This is comic for two reasons:

a) An umbrella is a mechanism designed by man to function in a particular manner, and its existence and effectiveness as a protection depend upon man's understanding of physical laws. An umbrella turning inside out is funnier than a hat blowing off because an umbrella is made to be opened, to change its shape when its owner wills. It now continues to change its shape, in obedience to the same laws, but against his will.

b) The activating agent, the wind, is invisible, so the cause of the umbrella turning inside out appears to lie in the umbrella itself. It is not particularly funny if a tile falls and makes a hole in the umbrella, because the cause is visibly natural.

When a film is run backwards, reversing the historical succession of events, the flow of volition is likewise reversed and proceeds from the object to the subject. What was originally the action of a man taking off his coat becomes the action of a coat putting itself on a man.

The same contradiction is the basis of most of the comic effects of the clown. In appearance he is the clumsy man whom inanimate objects conspire against to torment; this in itself is funny to watch, but our profounder amusement is derived from our knowledge that this is only an appearance, that, in reality, the accuracy with which the objects trip him up or hit him on the head is caused by the clown's own skill.

2) A clash between the laws of the inorganic which has no *telos*, and the behavior of living creatures who have one.

Example: A man walking down the street, with his mind concentrated upon the purpose of his journey, fails to notice a banana skin, slips and falls down. Under the obsession of his goal—it may be a goal of thought—he forgets his subjection to the law of gravity. His goal need not necessarily be a unique and personal one; he may simply be looking for a public lavatory. All that matters is that he should be ignoring the present for the sake of the future. A child learning to walk, or an adult picking his way carefully over an icy surface, are not funny if they fall down, because they are conscious of the present.

Comic Situations in the Relationship Between the Sexes

As a natural creature a human being is born either male or female and endowed with an impersonal tendency to reproduce the human species by mating with any member of the opposite sex who is neither immature nor senile. In this tendency the individuality of any given male or female is subordinate to its general reproductive function. (*Male and female created He them . . . Be fruitful and multiply.*)

As a historical person, every man and woman is a unique individual, capable of entering into a unique relation of love with another person. As a person, the relationship takes precedence over any function it may also have. (*It is not good for man to be alone.*)

The ideal of marriage is a relationship in which both these elements are synthesized; husband and wife are simultaneously involved in relations of physical love and the love of personal friendship.

The synthesis might be easier to achieve if the two elements remained distinct, if the physical, that is, remained as impersonal as it is among the animals, and the personal relation was completely unerotic.

In fact, however, we never experience sexual desire as a blind need which is indifferent to its sexual object; our personal history and our culture introduce a selective element so that, even on the most physical level, some types are more desirable than others. Our sexual desire, as such, is impersonal in that it lacks all consideration for the person who is our type, but personal in that our type is our personal taste, not a blind need.

This contradiction is fertile ground for self-deception. It allows us to persuade ourselves that we value the person of another, when, in fact, we only value her (or him) as a sexual object, and it allows us to endow her with an imaginary personality which has little or no relation to the real one.

From the personal point of view, on the other hand, sexual desire, because of its impersonal and unchanging character, is a comic contradiction. The relation between every pair of lovers is unique, but in bed they can only do what all mammals do.

Comic Travesties

Twelfth Night. The pattern of relationships is as follows:

1) Viola (Caesario) is wholly in the truth. She knows who she is, she knows that the Duke is a man for whom she feels personal love, and her passionate image of him corresponds to the reality.

2) The Duke is in the truth in one thing; he knows that he feels a personal affection for Caesario (Viola). This is made easier for him by his boylike appearance—did he look like a nature man, he would fall into a class, the class of potential rivals in love. The fact that he feels personal affection for the illusory Caesario guarantees the authenticity of his love for the real Viola as a person, since it cannot be an illusion provoked by sexual desire.

His relation to Olivia, on the other hand, is erotic-fantastic in one of two ways, and probably in both: either his image of her does not correspond to her real nature or, if it does correspond, it is fantastic in relation to himself; the kind of wife he really desires is not what he imagines. The fact that, though she makes it clear that she does not return his passion, he still continues to pursue her and by devious strategies, demonstrates that he lacks respect for her as a person.

3) Olivia has an erotic-fantastic image of Caesario (Viola). Since she is able to transfer her image successfully to Caesario's double, Sebastian, and marry him, we must assume that the image of the kind of husband she desires is real in relation to herself and only accidentally fantastic because Caesario happens to be, not a man, but a woman in disguise.

4) The illusion of Antonio and Sebastian is not concerned with the erotic relationship, but with the problem of body-soul identity. It is a general law that a human face is the creation of its owner's past and that, since two persons cannot have the same past, no two faces are alike. Identical twins are the exception to this rule. Viola and Sebastian are twins, but not identical twins, for one is female and the other male; dress them both, however, in male or female clothing, and they appear to be identical twins.

It is impossible to produce *Twelfth Night* today in an ordinary theatre since feminine roles are no longer played, as they were in Shakespeare's time, by boys. It is essential to the play that, when Viola appears dressed as a boy, the illusion should be perfect; if it is obvious to the audience that Caesario is really a girl, the play becomes a farce, and a farce in bad taste, for any serious emotion is impossible in a farce, and some of the characters in *Twelfth Night* have serious emotions. A boy whose voice has not yet broken can, when dressed as a girl, produce a perfect illusion of a girl; a young woman, dressed as a boy, can never produce a convincing illusion of a boy.

Der Rosenkavalier and Charley's Aunt. To Baron Lerchenau, the seduction of young chambermaids has become a habit, i.e., what was once a combination of desire and personal choice has become almost an automatic reflex. A costume suggests to him the magic word *chambermaid,* and the word issues the command *Seduce her.* The baron, however, is not quite a farce character; he knows the difference between a pretty girl and an ugly one. The mezzo-soprano who plays Octavian should be good-looking enough to give the illusion of a good-looking young man, when dressed as one. In the third act, when she is dressed as what she really is, a girl, she will be pretty, but her acting the role of a chambermaid must be farcical, and give the impression of a bad actor impersonating a girl, so that only a man as obsessed by habit as the Baron could fail to notice it.

Charley's Aunt is pure farce. The fortune-hunting uncle is not a slave of habit; he really desires to marry a rich widow, but her riches are all he desires; he is totally uninterested in sex or in individuals. He has been told that he is going to meet a rich widow, he sees widow's weeds and this is sufficient to set him in motion. To the audience, therefore, it must be obvious that she is neither female nor elderly, but a young undergraduate pretending, with little success, to be both.

The Lover and the Citizen

Marriage is not only a relation between two individuals; it is also a social institution, involving social emotions concerned with class status and prestige among one's fellows. This is not in itself comic; it only becomes comic if social emotion is the only motive for a marriage, so that the essential motives for marriage, sexual intercourse, procreation and personal affection, are lacking. A familiar comic situation is that of *Don Pasquale*. A rich old man plans to marry a young girl against her will, for she is in love with a young man of her own age; the old man at first looks like succeeding, but in the end he is foiled. For this to be comic, the audience must be convinced that Don Pasquale does not really feel either desire or affection for Norina, that his sole motive is a social one, to be able to boast to other old men that he can win a young wife when they cannot. He wants the prestige of parading her and making others envy him. If he really feels either desire or affection, then he will really suffer when his designs are foiled, and the situation will be either pathetic or satiric. In *Pickwick Papers,* the same situation occurs, only this time it is the female sex which has the social motive. Widow after widow pursues Weller, the widower, not because she wants to be married to him in particular, but because she wants the social status of being a married woman.

The Law of the City and the Law of Justice
Example: Falstaff's speech on Honour (*Henry IV*, Part I, Act V, Scene II.)

If the warrior ethic of honor, courage and personal loyalty were believed by an Elizabethan or a modern audience to be the perfect embodiment of justice, the speech would not be sympathetically comic, but a satirical device by which Falstaff was held up to ridicule as a coward. If, on the other hand, the warrior ethic were totally unjust, if there were no occasions on which it was a true expression of moral duty, the speech would be, not comic, but a serious piece of pacifist propaganda. The speech has a sympathetically comic effect for two reasons, the circumstances under which it is uttered, and the character of the speaker.

Were the situation one in which the future of the whole community is at stake, as on the field of Agincourt, the speech would strike an unsympathetic note, but the situation is one of civil war, a struggle for power among the feudal nobility in which the claims of both sides to be the legitimate rulers are fairly equal—Henry IV was once a rebel who deposed his King—and a struggle in which their feudal dependents are compelled to take part and risk their lives without having a real stake in the outcome. Irrespective of the speaker, the speech is a comic criticism of the feudal ethic as typified by Hotspur. Courage is a personal virtue, but military glory for military glory's sake can be a social evil; unreasonable and unjust wars create the paradox that the personal vice of cowardice can become a public virtue.

That it should be Falstaff who utters the speech increases its comic effect. Falstaff has a fantastic conception of himself as a daredevil who plays highwayman, which, if it were true, would require exceptional physical courage. He tries to keep up this illusion, but is always breaking down because of his moral courage which keeps forcing him to admit that he is afraid. Further, though he lacks courage, he exemplifies the other side of the warrior ethic, personal loyalty, as contrasted with Prince Hal's Machiavellian manipulation of others. When Falstaff is rejected by the man to whom he has pledged his whole devotion, his death may truly be called a death for the sake of his wounded honor.

The Banal

The human person is a unique singular, analogous to all other persons, but identical with none. Banality is an illusion of identity for, when people describe their experiences in clichés, it is impossible to distinguish the experience of one from the experience of another.

The cliché user is comic because the illusion of being identical with others is created by his own choice. He is the megalomaniac in reverse. Both have fantastic conceptions of themselves but, whereas the megalomaniac thinks of himself as being somebody else—God, Napoleon, Shakespeare—the banal man thinks of himself as being everybody else, that is to say, nobody in particular.

VERBAL HUMOR

Verbal humor involves a violation in a particular instance of one of the following general principles of language.

1) Language is a means of denoting things or thoughts by sounds. It is a law of language that any given verbal sound always means the same thing and only that thing.

2) Words are man-made things which men use, not persons with a will and consciousness of their own. Whether they make sense or nonsense depends upon whether the speaker uses them correctly or incorrectly.

3) Any two or more objects or events which language seeks to describe are members, either of separate classes, or of the same class, or of overlapping classes. If they belong to separate classes, they must be described in different terms, and if they belong to the same class they must be described in the same terms. If, however, their classes overlap, either class can be described metaphorically in terms which describe the other exactly, e.g., it is equally possible to say—the plough swims through the soil—and—the ship ploughs through the waves.

4) In origin all language is concrete or metaphorical. In order to use language to express abstractions, we have to ignore its original concrete and metaphorical meanings.

The first law is violated by the pun, the exceptional case in which one verbal sound has two meanings.

When I am dead I hope it may be said:
His sins were scarlet, but his books were read.

For the pun to be comic, the two meanings must both make sense in the context. If all books were bound in black, the couplet would not be funny.

Words which rhyme, that is to say, words which denote different things but are partially similar in sound, are not necessarily comic. To be comic, the two things they denote must either be so incongruous with each other that one cannot imagine a real situation in which a speaker would need to bring them together, or so irrelevant to each other, that they could only become associated by pure chance. The effect of a comic rhyme is as if the words, on the basis of their auditory friendship, had taken charge of the situation, as if, instead of an event requiring words to describe it, words had the power to create an event. Reading the lines

There was an Old Man of Whitehaven
Who danced a quadrille with a raven

one cannot help noticing upon reflection that, had the old gentleman lived in Ceylon, he would have had to dance with a swan; alternatively, had his dancing partner been a mouse, he might have had to reside in Christ Church, Oxford.

The comic rhyme involves both the first two laws of language; the spoonerism only the second. *Example:* a lecturing geologist introduces a lantern slide with the words: "And here, gentlemen, we see a fine example of erotic blacks."

So far as the speaker is concerned he has used the language incorrectly, yet what he says makes verbal sense of a kind. Unlike the pun however, where both meanings are relevant, in the spoonerism the accidental meaning is nonsense in the context. Thus, while the comic nature of the pun should be immediately apparent to the hearer, it should take time before he realizes what the speaker of the spoonerism intended to say. A pun is witty and intended; a spoonerism, like a comic rhyme, is comic and should appear to be involuntary. As with the clown, the speaker appears to be the slave of language, but in reality is its master.

Just as there are people who are really clumsy so there are incompetent poets who are the slaves of the only rhymes they know; the kind of poet caricatured by Shakespeare in the play of *Pyramus and Thisbe:*

> Those lily lips,
> This cherry nose,
> These yellow cowslip cheeks,
> Are gone, are gone,
> Lovers make moan;
> His eyes were green as leeks.
> O Sisters Three,
> Come, come to me
> With hands as pale as milk;
> Lay them in gore,
> Since you have shore
> With shears his thread of silk.

In this case we laugh at the rustic poet, not with him.

One of the most fruitful of witty devices is a violation of the third law, namely, to treat members of overlapping classes as if they were members of the same class. For example, during a period of riots and social unrest when the mob had set fire to hayricks all over the country Sidney Smith wrote to his friend, Mrs. Meynell:

> What do you think of all these burnings? and have you heard of the new sort of burnings? Ladies' maids have taken to setting their mistresses on fire. Two dowagers were burned last week, and large rewards are offered. They are inventing little fire-engines for the toilet table, worked with lavender water.

The fourth law, which distinguishes between the occasions when speech is used to describe concrete things and those in which it is used for abstract purposes, provides an opportunity for wit, as in Wilde's epigram:

> Twenty years of romance make a woman look like a ruin, and twenty years of marriage make her look like a public building.

Ruin has become a "dead" metaphor, that is to say, a word which normally can be used as an abstraction, but public building is still a concrete description.

Literary Parody, and Visual Caricature

Literary parody presupposes a) that every authentic writer has a unique perspective on life and b) that his literary style accurately expresses that perspective. The trick of the parodist is to take the unique style of the author, *how* he expresses his unique vision, and make it express utter banalities; *what* the parody expresses could be said by anyone. The effect is of a reversal in the relation between the author and his style. Instead of the style being the creation of the man, the man becomes the puppet of the style. It is only possible to caricature an author one admires because, in the case of an author one dislikes, his own work will seem a better parody than one could hope to write oneself.

Example: As we get older we do not get any younger.
Seasons return, and to-day I am fifty-five,
And this time last year I was fifty-four,
And this time next year I shall be sixty-two.
And I cannot say I should like (to speak for
myself)
To see my time over again—if you can call it
time:
Fidgeting uneasily under a draughty stair,
Or counting sleepless nights in the crowded
tube.

(HENRY REED, *Chard Whitlow*.)

Every face is a present witness to the fact that its owner has a past behind him which might have been otherwise, and a future ahead of him in which some possibilities are more probable than others. To "read" a face means to guess what it might have been and what it still may become. Children, for whom most future possibilities are equally probable, the dead for whom all possibilities have been reduced to zero, and animals who have only one possibility to realize and realize it completely, do not have faces which can be read, but wear inscrutable masks. A caricature of a face admits that its owner has had a past, but denies that he has a future. He has created his features up to a certain point, but now they have taken charge of him so that he can never change; he has become a single possibility completely realized. That is why, when we go to the zoo, the faces of the animals remind one of caricatures of human beings. A caricature doesn't need to be read; it has no future.

We enjoy caricatures of our friends because we do not want to think of their changing, above all, of their dying; we enjoy caricatures of our enemies because we do not want to consider the possibility of their having a change of heart so that we would have to forgive them.

Flyting

Flyting seems to have vanished as a studied literary art and only to survive in the impromptu exchanges of truckdrivers and cabdrivers. The comic effect arises from the contradiction between the insulting nature of what is said which appears to indicate a passionate relation of hostility and agression, and the calculated skill of verbal invention which indicates that the protagonists are not thinking about each other but about language and their pleasure in employing it inventively. A man who is really passionately angry is speechless and can only express his anger by physical violence. Playful anger is intrinsically comic because, of all emotions, anger is the least compatible with play.

Satire

The object of satire is a person who, though in possession of his moral faculties, transgresses the moral law beyond the normal call of temptation. The lunatic cannot be an object of satire, since he is not morally responsible for his actions, and the wicked man cannot be an object because, while morally responsible, he lacks the normal faculty of conscience. The commonest object of satire is the rogue. The rogue transgresses the moral law at the expense of others, but he is only able to do this because of the vices of his victims; they share in his guilt. The wicked man transgresses the moral law at the expense of others, but his victims are innocent. Thus a black marketeer in sugar can be satirized because the existence of such a black market depends upon the greed of others for sugar, which is a pleasure but not a necessity; a black marketeer in penicillin cannot be satirized because, for the sick, it is a necessity and, if they cannot pay his prices, they will die.

After the rogue, the commonest object of satire is the monomaniac. Most men desire money and are not always too scrupulous in the means by which they obtain it, but this does not make them objects of satire, because their desire is tempered by a number of competing interests. A miser is satirizable because his desire overrides all desires which normal selfishness feels, such as sex or physical comfort.

The Satirical Strategy

There is not only a moral human norm, but also a normal way of transgressing it. At the moment of yielding to temptation, the normal human being has to exercise self-deception and rationalization, for in order to yield he requires the illusion of acting with a good conscience: after he has committed the immoral act, when desire is satisfied, the normal human being realizes the nature of his act and feels guilty. He who is incapable of realizing the nature of his act is mad, and he who, both before, while, and after committing it, is exactly conscious of what he is doing yet feels no guilt, is wicked.

The commonest satirical devices therefore, are two: 1) To present the object of satire *as if* he or she were mad and unaware of what he is doing.

Now Night descending, the proud scene was o'er,
But lived in Settle's numbers, one day more.
(POPE.)

The writing of poetry which, even in the case of the worst of poets, is a personal and voluntary act, is presented as if it were as impersonal and necessary as the revolution of the earth, and the value of the poems so produced which, even in a bad poet, varies, is presented as invariable and therefore subject to a quantitative measurement like dead matter.

The satiric effect presupposes that the reader knows that in real life Settle was not a certifiable lunatic, for lunacy overwhelms a man against his will: Settle is, as it were, a self-made lunatic.

2) To present the object of satire as if he or she were wicked and completely conscious of what he is doing without feeling any guilt.

Although, dear Lord, I am a sinner,
I have done no major crime;
Now I'll come to Evening Service
Whensoever I have time.
So, Lord, reserve for me a crown,
And do not let my shares go down.
(John Betjeman.)

Again, the satiric effect depends upon our knowing that in real life the lady is not wicked, that, if she were really as truthful with herself as she is presented, she could not go to Church.

Satire flourishes in a homogeneous society where satirist and audience share the same views as to how normal people can be expected to behave, and in times of relative stability and contentment, for satire cannot deal with serious evil and suffering. In an age like our own, it cannot flourish except in intimate circles as an expression of private feuds: in public life the evils and sufferings are so serious that satire seems trivial and the only possible kind of attack is prophetic denunciation.

DON JUAN

Hört ihr Kindeslieder singen,
Gleich ists euer eigner Scherz;
Seht ihr mich im Takte springen,
Hüpft euch elterlich das Herz.
FAUST, Part II, Act III

Most of the literary works with which we are acquainted fall into one of two classes, those we have no desire to read a second time—sometimes, we were never able to finish them—and those we are always happy to reread. There are a few, however, which belong to a third class; we do not feel like reading one of them very often but, when we are in the appropriate mood, it is the only work we feel like reading. Nothing else, however good or great, will do instead.

For me, Byron's *Don Juan* is such a work. In trying to analyze why this should be so, I find helpful a distinction which, so far as I have been able to discover, can only be made in the English language, the distinction between saying, "So-

and-so or such-and-such is *boring,*" and saying, "So-and-so or such-and-such is a *bore.*"

In English, I believe, the adjective expresses a subjective judgment; *boring* always means *boring-to-me*. For example, if I am in the company of golf enthusiasts, I find their conversation boring but they find it fascinating. The noun, on the other hand, claims to be an objective, universally valid statement; X *is a bore* is either true or false.

Applied to works of art or to artists, the distinction makes four judgments possible.

1) Not (or seldom) boring but a bore. *Examples:* The last quartets of Beethoven, the Sistine frescoes of Michelangelo, the novels of Dostoievski.

2) Sometimes boring but not a bore. Verdi, Degas, Shakespeare.

3) Not boring and not a bore. Rossini, the drawings of Thurber, P. G. Wodehouse.

4) Boring and a bore. Works to which one cannot attend. It would be rude to give names.

Perhaps the principle of the distinction can be made clearer by the following definitions:

A. The absolutely boring but absolutely not a bore: the time of day.

B. The absolutely not boring but absolute bore: God.

Don Juan is sometimes boring but pre-eminently an example of a long poem which is not a bore. To enjoy it fully, the reader must be in a mood of distaste for everything which is to any degree a bore, that is, for all forms of passionate attachment, whether to persons, things, actions or beliefs.

This is not a mood in which one can enjoy satire, for satire, however entertaining, has its origin in passion, in anger at what is the case, desire to change what is the case into what ought to be the case, and belief that the change is humanly possible. The *Dunciad,* for example, presupposes that the Goddess of Dullness is a serious enemy of civilization, that it is the duty of all good citizens to rally to the defense of the

City against her servants, and that the cause of Commonsense is not hopeless.

In defending his poem against the charge of immorality, Byron said on one occasion: "Don Juan will be known bye-a-bye for what it is intended—a Satire on abuses of the present state of Society": but he was not telling the truth. The poem, of course, contains satirical passages. When Byron attacks Wordsworth, Southey or Wellington, he is certainly hoping to deprive them of readers and admirers and behind his description of the siege of Ismail lies a hope that love of military glory and adulation of the warrior are not incurable defects in human nature but evils against which the conscience of mankind can, in the long run, be persuaded to revolt.

But, as a whole, *Don Juan* is not a satire but a comedy, and Byron knew it, for in a franker mood he wrote to Murray:

> I have no plan—I had no plan; but I had or have materials; though if, like Tony Lumpkin, I am to be "snubbed so when I am in spirits," the poem will be naught and the poet turn serious again . . . You are too earnest and eager about a work which was never intended to be serious. Do you suppose that I could have any intention but to giggle and make giggle.

Satire and comedy both make use of the comic contradiction, but their aims are different. Satire would arouse in readers the desire to act so that the contradictions disappear; comedy would persuade them to accept the contradictions with good humor as facts of life against which it is useless to rebel.

> Poor Julia's heart was in an awkward state,
>   She felt it going and resolved to make
> The noblest efforts for herself and mate,
>   For honour's, pride's, religion's, virtue's sake;
> Her resolutions were most truly great;
>   And almost might have made a Tarquin quake;
> She prayed the Virgin Mary for her grace
> As being the best judge in a lady's case.

She vow'd she never would see Juan more
  And next day paid a visit to his mother;
And looked extremely at the opening door,
  Which by the Virgin's grace, let in another;
Grateful she was, and yet a little sore—
  Again it opens—it can be no other.
'Tis surely Juan now—No! I'm afraid
That night the Virgin was no longer prayed.

Julia is presented, neither as a pious hypocrite nor as a slut, but as a young woman, married to an older man she does not like, tempted to commit adultery with an attractive boy. The conflict between her conscience and her desire is perfectly genuine. Byron is not saying that it is silly of Julia to pray because there is no God, or that marriage is an unjust institution which should be abolished in favor of free love. The comedy lies in the fact that the voice of conscience and the voice of desire can both be expressed in the verbal form of a prayer, so that, while Julia's conscience is praying to the Madonna, her heart is praying to Aphrodite. Byron does not pass judgment on this; he simply states that human nature is like that and implies, perhaps, that, in his experience, if Aphrodite has opportunity on her side, the Madonna is seldom victorious, so that, in sexual matters, we ought to be tolerant of human frailty.

Byron's choice of the word *giggle* rather than *laugh* to describe his comic intention deserves consideration.

All comic situations show a contradiction between some general or universal principle and an individual or particular person or event. In the case of the situation at which we giggle, the general principles are two:

1) The sphere of the sacred and the sphere of the profane are mutually exclusive.
2) The sacred is that at which we do not laugh.

Now a situation arises in which the profane intrudes upon the sacred but without annulling it. If the sacred were annulled, we should laugh outright, but the sacred is still felt to be present, so that a conflict ensues between the desire to laugh and the feeling that laughter is inappropriate. A person to whom the distinction between the sacred and the profane had no meaning could never giggle.

If we giggle at Julia's prayer, it is because we have been brought up in a culture which makes a distinction between sacred and profane love. Similarly, we miss the comic point if we read the following lines as a satire on Christian dogma.

> as I suffer from the shocks
> of illness, I grow much more orthodox.
>
> The first attack at once proved the Divinity;
> (But *that* I never doubted, nor the Devil);
> The next, the Virgin's mystical Virginity;
> The third, the usual Origin of Evil;
> The fourth at once established the whole Trinity
> On so uncontrovertible a level,
> That I devoutly wished the three were four
> On purpose to believe so much the more.

If these lines were satirical, they would imply that all people in good health are atheists. But what Byron says is that when people are well, they tend to be frivolous and forget all those questions about the meaning of life which are of sacred importance to everybody, including atheists, and that when they are ill, they can think of nothing else. One could imagine a similar verse by Shelley (if he had had any sense of humor) in which he would say: "The iller I get, the more certain I become that there is no God." Shelley, as a matter of fact, complained that he was powerless "to eradicate from his friend's great mind the delusions of Christianity which in spite of his reason seem perpetually to recur and to lie in ambush for his hours of sickness and distress," and, had Bryon lived longer, the prophecy Sir Walter Scott made in 1815 might well have come true.

> I remember saying to him that I really thought that, if he lived a few years longer, he would alter his senti-

> ments. He answered rather sharply. "I suppose you are one of those who prophesy that I will turn Methodist." I replied—"No. I don't expect your conversion to be of such an ordinary kind. I would rather look to see you retreat upon the Catholic faith and distinguish yourself by the austerity of your penances."

The terms "sacred" and "profane" can be used relatively as well as absolutely. Thus, in a culture that puts a spiritual value upon love between the sexes, such a love, however physical, will seem sacred in comparison with physical hunger. When the shipwrecked Juan wakes and sees Haidée bending over him, he sees she is beautiful and is thrilled by her voice, but the first thing he longs for is not her love but a beefsteak.

The sacred can be evil as well as good. In our culture it is considered normal (the normal is always profane) for men to be carnivorous, and vegetarians are looked upon as cranks.

> Although his anatomical construction
> Bears vegetables in a grumbling way,
> Your laboring people think beyond all question
> Beef, veal, and mutton better for digestion.

Cannibalism, on the other hand, is a crime which is regarded with sacred horror. The survivors from the shipwreck in Canto II are not only starving but also have a craving for meat to which their upbringing has conditioned them. Unfortunately, the only kind of meat available is human. One can imagine a group of men in similar circumstances who would not have become cannibals because they had been brought up in a vegetarian culture and were unaware that human beings could eat meat. The men in Byron's poem pay with their lives for their act, not because it is a sacred crime but for the profane reason that their new diet proves indigestible.

> By night chilled, by day scorched, there one by one
>   They perished until withered to a few,
> But chiefly by a species of self-slaughter
> In washing down Pedrillo with salt water.

It is the silly mistake of drinking salt water, not the sacred crime of consuming a clergyman, that brings retribution.

Most readers will probably agree that the least interesting figure in *Don Juan* is its official hero, and his passivity is all the more surprising when one recalls the legendary monster of depravity after whom he is named. The Don Juan of the myth is not promiscuous by nature but by will; seduction is his vocation. Since the slightest trace of affection will turn a number on his list of victims into a name, his choice of vocation requires the absolute renunciation of love. It is an essential element in the legend, therefore, that Don Juan be, not a sinner out of weakness, but a defiant atheist, the demonic counter-image of the ascetic saint who renounces all personal preference for one neighbor to another in order that he may show Christian charity to all alike.

When he chose the name Don Juan for his hero, Byron was well aware of the associations it would carry for the public, and he was also aware that he himself was believed by many to be the heartless seducer and atheist of the legend. His poem is, among other things, a self-defense. He is saying to his accusers, as it were: "The Don Juan of the legend does not exist. I will show you what the sort of man who gets the reputation for being a Don Juan is really like."

Byron's hero is not even particularly promiscuous. In the course of two years he makes love with five women, a poor showing in comparison with the 1003 Spanish ladies of Leporello's Catalogue aria, or even with Byron's own "200 odd Venetian pieces." Furthermore, he seduces none of them. In three cases he is seduced—by Julia, Catherine, the Duchess of Fitz-Fulk—and in the other two, circumstances outside his control bring him together with Haidée and Dudù, and no persuasion on his part is needed. Then, though he cannot quite play Tristan to her Isolde and commit suicide when he is parted from Haidée, he has been genuinely in love with her.

Far from being a defiant rebel against the laws of God and man, his most conspicuous trait is his gift for social conformity. I cannot understand those critics who have seen in him a kind of Rousseau child of Nature. Whenever chance takes him, to a pirate's lair, a harem in Mohammedan Constantinople, a court in Greek Orthodox Russia, a country house in Protestant England, he immediately adapts himself and is accepted as an agreeable fellow. Had Byron continued the poem as he planned and taken Juan to Italy to be a *cavaliere servente* and to Germany to be a solemn Werther-faced man, one has no doubt that he would have continued to play the roles assigned to him with tact and aplomb. In some respects Juan resembles the Baudelairian dandy but he lacks the air of *insolent* superiority which Baudelaire considered essential to the true dandy; he would never, one feels, say anything outrageous or insulting. Aside from the stylistic impossibility of ending a comic poem on a serious note, it is impossible to imagine Juan, a man without enemies, ending on the guillotine, as apparently Byron was considering doing with him.

When one compares Don Juan with what we know of his creator, he seems to be a daydream of what Byron would have liked to be himself. Physically he is unblemished and one cannot imagine him having to diet to keep his figure; socially, he is always at his ease and his behavior in perfect taste. Had Juan set out for Greece, he would not have had made for himself two Homeric helmets with overtowering plumes nor had engraved on his coat of arms the motto *Crede Don Juan*.

Byron, though very conscious of his rank, never felt fully at ease in the company of his social equals (Shelley was too odd to count). Even when he was the social lion of London, Lord Holland observed:

> It was not from his birth that Lord Byron had taken the station he held in society for, till his talents were known, he was, in spite of his birth, in anything but good society and *but* for his talents would never, perhaps, have been in any better.

And Byron himself confessed to Lady Blessington:

> I am so little fastidious in the selection or rather want of selection of associates, that the most stupid men satisfy me as well, nay, perhaps, better than the most brilliant. The effort of letting myself down to them costs me nothing, though my pride is hurt that they do not seem more sensible of the condescension.

Juan, though by birth a Spaniard and a Catholic and therefore an outsider from an Englishman's point of view, is the perfect embodiment of the very English ideal of succeeding at anything he does without appearing to be ambitious of success.

Characters which are daydream projections of their authors are seldom very interesting and, had Byron written *Don Juan* as a straightforward narrative poem in the style of *The Corsair* or *Lara,* it would probably have been unreadable. Fortunately, he had discovered a genre of poetry which allows the author to enter the story he is telling. Juan is only a convenience: the real hero of the poem is Byron himself.

Byron's poetry is the most striking example I know in literary history of the creative role which poetic form can play. If William Stewart Rose had arrived in Venice in September 1817 with nothing for him but magnesia and red tooth powder, Byron would probably today be considered a very minor poet. He knew Italian well, he had read Casti's *Novelle Galanti* and loved them, but he did not realize the poetic possibilities of the mock-heroic ottava-rima until he read Frere's *The Monks and the Giants.*

Take away the poems he wrote in this style and meter, *Beppo, The Vision of Judgment, Don Juan,* and what is left of lasting value? A few lyrics, though none of them is as good as the best of Moore's, two adequate satires though inferior to Dryden or Pope, "Darkness," a fine piece of blank verse marred by some false sentiment, a few charming occasional pieces, half a dozen stanzas from *Childe Harold,* half a dozen lines from *Cain,* and that is all. Given his production up till that date, he showed better judgment than his readers when he wrote to Moore in 1817:

> If I live ten years longer, you will see, however, that all is not over with me—I don't mean in literature, for that is nothing: and it may seem odd enough to say I do not think it is my vocation.

Soon afterwards, he read Frere: as he had foretold, it was not all over with him but, as he had not foreseen, his vocation was to be literature. The authentic poet was at last released.

So long as Byron tried to write Poetry with a capital P, to express deep emotions and profound thoughts, his work deserved that epithet he most dreaded, *una seccatura.* As a thinker he was, as Goethe perceived, childish, and he possessed neither the imaginative vision—he could never invent anything, only remember—nor the verbal sensibility such poetry demands. Lady Byron, of all people, put her finger on his great defect as a serious poet.

> He is the absolute monarch of words, and uses them as Bonaparte did lives, for conquest without regard to their intrinsic value.

The artistic failure of *Childe Harold* is due in large measure to Byron's disastrous choice of the Spenserian stanza. At the time, he had only read a few verses of *The Faerie Queene* and when, later, Leigh Hunt tried to make him read the whole of it, one is not surprised to learn that he hated the poem. Nothing could be further removed from Byron's cast of mind than its slow, almost timeless, visionary quality.

His attempt to write satirical heroic couplets were less unsuccessful but, aside from the impossibility of equaling Dryden and Pope in their medium, Byron was really a comedian, not a satirist. Funny things can be said in heroic couplets, but the heroic couplet as a *form* is not comic, that is to say, it does not itself make what it says funny.

Before *Beppo,* the authentic Byron emerges only in light occasional verse such as "Lines to a Lady who appointed a night in December to meet him in the garden."

> Why should you weep like Lydia Languish
> And fret with self-created anguish

Or doom the lover you have chosen
On winter nights to sigh half-frozen;
In leafless shades to sue for pardon,
Only because the scene's a garden?
For gardens seem, by one consent,
Since Shakespeare set the precedent,
Since Julia first declared her passion,
To form the place of assignation,
Oh, would some modern muse inspire
And seat her by a sea-coal fire;
Or had the bard at Christmas written
And laid the scene of love in Britain,
He, surely, in commiseration
Had changed the place of declaration.
In Italy I've no objection,
Warm nights are proper for reflection:
But here our climate is so rigid
That love itself is rather frigid:
Think on our chilly situation,
And curb this rage for imitation.

In this, a very early poem, one can note already the speed and the use of feminine rhymes which were to become Byron's forte. Feminine rhymes are as possible in a five-foot line as in a four-foot but, at this date, the tune of the Pope couplet was still too much in his ear to allow him to use them. There are only three couplets with feminine rhymes in *English Bards and Scotch Reviewers* and only one in *Hints from Horace*.

Frere was not a great poet, but his perception of the comic possibilities of an *exact* imitation in English of Italian ottava-rima was a stroke of genius. Italian is a polysyllabic language, most of its words end on an unaccented syllable and rhymes are very common. Italian ottava-rima, therefore, is usually hendecasyllabic with feminine rhymes and, because three rhymes can be found without any effort, it became a maid-of-all-work stanza which would fit any subject. An Italian poet could use it for comic or satirical purposes, but he could also be serious and pathetic in it. There is nothing comic, for example, about this stanza from *Gerusalemme Liberata.*

Lei nel partir, lei nel tornar del sole
Chiama con voce mesta e prega e plora;
Come usignol cui villan duro invole
Dal nido i figli non pennuti ancora
Che in miserabil canto afflite e sole
Piange le notte, e n'empie, boschi e l'ora.
Alfin col nuovo di rinchiude alquanto
I lumi; e il sonno in lor serpe fra il pianto.

When English poets first copied the stanza, they instinctively shortened the lines to decasyllabics with masculine rhymes.

All suddenly dismaid, and hartless quite
He fled abacke and catching hastie holde
Of a young alder hard behinde him pight,
It rent, and streight aboute him gan beholde
What God or Fortune would assist his might.
But whether God or Fortune made him bold
It's hard to read; yet hardie will he had
To overcome, that made him less adrad.

("Vergil's Gnat.")

The frequent monosyllables, the abruptness of the line endings and the absence of elision completely alter the movement. Further, because of the paucity of rhymes in English, it is almost impossible to write a poem of any length in this stanza without either using banal rhymes or padding the line in order to get a rhyme. If, from Chaucer to Sackville, it was not ottava-rima but rhyme-royal which was the staple vehicle for a long poem, one reason, at least, was that rhyme-royal calls for only one rhyme triplet, not two. So far as I know, the first English poet to combine ottava-rima with the high style was Yeats who, in his later years, wrote many of his finest poems in it. He gets round the rhyming problem by a liberal use of half-rhymes and by ending lines with words which are almost dactyls, so that the rhyming syllable is only lightly accented. For example, in the opening stanza of "Nineteen Hundred and Nineteen," only two of the lines rhyme exactly.

> Many ingenious lovely things are gone
> That seemed sheer miracle to the multitude,
> Protected from the circle of the moon
> That pitches common things about. There stood
> Amid the ornamental bronze and stone
> An ancient image made of olive wood—
> And gone are Phidias' famous ivories
> And all the golden grasshoppers and bees.

Frere was the first fully to realize (though, as W. P. Ker has pointed out, there are anticipations in Gay's "Mr. Pope's Welcome from Greece") that the very qualities of the stanza which make it an unsuitable vehicle for serious poetry make it an ideal one for comic verse since in English, unlike Italian, the majority of double or triple rhymes are comic.

Our association of the word *romantic* with the magical and dreamlike is so strong that we are apt to forget that the literary period so classified is also a great age for comic poetry. The comic verse of poets like Canning, Frere, Hood, Praed, Barham, and Lear was a new departure in English poetry, and not least in its exploitation of comic rhyme. Indeed, before them, the only poets I can think of who used it intentionally and frequently were Skelton and Samuel Butler.

The very qualities of English ottava-rima which force a serious poet to resort to banal rhymes and padding are a stimulus to the comic imagination, leading to the discovery of comic rhymes and providing opportunities for the interpolated comment and conversational aside, and Byron developed this deliberate looseness of manner to the full.

> An Arab horse, a stately stag, a barb
>   New broke, a camelopard, a gazelle.
> No—none of these will do—and then their garb!
>   Their veil and petticoat—Alas! to dwell
> Upon such things would very near absorb
>   A canto—then their feet and ankles—well,

Thank heaven I've got no metaphor quite ready,
(And so, my sober Muse—come, let's be steady.)

He also exploited to the full the structural advantages of the stanza. As a unit, eight lines give space enough to describe a single event or elaborate on a single idea without having to run on to the next stanza. If, on the other hand, what the poet has to say requires several short sentences, the arrangement of the rhymes allows him to pause at any point he likes without the stanza breaking up into fragments, for his separate statements will always be linked by a rhyme. The stanza divides by rhyme into a group of six lines followed by a coda of two; the poet can either observe this division and use the couplet as an epigrammatic comment on the first part, or he can take seven lines for his theme and use the final one as a punch line.

Gulbeyaz, for the first time in her days,
  Was much embarrassed, never having met
In all her life with aught save prayers and praise;
  And as she also risked her life to get
Him whom she meant to tutor in love's ways
  Into a comfortable tête-à-tête,
To lose the hour would make her quite a martyr.
And they had wasted now about a quarter.

Her form had all the softness of her sex,
  Her features all the sweetness of the devil,
When he put on the cherub to perplex
  Eve, and paved (God knows what) the road to evil;
The sun himself was scarce more free from specks
  Than she from aught at which the eye could cavil;
Yet, somehow, there was something somewhere wanting,
As if she rather ordered than was granting.

What had been Byron's defect as a serious poet, his lack of reverence for words, was a virtue for the comic poet. Serious poetry requires that the poet treat words as if they were persons, but comic poetry demands that he treat them as things and few, if any, English poets have rivaled Byron's ability to put words through the hoops.

Needless to say, the skill of the comic poet, like that of the lion tamer or the clown, takes hard work to perfect. Byron chose to give others the impression that he dashed off his poetry, like a gentleman, without effort, but the publication of the Variorum edition of *Don Juan* demonstrates that, although he wrote with facility, he took a great deal more pains than he pretended. The editors, with an industrious devotion which is as admirable as it is, to me, incredible, have provided statistical tables. Thus, 87 out of the 172 stanzas in Canto I show revisions in four or more lines, and 123 revisions in the concluding couplet. A few examples will suffice.

Canto I, st. 103.
First draft:
They are a sort of post-house, where the Fates
Change horses every hour from night till noon;
Then spur away with empires and oe'r states,
Leaving no vestige but a bare chronology,
Except the hopes derived from true theology.

First Revision:
Except the promises derived from true theology.

Final version:
They are a sort of post-house where the Fates
Change horses, making history change its tune;
Then spur away o'er empires and o'er states,
Leaving at last not much besides chronology
Excepting the post-obits of theology.

Canto IX, st. 33.
First draft:
O ye who build up statues all defiled
With gore, like Nadir Shah, that costive Sophy,
Who after leaving Hindostan a wild,
And leaving Asia scarce a cup of coffee,
To soothe his woes withal, went mad and was
Killed because what he swallowed would not pass.

Final version:
O! ye who build up monuments defiled
With gore, like Nadir Shah, that costive Sophy
Who, after leaving Hindostan a wild,
And scarce to the Mogul a cup of coffee,
To soothe his woes withal, was slain—the sinner!
Because he could no more digest his dinner.

Canto XI, st. 60.
First version:
'Tis strange the mind should let such phrases quell its
Chief impulse with a few frail paper pellets.

Second Version:
'Tis strange the mind, that all celestial Particle,
Should let itself be put out by an Article.

Final Version:
'Tis strange the mind, that very fiery Particle,
Should let itself be snuffed out by an Article.

One should be wary, when comparing an author's various productions, of saying: this piece is an expression of the real man and that piece is not—for nobody, not even the subject himself, can be certain who he is. All we can say is that this piece is the expression of a person who might possibly exist but nobody could possibly exist of whom that piece would be the expression.

There have been poets—Keats is the most striking example—whose letters and poems are so different from each other that they might have been written by two different people, and yet both seem equally authentic. But, with Byron, this is not the case. From the beginning, his letters seem authentic but, before *Beppo*, very little of his poetry; and the more closely his poetic *persona* comes to resemble the epistolary *persona* of his letters to his male friends—his love letters are another matter—the more authentic his poetry seems.

So Scrope is gone—down diddled—as Doug K writes it,
the said Doug being like the man who, when he lost a

> friend, went down to St. James Coffee House and took a new one; 'the best of men'. Gone to Bruges where he will get tipsy with Dutch beer and shoot himself the first foggy morning.

Reading this letter to Hobhouse, one immediately recognizes its likeness to *Don Juan* and its unlikeness to *Manfred* and one feels that, while the letter and *Don Juan* have been written by someone-in-particular, *Manfred* must have been written, as it were, by a committee.

If one can say that the authentic poet in Byron is Byron the Friend, it is worth asking what are the typical characteristics of friendship. (I am thinking, of course, of friendship between men. To me, as to all men, the nature of friendship between women remains a mystery, which is probably a wise provision of nature. If we ever discovered what women say to each other when we are not there, our male vanity might receive such a shock that the human race would die out.)

The basis of friendship is similarity: it is only possible between persons who regard each other as equals and who have some interests and tastes in common, so that they can share each other's experiences. We can speak of a false friendship but not of an unreciprocated one. In this, friendship differs from sexual love which is based on difference and is all too often unreciprocated. Further, friendship is a nonexclusive, nonpossessive relationship; we can speak of having friends in common, while we cannot speak of having lovers, husbands or wives in common. Between two friends, therefore, there is an indifference towards, even an impatience with, those areas of human experience which they cannot share with each other, religious experiences, for example, which are unsharable with anybody, and feelings of passionate devotion which can be shared, if at all, only with the person for whom they are felt. André Gide was being unduly cynical, perhaps, when he defined a friend as someone with whom one does something disgraceful; it is true, however, that a vice in common can be the ground of a friendship but not a virtue in common. X and Y may be friends *because* they are both drunkards or womanizers but, if they are both sober and chaste, they are friends for some other reason.

The experiences which friends can share range from the grossest to the most subtle and refined, but nearly all of them belong to the category of the Amusing. No lover worries about boring his beloved; if she loves him, she cannot be bored and if she doesn't love him, he is too unhappy to care if she is. But between two friends, their first concern is not to bore each other. If they are persons of heart and imagination, they will take it for granted that the other has beliefs and feelings which he takes seriously and problems of his own which cause him suffering and sorrow, but in conversation they will avoid discussing them or, if they do discuss them, they will avoid the earnest note. One laughs with a friend; one does not weep with him (though one may weep *for* him).

Most poetry is the utterance of a man in some state of passion, love, joy, grief, rage, etc., and no doubt this is as it should be. But no man is perpetually in a passion and those states in which he is amused and amusing, detached and irreverent, if less important, are no less human. If there were no poets who, like Byron, express these states, Poetry would lack something.

An authentic and original work nearly always shocks its first readers and Byron's "new manner" was no exception.

> Beppo is just imported but not perused. The greater the levity of Lord Byron's Compositions, the more I imagine him to suffer from the turbid state of his mind.
> (Lady Byron.)

> Frere particularly observed that the world had now given up the foolish notion that you were to be identified with your sombre heroes, and had acknowledged with what great success and good keeping you had portrayed a grand imaginary being. But the same admiration cannot be bestowed upon, and will not be due to the Rake Juan. . . . All the idle stories about your Venetian life will be more than confirmed. (Hobhouse.)

Dear *Adorable* Lord Byron, *don't* make a more *coarse* old libertine of yourself . . . When you don't feel quite up to a spirit of benevolence . . . throw away your pen, my love, and take a little *calomel.* (Hariette Wilson, who shortly afterwards offered to come and pimp for him.)

I would rather have the fame of Childe Harold for THREE YEARS *than an* IMMORTALITY *of Don Juan.*

(Teresa Guiccoli.)

Some of his friends, among them Hobhouse, admired parts of *Don Juan,* but the only person who seems to have realized how utterly different in kind it was from all Byron's previous work was John Lockhart:

Stick to Don Juan; it is the only sincere thing you have ever written . . . out of all sight the best of your works; it is by far the most spirited, the most straightforward, the most interesting, and the most poetical . . . the great charm of its style, is that it is not much like the style of any other poem in the world.

Byron was not normally given to praising his own work, but of *Don Juan* he was openly proud:

Of the fate of the "pome" I am quite uncertain, and do not anticipate much brilliancy from your silence. But I do not care. I am as sure as the Archbishop of Granada that I never wrote better, and I wish you all better taste.

As to "Don Juan," confess, confess—you dog be candid—that it is the sublime of *that there* sort of writing—it may be bawdy but is it not good English? It may be profligate, but is it not life, is it not the *thing?* Could any man have written it who has not lived in the world?—and tooled in a post-chaise?—in a hackney coach?—in a gondola?—against a wall?—in a court carriage?—in a vis-a-vis?—on a table?—and under it?

There is an element of swank in this description, for the poem is far less bawdy than he makes it sound. Only a small part of the experience upon which Byron drew in writing it was amorous.

What Byron means by life—which explains why he could never appreciate Wordsworth or Keats—is the motion of life, the *passage* of events and thoughts. His visual descriptions of scenery or architecture are not particularly vivid, nor are his portrayal of states of mind particularly profound, but at the description of things in motion or the way in which the mind wanders from one thought to another he is a great master.

Unlike most poets, he must be read very rapidly as if the words were single frames in a movie film; stop on a word or a line and the poetry vanishes—the feeling seems superficial, the rhyme forced, the grammar all over the place—but read at the proper pace, it gives a conviction of watching the real thing which many profounder writers fail to inspire for, though motion is not the only characteristic of life, it is an essential one.

If Byron was sometimes slipshod in his handling of the language, he was a stickler for factual accuracy; "I don't care one lump of sugar," he once wrote, "for my poetry; but for my *costume*, and my *correctness* . . . I will combat lustily," and, on another occasion, "I hate things *all fiction* . . . There should always be some foundation of fact for the most airy fabric, and pure invention is but the talent of a liar." He was furious when the poem "Pilgrimage to Jerusalem" was attributed to him: "How the devil should I write about *Jerusalem*, never having been yet there?" And he pounced, with justice, on Wordsworth's lines about Greece:

> Rivers, fertile plains, and sounding shores,
> Under a cope of variegated sky.

The rivers are dry half the year, the plains are barren, and the shores as "still" and "tideless" as the Mediterranean can make them; the sky is anything but variegated, being for months and months "darkly, deeply, beautifuly blue."

The material of his poems is always drawn from events that actually happened, either to himself or to people he knew, and he took great trouble to get his technical facts, such as sea terms, correct.

When he stopped work on *Don Juan,* he had by no means exhausted his experience. Reading through Professor Marchand's recent biography, one comes across story after story that seems a natural for the poem; Caroline Lamb, for example, surrounded by little girls in white, burning effigies of Byron's pictures and casting into the flames copies of his letters because she could not bear to part with the originals; Byron himself, at Shelley's cremation, getting acutely sunburned, and Teresa preserving a piece of skin when he peeled; Teresa forbidding an amateur performance of *Othello* because she couldn't speak English and wasn't going to have anybody else play Desdemona. And, if Byron's shade is still interested in writing, there are plenty of posthumous incidents. The Greeks stole his lungs as a relic and then lost them; at his funeral, noble carriage after noble carriage lumbered by, all empty, because the aristocracy felt they must show some respect to a fellow-peer but did not dare seem to show approval of his politics or his private life; Fletcher, his valet, started a macaroni factory and failed; Teresa married a French marquis who used to introduce her as "*La Marquise de Boissy, ma femme, ancienne maîtresse de Byron*" and after his death maîtresse devoted herself to spiritualism, talking with the spirits of both Byron and her first husband. What stanzas they could all provide! How suitable, too, for a *that-there* poet that the room in which his "Memoirs" were burned should now be called the Byron Room, how perfect the scene John Buchan describes of himself and Henry James setting down to examine the archives of Lady Lovelace:

> . . . during a summer weekend, Henry James and I waded through masses of ancient indecency, and duly wrote an opinion . . . My colleague never turned a hair. His only words for some special vileness were "singular"—"most curious"—"nauseating, perhaps, but how quite inexpressibly significant."

DINGLEY DELL & THE FLEET

To become mature is to recover that sense of seriousness which one had as a child at play.

F. W. NIETZSCHE

All characters who are products of the mythopeoic imagination are instantaneously recognizable by the fact that their existence is not defined by their social and historial context; transfer them to another society or another age and their characters and behavior will remain unchanged. In consequence, once they have been created, they cease to be their author's characters and become the reader's; he can continue their story for himself.

Anna Karenina is not such a character for the reader cannot imagine her apart from the particular milieu in which Tolstoi places her or the particular history of her life which he records; Sherlock Holmes, on the other hand, is: every reader, according to his fancy, can imagine adventures for him which Conan Doyle forgot, as it were, to tell us.

Tolstoi was a very great novelist, Conan Doyle a very minor one, yet it is the minor not the major writer who possesses the mythopoeic gift. The mythopoeic imagination is only accidentally related, it would seem, to the talent for literary expression; in Cervantes' *Don Quixote* they are found together, in Rider Haggard's *She* literary talent is largely absent. Indeed, few of the writers whom we call great have created mythical characters. In Shakespeare's plays we find five, Prospero, Ariel, Caliban, Falstaff and Hamlet, and Hamlet is a myth for actors only; the proof that, for actors, he is a myth is that all of them without exception, irrespective of age, build, or even sex, wish to play the part.

After Cervantes, as a writer who combines literary talent and a mythopoeic imagination, comes Dickens and, of his many mythical creations, Mr. Pickwick is one of the most memorable. Though the appeal of mythical characters transcends all highbrow-lowbrow frontiers of taste, it is not unlimited; every such character is symbolic of some important and perpetual human concern, but a reader must have experienced this concern, even if he cannot define it to himself, before the character can appeal to him. Judging by my own experience, I would say that *Pickwick Papers* is emphatically *not* a book for children and the reflections which follow are the result of my asking myself: "Why is it that I now read with such delight a book which, when I was given it to read as a boy, I found so boring, although it apparently contains nothing which is too 'grown-up' for a twelve-year-old?" The conclusion I have come to is that the real theme of *Pickwick Papers*—I am not saying Dickens was consciously aware of it and, indeed, I am pretty certain he was not—is the Fall of Man. It is the story of a man who is innocent, that is to say, who has not eaten of the Tree of the Knowledge of Good and Evil and is, therefore, living in Eden. He then eats of the Tree, that is to say, he becomes conscious of the reality of Evil but, instead of falling from innocence into sin—this is what makes him a mythical character—he changes from an innocent child into an innocent adult who no longer lives in an imaginary Eden of his own but in the real and fallen world.

If my conclusion is correct, it explains why *Pickwick Papers* said nothing to me as a boy because, though no boy is innocent, he has no clear notion of innocence, nor does he know that to be no longer innocent, but to wish that one were, is part of the definition of an adult.

However he accounts for it, every adult knows that he lives in a world where, though some are more fortunate than others, no one can escape physical and mental suffering, a world where everybody experiences some degree of contradiction between what he desires to do and what his conscience tells him he ought to do or others will allow him to do. Everybody wishes that this world were not like that, that he could live in a world where desires would conflict neither with each other nor with duties nor with the laws of nature, and a great number of us enjoy imagining what such a world would be like.

Our dream pictures of the Happy Place where suffering and evil are unknown are of two kinds, the Edens and the New Jerusalems. Though it is possible for the same individual to imagine both, it is unlikely that his interest in both will be equal and I suspect that between the Arcadian whose favorite daydream is of Eden, and the Utopian whose favorite daydream is of New Jerusalem there is a characterological gulf as unbridgeable as that between Blake's Prolifics and Devourers.

In their relation to the actual fallen world, the difference between Eden and New Jerusalem is a temporal one. Eden is a past world in which the contradictions of the present world have not yet arisen; New Jerusalem is a future world in which they have at last been resolved. Eden is a place where its inhabitants may do whatever they like to do; the motto over its gate is, "Do what thou wilt is here the Law." New Jerusalem is a place where its inhabitants like to do whatever they ought to do, and its motto is, "In His will is our peace."

In neither place is the moral law felt as an imperative; in Eden because the notion of a universal law is unknown, in New Jerusalem because the law is no longer a law-for, commanding that we do this and abstain from doing that, but a law-of, like the laws of nature, which describes how, in fact, its inhabitants behave.

To be an inhabitant of Eden, it is absolutely required that one be happy and likable; to become an inhabitant of New Jerusalem it is absolutely required that one be happy and good. Eden cannot be entered; its inhabitants are born there. No unhappy or unlikable individual is ever born there and, should one of its inhabitants become unhappy or unlikable, he must leave. Nobody is born in New Jerusalem but, to enter it, one must, either through one's own acts or by Divine Grace, have become good. Nobody ever leaves New Jerusalem, but the evil or the unredeemed are forever excluded.

The psychological difference between the Arcadian dreamer and the Utopian dreamer is that the backward-looking Arcadian knows that his expulsion from Eden is an irrevocable fact and that his dream, therefore, is a wish-dream which cannot become real; in consequence, the actions which led to his expulsion are of no concern to his dream. The forward-looking Utopian, on the other hand, necessarily believes that his New Jerusalem is a dream which ought to be realized so that the actions by which it could be realized are a necessary element in his dream; it must include images, that is to say, not only of New Jerusalem itself but also images of the Day of Judgment.

Consequently, while neither Eden nor New Jerusalem are places where aggression can exist, the Utopian dream permits indulgence in aggressive fantasies in a way that the Arcadian dream does not. Even Hitler, I imagine, would have defined his New Jerusalem as a world where there are no Jews, not as a world where they are being gassed by the million day after day in ovens, but he was a Utopian, so the ovens had to come in.

How any individual envisages Eden is determined by his temperament, personal history and cultural milieu, but to all dream Edens the following axioms, I believe, apply.

1) Eden is a world of pure being and absolute uniqueness. Change can occur but as an instantaneous trans-

formation, not through a process of becoming. Everyone is incomparable.
2) The self is satisfied whatever it demands; the ego is approved of whatever it chooses.
3) There is no distinction between the objective and the subjective. What a person appears to others to be is identical with what he is to himself. His name and his clothes are as much *his* as his body, so that, if he changes them, he turns into someone else.
4) Space is both safe and free. There are walled gardens but no dungeons, open roads in all directions but no wandering in the wilderness.
5) Temporal novelty is without anxiety, temporal repetition without boredom.
6) Whatever the social pattern, each member of society is satisfied according to his conception of his needs. If it is a hierarchical society, all masters are kind and generous, all servants faithful old retainers.
7) Whatever people do, whether alone or in company, is some kind of play. The only motive for an action is the pleasure it gives the actor, and no deed has a goal or an effect beyond itself.
8) Three kinds of erotic life are possible, though any particular dream of Eden need contain only one. The polymorphous-perverse promiscuous sexuality of childhood, courting couples whose relation is potential, not actual, and the chastity of natural celibates who are without desire.
9) Though there can be no suffering or grief, there can be death. If a death occurs, it is not a cause for sorrow —the dead are not missed—but a social occasion for a lovely funeral.
10) The Serpent, acquaintance with whom results in immediate expulsion—any serious need or desire.

The four great English experts on Eden are Dickens, Oscar Wilde, Ronald Firbank and P. G. Wodehouse.[1]

[1] N. B. To my surprise, the only creators of Edens during the last three centuries I can think of, have all been English.

If, in comparing their versions of Eden with those of the Ancient World, I call theirs Christian, I am not, of course, asserting anything about their own beliefs. I only mean that their versions presuppose an anthropology for which Christianity is, historically, responsible. Whether it can exist in a society where the influence of Christianty has never been felt or has been eradicated, I do not know. I suspect that works like *Pickwick Papers, The Importance of Being Earnest, The Flower Beneath the Foot,* and *Blandings Castle* would bewilder a Russian Communist as much as they would have bewildered an Ancient Greek. The Communist would probably say: "It is incredible that anybody should *like* people so silly and useless as Mr. Pickwick, Miss Prism, Madame Wetme and Bertie Wooster." The Greek would probably have said: "It is incredible that such people, so plain, middle-aged and untalented, should be *happy.*"

When the Greeks pictured Eden, they thought of it as a place which the gods or Chance might permit to exist. In his tenth Pythian Ode, Pindar describes the life of the Hyperboreans.

> Never the Muse is absent
> from their ways: lyres clash and the flutes cry
> and everywhere maiden choruses whirling.
> They bind their hair in golden laurel and take their
> holiday.
> Neither disease nor bitter old age is mixed
> In their sacred blood; far from labor and battle
> they live; they escape Nemesis
> the overjust.

Or it might exist, like the Islands of the Blessed, as a place of rest and reward for dead heroes. The Greek poets speak of it, not as an imaginary poetic world, but as a distant region of the real world which they have not visited but of which they have heard reports. Pindar's description of the Hyperboreans is related to his definition of the difference between gods and men in the sixth Nemean:

> There is one
> race of men, one race of gods; both have breath
> of life from a single mother. But sundered power
> holds us divided, so that the one is nothing, while
> for the other the brazen sky is established
> their sure citadel for ever. Yet we have some likeness in great
> intelligence or strength to the immortals,
> though we know not what the day will bring, what course
> after nightfall
> destiny has written that we must run to the end.

Gods and men do not differ in nature, only in power; the gods are immortal and can do what they like, men are mortal and can never foresee the consequences of their actions. Therefore, the more powerful a man is, the more godlike he becomes. It is possible to conceive of men so gifted by fortune that, like the Hypoboreans, their life would be indistinguishable from that of the gods.

This is a conception natural to a shame-culture in which who a man is is identical with what he does and suffers. The happy man is the fortunate man, and fortune is objectively recognizable; to be fortunate means to be successful, rich, powerful, beautiful, admired. When such a culture imagines Eden, therefore, it automatically excludes the weak and the ungifted, children, old people, poor people, ugly people.

The first significant difference between the conception of man held by a shame-culture and that of a guilt-culture is that a guilt-culture distinguishes between what a man is to other men, the self he manifests in his body, his actions, his words, and what he is to himself, a unique ego which is unchanged by anything he does or suffers. In a shame-culture, there is no real difference between statements in the third person and statements in the first; in a guilt-culture, they are totally distinct. In the statement *Jones is six feet tall,* the predicate qualifies the subject; in the statement *I am six feet tall,* it does not. It qualifies a self which the subject recognizes to be six feet tall; the *I* has no height.

In a shame-culture, the moral judgment a man passes upon himself is identical with that which others pass on him; the virtue or shamefulness of an act lies in the nature of the act itself, irrespective or the doer's personal intention or responsibility. In a guilt-culture, the subject passes moral judgment upon his thoughts and feelings even if they are never realized in action, and upon his acts irrespective of whether others know of them or not, approve of them or not.

In a guilt-culture, therefore, there are a special series of first-person propositions in which the predicate does qualify the subject. For example:

I am innocent/guilty
I am proud/humble
I am penitent/impenitent
I am happy/unhappy.

(I am in a state of pleasure/pain is not, of course, one of them. Pain and pleasure are states of the self, not of the ego.)

If I make any such assertion, it must be true or false, but no person except myself can know which; there is no way in which, from observing me, another can come to any conclusion.

A writer brought up in a Christian society who would describe Eden has, therefore, to cope with a problem which his pagan predecessors were spared. As an artist he can only deal in the manifest and objective—his Eden, like the pagan one, must be a fortunate place where there is no suffering and everybody has a good time—but he has to devise a way of making outward appearances signify subjective states of innocence and happiness to which, in the real world, they are not necessarily related.

If one compares versions of Eden by pagan writers with Christian versions, it is noticeable that the former are beautiful in a serious way and that the latter are for the most part comic, even grotesque; they reserve the serious for descriptions of New Jerusalem.

Suppose a writer wishes to show that every man loves himself, not because of this or that quality he possesses, but simply because he is uniquely he, what can he do? One possible image is that of an exceptionally ugly man—prodigiously fat, let us say—who is nevertheless convinced that he is irresistible to the ladies.

Here the exceptional obesity is an indirect sign for the uniqueness of the subject, and the fantastic vanity—in real life, a man must be reasonably good-looking before he can become vain in this way—an indirect sign for the independence of self-love from any quality of the self. But both signs remain indirect; the ugliest, the most average-looking and the most beautiful human beings all love themselves in the same way.

Suppose he wishes to portray a humble man. The writer can show someone engaging by his own choice—he is perfectly free to refuse—in activities for which he has no talent whatsoever and at which, therefore, he is bound to fail and look ridiculous, and then show him as radiant with self-esteem in his failure as if he had triumphed. Here self-esteem in a situation which in real life would destroy it is an indirect sign for humility; but not a direct sign, for a successful man can be humble too.

Or again, suppose a writer wishes to portray an innocent man. No human being is innocent, but small children are not yet personally guilty. It is possible that they have some knowledge of good and evil, but it is certain they have no innate knowledge of what their parents and society call right and wrong, and apply alike to such diverse matters as toliet habits, social manners, stealing and cruelty.

Compared with a normal adult, a small child is lacking in a sense of honor and a sense of shame. One way, therefore, in which a writer can portray an innocent man is to show an adult behaving in a way which his society considers outrageous without showing the slightest awareness of public opinion. A normal adult might wish to behave in the same way and even do so if he were certain that nobody else would get to hear of his behavior, but fear of social disapproval will prevent him from behaving so in public. The lack of shame is an indirect sign of innocence but, once again, not a direct sign, because lunatics show the same lack of shame.

When the novel opens, Mr. Pickwick is middle-aged. In his farewell speech at the Adelphi, he says that nearly the whole of his previous life had been devoted to business and the pursuit of wealth, but we can no more imagine what he did during those years than we can imagine what Don Quixote did before he went mad or what Falstaff was like as a young man. In our minds Mr. Pickwick is born in middle age with independent means; his mental and physical powers are those of a middle-aged man, his experience of the world that of a newborn child. The society into which he is born is a commercial puritanical society in which wealth is honored, poverty despised, and any detected lapse from the strictest standards of propriety severely punished. In such a society, Mr. Pickwick's circumstances and nature make him a fortunate individual. He is comfortably off and, aside from a tendency at times to overindulge in food and drink, without vices. Sex, for example, is no temptation to him. One cannot conceive of him either imagining himself romantically in love with a girl of the lower orders, like Don Quixote, or consorting with whores, like Falstaff. So far as his experience goes, this world is an Eden without evil or suffering.

> His sitting-room was the first floor front, his bedroom the second floor front; and thus, whether he was sitting at his desk in his parlour or standing before the dressing-glass in his dormitory, he had an equal opportunity of contemplating human nature in all the numerous phases it exhibits, in that not more populous than popular thoroughfare. His landlady, Mrs. Bardell—the relict and sole executrix of a deceased custom-house officer—

was a comely woman of bustling manners and agreeable appearance, with a natural genius for cooking, improved by study and long practice, into an exquisite talent. There were no children, no servants, no fowls—cleanliness and quiet reigned throughout the house; and in it Mr. Pickwick's will was law.

His three young friends, Tupman, Snodgrass and Winkle, are equally innocent. Each has a ruling passion, Tupman for the fair sex, Snodgrass for poetry, and Winkle for sport, but their talents are not very formidable. We are not given any specimen of Snodgrass's poems, but we may presume that, at their best, they reach the poetic level of Mrs. Leo Hunter's "Ode to an Expiring Frog."

> Say, with fiends in spare of boys
> With wild halloo and brutal noise
> Hunted thee from marshy joys
> With a dog,
> Expiring frog?

We are shown Winkle at a shoot and learn that the birds are in far less danger than the bystanders. Tupman's age and girth are hardly good qualifications for a Romeo or a Don Juan. Contact with the world cures them of their illusions without embittering them, Eros teaches the two young men that the favors of Apollo and Artemis are not what they desire—Snodgrass marries Emily and becomes a gentleman farmer, Winkle marries Arabella Allen and goes into his father's business—and Tupman comes to acquiesce cheerfully in the prospect of a celibate old age.

The results of Mr. Pickwick's scientific researches into the origin of the Hampstead Ponds and the nature of Tittlebats were no more reliable, we may guess, than his archaeology but, as the book progresses, we discover that, if his ability at enquiry is less than he imagines, his capacity to learn is as great. What he learns is not what he set out to learn but is forced upon him by fate and by his decision to go to prison, but his curiosity about life is just as eager at the end of the book as it was at the beginning; what he has been taught is the difference between trivial and important truths.

From time to time, Dickens interrupts his narrative to let Mr. Pickwick read or listen to a tale. Some, like the Bagman's story, the story of the goblins who stole a sexton, the anecdote of the tenant and the gloomy ghost, are tall tales about the supernatural, but a surprising number are melodramas about cases of extreme suffering and evil: a broken-down clown beats his devoted wife and dies of D.T.'s; the son of a wicked father breaks his mother's heart, is transported, returns after seventeen years and is only saved from parricide by his father dying before he can strike him; a madman raves sadistically; a man is sent to prison for debt by his father-in-law, his wife and child die, he comes out of prison and devotes the rest of his life to revenge, first refusing to save his enemy's son from drowning and then reducing him to absolute want.

Stories of this kind are not tall; they may be melodramatically written, but everybody knows that similar things happen in real life. Dickens' primary reason for introducing them was, no doubt, that of any writer of a serial—to introduce a novel entertainment for his readers at a point when he feels they would welcome an interruption in the main narrative—but, intentionally or unintentionally, they contribute to our understanding of Mr. Pickwick.

Mr. Pickwick is almost as fond of hearing horror tales and curious anecdotes as Don Quixote is of reading Courtly Romances, but the Englishman's illusion about the relationship of literature to life is the opposite of the Spaniard's.

To Don Quixote, literature and life are identical; he believes that, when his senses present him with facts which are incompatible with courtly romance, his senses must be deceiving him. To Mr. Pickwick, on the other hand, literature and life are separate universes; evil and suffering do not exist in the world he perceives with his senses, only in the world of entertaining fiction.

Don Quixote sets out to be a Knight Errant, to win glory and the hand of his beloved by overthrowing the wicked and unjust and rescuing the innocent and afflicted. When Mr.

Pickwick and his friends set out for Rochester, they have no such noble ambitions; they are simply looking for the novel and unexpected. Their reason for going to Bath or to Ipswich is that of the tourist—they have never been there.

Don Quixote expects to suffer hardship, wounds and weariness in the good cause, and is inclined to suspect the pleasant, particularly if feminine, as either an illusion or a temptation to make him false to his vocation. The Pickwick Club expects to have nothing but a good time, seeing pretty towns and countrysides, staying in well-stocked inns and making pleasant new acquaintances like the Wardles. However, the first new new acquaintance they make in their exploration of Eden is with the serpent, Jingle, of whose real nature they have not the slightest suspicion. When Jingle's elopement with Rachel Wardle opens his eyes, Mr. Pickwick turns into a part-time Knight Errant: he assumes that Jingle, the base adventurer, is a unique case and, whenever he comes across his tracks, he conceives it his duty not to rest until he has frustrated his fell designs, but his main purpose in travel is still to tour Eden. Rescuing unsuspecting females from adventurers has not become his vocation.

During his first pursuit of Jingle, Mr. Pickwick meets Sam Weller, decides to engage him as a personal servant, and in trying to inform Mrs. Bardell of his decision creates the misunderstanding which is to have such unfortunate consequences. Sam Weller is no innocent; he has known what it is like to be destitute and homeless, sleeping under the arches of Waterloo Bridge, and he does not expect this world to be just or its inhabitants noble. He accepts Mr. Pickwick's offer, not because he particularly likes him, but because the job promises to be a better one than that of the Boots at an inn.

> I wonder whether I'm meant to be a footman, or a groom, or a gamekeeper or a seedsman? I look like a sort of compo of every one of 'em. Never mind; there's change of air, plenty to see, and little to do; and all this suits my complaint uncommon.

But before the story ends, he is calling Mr. Pickwick an angel, and his devotion to his master has grown so great that he insists upon being sent to prison in order to look after him. For Sam Weller had, after all, his own kind of innocence: about the evil in the world he had learned as much as anybody, but his experience had never led him to suspect that a person so innocent of evil as Mr. Pickwick could inhabit it.

Mr. Pickwick has hardly engaged Sam Weller when the letter arrives from Dodson and Fogg, announcing that Mrs. Bardell is suing him for Breach of Promise, and his real education begins.

If, hitherto, he had ever thought about the Law at all, he had assumed that it was what the Law must always claim to be:

1) Just. Those acts which the Law prohibits and punishes are always unjust; no just or innocent act is ever prohibited or punished.
2) Efficient. There are no unjust acts or persons that the Law overlooks or allows to go unpunished.
3) Infallible. Those whom the Law finds guilty are always guilty; no innocent person is ever found guilty.

He has got to learn that none of these claims is fulfilled, and why, in this world, they cannot be fulfilled.

Even were the Law formally perfect, its administration cannot be, because it has to be administered, not by angels or machines, but by human individuals who, like all human beings, vary in intelligence, temperament and moral character: some are clever, some stupid, some kind, some cruel, some scrupulous, some unscrupulous.

Moreover, lawyers are in the morally anomalous position of owing their livelihood and social status to the criminal, the unjust and the ignorant; if all men knew the Law and kept it, there would be no work for lawyers. Doctors also owe their livelihood to an evil, sickness, but at least sickness is a natural evil—men do not desire ill health—but crimes and civil wrongs are acts of human choice, so that the contradiction between the purpose of Law and the personal interest of lawyers is more glaring. And then the complexity of the Law and the nature of the legal process make those who practice law peculiarly liable to a vice which one might call the vice of Imaginary Innocence.

No human being is innocent, but there is a class of innocent human actions called Games.

A game is a closed world of action which has no relation to any other actions of those who play it; the players have no motive for playing the game except the pleasure it gives them, and the outcome of the game has no consequences beyond itself. Strictly speaking, a game in which the players are paid to play, or in which they play for money stakes, ceases to be a game, for money exists outside the closed world of the game. In practice, one may say that a game played for stakes remains a game so long as the sums of money won or lost are felt by the players to be, not real, but token payments, that is to say, what they win or lose has no sensible effect upon their lives after the game is over.

The closed world of the game is one of mock passions, not real ones. Many games are, formally, mock battles, but if any one of the players should feel or display real hostility, he immediately ceases to be a player. Even in boxing and wrestling matches, in which the claim to be called games at all is doubtful, the ritual of shaking hands at the beginning and end asserts that they are not fights between real enemies.

Within the closed world of the game the only human beings are the players; the other inhabitants are things, balls, bats, chessman, cards, etc.

Like the real world, the game world is a world of laws which the players must obey because obedience to them is a necessary condition for entering it. In the game world there is only one crime, cheating, and the penalty for this is exclusion; once a man is known to be a cheat, no other player will play with him.

In a game the pleasure of playing, of exercising skill, takes precedence over the pleasure of winning. If this were not so, if victory were the real goal, a skillful player would prefer to have an unskillful one as his opponent, but only those to whom, like cardsharpers, a game is not a game but a livelihood, prefer this. In the game world the pleasure of victory is the pleasure of *just* winning. The game world, therefore, is an innocent world because the ethical judgment good-or-bad does not apply to it; a good game means a game at the conclusion of which all the players, whether winners or losers, can truthfully say that they have enjoyed themselves, a point which is made by the Little Man's speech after the cricket match between Dingley Dell and Muggleton.

> Sir, while we remember that Muggleton has given birth to a Dumkins and a Podder, let us never forget that Dingley Dell can boast of a Luffey and a Struggles. Every gentleman who hears me, is probably acquainted with the reply made by an individual who—to use an ordinary figure of speech—"hung out" in a tub, to the Emperor Alexander:—"If I were not Diogenes," said he, "I would be Alexander": I can well imagine these gentlemen to say. If I were not Dumkins, I would be Luffey; If I were not Podder, I would be Struggles.

The vice of Imaginary Innocence consists in regarding an action in the open world of reality as if it were an action in the closed world of the game.

If this world were the worst of all possible worlds, a world where everybody was obliged to do what he dislikes doing and prohibited from doing anything he enjoyed, this vice would be impossible. It is only possible because some people have the good fortune to enjoy doing something which society requires to be done; what, from the point of view of society, is their necessary labor, is, from their own, voluntary play. Men fall into this vice when, because of the pleasure which the exercise of their calling gives them, they forget that what is play for them may for others concern real needs and passions.

Before Mr. Pickwick has to suffer in person from this human failing, he has already witnessed a manifestation of it in the party politics of Eatonswill.

Party politics presupposes that it is possible for two people, equally rational and well-meaning, to hold different opinions about a policy and possible for a man to be convinced by argument that his opinion has been mistaken. It is also presupposes that, however widely their political opinions may differ, all voters are agreed that the goal of politics is the establishment of a just and smoothly running society. But in Eatonswill the pleasure of party rivalry and debate has become an end in itself to both parties, a closed game world, and the real goal of politics has been forgotten.

> The Blues lost no opportunity of opposing the Buffs and the Buffs lost no opportunity of opposing the Blues . . . If the Buffs proposed to new skylight the market place, the Blues got up public meeting and denounced the proceeding; if the Blues proposed the erection of an additional pump in the High Street, the Buffs rose as one man and stood aghast at the enormity. There were Blue shops and Buff shops, Blue Inns and Buff Inns; there was a Blue aisle and a Buff aisle in the very church itself.

On such a parochial scale politics as a game is relatively harmless, though on a national scale it is vicious, but there can be no circumstances in which the practice of Law as a game is not vicious. People who are not lawyers never come into court for fun; they come, either because they have been arrested or because they believe they have been wronged and see no other way of redress. Winning or losing their case is never a mock victory or defeat but always a real one; if they lose, they go to prison or suffer social disgrace or are made to pay money.

Rightly or wrongly, it is believed in our culture that, in most criminal and civil trials, the best means of arriving at the ethical judgment guilty-or-not-guilty is through a kind of aesthetic verbal combat between a prosecuting and a defending counsel, to which the judge acts as a referee, and the verdict is given by a jury. To say that a lawyer is a good lawyer, therefore, is an aesthetic not an ethical description; a good lawyer is not one who causes justice to be done, but one who wins his cases, whether his client be innocent or guilty, in the right or in the wrong, and nothing will enhance his reputation for being a good lawyer so much as winning a case against apparently hopeless odds, a state of affairs which is more likely to arise if his client is really guilty than if he is really innocent. As men, Dodson and Fogg are scoundrels but, as lawyers, their decent colleague Mr. Perkins has to admit that they are very good.

> Mrs. Bardell, supported by Mrs. Chappins, was led in and placed in a drooping state at the other end of the seat on which Mr. Pickwick sat . . . Mrs. Saunders then appeared, leading in Master Bardell. At sight of her child, Mrs. Bardell started: suddenly recollecting herself, she kissed him in a frantic manner; then relapsing into a state of hysterical imbecility the good lady requested to be informed where she was. In reply to this, Mrs. Chappins and Mrs. Saunders turned their heads away and wept, while Messrs Dodson and Fogg intreated the plaintiff to compose herself . . . "Very good notion, that indeed," whispered Perkins to Mr. Pickwick. "Capital fellows those Dodson and Fogg; excellent ideas of effect, my dear sir, excellent."

Dodson and Fogg may be scoundrels but they are not wicked men; though they cause undeserved suffering in others, they have no malevolent intent—the suffering they cause gives them no pleasure. To them, their clients are the pieces with which they play the legal game, which they find as enjoyable as it is lucrative. So, too, when Sergeant Buzzfuzz expresses his detestation of Mr. Pickwick's character, or Mr. Sumpkins bullies the unfortunate witness Winkle, what their victims feel as real hostility is, in fact, the mock hostility of the player: had they been engaged for the Defense, their abuse would have been directed against Mrs. Bardell and Mrs. Chappins, and they will have completely forgotten about the whole case by the next morning. The Guild Hall which is a Purgatory to Mr. Pickwick is to them what Dingley Dell is to him, an Arcadia.

When he is found guilty, Mr. Pickwick takes a vow that he will never pay the damages. In so doing he takes his first step out of Eden into the real world, for to take a vow is to commit one's future, and Eden has no conception of the future for it exists in a timeless present. In Eden, a man always does what he likes to do at the moment, but a man who takes a vow commits himself to doing something in the future which, when the time comes, he may dislike doing. The consequence of Mr. Pickwick's vow is that he has to leave his Eden of clean linen and polished silver for a Limbo of dirty crockery and rusty broken toasting forks where, in the eyes of the Law, he is a guilty man, a lawbreaker among other lawbreakers.

The particular class of lawbreakers among whom Mr. Pickwick finds himself in The Fleet are debtors. In selecting this class of offender rather than another for him to encounter, one of Dickens' reasons was, of course, that he considered the English laws of his day concerning debt to be monstrously unjust and sending his fictional hero there gave him an opportunity for satirical exposure of a real social abuse. But in a world where money is the universal medium of exchange, the notion of debt has a deep symbolic resonance. Hence the clause in the Lord's Prayer as it appears in the Authorized Version of St. Matthew—"Forgive us our debts as we forgive our debtors"—and the parable of the forgiving and unforgiving creditor.

To be in debt means to have taken more from someone than we have given whether the *more* refers to material or to spiritual goods. Since we are not autonomous beings who can create and sustain our lives by ourselves, every human being is in debt to God, to Nature, to parents and neighbors for his existence, and it is against this background of universal human debt that we view the special case of debt and credit between one individual and another. We are born unequal; even if all social inequalities were abolished, there would remain the natural inequalities of talent and inherited tendencies, and circumstance outside our control will always affect both our need to receive and our capacity to give. A rich man, in whatever sense he is rich, can give more than a poor man; a baby and a sick person need more from others than a healthy adult. Debt or credit cannot be measured in quantitative terms; a relation between two persons is just if both take no more than they need and give as much as they can, and unjust if either takes more or gives less than this.

In prison, Mr. Pickwick meets three kinds of debtors. There are those like Smangle who are rather thieves than debtors for they have borrowed money with the conscious intention of not paying it back. There are the childish who believe in magic; they intended to return what they borrowed when their luck changed, but had no rational reason to suppose that it would. And there are those like the cobbler who have fallen into debt through circumstances which they could neither foresee nor control.

> An old gentleman that I worked for, down in the country, and died well off, left five thousand pounds behind him, one of which he left to me, 'cause I'd married a humble relation of his. And being surrounded by a great number of nieces and nephews, as well always quarrelling and fighting among themselves for the property, he makes me his executor to divide the rest among 'em as the will provided, and I paid all the legacies. I'd hardly done it when one nevy brings an action to set the will aside. The case comes on, some months afterwards, afore a deaf old gentleman in a back room somewhere down by Paul's Churchyard . . . and arter four counsels had taken a day a piece to both him regularly, he takes a week or two to consider and then gives his judgment that the testator was not quite right in the head, and I must pay all the money back again, and all the costs. I appealed; the case comes on before three or four very sleepy gentlemen, who had heard it all before in the other court and they very dutifully confirmed the decision of the old gentleman below. After that we went into Chancery, where we are still. My lawyers have had all my thousand pounds long ago; and what between the estate as they call it and the costs, I'm here for ten thousand, and shall stop here till I die, mending shoes.

Yet, in the eyes of the Law, all three classes are equally guilty. This does not mean, however, that all debtors receive the same treatment.

> The three chums informed Mr. Pickwick in a breath that money was in the Fleet, just what money was out of it; that it would instantly procure him almost anything

> he desired; and that, supposing he had it, and had no objection to spend it, if he only signified his wish to have a room to himself, he might take possession of one, furnished and fitted to boot, in half an hour's time.

The lot of the penniless debtor, like the Chancery Prisoner, was, in Dickens' time, atrocious, far worse than that of the convicted criminal, for the convict was fed gratis by the State but the debtor was not, so that, if penniless, he must subsist on the charity of his fellow prisoners or die of starvation. On the other hand, for those with a little money and no sense of shame, the Fleet Prison could seem a kind of Eden.

> There were many classes of people here, from the laboring man in his fustian jacket, to the broken down spendthrift in his shawl dressing-gown, most appropriately out at elbows; but there was the same air about them all—a listless jail-bird careless swagger, a vagabondish who's afraid sort of bearing which is indescribable in words . . . "It strikes me, Sam," said Mr. Pickwick, "that imprisonment for debt is scarcely any punishment at all." "Think not, sir?," inquired Mr. Weller. "You see how these fellows drink and smoke and roar," replied Mr. Pickwick, It's quite impossible that they can mind it much." "Ah, that's just the very thing sir," rejoined Sam, "*they* don't mind it; it's a regular holiday to them—all porter and skittles. It is t'other wuns as gets down over, with this sort of thing: them down-hearted fellers as can't swig away at the beer, nor play at skittles neither: them as would pay as they could, and get's low by being boxed up. I'll tell you wot it is, sir; them as is always a idlin' in public houses it don't damage at all, and them as is always a working wen they can, it damages too much."

His encounter with the world of the Fleet is the end of Mr. Pickwick's innocence. When he started out on his adventures, he believed the world to be inhabited only by the well-meaning, the honest and the entertaining; presently he discovered that it also contains malevolent, dishonest and boring inhabitants, but it is only after entering the Fleet that he realizes it contains persons who suffer, and that the division between those who are suffering and those who are not is more significant than the division between the just and the unjust, the innocent and the guilty. He himself, for instance, has been unjustly convicted, but he is in prison by his own choice and, though he does not enjoy the Fleet as much as Dingley Dell, by the standards of comfort within the Fleet, he enjoys the advantages of a king, not because he is morally innocent while Jingle and Trotter are morally guilty, but because he happens to be the richest inmate while they are among the poorest. Then Mrs. Bardell, who through stupidity rather than malice is responsible for the injustice done to him, becomes a fellow prisoner. Mr. Pickwick is compelled to realize that he, too, is a debtor, because he has been more fortunate than most people, and that he must discharge his debt by forgiving his enemies and relieving their suffering. In order to do his duty, he has to do in fact what he had been falsely accused of doing, commit a breach of promise by breaking his vow and putting money into the pockets of Dodson and Fogg; for the sake of charity, he has to sacrifice his honor.

His loss of innocence through becoming conscious of the real world has the same consequences for Mr. Pickwick as a fictional character as recovering his sanity has for Don Quixote; in becoming ethically serious, both cease to be aesthetically comic, that is to say, interesting to the reader, and they must pass away, Don Quixote by dying, Mr. Pickwick by retiring from view.

Both novels are based upon the presupposition that there is a difference between the Law and Grace, the Righteous man and the Holy man: this can only be expressed indirectly by a comic contradiction in which the innocent hero comes into collision with the law without appearing, in his own eyes, to suffer. The only way in which their authors can compel the reader to interpret this correctly—neither to ignore the sign nor to take it as a direct sign—is, in the end, to take off the comic mask and say: "The Game, the make-believe is over: players and spectators alike must now return to reality. What you have heard was but a tall story."

POSTSCRIPT: THE FRIVOLOUS & THE EARNEST

An aesthetic religion (polytheism) draws no distinction between what is frivolous and what is serious because, for it, all existence is, in the last analysis, meaningless. The whims of the gods and, behind them, the whim of the Fates, are the ultimate arbiters of all that happens. It is immediately frivolous because it is ultimately in despair.

A frivolity which is innocent, because unaware that anything serious exists, can be charming, and a frivolity which, precisely because it is aware of what is serious, refuses to take seriously that which is not serious, can be profound. What is so distasteful about the Homeric gods is that they are well aware of human suffering but refuse to take it seriously. They take the lives of men as frivolously as their own; they meddle with the former for fun, and then get bored.

> When Zeus had brought the Trojans and Hector close to the ships, he left them beside the ships to bear the toil and woe unceasingly, and he himself turned his shining eyes away, gazing afar at the land of the horse-rearing Thracians and the Mysians, who fight in close array, and the noble Hippomolgoi who live on milk, and the Abioi, most righteous of men.
>
> (*Iliad*, Book XIII.)

They kill us for their sport. If so, no human sportsman would receive one of the gods in his house: they shoot men sitting and out of season.

If Homer had tried reading the *Iliad* to the gods on Olympus, they would either have started to fidget and presently asked if he hadn't got something a little lighter, or, taking it as a comic poem, would have roared with laughter or possibly, even, reacting like ourselves to a tear-jerking movie, have poured pleasing tears.

The songs of Apollo: the lucky improvisations of an amateur.

The only Greek god who does any work is Hephaestus, and he is a lame cuckold.

Render unto Caesar the things that are Caesar's and unto God the things that are God's. Christianity draws a distinction between what is frivolous and what is serious, but allows the former its place. What it condemns is not frivolity but idolatry, that is to say, taking the frivolous seriously.

The past is not to be taken seriously (*Let the dead bury their dead*) nor the future (*Take no thought for the morrow*), only the present instant and that, not for its aesthetic emotional content but for its historic decisiveness. (*Now is the appointed time.*)

Man desires to be free and he desires to feel important. This places him in a dilemma, for the more he emancipates himself from necessity the less important he feels.

That is why so many *actes gratuites* are criminal: a man asserts his freedom by disobeying a law and retains a sense of self-importance because the law he has disobeyed is an important one. Much crime is magic, an attempt to make free with necessity.

An alternative to criminal magic is the innocent game. Games are *actes gratuites* in which the players obey rules chosen by themselves. Games are freer than crimes because the rules of a game are arbitrary and moral laws are not; but they are less important.

The rules of a game give it importance to those who play it by making it difficult, a test of skill. This means, however, that a game can only be important to those who have the particular physical or mental skills which are required to play it, and the gift of such skills is a matter of chance.

To the degree that a vocation or a profession requires some gift, it partakes, for him who is able to practice it, of the nature of a game, however serious the social need it serves. The famous brain surgeon, Dr. Cushing, was once consulted by a student as to whether or not he should specialize in surgery: the doctor settled the question for him in the negative by asking; "Do you enjoy the sensation of putting a knife into living flesh?"

To witness an immoral act, like a man beating his wife, makes a spectator angry or unhappy. To witness an untalented act, like a clumsy man wrestling with a window blind or a piece of bad sculpture, makes him laugh.

Life is not a game because one cannot say: "I will live on condition that I have a talent for living." Those who cannot play a game can always be spectators, but no one can hire somebody else to live his life for him while he looks on.

In a game, just losing is almost as satisfying as just winning. But no man ever said with satisfaction, "I almost married the girl I love," or a nation, "We almost won the war." In life the loser's score is always zero.

Nothing can be essentially serious for man except that which is given to all men alike, and that which is commanded of all men alike.

All men alike are given a physical body with physical needs which have to be satisfied if they are to survive, and all men alike are given a will which has the power to make choices. (To say of someone that his will is strong or weak is not like saying that he is tall or short, or even that he is clever or stupid: it is a description of how his will functions, not an assessment of the amount of will power he possesses.)

Corresponding to these gifts are two commands: "In the sweat of thy face shalt thou eat bread," and "Thou shalt love the Lord thy God and thy neighbor as thyself," are both commanded of all men alike.

Thus the only two occupations which are intrinsically serious are the two which do not call for any particular natural gifts, namely, unskilled manual labor and the priesthood (in its ideal aspects as the Apostolate). Any unskilled laborer and any priest is interchangeable with every other. Any old porter can carry my bag, any trumpery priest absolve me of a mortal sin. One cannot say of an unskilled laborer or of a priest that one is better or worse than another; one can only say, in the case of the laborer, that he is employed, in the case of the priest, that he has been ordained.

Of all other occupations, one must say that, in themselves, they are frivolous. They are only serious in so far that they are the means by which those who practice them earn their bread and are not parasites on the labor of others, and to the degree that they permit or encourage the love of God and neighbor.

There is a game called Cops and Robbers, but none called Saints and Sinners.

It is incorrect to say, as the Declaration of Independence says, that all men have a right to the pursuit of happiness. All men have a right to avoid unnecessary pain if they can, and no man has a right to pleasure at the cost of another's pain. But happiness is not a right; it is a duty. To the degree that we are unhappy, we are in sin. (And vice versa.) A duty cannot be pursued because its imperative applies to the present instant, not to some future date.

My duty towards God is to be happy; my duty towards my neighbor is to try my best to give him pleasure and alleviate his pain. No human being can *make* another one happy.

GENIUS & APOSTLE

No genius has an in order that: *the Apostle has absolutely and paradoxically an* in order that.

SØREN KIERKEGAARD

I

In such theoretical discussions concerning the nature of drama as I have read, it has always seemed to me that insufficient attention was paid to the nature of the actor. What distinguishes a drama from both a game and a rite is that, in a game, the players play themselves and, in a rite, though the participants may *represent* somebody else, a god, for instance, they do not have to *imitate* him, any more than an ambassador to a foreign country has to imitate the sovereign whom he represents. Further, in both a game and a rite, the actions are real actions, or at least, real to the participants—goals are scored, the bull is killed, the bread and wine are transubstantiated—but, in a drama, all actions are mock actions—the actor who plays Banquo is not really murdered, the singer who plays Don Giovanni may himself be a henpecked husband.

No other human activity seems as completely gratuitous as "acting"; games are gratuitous acts, but it can be argued that they have a utile value—they develop the muscles or sharpen the wits of those who play them—but what conceivable purpose could one human being have for imitating another?

The fact that dramatic action is mock action and mimetic art completely gratuitous makes the dramatic picture of human life a peculiar one. In real life, we exist as bodies, social individuals and unique persons simultaneously, so that there can be no human deed or act of personal choice which is without an element of human behavior, what we do from necessity, either the necessities of our physical nature or the habits of our socially acquired "second nature." But on the stage, the kind of human life we see is a life of pure deeds from which every trace of behavior has been eliminated. Consequently, any human activity which cannot be imagined without its element of necessity, cannot be represented on the stage. Actors, for example, can toy with cucumber sandwiches, but they cannot eat a hearty meal because a hearty meal cannot be imagined taking less than three quarters of an hour to consume. Dramatists have been known to expect an actor to write a letter on stage, but it always looks ridiculous; on stage a letter can be read aloud but not written in silence. Nor can an actor do any serious piece of work, for real work cannot be imagined apart from the real time it takes. Only deeds can be divorced from real time. Thus, a man might write in his diary, "I began or I finished work at 9:15," but he would never write "I worked at 9:15"; (as a court witness he might say, "I was working at 9:15"); on the other hand, he might very well write, "At 9:15 I proposed to Julia and she accepted me" because, although his words of proposal and hers of acceptance must have taken a certain length of time to utter, this is irrelevant to the dramatic significance of the event.

Since human life, as the stage can present it, is, firstly, a life of pure action and, secondly, a public life—the actors play to an audience, not to themselves—the characters best-suited to drama are men and women who by fate or choice lead a public existence and whose deeds are of public concern. Worldly ambition, for example, is a more dramatic motive than sexual passion, because worldly ambition can only be realized in public, while sexual passion unless, like that of Antony and Cleopatra, it has political consequences, affects only a handful of persons. Unfortunately for the modern dramatist, during the past century and a half the public realm has been less and less of a realm where human deeds are done, and more and more a realm of mere human behavior. The contemporary dramatist has lost his natural subject.

This process was already far advanced in the nineteenth century and dramatists, like Ibsen, who took their art seriously, were beginning to look for new kinds of heroes. The romantic movement had brought to public notice a new kind of hero, the artist-genius. The public interest taken in figures like Victor Hugo, Dickens and Wagner would have been unthinkable two centuries earlier.

It was inevitable that, sooner or later, a dramatist would ask himself if the artist-genius could be substituted for the traditional man-of-action as a dramatic hero. A sensible dramatist, however, would immediately realize that a direct treatment would be bound to fail. An artist is not a doer of deeds but a maker of things, a worker, and work cannot be represented on stage because it ceases to be work if the time it takes is foreshortened, so that what makes an artist of interest, his art—aside from which he is not an artist but simply a man—will have to take place off stage. Secondly, the audience will have to be convinced that the figure they are told is a genius really is one, not somebody without any talent who says he is a genius. If he is a poet, for example, the poetry of his which the audience hear must be of the first order. But, even if the dramatist is himself a great poet, the only kind of poetry he can write is his own; he cannot make up a special kind of poetry for his hero, unlike his own yet equally great. Lastly, while deeds and character are identical, works and character are not; the relation between who an artist is as a person and what he makes is too vague to discuss. To say that Lesbia's treatment of Catullus and his love for her were the cause of his poetry is a very different thing from saying that Macbeth's ambition and the prophecies of the witches were the cause of Banquo's murder. Had both their characters been different, the poems would, no doubt, have been different, but their characters do not explain why Catullus wrote the actual poems he did, and not an infinite number of others which he might equally well have written but did not.

In order to become an artist, a man must be endowed with an exceptional talent for fabrication or expression, but what makes it possible for him to exercise this talent and for his public to appreciate it is the capacity of all human beings to imagine anything which is the case as being otherwise; every man, for example, can imagine committing a murder or laying down his life for a friend's without actually doing so. Is there, one can picture Ibsen asking himself, perhaps subconsciously, any figure traditionally associated with the stage who could be made to stand for this imaginative faculty? Yes, there is: the actor. Keats' famous description of the poet applies even more accurately to the actor.

> As to the poetic character itself, it is not itself: it has no self—it is everything and nothing. The Sun, the Moon, the sea, and men and women who are creatures of impulse, are poetical and have about them an unchangeable attribute—the poet has none: no identity.

Throughout *Peer Gynt,* one question keeps being asked and answered in various ways, namely, *Who am I? What is my real self?* For the animals, the question does not arise.

> What innocence is in the life of beasts.
> They perform the behest of their great creator.
> They are themselves.

The nearest human approximation to this animal selfhood is the "second nature" a man acquires through heredity and social custom.

> My father thieves,
> His son must steal.
> My father received,
> And so must I.
> We must bear our lot,
> And be ourselves.

So, too, with the drowning cook who gets as far in the Lord's Prayer as *Give us this day our daily bread* and then sinks.

> Amen, lad.
> You were yourself to the end.

Next comes the social "idiot" in the Greek sense, the individual whose life is as conditioned by one personal overriding interest as the conventional individual's is by social habit. In the first act Peer sees a young peasant cutting off a finger in order to escape conscription; Peer is fascinated and shocked:

> The thought perhaps—the wish to will,
> That I can understand, but really
> To do the deed. Ah me, that beats me.

In the last act he hears a funeral sermon about the same peasant in which the parson says:

> He was a bad citizen, no doubt,
> For Church and State alike, a sterile tree—
> But up there on the rocky mountain side
> Where his work lay, *there* I say he was great
> Because he was himself.

Neither of these human ways of being oneself, however, satisfy Peer. He tells his mother he means to be a King and Emperor, but there is only one kind of empire which nobody else can threaten or conquer, the empire of one's own consciousness, or, as Peer defines it:

> The Gyntian Self—An army that,
> Of wishes, appetites, desires!
> The Gyntian Self—It is a sea
> Of fancies, claims, and aspirations.

But the Peer we see on stage has no appetites or desires in the ordinary sense; he plays at having them. Ibsen solves the problem of presenting a poet dramatically by showing us a man who treats nearly everything he does as a role, whether it be dealing in slaves and idols or being an Eastern Prophet. A poet in real life would have written a drama about slave trading, then another drama about a prophet but, on the stage, play acting stands for making.

The kinship of the poet to the dreamer on the one hand and the madman on the other and his difference from them both is shown by Peer's experiences, first in the kingdom of the trolls and then in the asylum. The kingdom of dreams is ruled by wish or desire; the dreaming ego sees as being the case whatever the self desires to be the case. The ego, that is to say, is the helpless victim of the self; it cannot say, "I'm dreaming." In madness it is the self which is the helpless victim of the ego: a madman says, "I am Napoleon," and his self cannot tell him, "You're a liar." (One of the great difficulties in translating *Peer Gynt* is, I understand, that Norwegian has two words, one for the I *which is conscious* and another for the self *of which it is conscious,* where English has only one. *Myself* can mean either.)

Both the dreamer and the madman are in earnest; neither is capable of play acting. The dreamer is like the moviegoer who writes abusive letters to the actor he has seen playing a villain; the madman is like the actor who believes the same thing about himself, namely, that he is identical with his role.

But the poet pretends for fun; he asserts his freedom by lying—that is to say, by creating worlds which he *knows* are imaginary. When the troll king offers to turn Peer into a real troll by a little eye operation, Peer indignantly refuses. He is perfectly willing, he says, to swear that a cow is a beautiful maiden, but to be reduced to a condition in which he could not tell one from the other—that he will never submit to.

The difference between trolls and men, says the king, is that the Troll Motto is *To Thyself Be Enough,* while the Human Motto is *To Thyself Be True.* The Button-Moulder and the Lean One both have something to say about the latter.

> To be oneself is: to slay oneself.
> But on you that answer is doubtless lost;
> And therefore we'll say: to stand forth everywhere
> With Master's intention displayed like a sign-board.
>
> Remember, in two ways a man can be
> Himself—there's a right and wrong side to the jacket.
> You know they have lately discovered in Paris
> A way to take portraits by help of the sun.
> One can either produce a straightforward picture,
> Or else what is known as a negative one.
> In the latter the lights and the shades are reversed.

But suppose there is such a thing as a poetic vocation or, in terms of Ibsen's play, a theatrical vocation; how do their words apply? If a man can be called to be an actor, then the only way he can be "true" to himself is by "acting," that is to say, pretending to be what he is not. The dreamer and the madman are "enough" to themselves because they are unaware that anything exists except their own desires and hallucinations; the poet is "enough" to himself in the sense that, while knowing that others exist, as a poet he does without them. Outside Norway, Peer has no serious relations with others, male or female. On the subject of friendship, Ibsen once wrote to Georg Brandes:

> Friends are a costly luxury, and when one invests one's capital in a mission in life, one cannot afford to have friends. The expensiveness of friendship does not lie in what one does for one's friends, but in what, out of regard for them, one leaves undone. This means the crushing of many an intellectual germ.

But every poet is also a human being, distinguishable from what he makes, and through Peer's relations to Ase and Solveig, Ibsen is trying to show us, I believe, what kind of person is likely to become a poet—assuming, of course, that he has the necessary talent. According to Ibsen, the predisposing factors in childhood are, first, an isolation from the social group—owing to his father's drunkenness and spendthrift habits, he is looked down on by the neighbors—and second, a playmate who stimulates and shares his imaginative life—a role played by his mother.

> Ay, you must know that my husband, he drank,
> Wasted and trampled our gear under foot.
> And meanwhile at home there sat Peerkin and I—
> The best we could do was to try to forget. . . .
> Some take to brandy, and others to lies;
> And we—why, we took to fairy-tales.

It is not too fanciful, I believe, to think of laboring as a neuter activity, doing as masculine, and making as feminine. All fabrication is an imitation of motherhood and, whenever we have information about the childhood of an artist, it reveals a closer bond with his mother than with his father: in a poet's development, the phrase *The milk of the Word* is not a mere figure of speech.

In their games together, it is the son who takes the initiative and the mother who seems the younger, adoring child. Ase dies and bequeaths to Solveig, the young virgin, the role of being Peer's Muse. If the play were a straight realistic drama, Peer's treatment of Solveig would bear the obvious psychoanalytic explanation—namely, that he suffers from a mother-fixation which forbids any serious sexual relation: he cannot love any women with whom he sleeps. But the play is a parable and, parabolically, the mother-child relationship has, I believe, another significance: it stands for the kind of love that is unaffected by time and remains unchanged by any act of the partners. Many poets, it would seem, do their best work when they are "in love," but the psychological condition of being "in love" is incompatible with a sustained historical relationship like marriage. The poet's Muse must either be dead like Dante's Beatrice, or far away like Peer's Solveig, or keep on being reincarnated in one lady after another. Ase's devotion gives Peer his initial courage to be a poet and live without an identity of his own, Solveig gives him the courage to continue to the end. When at the end of the play he asks her, "Where is the real Peer?"—the human being as distinct from his poetic function—she answers, "In my faith, in my hope, in my love." This is an echo of his own belief. Ibsen leaves in doubt the question whether this faith is justified or not. It may be that, after all, the poet must pay for his vocation by ending in the casting-ladle. But Peer has so far been lucky: "He had women behind him."

The insoluble difficulty about the artist as a dramatic character is that, since his relations with others are either momentary or timeless, he makes any coherent plot impossible. *Peer Gynt* is a fascinating play, but one cannot say its structure is satisfying. Practically the whole of the drama (and nearly all of the best scenes) is a Prologue and an Epilogue: the Prologue shows us how a boy comes to be destined for the vocation of poet rather than a career as a statesman or an engineer, the Epilogue shows us the moral and psychological crisis for a poet in old age when death faces him and he must account for his life. Only in the Fourth Act are we shown, so to speak, the adult poet at work, and in this act the number of scenes and the number of characters introduced are purely arbitrary. Ibsen uses the act as an opportunity to make satirical comments on various aspects of Norwegian life, but Peer himself is only accidentally related to the satire.

II

Two years before *Peer Gynt*, Ibsen wrote *Brand*. Both were composed in Italy, and Ibsen said of them:

> May I not like Christoff in Jacob von Tyboe, point to Brand and Peer Gynt and say—See, the wine cup has done this.

The heroes of these two plays are related to each other by being each other's opposite. To Peer the Devil is a dangerous viper who tempts man to do the irretrievable; to Brand the Devil is Compromise.

Brand is a priest. Ibsen once said that he might equally well have made him a sculptor or a politician, but this is not true. In Rome Ibsen had met and been deeply impressed by a young Norwegian theological student and Kierkegaard enthusiast, Christopher Brunn. At the time Ibsen was very angry with his fellow countrymen for having refused to come to the aid of Denmark when Germany attacked her and annexed Schleswig-Holstein. Brunn had actually fought as a volunteer in the Danish army and he asked Ibsen why, if he had felt as strongly as he professed, he had not done likewise. Ibsen made the answer one would expect—a poet has other tasks to perform—but it is clear that the question made him very uncomfortable and *Brand* was a product of his discomfort.

Whether he had read it for himself or heard of it from Brunn, it seems evident that Ibsen must have been aware of Kierkegaard's essay on the difference between a genius and an apostle. In *Peer Gynt* he deals with the first; in *Brand*, which he wrote first, with the second.

An apostle is a human individual who is called by God to deliver a message to mankind. Oracles and shamans are divine mouthpieces, but they are not apostles. An oracle or a shaman is an accredited public official whose spiritual authority is recognized by all; he does not have to seek out others but sits and waits for them to consult him—Delphi is the navel of the world. He receives a professional training and, in order to qualify, he must exhibit certain talents, such as an ability to enter into a trance state.

An apostle, on the other hand, is called to preach to others a divine message which is new to them, so that he cannot expect others to come looking for him nor expect to have any official spiritual status. While oracle and shaman are, so to speak, radio sets through which at certain moments a god may speak, an apostle is an ordinary human messenger like a man who delivers mail; he cannot wait for certain divinely inspired moments to deliver his message and, if his audience should ask him to show his credentials, he has none.

In the case of any vocation of Genius, a man is called to it by a natural gift with which he is already endowed. A young man, for example, who tells his parents, "I am going to be a sculptor, cost what it may," bases his statement on the conviction that he has been born with a talent for making beautiful, three-dimensional objects. It makes no difference to his decision whether he is a Christian who believes that this talent is a gift of God or an atheist who attributes it to blind Nature or Chance for, even if he is a believer, he knows that he is called by his gift, not by God directly. Since the gift is *his,* to say "I must become a sculptor" and "I want to become one" means the same thing: it is impossible to imagine anyone's saying, "A sculptor is the last thing on earth I want to be, but I feel it is my duty to become one."

An Apostle, on the other hand, is called by God directly. Jehovah says to Abraham: "Go get thee up out of the land"; Christ says to Matthew, the tax-collector; "Follow me!" If one asks, "Why Abraham or Matthew and not two other people?" there is no human answer; one cannot speak of a talent for being an Apostle or of the apostolic temperament. Whatever ultimate spiritual rewards there may be for an Apostle, they are unknowable and unimaginable; all he knows is that he is called upon to forsake everything he has been, to venture into an unknown and probably unpleasant future. Hence it is impossible to imagine the apostolic calling's being echoed by a man's natural desire. Any genuine Apostle must, surely, say, "I would not but, alas, I must." The prospective sculptor can correctly be said to *will* to become a sculptor—that is to say, to submit himself to the study, toil and discipline which becoming a sculptor involves—but an Apostle cannot correctly be said to will anything; he can only say, "Not as I will, but as Thou wilt." It is possible for a man to be deceived about a secular calling—he imagines he has a talent when in fact he has none—but there is an objective test to prove whether his calling is genuine or imaginary: either he produces valuable works or he does not. A great sculptor may die with his works totally unrecognized by the public but, in the long run, the test of his greatness is worldly recognition of his work. But in the case of an Apostle there is no such objective test: he may make a million converts or he may make none, and we are still no nearer knowing whether his vocation was genuine or not. He may give his body to be burned and still we do not know. What makes an apostle a hero in a religious sense is not what he does or fails to do for others, but the constancy of his faith that God has called him to speak in His name.

The message Brand has to deliver is drawn for the most part from Kierkegaard and may be summed up in two passages from Kierkegaard's *Journals*.

> The Christianity of the majority consists roughly of what may be called the two most doubtful extremities of Christianity (or, as the parson says, the two things which must be clung to in life and death), first of all the saying about the little child, that one becomes a Christian as a little child and that of such is the Kingdom of Heaven; the second is the thief on the cross. People live by virtue of the former—in death they reckon upon consoling themselves with the example of the thief.
>
> This is the sum of their Christianity; and, correctly defined, it is a mixture of childishness and crime. . . .

> Most people think that the Christian commandments, "Thou shalt love thy neighbor as thyself, etc." are intentionally oversevere, like putting one's clock ahead to make sure of getting up in the morning.

In some of Brand's speeches, however, there is an emphasis on the human will which is Nietzschean rather than Kierkegaardian.

A whole shall rise which God shall recognize,
Man, His greatest creation, His close heir,
Adam, young and strong.

It is not
Martyrdom to die in agony upon a cross
But to will that you shall die upon a cross.

These are not statements which Kierkegaard would have made. Indeed, he expressly says that there is a great difference between willing a martyrdom which God has willed for you and willing one for yourself before you know whether or not it is required of you, and that to will the second is spiritual pride of an extreme kind.

Brand's prophetic denunciations are directed against three kinds of life, the aesthetic life governed by the mood of the moment, the conventional life of social and religious habit, and the insane life of "The wild of heart in whose broken mind evil seems beautiful," which, presumably, refers to the criminal as well as to the clinically insane.

Ibsen did not, as Shaw might have done, make his play an intellectual debate. Brand has no trouble in demolishing the arguments of his opponents. There is a great deal more to be said for the aesthetic life than a ninny like Ejnar can put forward, and a belief in the value of habit, both in social and religious life, can and is held by wise good people; it is not confined to cowardly crooks like the Mayor and the Provost. The only antagonist who is in any way his equal is the doctor.

DOCTOR: . . . . . I've got to visit a patient.
BRAND: My mother?
DOCTOR: Yes . . . You've been to see her already perhaps?
BRAND: No.
DOCTOR: You're a hard man. I've struggled all the way.
Across the moor, through mist and sleet,
Although I know she pays like a pauper.

BRAND: May God bless your energy and skill.
Ease her suffering, if you can. . . .
DOCTOR: Don't wait for her to send for you.
Come now, with me.
BRAND: Until she sends for me, I know no duty there.
DOCTOR: . . . your credit account
For strength of will is full, but, priest,
Your love account is a white virgin page,

Brand replies with an outburst against the popular use of the word *love* as a veil to cover and excuse weakness, but this does not refute the doctor because the latter, by risking his life to ease the suffering of a dying woman, has proved that he means something quite different by the word. There is, however, no dialectical relation between his position and Brand's because his ethics are those of his profession. Brand has just refused to go and give his dying mother the sacrament because she will not renounce her property. To the Doctor this seems gratuitous cruelty because he can only think about the care of sick souls in terms of the cure of sick bodies. In his world of experience a patient is either in pain or not in pain, and every patient desires to be well. He cannot grasp, because it is outside his professional experience, that, in the soul, a desire may be the sickness itself. Brand's mother clings to her possessions with passionate desire, and to relinquish them will cause her great suffering but, unless she suffers, she can never know true joy. (The analogy to surgery does not hold. The patient must suffer now at the hands of the surgeon in order that he may be free from pain in the future, but he already knows what it means to be free from pain. The sinner does not know what it means to be spiritually happy; he only knows that to give up his sin will be a great suffering.)

In the character of Brand Ibsen shows us an individual of heroic courage who exemplifies in his own life what he preaches and who suffers and dies for what he believes, but, as a religious hero, he won't quite do. Our final impression is of a tragic hero of the conventional kind whose field of action happens to be religion, but whose motives are the same pride and self-will that motivate the tragic heroes of this world.

If, as an apostle, Brand fails to convince us, the fault, I believe, is not due to lack of talent on Ibsen's part, but to his mistaken approach. While, when he came to write *Peer Gynt,* he approached the dramatic portrayal of a genius indirectly, in tackling the portrayal of an apostle, he tried a direct approach and this was bound to fail.

Thus, he gives us a picture of Brand's childhood. Unlike Peer, poor Brand did not have women behind him, and in the end he has to drag Agnes after him. His mother had renounced marriage to the man she loved in order to marry one who was expected to make money. He failed and died, and she had denied all love and happiness both to herself and her son and devoted herself with absolute passion to the acquisition and hoarding of wealth. The relation between mother and son is one of defiant hostility mingled with respect for the other's strength of will and contempt for sentimentality masquerading as love. In preferring damnation to the surrender of all her goods, she shows herself every bit as much a believer in All-or-Nothing as Brand does in refusing to give her the Sacrament unless she renounces her idol. Psychologically, mother and son are alike; the only difference between them is in the God whom each worships.

Such a situation is dramatically interesting and psychologically plausible, but it inevitably makes us suspect Brand's claim to have been called by the True God, since we perceive a personal or hereditary motivation in his thought and conduct. Peer's relation to his mother is a possible psychological background for a certain class of human being, the class of artist-geniuses. But every apostle is a member of a class of one and no psychological background can throw any light on a calling which is initiated by God directly.

It is very difficult to conceive of a successful drama without important personal relations, and of such, the most intense is, naturally, the relation between a man and a woman. The scenes between Brand and Agnes are the most exciting and moving parts of the poem, but their effect is to turn

Brand into a self-torturing monster for whose sufferings we can feel pity but no sympathy. Whether one agrees or disagrees with the insistence of the Roman Church that its priests be celibate—The Church Visible, after all, requires administrators, theologians, diplomats, etc., as well as apostles —the apostolic calling, ideally considered, is incompatible with marriage. An apostle exists for the sake of others but not as a person, only as a mouthpiece and a witness to the Truth; once they have received the Truth and he has borne his witness, his existence is of no account to others. But a husband and wife are bound by a personal tie, and the demands they make upon each other are based on this. If a husband asks his wife to make this or that sacrifice, he asks her to make it for his sake, and his right to ask comes from their mutual personal love. But when an apostle demands that another make a sacrifice, it cannot be for his sake; he cannot say, "If you love me, please do this," but can only say, "Thus saith the Lord. Your salvation depends upon your doing this."

When Brand first meets Agnes, he is already convinced of his calling and aware that suffering, certainly, and a martyr's death, possibly, will be required of him. His words and his risking of his life to bring consolation to a dying man reveal to her the falseness of her relation to Ejnar. At this point I do not think she is in love with Brand, but she is overwhelmed with admiration for him as a witness to the truth and prepared to fall in love with him if he should show any personal interest in her. He does show a personal interest—he is lonely and longing for personal love—they marry, they are mutually happy and they have a son, Ulf. Then comes disaster. Either they must leave the fjord and his work as the village priest—an act which Brand believes would be a betrayal of his calling —or their child must die. Brand decides that they shall remain, and Ulf does die. One would have thought that the obvious solution was to send his wife and child away to a sunnier climate and remain himself (since he inherited his mother's money, he has the means) but this solution does not seem to have occurred to him. (Of course if it had, the big dramatic scenes which follow could not have been written.)

Later, he accuses Agnes of idolatry in not accepting Ulf's death as the will of God and makes her give away all his clothes to a gypsy child. Possibly she is guilty of idolatry and should give the clothes away for the sake of her own soul and, were Brand a stranger, he could tell her so. But he is both the husband whom she loves and the father of her child who took the decision which caused the child's death and so led her into the temptation of idolatry, so that when he tells her:

> You are my wife, and I have the right to demand
> That you shall devote yourself wholly to our calling

the audience feels that he has no such right. This is only the most obvious manifestation of a problem which besets Ibsen throughout the play, namely, the problem of how to make an apostle dramatically interesting. To be dramatically viable, a character must not only act, but also talk about his actions and his feelings and talk a great deal: he must address others as a person—a messenger cannot be a major character on the stage. For dramatic reasons, therefore, Ibsen has to allow Brand to speak in the first person and appear the author of his acts, to say "I will this." But an apostle is a messenger, and he acts not by willing but by submitting to the will of God who cannot appear on the stage. It is inevitable, therefore, that our final impression of Brand is of an idolator who worships not God, but *his* God. It makes no difference if the God he calls his happens to be the true God; so long as he thinks of Him as his, he is as much an idolator as the savage who bows down to a fetish. To me, one of the most fascinating scenes of the play is Brand's final encounter with Ejnar. Ejnar has had some sort of evangelical conversion, believes that he is saved, and is going off to be a missionary in Africa. Brand tells him of Agnes' death, but he shows no sorrow, though he had once loved her.

> EJNAR: How was her faith?
> BRAND: Unshakeable.
> EJNAR: In whom?
> BRAND: In her God.

EJNAR: Her God cannot save her. She is damned. . . .
BRAND: You dare to pronounce judgment on her and me,
Poor, sinning fool?
EJNAR: My faith has washed me clean.
BRAND: Hold your tongue.
EJNAR: Hold yours.

Ejnar, is, as it were, a caricature of Brand, but the likeness is cruel.

Though a direct portrayal of an apostle is not possible in art, there exists, though not in drama, one great example of a successful indirect portrayal, Cervantes' *Don Quixote*.

III

The Knight-Errant

The Knight-Errant, whom Don Quixote wishes to become and actually parodies, was an attempt to Christianize the pagan epic hero.

1) He possesses epic *arete* of good birth, good looks, strength, etc.
2) This *arete* is put in the service of the Law, to rescue the unfortunate, protect the innocent, and combat the wicked.
3) His motives are three: a) the desire for glory
   b) the love of justice
   c) the love of an individual woman who judges and rewards.
4) He suffers exceptionally; first, in his adventures and collisions with the lawless; secondly, in his temptations to lawlessness in the form of unchastity; and thirdly, in his exceptionally difficult erotic romance.
5) In the end he succeeds in this world. Vice is punished and virtue is rewarded by the lady of his heart.

When we first meet Don Quixote he is a) poor, b) not a knight, c) fifty, d) has nothing to do except hunt and read romances about Knight-Errantry. Manifestly, he is the opposite of the heroes he admires, i.e., he is lacking in the epic *arete* of birth, looks, strength, etc. His situation, in fact, is aesthetically uninteresting except for one thing: his passion is great enough to make him sell land to buy books. This makes him aesthetically comic. Religiously he is tragic, for he is a hearer not a doer of the word, the weak man guilty in his imagination of Promethean pride. Now suddenly he goes mad, i.e., he sets out to become what he admires. Aesthetically this looks like pride; in fact, religiously, it is a conversion, an act of faith, a taking up of his cross.

The Quixotic Madness and the Tragic Madness

The worldly villain like Macbeth is tempted by an *arete* he possesses to conquer this world of the nature of which he has a shrewd idea. His decisions are the result of a calculation of the probabilities of success, each success increases his madness but in the end he fails and is brought to despair and death. (Don Quixote is a) lacking in *arete,* b) has a fantastic conception of this world, c) always meets with failure yet is never discouraged, d) suffers himself intentionally and makes others suffer only unintentionally.

The Quixotic Madness and the Comic Madness

The comic rogue declares: the world=that which exists to give me money, beauty, etc. I refuse to suffer by being thwarted. He is cured by being forced to suffer through collision with the real world.

Don Quixote declares: The world=that which needs my existence to save it at whatever cost to myself. He comes into collision with the real world but insists upon continuing to suffer. He becomes the Knight of the Doleful Countenance but never despairs.

Don Quixote and Hamlet

Hamlet lacks faith in God and in himself. Consequently he must define his existence in terms of others, e.g., I am the man whose mother married his uncle who murdered his father. He would like to become what the Greek tragic hero is, a creature of situation. Hence his inability to act, for he can only "act," i.e., play at possibilities.

Don Quixote is the antithesis of an actor, being completely incapable of seeing himself in a role. Defining his situation in terms of his own character, he is completely unreflective.

Madness and Faith

To have faith in something or someone means

a) that the object of faith is not manifest. If it becomes manifest, then faith is no longer required.

b) the relation of faith between subject and object is unique in every case. Hundreds may believe, but each has to believe by himself.

Don Quixote exemplifies both. a) He never sees things that aren't there (delusion) but sees them differently, e.g., windmills as giants, sheep as armies, puppets as Moors, etc. b) He is the only individual who sees them thus.

Faith and Idolatry

The idolater makes things out to be stronger than they really are so that they shall be responsible for him, e.g., he might worship a windmill for its giantlike strength. Don Quixote never expects things to look after him; on the contrary he is always making himself responsible for things and people who have no need of him and regard him as an impertinent old meddler.

Faith and Despair

People are tempted to lose faith a) when it fails to bring worldly success, b) when the evidence of their senses and feelings seem against it. Don Quixote a) is consistently defeated yet persists, b) between his fits of madness he sees that the windmills are not giants but windmills, etc., yet, instead of despairing, he says, "Those cursed magicians delude me, first drawing me into dangerous adventures by the appearance of things as they really are, and then presently changing the face of things as they please." His supreme test comes when Sancho Panza describes a country wench, whom Don Quixote sees correctly as such, as the beautiful Princess Dulcinea and in spite of his feelings concludes that he is enchanted and that Sancho Panza is right.

Don Quixote and the Knight-Errant

Don Quixote's friends attack the Romances he loves on the grounds that they are historically untrue, and lacking in style.

Don Quixote, on the other hand, without knowing it, by his very failure to imitate his heroes exactly, at once reveals that the Knight-Errant of the Romances is half-pagan, and becomes himself the true Christian Knight.

Epic Dualism

The world of the Romances is a dualistic world where the completely good and innocent fight the completely evil and guilty. The Knight-Errant comes into collision only with those who are outside the Law: giants, heretics, heathens, etc. When he is in one of his spells, Don Quixote, under the illusion that he is showing the righteous anger of the Knight-Errant, comes into collision with the law, i.e., he attacks innocent clerics and destroys other people's property.

When he is not deluded as to the nature of those he is trying to help, e.g., the convicts or the boy being thrashed, he only succeeds in making things worse and earns enmity, not gratitude.

Frauendienst

Don Quixote affirms all the articles of the Amor religion, namely, that a) the girl must be noble and beautiful, b) there must be some barrier, c) the final goal of the Knight's trials is to be rewarded by having his love reciprocated.

In fact, the girl he calls Dulcinea del Toboso is "a good likely country lass for whom he had formerly had a sort of inclination, though 'tis believed she never heard of it." She is of lower social status, and he is past the age when sexual love means anything to him. Nevertheless, his behavior has all the courage that might be inspired by a great passion.

Again, Don Quixote expects to be tempted to unchastity so that, in the inn when the hunchback maid is trying to reach the carter's bed, he fancies that she is the daughter of the

Governor of the Castle, who has fallen in love with him and is trying to seduce him. Bruised and battered as he is, even Don Quixote has to admit that for the moment he has no capacity.

The language is the language of Eros, the romantic idolization of the fair woman, but its real meaning is the Christian agape which loves all equally irrespective of their merit.

Snobbery

The true Knight-Errant has nothing to do with the Lower Orders and must never put himself in an undignified position, e.g., Launcelot is disgraced by riding in a cart. Don Quixote attempts to do likewise but with singular unsuccess. He is constantly having to do with the Lower Orders under the illusion that they are the nobility. His aristocratic refusal to pay, which he adopts out of literary precedence, not personal feeling, never works out—he ends by overpaying. Again the language is the language of the feudal knight, but the behavior is that of the Suffering Servant. This may be compared with the reverse situation in *Moby Dick* when Captain Ahab leaves his cabin boy in his captain's cabin and mounts the lookout like an ordinary seaman: here the behavior is apparently humble, but is in fact the extremity of pride.

This-Worldliness

The Knight-Errant is this-worldly in that he succeeds in arms and in love. Don Quixote professes a similar hope but in fact is not only persistently defeated but also cannot in the end even maintain in combat that Dulcinea is without a rival. Thus, he not only has to suffer the Knight's trials but also must suffer the consciousness of defeat. He is never able to think well of himself. He uses the language of the epic hero, but reveals himself to us as the Knight of Faith whose kingdom is not of this world.

Don Quixote's Death

However many further adventures one may care to invent for Don Quixote—and, as in all cases of a true myth, they are potentially infinite—the conclusion can only be the one which Cervantes gives, namely, that he recovers his senses and dies. Despite the protestations of his friends, who want him to go on providing them with amusement, he must say: "Ne'er look for birds of this year in the nests of the last: I was mad but I am now in my senses: I was once Don Quixote de la Mancha but am now the plain Alonso Quixano, and I hope the sincerity of my words and my repentance may restore me the same esteem you have had for me before."

For, in the last analysis, the saint cannot be presented aesthetically. The ironic vision gives us a Don Quixote who is innocent of every sin but one; and that one sin he can put off only by ceasing to exist as a character in a book, for all such characters are condemned to it, namely, the sin of being at all times and under all circumstances interesting.

POSTSCRIPT: CHRISTIANITY & ART

Art is compatible with polytheism and with Christianity, but not with philosophical materialism; science is compatible with philosophical materialism and with Christianity, but not with polytheism. No artist or scientist, however, can feel comfortable as a Christian; every artist who happens also to be a Christian wishes he could be a polytheist; every scientist in the same position that he could be a philosophical materialist. And with good reason. In a polytheist society, the artists are its theologians; in a materialist society, its theologians are the scientists. To a Christian, unfortunately, both art and science are secular activities, that is to say, small beer.

No artist, qua artist, can understand what is meant by *God is Love* or *Thou shalt love thy neighbor* because he doesn't care whether God and men are loving or unloving; no scientist, qua scientist, can understand what is meant because he doesn't care whether to-be-loving is a matter of choice or a matter of compulsion.

To the imagination, the sacred is self-evident. It is as meaningless to ask whether one believes or disbelieves in Aphrodite or Ares as to ask whether one believes in a character in a novel; one can only say that one finds them true or untrue to life. To believe in Aphrodite and Ares merely means that one believes that the poetic myths about them do justice to the forces of sex and aggression as human beings experience them in nature and their own lives. That is why it is possible for an archaeologist who digs up a statuette of a god or goddess to say with fair certainty what kind of divinity it represents.

Similarly, to the imagination, the godlike or heroic man is self-evident. He does extraordinary deeds that the ordinary man cannot do, or extraordinary things happen to him.

The Incarnation, the coming of Christ in the form of a servant who cannot be recognized by the eye of flesh and blood, but only by the eye of faith, puts an end to all claims of the imagination to be the faculty which decides what is truly sacred and what is profane. A pagan god can appear on earth in disguise but, so long as he wears his disguise, no man is expected to recognize him nor can. But Christ appears looking just like any other man, yet claims that He is the Way, the Truth and the Life, and that no man can come to God the Father except through Him. The contradiction between the profane appearance and the sacred assertion is impassible to the imagination.

It is impossible to represent Christ on the stage. If he is made dramatically interesting, he ceases to be Christ and turns into a Hercules or a Svengali. Nor is it really possible to represent him in the visual arts for, if he were visually recognizable, he would be a god of the pagan kind. The best the painter can do is to paint either the Bambino with the Madonna or the dead Christ on the cross, for every baby and every corpse seems to be both individual and universal, *the* baby, *the* corpse. But neither a baby nor a corpse can say *I am the Way, etc.*

To a Christian, the godlike man is not the hero who does extraordinary deeds, but the holy man, the saint, who does good deeds. But the gospel defines a good deed as one done in secret, hidden, so far as it is possible, even from the doer, and forbids private prayer and fasting in public. This means that art, which by its nature can only deal with what can and should be manifested, cannot portray a saint.

There can no more be a "Christian" art than there can be a Christian science or a Christian diet. There can only be a Christian spirit in which an artist, a scientist, works or does not work. A painting of the Crucifixion is not necessarily more Christian in spirit than a still life, and may very well be less.

I sometimes wonder if there is not something a bit questionable, from a Christian point of view, about all works of art which make overt Christian references. They seem to assert that there is such a thing as a Christian culture, which there cannot be. Culture is one of Caesar's things. One cannot help noticing that the great period of "religious" painting coincided with the period when the Church was a great temporal power.

The only kind of literature which has gospel authority is the parable, and parables are secular stories with no overt religious reference.

There are many hymns I like as one likes old song hits, because, for me, they have sentimental associations, but the only hymns I find poetically tolerable are either versified dogma or Biblical ballads.

Poems, like many of Donne's and Hopkins', which express a poet's personal feelings of religious devotion or penitence, make me uneasy. It is quite in order that a poet should write a sonnet expressing his devotion to Miss Smith because the poet, Miss Smith, and all his readers know perfectly well that, had he chanced to fall in love with Miss Jones instead, his feelings would be exactly the same. But if he writes a sonnet expressing his devotion to Christ, the important point, surely, is that his devotion is felt for Christ and not for, say, Buddha or Mahomet, and this point cannot be made in poetry; the Proper Name proves nothing. A penitential poem is even more questionable. A poet must intend his poem to be a good one, that is to say, an enduring object for other people to admire. Is there not something a little odd, to say the least, about making an admirable public object out of one's feelings of guilt and penitence before God?

A poet who calls himself a Christian cannot but feel uncomfortable when he realizes that the New Testament contains no verse (except in the apochryphal, and gnostic, *Acts of John*), only prose. As Rudolf Kassner has pointed out:

> The difficulty about the God-man for the poet lies in the Word being made Flesh. This means that reason and imagination are one. But does not Poetry, as such, live from their being a gulf between them?
>
> What gives us so clear a notion of this as metre, verse measures? In the magical-mythical world, metre was sacred, so was the strophe, the line, the words in the line, the letters. The poets were prophets.
>
> That the God-man did not write down his words himself or show the slightest concern that they should be written down in letters, brings us back to the Word made Flesh.
>
> Over against the metrical structures of the poets stand the Gospel parables in prose, over against magic a freedom which finds its limits within itself, is itself limit, over against poetic fiction (*Dichtung*), pointing to and interpreting fact (*Deutung*). (*Die Geburt Christi.*)

I hope there is an answer to this objection, but I don't know what it is.

The imagination is a natural human faculty and therefore retains the same character whatever a man believes. The only difference can be in the way that he interprets its data. At all times and in all places, certain objects, beings and events arouse in his imagination a feeling of sacred awe, while other objects, beings and events leave his imagination unmoved. But a Christian cannot say, as a polytheist can: "All before which my imagination feels sacred awe is sacred-in-itself, and all which leaves it unmoved is profane-in-itself. There are two possible interpretations a Christian can make, both of them, I believe, orthodox, but each leaning towards a heresy. Either he can say, leaning towards Neoplatonism: "That which arouses in me a feeling of sacred awe is a channel through which, to me as an individual and as a member of a certain culture, the sacred which I cannot perceive directly is revealed to me." Or he can say, leaning towards pantheism: "All objects, beings and events are sacred but, because of my individual and cultural limitations, my imagination can only recognize these ones." Speaking for myself, I would rather, if I must be a heretic, be condemned as a pantheist than as a Neoplatonist.

In our urbanized industrial society, nearly everything we see and hear is so aggressively ugly or emphatically banal that it is difficult for a modern artist, unless he can flee to the depths of the country and never open a newspaper, to prevent his imagination from acquiring a Manichaean cast, from *feeling*, whatever his religious convictions to the contrary, that the physical world is utterly profane or the abode of demons. However sternly he reminds himself that the material universe is the creation of God and found good by Him, his mind is haunted by images of physical disgust, cigarette butts in a half-finished sardine can, a toilet that won't flush, etc.

Still, things might be worse. If an artist can no longer put on sacred airs, he has gained his personal artistic liberty instead. So long as an activity is regarded as being of sacred importance, it is controlled by notions of orthodoxy. When art is sacred, not only are there orthodox subjects which every artist is expected to treat and unorthodox subjects which no artist may treat, but also orthodox styles of treatment which must not be violated. But, once art becomes a secular activity, every artist is free to treat whatever subject excites his imagination, and in any stylistic manner which he feels appropriate.

We cannot have any liberty without license to abuse it. The secularization of art enables the really gifted artist to develop his talents to the full; it also permits those with little or no talent to produce vast quantities of phony or vulgar trash. When one looks into the window of a store which sells devotional art objects, one can't help wishing the iconoclasts had won.

For artists, things may very well get worse and, in large areas of the world, already have.

So long as science regards itself as a secular activity, materialism is not a doctrine but a useful empirical hypothesis. A scientist, qua scientist, does not need, when investigating physical nature, to bother his head with ontological or teleological questions any more than an artist, qua artist, has to bother about what his feelings of sacred awe may ultimately signify.

As soon, however, as materialism comes to be regarded as sacred truth, the distinction between the things of God and the things of Caesar is reabolished. But the world of sacred materialism is very different from the world of sacred polytheism. Under polytheism, everything in life was, ultimately, frivolous, so that the pagan world was a morally tolerant world—far too tolerant, for it tolerated many evils, like slavery and the exposure of infants, which should not be tolerated. It tolerated them, not because it did not know that they were evil, but because it did not believe that the gods were necessarily good. (No Greek, for example, ever defended slavery, as slave owners in the Southern States defended it, on the grounds that their slaves were happier as slaves than they would be as freemen. On the contrary, they argued that the slave must be subhuman because, otherwise, he would have killed himself rather than endure life as a slave.)

But, under religious materialism, everything in life is, ultimately, serious, and therefore subject to moral policing. It will not tolerate what it knows to be evil with a heartless shrug—that is how life is, always has been and always will be—but it will do something which the pagan world never did; it will do what it knows to be evil for a moral purpose, do it deliberately now so that good may come in the future.

Under religious materialism, the artist loses his personal artistic liberty again, but he does not recover his sacred importance, for now it is not artists who collectively decide what is sacred truth, but scientists, or rather the scientific politicians, who are responsible for keeping mankind in the true faith. Under them, an artist becomes a mere technician, an expert in effective expression, who is hired to express effectively what the scientific politician requires to be said.

PART EIGHT

Homage to Igor Stravinsky

NOTES ON MUSIC AND OPERA

Opera consists of significant situations in artificially arranged sequence.

GOETHE

Singing is near miraculous because it is the mastering of what is otherwise a pure instrument of egotism: the human voice.

HUGO VON HOFMANNSTHAL

What is music about? What, as Plato would say, does it imitate? Our experience of Time in its twofold aspect, natural or organic repetition, and historical novelty created by choice. And the full development of music as an art depends upon a recognition that these two aspects are different and that choice, being an experience confined to man, is more significant than repetition. A succession of two musical notes is an act of choice; the first causes the second, not in the scientific sense of making it occur necessarily, but in the historical sense of provoking it, of providing it with a motive for occurring. A successful melody is a self-determined history; it is freely what it intends to be, yet is a meaningful whole, not an arbitrary succession of notes.

Music as an art, i.e., music that has come to a conscious realization of its true nature, is confined to Western civilization alone and only to the last four or five hundred years at that. The music of all other cultures and epochs bears the same relation to Western music that magical verbal formulas bear to the art of poetry. A primitive magic spell may be poetry but it does not know that it is, nor intend to be. So, in all but Western music, history is only implicit; what it thinks it is doing is furnishing verses or movements with a repetitive accompaniment. Only in the West has chant become song.

Lacking a historical consciousness, the Greeks, in their theories of music, tried to relate it to Pure Being, but the becoming implicit in music betrays itself in their theories of harmony in which mathematics becomes numerology and one chord is intrinsically "better" than another.

Western music declared its consciousness of itself when it adopted time signatures, barring and the metronome beat. Without a strictly natural or cyclical time, purified from every trace of historical singularity, as a framework within which to occur, the irreversible historicity of the notes themselves would be impossible.

In primitive proto-music, the percussion instruments which best imitate recurrent rhythms and, being incapable of melody, can least imitate novelty, play the greatest role.

The most exciting rhythms seem unexpected and complex, the most beautiful melodies simple and inevitable.

Music cannot imitate nature: a musical storm always sounds like the wrath of Zeus.

A verbal art like poetry is reflective; it stops to think. Music is immediate, it goes on to become. But both are active, both insist on stopping or going on. The medium of passive reflection is painting, of passive immediacy the cinema, for the visual world is an immediately given world where Fate is mistress and it is impossible to tell the difference between a chosen movement and an involuntary reflex. Freedom of choice lies, not in the world we see, but in our freedom to turn our eyes in this direction, or that, or to close them altogether.

Because music expresses the opposite experience of pure volition and subjectivity (the fact that we cannot shut our ears at will allows music to assert that we cannot *not* choose), film music is not music but a technique for preventing us from using our ears to hear extraneous noises and it is bad film music if we become consciously aware of its existence.

Man's musical imagination seems to be derived almost exclusively from his primary experiences—his direct experience of his own body, its tensions and rhythms, and his direct experience of desiring and choosing—and to have very little to do with the experiences of the outside world brought to him through his senses. The possibility of making music, that is, depends primarily, not upon man's possession of an auditory organ, the ear, but upon his possession of a sound-producing instrument, the vocal cords. If the ear were primary, music would have begun as program pastoral symphonies. In the case of the visual arts, on the other hand, it is a visual organ, the eye, which is primary for, without it, the experiences which stimulate the hand into becoming an expressive instrument could not exist.

The difference is demonstrated by the difference in our sensation of motion in musical space and visual space.

An increase in the tension of the vocal cords is conceived in musical space as a going "up," a relaxation as a going "down." But in visual space it is the bottom of the picture (which is also the foreground) which is felt as the region of greatest pressure and, as the eye rises up the picture, it feels an increasing sense of lightness and freedom.

The association of tension in hearing with up and seeing with down seems to correspond to the difference between our experience of the force of gravity in our own bodies and our experience of it in other bodies. The weight of our own bodies is felt as inherent in us, as a personal wish to fall down, so that rising upward is an effort to overcome the desire for rest in ourselves. But the weight (and proximity) of other objects is felt as weighing down on us; they are "on top" of us and rising means getting away from their restrictive pressure.

All of us have learned to talk, most of us, even, could be taught to speak verse tolerably well, but very few have learned or could ever be taught to sing. In any village twenty people could get together and give a performance of *Hamlet* which, however imperfect, would convey enough of the play's greatness to be worth attending, but if they were to attempt a similar performance of *Don Giovanni,* they would soon discover that there was no question of a good or a bad performance because they could not sing the notes at all. Of an actor, even in a poetic drama, when we say that his performance is good, we mean that he simulates by art, that is, consciously, the way in which the character he is playing would, in real life, behave by nature, that is, unconsciously. But for a singer, as for a ballet dancer, there is no question of simulation, of singing the composer's notes "naturally"; his behavior is unabashedly and triumphantly art from beginning to end. The paradox implicit in all drama, namely, that emotions and situations which in real life would be sad or painful are on the stage a source of pleasure becomes, in opera, quite explicit. The singer may be playing the role of a deserted bride who is about to kill herself, but we feel quite certain as we listen that not only we, but also she, is having a wonderful time. In a sense, there can be no tragic opera because whatever errors the characters make and whatever they suffer, they are doing exactly what they wish. Hence the feeling that *opera seria* should not employ a contemporary subject, but confine itself to mythical situations, that is, situations which, as human beings, we are all of us necessarily in and must, therefore, accept, however tragic they may be. A contemporary tragic situation like that in Menotti's *The*

Consul is too actual, that is, too clearly a situation some people are in and others, including the audience, are not in, for the latter to forget this and see it as a symbol of, say, man's existential estrangement. Consequently the pleasure we and the singers are obviously enjoying strikes the conscience as frivolous.

On the other hand, its pure artifice renders opera the ideal dramatic medium for a tragic myth. I once went in the same week to a performance of *Tristan und Isolde* and a showing of *L'Eternal Retour,* Jean Cocteau's movie version of the same story. During the former, two souls, weighing over two hundred pounds apiece, were transfigured by a transcendent power; in the latter, a handsome boy met a beautiful girl and they had an affair. This loss of value was due not to any lack of skill on Cocteau's part but to the nature of the cinema as a medium. Had he used a fat middle-aged couple the effect would have been ridiculous because the snatches of language which are all the movie permits have not sufficient power to transcend their physical appearance. Yet if the lovers are young and beautiful, the cause of their love looks "natural," a consequence of their beauty, and the whole meaning of the myth is gone.

> The man who wrote the Eighth Symphony has a right to rebuke the man who put his rapture of elation, tenderness, and nobility into the mouths of a drunken libertine, a silly peasant girl, and a conventional fine lady, instead of confessing them to himself, glorying in them, and uttering them without motley as the universal inheritance. (BERNARD SHAW.)

Shaw, and Beethoven, are both wrong, I believe, and Mozart right. Feelings of joy, tenderness and nobility are not confined to "noble" characters but are experienced by everybody, by the most conventional, most stupid, most depraved. It is one of the glories of opera that it can demonstrate this and to the shame of the spoken drama that it cannot. Because we use language in everyday life, our style and vocabulary become identified with our social character as others see us, and in a play, even a verse play, there are narrow limits to the range in speech possible for any character beyond which the playwright cannot go without making the character incredible. But precisely because we do not communicate by singing, a song can be out of place but not out of character; it is just as credible that a stupid person should sing beautifully as that a clever person should do so.

If music in general is an imitation of history, opera in particular is an imitation of human willfulness; it is rooted in the fact that we not only have feelings but insist upon having them at whatever cost to ourselves. Opera, therefore, cannot present character in the novelist's sense of the word, namely, people who are potentially good *and* bad, active *and* passive, for music is immediate actuality and neither potentiality nor passivity can live in its presence. This is something a librettist must never forget. Mozart is a greater composer than Rossini but the Figaro of the *Marriage* is less satisfying, to my mind, than the Figaro of the *Barber* and the fault, is, I think, Da Ponte's. His Figaro is too interesting a character to be completely translatable into music, so that co-present with the Figaro who is singing, one is conscious of a Figaro who is not singing but thinking to himself. The barber of Seville, on the other hand, who is not a person but a musical busybody, goes into song exactly with nothing over.

Again, I find *La Bohème* inferior to *Tosca,* not because its music is inferior, but because the characters, Mimi in particular, are too passive; there is an awkward gap between the resolution with which they sing and the irresolution with which they act.

The quality common to all the great operatic roles, e.g., Don Giovanni, Norma, Lucia, Tristan, Isolde, Brünnhilde, is that each of them is a passionate and willful state of being. In real life they would all be bores, even Don Giovanni.

In recompense for this lack of psychological complexity, however, music can do what words cannot, present the immediate and simultaneous relation of these states to each other. The crowning glory of opera is the big ensemble.

The chorus can play two roles in opera and two only, that of the mob and that of the faithful, sorrowing or rejoicing community. A little of this goes a long way. Opera is not oratorio.

Drama is based on the Mistake. I think someone is my friend when he really is my enemy, that I am free to marry a woman when in fact she is my mother, that this person is a chambermaid when it is a young nobleman in disguise, that this well-dressed young man is rich when he is really a penniless adventurer, or that if I do this such and such a result will follow when in fact it results in something very different. All good drama has two movements, first the making of the mistake, then the discovery that it was a mistake.

In composing his plot, the librettist has to conform to this law but, in comparison to the dramatist, he is more limited in the kinds of mistake he can use. The dramatist, for instance, procures some of his finest effects from showing how people deceive themselves. Self-deception is impossible in opera because music is immediate, not reflective; whatever is sung is the case. At most, self-deception can be suggested by having the orchestral accompaniment at variance with the singer, e.g., the jolly tripping notes which accompany Germont's approach to Violetta's deathbed in *La Traviata*, but unless employed very sparingly such devices cause confusion rather than insight.

Again, while in the spoken drama the discovery of the mistake can be a slow process and often, indeed, the more gradual it is the greater the dramatic interest, in a libretto the drama of recognition must be tropically abrupt, for music cannot exist in an atmosphere of uncertainty; song cannot walk, it can only jump.

On the other hand, the librettist need never bother his head, as the dramatist must, about probability. A credible situation in opera means a situation in which it is credible that someone should sing. A good libretto plot is a melodrama in both the strict and the conventional sense of the word; it offers as many opportunities as possible for the characters to be swept off their feet by placing them in situations which are too tragic or too fantastic for "words." No good opera plot can be sensible for people do not sing when they are feeling sensible.

The theory of "music-drama" presupposes a libretto in which there is not one sensible moment or one sensible remark: this is not only very difficult to manage, though Wagner managed it, but also extremely exhausting on both singers and the audience, neither of whom may relax for an instant.

In a libretto where there are any sensible passages, i.e., conversation not song, the theory becomes absurd. If, for furthering the action, it becomes necessary for one character to say to another "Run upstairs and fetch me a handkerchief," then there is nothing in the words, apart from their rhythm, to make one musical setting more apt than another. Wherever the choice of notes is arbitrary, the only solution is a convention, e.g., *recitativo secco.*

In opera the orchestra is addressed to the singers, not to the audience. An opera-lover will put up with and even enjoy an orchestral interlude on condition that he knows the singers cannot sing just now because they are tired or the scene-shifters are at work, but any use of the orchestra by itself which is not filling in time is, for him, wasting it. Leonora III is a fine piece to listen to in the concert hall, but in the opera house, when it is played between scenes one and two of the second act of *Fidelio,* it becomes twelve minutes of acute boredom.

If the librettist is a practicing poet, the most difficult problem, the place where he is most likely to go astray, is the composition of the verse. Poetry is in its essence an act of reflection, of refusing to be content with the interjections of immediate emotion in order to understand the nature of what is felt. Since music is in essence immediate, it follows that the words of a song cannot be poetry. Here one should draw a distinction between lyric and song proper. A lyric is a poem intended to be chanted. In a chant the music is subordinate to the words which limit the range and tempo of the notes. In song, the notes must be free to be whatever they choose and the words must be able to do what they are told.

The verses of *Ah non credea* in *La Sonnambula*, though of little interest to read, do exactly what they should: suggest to Bellini one of the most beautiful melodies ever written and then leave him completely free to write it. The verses which the librettist writes are not addressed to the public but are really a private letter to the composer. They have their moment of glory, the moment in which they suggest to him a certain melody; once that is over, they are as expendable as infantry to a Chinese general: they must efface themselves and cease to care what happens to them.

There have been several composers, Campion, Hugo Wolf, Benjamin Britten, for example, whose musical imagination has been stimulated by poetry of a high order. The question remains, however, whether the listener hears the sung words as words in a poem, or, as I am inclined to believe, only as sung syllables. A Cambridge psychologist, P. E. Vernon, once performed the experiment of having a Campion song sung with nonsense verses of equivalent syllabic value substituted for the original; only six per cent of his test audience noticed that something was wrong. It is precisely because I believe that, in listening to song (as distinct from chant), we hear, not words, but syllables, that I am not generally in favor of the performances of operas in translation. Wagner or Strauss in English sounds intolerable, and would still sound so if the poetic merits of the translation were greater than those of the original, because the new syllables have no apt relation to the pitch and tempo of the notes with which they are associated. The poetic value of the words may provoke a composer's imagination, but it is their syllabic values which determine the kind of vocal line he writes. In song, poetry is expendable, syllables are not.

"History," said Stephen Dedalus, "is the nightmare from which I must awake." The rapidity of historical change and the apparent powerlessness of the individual to affect Collective History has led in literature to a retreat from history.

Instead of tracing the history of an individual who is born, grows old and dies, many modern novelists and short story writers, beginning with Poe, have devoted their attention to timeless passionate moments in a life, to states of being. It seems to me that, in some modern music, I can detect the same trend, a trend towards composing a static kind of music in which there is no marked difference between its beginning, its middle and its end, a music which sounds remarkably like primitive proto-music. It is not for me to criticize a composer who writes such music. One can say, however, that he will never be able to write an opera. But, probably, he won't want to.

The golden age of opera, from Mozart to Verdi, coincided with the golden age of liberal humanism, of unquestioning belief in freedom and progress. If good operas are rarer today, this may be because, not only have we learned that we are less free than nineteenth-century humanism imagined, but also have become less certain that freedom is an unequivocal blessing, that the free are necessarily the good. To say that operas are more difficult to write does not mean that they are impossible. That would only follow if we should cease to believe in free will and personality altogether. Every high C accurately struck demolishes the theory that we are the irresponsible puppets of fate or chance.

CAV & PAG

If a perfume manufacturer were to adopt the "naturalistic" aesthetic, what kind of scents would he bottle?

PAUL VALÉRY

While we all know that every moment of life is a living moment, it is impossible for us not to feel that some moments are more lively than others, that certain experiences are clues to the meaning and essential structures of the whole flux of experience in a way that others are not. This selection is, in part, imposed by experience itself—certain events overwhelm us with their importance without our knowing why —and in part is due to a predisposition on our side, by personal temperament and by social tradition, to be open to some kinds of events and closed to others. Dante's encounter with Beatrice, for example, was *given* him, but he would probably not have received or interpreted the revelation in exactly the way that he did if the love poetry of Provence had never been written. On the other hand, many people before Wordsworth must have experienced feelings about Nature similar to his, but they had dismissed them as not very relevant.

Every artist holds, usually in common with his contemporaries, certain presuppositions about the real *Nature* concealed behind or within the stream of phenomena, to which it is his artistic duty to be true, and it is these which condition the kind of art he produces as distinct from its quality.

Suppose that a dramatist believes that the most interesting and significant characteristic of man is his power to choose between right and wrong, his responsibility for his actions; then, out of the infinite number of characters and situations that life offers him, he will select situations in which the temptation to choose wrong is at its greatest and the actual consequences incurred by the choice are most serious, and he will select characters who are most free to choose, least in the position to blame their choice afterwards on circumstances or other people.

At most periods in history he could find both of these most easily among the lives of the rich and powerful, and least among the lives of the poor. A king can commit a murder without fear of punishment by human law; a poor man cannot, so that, if the poor man refrains from committing one, we feel that the law, not he, is largely responsible. A king who steals a country is more interesting dramatically than a starving peasant who steals a loaf, firstly because the country is so much bigger, and secondly because the king is not driven, like the peasant, by an impersonal natural need outside his control, but by a personal ambition which he could restrain.

For many centuries the dramatic role of the poor was to provide comic relief, to be shown, that is, in situations and with emotions similar to those of their betters but with this difference: that, in their case, the outcome was not tragic suffering. Needless to say, no dramatist ever believed that in real life the poor did not suffer but, if the dramatic function of suffering is to indicate moral guilt, then the relatively innocent cannot be shown on the stage as suffering. The comic similarity of their passions is a criticism of the great, a reminder that the king, too, is but a man, and the difference in destiny a reminder that the poor who, within their narrower captivity, commit the same crimes, are, by comparison, innocent.

Such a view might be termed the traditional view of Western culture against which naturalism was one form of revolt. As a literary movement, nineteenth-century naturalism was a corollary of nineteenth-century science, in particular of its biology. The evidence of Evolution, the discovery of some of the laws of genetics, for example, had shown that man was much more deeply embedded in the necessities of the natural order than he had imagined, and many began to believe that it was only a matter of time before the whole of man's existence, including his historical personality, would be found to be phenomena explicable in terms of the laws of science.

If the most significant characteristic of man is the complex of biological needs he shares with all members of his species, then the best lives for the writer to observe are those in which the role of natural necessity is clearest, namely, the lives of the very poor.

The difficulty for the naturalistic writer is that he cannot hold consistently to his principles without ceasing to be an artist and becoming a statistician, for an artist is by definition interested in uniqueness. There can no more be an art about the common man than there can be a medicine about the uncommon man. To think of another as common is to be indifferent to his personal fate; to the degree that one loves or hates another, one is conscious of his or her uniqueness. All the characters in literature with universal appeal, those that seem to reveal every man to himself, are in character and situation very uncommon indeed. A writer who is committed to a naturalist doctrine is driven by his need as an artist to be interesting to find a substitute for the tragic situation in the pathetic, situations of fantastic undeserved misfortune, and a substitute for the morally responsible hero in the pathological case.

The role of impersonal necessity, the necessities of nature

or the necessities of the social order in its totality upon the human person can be presented in fiction, in epic poetry and, better still, in the movies, because these media can verbally describe or visually picture that nature and that order; but in drama, where they are forced to remain offstage—there can be no dramatic equivalent to Hardy's description of Egdon Heath in *The Return of the Native*—this is very difficult. And in opera it is impossible, firstly, because music is in its essence dynamic, an expression of will and self-affirmation and, secondly, because opera, like ballet, is a virtuoso art; whatever his role, an actor who sings is more an uncommon man, more a master of his fate, even as a self-destroyer, than an actor who speaks. Passivity or collapse of the will cannot be expressed in song; if, for example, a tenor really sings the word *"Piango,"* he does not cry, a fact of which some tenors, alas, are only too aware. It is significant as a warning sign that the concluding line of *Cavalleria Rusticana, "Hanno ammazzato compare Turiddu,"* and the concluding line of Pagliacci, *"La commedia è finita,"* are spoken, not sung.

In practice, the theory of *verismo*, as applied to opera, meant substituting, in place of the heroic artistocratic setting of the traditional *opera seria*, various exotic settings, social and geographic. Instead of gods and princes, it gives us courtesans (*La Traviata, Manon*), gypsies and bullfighters (*Carmen*), a diva (*Tosca*), Bohemian artists (*La Bohème*), the Far East (*Madama Butterfly*), etc., social types and situations every bit as unfamiliar to the average operagoer as those of Olympus or Versailles.

Giovanni Verga was no doctrinaire naturalist. He wrote about the Sicilian peasants because he had grown up among them, knew them intimately, loved them and therefore could see them as unique beings. The original short story *Cavalleria Rusticana* which appeared in *Vita dei Campi* (1880) differs in several important respects from the dramatized version which Verga wrote four years later and upon which the libretto is based. In the short story the hero Turiddu is the relatively innocent victim of his poverty and his good looks. Santuzza is not the abused defenseless creature we know from the opera but a rich man's daughter who knows very well how to look after herself. Turiddu serenades her but he has no chance of marrying her since he has no money and though she likes him, she does not lose her head. Her betrayal to Alfio of Turiddu's affair with Lola is therefore much more malicious and unsympathetic than it is in the opera. Finally, the reason that Turiddu gives Alfio for insisting upon a fight to the death is not Santuzza's future—he has completely forgotten her—but the future of his penniless old mother.

Santuzza's seduction and pregnancy, Turiddu's brutal rejection of her, her curse upon him, his final remorse were all added by Verga when he had to build up Santuzza into a big and sympathetic role for Duse. As a subject for a short libretto, it is excellent. The situation is strong, self-contained and immediately clear; it provides roles for a convenient number and range of voices; and the emotions involved are both singable emotions and easy to contrast musically. The psychology is straightforward enough for song but not silly: how right it is, for instance, that Turiddu should reproach Santuzza for having let him seduce her—*"Pentirsi è vano dopo l'offesa."* Thanks to the swiftness with which music can express a change in feeling, even Turiddu's sudden switch of attitude from contempt to remorse becomes much more plausible in the opera than it seems in the spoken drama. Targioni-Tozzetti and Menasci quite rightly stuck pretty closely to Verga's story, their chief addition being the lines in which Turiddu begs Lucia to accept Santuzza as a daughter. But, having at their disposal as librettists what a dramatist no longer has, a chorus, they took full advantage of it. The choral episodes, the chorus of spring, the mule-driving song, the Easter hymn, the drinking song take up more than a quarter of the score. It might have been expected that, particularly in so short a work, to keep postponing and interrupting the action so much would be fatal; but, in fact, if one asks what was the chief contribution of the librettists towards giving the work the peculiar impact and popularity it has, I think one must say it was precisely these episodes. Thanks to them, the action of the protagonists, their personal tragedy, is seen against an immense background, the recurrent death and rebirth of nature, the liturgical celebration of the once-and-for-all death and resurrection of the redeemer of man, the age-old social rites of the poor, so that their local history takes on a ritual significance; Turiddu's death is, as it were, a ritual sacrifice in atonement for the sins of the whole community. One of the most moving moments in the opera, for example—and nothing could be less *verismo*—occurs when Santuzza, the excommunicated girl who believes that she is damned, is translated out of her situation and starts singing out over the chorus, like Deborah the Prophetess, "*Inneggiamo il Signor non è morto!*"

If the interplay of rite and personal action which is the secret of *Cavalleria Rusticana* is not a typical concern of the *verismo* school, the libretto interest of *Pagliacci* is even less naturalistic, for the subject is the psychological conundrum—"Who is the real me? Who is the real you?" This is presented through three contradictions. Firstly, the contradiction between the artist who creates his work out of real joys and sufferings and his audience whom it amuses, who enjoy through its imaginary joys and sufferings which are probably quite different from those of its creator. Secondly, the contradiction between the actors who do not feel the emotions they are portraying and the audience who do, at least imaginatively. And, lastly, the contradiction between the actors as professionals who have to portray imaginary feelings and the actors as men and women who have real feelings of their own. We are all actors; we frequently have to hide our real feelings for others and, alone with ourselves, we are constantly the victims of self-deception. We can never be certain that we know what is going on in the hearts of others, though we usually overestimate our knowledge—both the shock of discovering an infidelity and the tortures of jealousy are due to this. On the other hand, we are too certain that nobody else sees the real us.

In the Prologue, Tonio, speaking on behalf of Leoncavallo and then of the cast, reminds the audience that the artist and the actor are men. When we reach the play within the play all the contradictions are going simultaneously. Nedda is half-actress, half-woman, for she is expressing her real feelings in an imaginary situation; she is in love but not with Beppe who is playing Harlequin. Beppe is pure actor; as a man he is not in love with anybody. Tonio and Canio are themselves, for their real feelings and the situation correspond, to the greater amusement of the audience for it makes them *act* so convincingly. Finally there is Nedda's lover Silvio, the member of the audience who has got into the act, though as yet invisibly. When Nedda as Columbine recites to Harlequin the line written for her, *"A stannotte—e per sempre tua sarò!"* Canio as Pagliaccio is tortured because he has heard her use, speaking as herself, these identical words to the lover he has not seen. One has only to imagine what the opera would be like if, with the same situation between the characters, the *Commedia* were omitted, to see how much the interest of the opera depends on the question of Illusion and Reality, a problem which is supposed only to concern *idealists.*

About the music of these two operas, I can, of course, only speak as a layman. The first thing that strikes me on hearing them is the extraordinary strength and vitality of the Italian operatic tradition. Since 1800 Italian opera had already produced four fertile geniuses, Bellini, Rossini, Donizetti and Verdi, yet there was still enough left to allow, not only the lesser but still formidable figure of Puccini, but also the talents of Ponchielli, Giordano, Mascagni and Leoncavallo to create original and successful works. Today, indeed—it may have seemed different in the nineties—we are more conscious in the works of these later composers of the continuity of the tradition than of any revolutionary novelty. We do not emerge from the house, after hearing *Cavalleria* or *Pagliacci* for the first time, saying to ourselves, "What a strange new kind of opera!" No, before the first ten bars are over, we are thinking: "Ah, another Italian opera. How jolly!"

Comparing one with the other (a rather silly but inevitable habit), Leoncavallo strikes me as much more technically adroit. One of the strange things about Mascagni is the almost old-fashioned simplicity of his musical means; he writes as if he were scarcely aware of even the middle Verdi. There are dull passages in *Cavalleria Rusticana,* e.g., the music of the mule-driving song, but, in the dramatic passages, the very primitive awkwardness of the music seems to go *with* the characters and give them a conviction which Leoncavallo fails to give to his down-at-heel actors. For instance, when I listen to Turiddu rejecting Santuzza in the duet, *"No, no! Turiddu, rimani,"* I can believe that I am listening to a village Don Giovanni, but when I listen to Silvio making love to Nedda in the duet, *"Decidi, il mio destin,"* I know that I am listening to a baritone. As a listener, then, I prefer Mascagni; if I were a singer, I daresay my preference would be reversed.

In making their way round the world, *Cav & Pag* have had two great advantages: they are relatively cheap to produce and the vocal writing is effective but does not make excessive demands so that they are enjoyable even when performed by provincial touring companies, whereas works like *La Gioconda* or *Fedora* are intolerable without great stars. Take, for example, the famous aria *"Vesti la giubba"*: if the singer is in good voice, he has a fine opportunity to put it through its paces; if his voice is going, he can always throw away the notes and just bellow, a procedure which some audiences seem to prefer.

All the various artistic battle cries, Classicism, Romanticism, Naturalism, Surrealism, The-language-really-used-by-men, The-music-of-the-future, etc., are of interest to art historians because of the practical help which, however absurd they may seem as theories, they have been to artists in discovering how to create the kind of works which were proper to their powers. As listeners, readers and spectators, we should take them all with a strong dose of salt, remembering that a work of art is not *about* this or that kind of life; it *has* life, drawn, certainly, from human experience but transmuted, as a tree transmutes water and sunlight into treehood, into its own unique being. Every encounter with a work of art is a personal encounter; what it *says* is not information but a revelation of itself which is simultaneously a revelation of ourselves. We may dislike any particular work we encounter or prefer another to it but, to the degree that our dislike or our preference is genuine, we admit its genuineness as a work of art. The only real negative judgment—it may be ourselves, not the works, that are at fault—is indifference. As Rossini put it: "All kinds of music are good except the boring kind."

TRANSLATING OPERA LIBRETTI

(Written in collaboration with Chester Kallman)

SILVA: *The cup's prepared, and so rejoice;*
And more, I'll let thee have thy choice.
(He proudly presents him a dagger and a cup of poison)

from an old translation of *Ernani*

To discover just how arrogant and stupid reviewers can be, one must write something in collaboration with another writer. In a literary collaboration, if it is to be successful, the partners to it must surrender the selves they would be if they were writing separately and become one new author; though, obviously, any given passage must be written by one of them, the censor-critic who decides what will or will not do is this corporate personality. Reviewers think they know better, that they can tell who wrote what; I can only say that, in the case of our collaborations, their guesses as to which parts were actually written by Mr. Kallman and which my myself have been, at a conservative estimate, seventy-five per cent wrong.

Ten years ago, if anybody had prophesied that we would one day find ourselves translating libretti, we would have thought him crazy. We had always been fanatic advocates of the tradition upheld by British and American opera houses of giving opera in its original tongue as against the European tradition of translation. If people want to know what is going on, we said, let them buy a libretto with an English crib and read it before coming to the opera house; even if they know Italian and German well, they should still do this because, in a performance, one rarely hears more than one word in ten. As regards performances in opera houses, we still feel pretty much the same way, but televised opera for mass audiences is another matter. Whether the TV audience could ever be persuaded to tolerate operas in foreign languages is doubtful, not only because mass audiences are lazy but also because, on a television set, every syllable can be heard so that the irritation caused by failing to understand what is said is greater than in an opera house. (And then, of course, the big broadcasting companies are willing to pay handsomely for translations and we saw no reason why, if a translation *was* going to be made, we shouldn't get the money.) Once we started, we felt our aesthetic prejudices weakening for a reason which is not perhaps a valid one since it is purely selfish: we found ourselves completely fascinated by the task.

The three libretti we have translated together so far are Da Ponte's libretto for *Don Giovanni,* Schikaneder-and-Giesecke's libretto for *Die Zauberflöte* and Brecht's text for the song-ballet *Die sieben Todsünden* with music by Kurt Weill. Each has its special problems. *Don Giovanni* is in Italian, with sung recitatives and, stylistically, an *opera giocosa; Die Zauberflöte* is in German, written as a series of numbers with spoken dialogue in between and, stylistically, an *opera magica. Die sieben Todsünden* is not a traditional opera in which, as Mozart said, "poetry absolutely has to be the obedient daughter of music," but, like all the Brecht-Weill collaborations, a work in which the words are at least as important as the music, and its language is that of contemporary speech and full of popular idiom.

In comparison with the ordinary translater, the translator of a libretto is much more strictly bound in some respects and much freer in others. Since the music is so infinitely more important than the text, the translator must start with the premise that his translation must demand no change of musical intervals or rhythms in order to fit it. This law is absolute for arias and ensembles; in recitative, occasions may arise when the dropping or addition of a note is justified, but they are very rare. The translator of a libretto, therefore, has to produce a version which is rhythmically identical, not with the verse prosody of the original as it would be spoken, but with the musical prosody as it is sung. The difficulty in achieving this lies in the fact that musical prosody is both quantitative, like Greek and Latin verse, and accentual like English and German. In a quantitative prosody, syllables are either long or short and one long syllable is regarded as being equal in length to two short syllables; in an accentual prosody like our own, the length of the syllables is ignored—metrically, they are regarded as all being equal in length—and the distinction is between accented and unaccented syllables. This means that the rhythmical value of the trisyllabic feet and the dissyllabic feet are the reverse in a quantitative prosody from what they are in an accentual. Thus

> A quantitative dactyl or anapaest is in 4/4 or 2/4 time. (March time.)
> A quantitative trochee or iamb is in 3/4 or 6/8 time. (Waltz time.)
> An accentual dactyl or anapaest is in waltz time.
> An accentual trochee or iamb in march time.

But in music both quantity and accent count:

> A 2/4 bar made up of a half note followed by two quarter notes is, quantitatively, a dactyl but, accentually, a bacchic.
> A musical triplet  is, quantitatively, a tribrach but, accentually, a dactyl.

To add to the translators' troubles, the felt tempo of the spoken word and of musical notes is utterly different. If, timing myself with a stop watch, I recite, first the most rapid piece of verse I can think of—The Nightmare Song from *Iolanthe,* let us say—and then the slowest verse I can think of—Tennyson's *Tears, idle tears*—I find that the proportional difference between the time taken in each case to recite the same number of syllables is, at most, 2-1, and much of this difference is attributable, not to the change in speed of uttering the syllables but to the pauses in speaking which I make at the caesuras in the slow piece. Further, the two tempi at which I speak them both lie in what is in music the faster half of the tempo range. The tempo which in speaking verse is felt to be an adagio is felt in music as an allegretto. The consequence of this difference is that, when a composer sets verses to a slow tempo, verse dactyls and anapaests turn into molossoi, its trochees and iambs into spondees. The line *Now thank we all our God* is iambic when spoken but spondaic when sung.

This means that it is not enough for the translator to read the verses of the libretto, scan them, and produce a prosodic copy in English for, when he then matches his copy against the score, he will often find that the musical distortion of the spoken rhythm which sounded possible in the original tongue sounds impossible in English. This is particularly liable to happen when translating from Italian because, even when speaking, an Italian has a far greater license in prolonging or shortening the length of his syllables than an Englishman.

Two Examples

1) In Leporello's aria at the beginning of *Don Giovanni* occurs the line *Ma mi par che venga gente* (But it seems to me that people are coming).

To begin with, we decided that Leporello must say something else. He is on guard outside the house where Don Giovanni is raping or trying to rape Donna Anna. Da Ponte's line suggests that a crowd of strangers are about to come on stage; actually, it will only be Don Giovanni pursued by Donna Anna and some time will elapse before the Commendatore enters. Our first attempt was

What was that? There's trouble brewing.

Spoken, *che venga gente* and *there's trouble brewing* sound more or less metrically equivalent, but the phrase is set to three eighth notes and two quarter notes, so that *gente* which, when spoken, is a trochee becomes a spondee. But *brewing*, because of the lack of consonants between the syllables, sounds distorted as a spondee, so we had to revise the line to

What was that? We're in for trouble.

2) When Tamino approaches the doors of Sarastro's temple, a bodiless voice cries *Zurück!*, strongly accentuating the second syllable. This looks easy to translate literally by *Go Back!* and, were the tempo a slow one, it could be. Unfortunately, the tempo indication is *allegro assai* and at that speed, the two English monosyllables sound like a nonsense disyallable *geBACK*. Another solution had to be found; ours was *Beware!*

Sometimes the translator is forced to depart from the original text because of differences in the sound and association between the original and its exact English equivalent. Take, for example, the simple pair, *Ja* and *Nein, Si* and *No, Yes* and *No*. In the Leporello-Giovanni duet *Eh, via buffone* which is sung *allegro assai*, Leporello's two stanza's are built around the use of *no* in the first and *si* in the second.

Ed io non burlo, ma voglio andar.
No, no, padrone, v'andar vi dico.
No! No! No!
No, no, no, no, no, no, no, no, no, no, no.
Non vo' restar, si!
Si! Si! Si!
Si, si, si, si, si, si, si, si, si, si!

In English as in Italian, one can sing rapidly no, no, no, no . . . but one cannot sing yes, yes, yes, yes . . . The opening lines of Tamino's first aria run

Dies Etwas kann ich zwar nicht nennen,
Doch fühl ich's hier wie Feuer brennen;

Soll die Empfindung Liebe sein?
Ja, Ja,
Die Liebe ist's allein.

The tempo this time is moderate so that it is physically possible to sing *Yes, Yes,* but Yes-Yes in our culture has a comic or at least unromantic association with impatience or boredom. Similarly, one cannot translate *Komm, Komm* which occurs in one of the choruses in the same opera as *Come, Come,* without making the audience laugh.

Another problem is that feminine rhymes which are the commonest kind in Italian and frequent in German, are not only much rarer in English, but most of the ones that do exist are comic rhymes. It is possible for a competent versifier to copy the original rhyme scheme but often at the cost of making the English sound like Gilbert and Sullivan. On rare occasions such as Leporello's Catalogue aria, the tendency of double rhymes to be funnier in English than in Italian can be an advantage but, in any tender or solemn scene, it is better to have no rhyme at all than a ridiculous one. The marble statue rebukes Don Giovanni in the churchyard scene with the couplet

Ribalde, audace,
Lascia'l morti in pace.

Here any rhyme in English will sound absurd.

Then, languages differ not only in their verbal forms, but also in their rhetorical traditions, so that what sounds perfectly natural in one language, can, when literally translated, sound embarrassing in another. All Italian libretti are full of polysyllabic interjections; such as *Traditore! Scelerato! Sconsigliato! Sciugurato! Sventurato!* etc., and these sound effective, even at moments of high emotion. But in the English language, aside from the fact that most of our interjections are one or two syllables long, they are seldom, if ever, used in serious situations and are mostly employed in slanging matches between schoolboys or taxicab drivers. In serious situations we tend, I think, to make declarative statements; instead of shouting *Traditore!* (Vile seducer!) to shout *You betrayed me!*

Now and again the translator may feel that a change is necessary, not because the habits of two languages are different but because what the librettist wrote sounds too damn silly in any language. When Donna Anna, Donna Elvira, and Don Ottavio arrive at Don Giovanni's party in the finale of Act I, Donna Elvira sings

Bisogn' aver corraggio,
O cari' amici miei.

which is perfectly sensible, but Don Ottavio's reply is not.

L'amica dice bene!
Corragio' aver conviene.

that is to say:

Our lady friend says wisely;
Some courage would do nicely.

Nor in the finale to *Die Zauberflöte* when the Spirits see Pamina approaching distraught, can one allow them to say, as they do in German:

Where is she, then?
She is out of her senses.

With such alterations, no musician or musicologist is likely to quarrel. A more controversial matter is syllabification, for some purists consider the original syllabification and slurs to be as sacrosanct as the notes themselves. We believe, however, that there are occasions, at least in libretti written before 1850, when changes in syllabification are justifiable. In the days of Mozart and Rossini, the speed at which operas were expected to be turned out made any studied collaboration between librettist and composer impossible. The librettists produced his verses and the composer set them as best he could; he might ask for an extra aria but not for detailed revisions. The insistence shown by Verdi in his later years, by Wagner and by Strauss upon having a text which exactly matched their musical ideas was unknown. Mozart frequently spreads a syllable over two or more notes, and not in coloratura runs only. In many cases, his reason for doing so was, we believe, quite simple: his musical idea contained more notes than the verse he had been given contained syllables—just as, when he has not been given enough lines for his music, he repeats them.

Now it so happens that in English, on account of its vowels and its many monosyllabic words, there are fewer syllables which sing well and are intelligible when spread over several notes than there are in either Italian or German; English is, intrinsically, a more staccato tongue. The first stanza of the duet between Papageno and Pamina runs thus:

Bei Männern welche Liebe fühlen
Fehlt auch ein gutes Herze nicht.
Die süssen Triebe mitzufühlen
Ist dann des Weibes erste Pflicht.

The rhythm is iambic, that is to say in 4/4 time. But Mozart has set it to a tune in 6/8 time so, to make the words fit, he spreads each accented syllable over two notes linked by a slur. It is, of course, not difficult to write an English iambic quatrain.

When Love his dart has deep implanted,
The hero's heart grows kind and tame.
And by his passion soon enchanted,
The nymph receives the ardent flame.

But, to our ears, this sounded wrong somehow; they kept demanding an anapaestic quatrain which would give one syllable to every note of the melody.

When Love in his bosom desire has implanted,
The heart of the hero grows gentle and tame.
And soon by his passion enkindled, enchanted,
The nymph receives the impetuous flame.

This, of course, involves doing away with the slurs in the score, and some purists may object. One can only ask singers to sing both iambic and anapaestic versions several times without prejudice and then ask themselves which, in English, sounds the more Mozartian.

All such details which demand the translator's attention are part of the more general and important problem of finding the right literary style for any given opera. The kind of diction suitable to an *opera seria,* for example, is unsuitable in an *opera buffa,* nor can a supernatural character like the Queen of the Night use the speech of a courtesan like Violetta. In deciding upon a style for a particular opera, the translator has to trust his intuition and his knowledge of the literature, both in the original tongue and in his own, of the period in which the opera is supposed to be set. While he must obviously avoid solecisms, the literary traditions of any two languages are so different that a puristic exactness is often neither necessary nor even desirable; it does not follow that the best equivalent for the Italian spoken and written in 1790 is the English spoken in that year.

Scene Five of *Don Giovanni* shows the peasants dancing. Zerlina sings:

Giovinette, che fate, all'amore, che fate, all'amore,
Non lasciate, che passi l'età,
Che passi l'età,
Che passi l'età.
Se nel seno vi bulica il core, bulica il core,
Il rimedio vedetelo quà.
Che piacer, che piacer, che sarà.

Given the character of the music, it seemed to us that the natural English equivalent was not something late-eighteenth-century like Da Ponte's Italian, but Elizabethan pastoral.

Pretty maid with your graces adorning the dew-spangled morning,
The red rose and the white fade away,
Both wither away,
All fade in a day.
Of your pride and unkindness relenting, to kisses consenting,
All the pains of your shepherd allay.
As the cuckoo flies over the may.

A different kind of stylistic problem is presented by the Brecht-Weill ballet *Die sieben Todsünden* which is set in a contemporary but mythical America. A contemporary American diction is called for, but it must not be too specifically so or the mythical element will disappear. Thus, while the translation must not contain words which are only used in British English—*haus* must be translated as *home* not as *house*—it would be wrong, although the family are said to live in Louisiana, to translate the German into the speech of American Southerners.

In one chorus the family list various delicious foods.

> *Hörnchen! Schnitzel! Spargel! Hühnchen!*
> *Und die kleinen gelben Honigküchen*

that is:

> Muffins! Cutlets! Asparagus! Chickens!
> And those little yellow honey-buns!

Though Americans do eat all of these, they do not make a characteristic list of what Americans, particularly from the South, would think of with the greatest greedy longing. Accordingly, we changed the list to:

> Crabmeat! Porkchops! Sweet-corn! Chicken!
> And those golden biscuits spread with honey!

The images and metaphors characteristic of one culture and language are not always as effective in another. Thus, a literal translation of one of the verses sung by Anna in *Lust* would go:

> And she shows her little white backside,
> Worth more than a little factory,
> Shows it gratis to starers and corner-boys,
> To the profane look of the world.

The most powerful line in this verse is the second, but, in American English, "a little factory" makes no impact. Some other comparison must be thought of:

> Now she shows off her white little fanny,
> Worth twice a little Texas motel,

And for nothing the poolroom can stare at Annie
As though she'd nothing to sell.

Translating Arias

An aria very rarely contains information which it is essential for the audience to know in order to understand the action and which must, therefore, be translated literally; all that a translation of an aria must do is convey the emotion or conflict of emotions which it expresses. At the same time, the arias in an opera are as a rule its high points musically, so that it is in them that the quality of the translation matters most. So far as an original librettist is concerned, all that matters is that his verses should inspire the composer to write beautiful music, but the translator is in a different position. The music is already there, and it is his duty to make his verses as worthy of it as he can.

Before Wagner and Verdi in his middle years, no composer worried much about the libretto; he took what he was given and did the best he could with it. This was possible because a satisfactory convention had been established as to the styles and forms in which libretti should be written which any competent versifier could master. This meant, however, that, while a composer could be assured of getting a settable text, one libretto was remarkably like another; all originality and interest had to come from the music. Today, it is idle to pretend that we can listen to a Mozart opera with the ears of his contemporaries, as if we had never heard the operas of Wagner, the late Verdi and Strauss in which the libretto plays an important role. In listening to a Mozart opera, we cannot help noticing when the text is banal or silly, or becoming impatient when a line is repeated over and over again. Having the beautiful music in his ears, a modern translator must feel it his duty to make his version as worthy of it as he can.

1) *Don Ottavio's first aria*

Dalla sua pace
La mia depende,
Quelch'al lei piace
Vita mi rende,

Quel che l'incresce
Morte mi da.
S'ella sospira
Sospir' anchio,
E mia quell'ira
Qu'e pianto è mio,
E non ho bene
S'ella non l'ha

Upon her peace / my peace depends / what pleases her / grants me life / and what saddens her / gives me death. If she sighs / I also sigh / mine is her anger / and her grief is mine / I have no joy / if she has none.

When one compares English poetry with Italian or that of any Romance language, one sees that English poetic speech is more concrete in its expressions; an English poet writing a love lyric tends to express his feelings in terms of imagery and metaphors drawn from nature, rather than stating them directly. Further, English and Italian notions of what it is proper for an amorous male to say and do are different. To an English sensibility, Ottavio's exclusive concentration upon himself—she mustn't be unhappy because it makes him unhappy—is a bit distasteful. Lastly, Da Ponte's lyric contains only a single idea repeated over and over again with but slight variations, but Mozart has given his second stanza a completely different musical treatment. Accordingly we tried to write a lyric which should be a) more concrete in diction, b) make Ottavio think more about Donna Anna than himself and c) less repetitive.

Shine, Lights of Heaven,
Guardians immortal,
Shine on my true love,
Waking or sleeping,
Sun, moon and starlight,
Comfort her woe.

O nimble breezes,
O stately waters,

Obey a lover,
Proclaim her beauty
And sing her praises
Where'er you go.

(da capo)
When grief beclouds her,
I walk in shadow,
My thoughts are with her,
Waking or sleeping;
Sun, moon and starlight,
Comfort her woe.

2) *Pamina's Aria in Die Zauberflöte, Act II*
Ach, ich fühl's, es ist verschwunden
Ewig hin, mein ganzes Glück, der Liebe Glück.
Nimmer kommt ihr, Wonne-stunden
Meinem Herzen mehr zurück.
Sieh, Tamino
Diese Tränen fliessen, Trauter, dir allein, dir allein.
Fühlst du nicht der Liebe Sehnen, Liebe Sehnen,
So wird Ruhe im Tode sein.
Fühlst du nicht der Liebe Sehnen,
Fühlst du nicht der Liebe Sehnen,
So wird Ruhe im Tode sein,
Im Tode sein.

(Ah, I feel it / it has vanished / for ever away / the joy of love. Never will you come / hours of wonder / back to my heart / See, Tamino / these tears flowing, beloved, for you alone / If you do not feel the sighs of love / then there will be peace in death.)

The aria contains a number of high notes, long runs and phrases which repeat like an echo. Any English version, therefore, must provide open vowels for the high notes and runs, and phrases which can sound like echoes. There is a certain kind of English poetry which is based upon the repetition of a word or words in slightly different context, for instance, Donne's "The Expiation."

Go, go, and if that word hath not quite killed thee,
Ease me with death by bidding me go too,
Or, if it have, let my word work on me
And a just office on a murderer do;
Except it be too late to kill me so,
Being double dead, going and bidding go.

Given Pamina's situation it seemed to us that we might make use of this style and build our lyric round the words *silent* and *grief*.

Hearts may break though grief be silent,
True hearts make their love their lives,
Silence love with ended lives;
Love that dies in one false lover
Kills the heart where love survives.

O Tamino, see the silence
Of my tears betray my grief,
Faithful grief.
If you flee my love in silence,
In faithless silence,
Let my sorrow die with me.
If you can betray Pamina,
If you love me not, Tamino,
Let my sorrow die with me
And silent be.

3) *Donna Anna's last aria in Don Giovanni.*
This consists of an orchestral recitative, a cavatina and a cabaletta.

RECIT: *Crudele? Ah no, mia bene. Troppo mi spiace*
allontanarti un ben che lungamente la nostra
alma desia . . . Ma, il mondo . . . O Dio! . . . Abbastanza

per te mi parla amore. Non sedur la constanza
del sensibil mio core!

CAVATINA: *Non mi dir, bell'idol mio,*
Che son io crudel con te;
Tu ben sai quant'io t'amai,
Tu conosci la mia fè,
Tu conosci la mia fè.
Calma, calm'il tuo tormento,
Se di duol non vuoi ch'io mora,
Non vuoi ch'io mora
Non mi dir, bell'idol mio,
Che son io crudel con te;
Calma, calm'il, etc. . . .

CABALETTA: *Forsè, forsè un giorn'il cielo*
Sentirà pietà di mè.

(Cruel? O no, my dear. Too much it grieves me to withhold from you a joy that for a long time our soul desires. But, the world . . . O God! Do not weaken the constancy of my suffering heart. Sufficiently for you Love speaks to me.

Do not tell me, my dearest dear,
That I am cruel to you;
You know well how much I love you,
You know my fidelity,
Calm your torment
If you do not wish me to die of grief.

Perhaps, one day, Heaven
Will take pity on me.

The aria is one of the most beautiful which Mozart ever wrote, but the words are of an appalling banality and make Donna Anna very unsympathetic, now leading poor Don Ottavio on, now repulsing him. We felt, therefore, that we must forget the orginal text entirely and write something quite new. In a coloratura aria of this kind, it is wise to start with translating or reinventing the cabaletta which, like a cadenza, is written to provide the singer with the opportunity to display her vocal virtuosity in runs and range of pitch. This means that, whatever lines one writes, the key syllables must contain long open vowels, preferably ā, e͞ɪ and a͞e. Accordingly, the first line of the aria we composed was the last, after taking a hint from the *cielo* in the preceding line.

On my dark His light shall break.

We then wrote a line to precede it and complete the cabaletta:

God will surely wipe away thy tears, my daughter,
On thy (my) dark His light shall break.

These lines suggested the idea that they might be some kind of message from Heaven, so that some lines, at least, of the cavatina would be concerned with where the message was coming from. We then remembered that, in the graveyard scene which immediately precedes it, Don Giovanni mentions that it is a cloudless night with a full moon, and that the supper scene which immediately follows it opens with the Don's hired musicians playing suitable supper music. These two facts suggested two ideas: a) that Donna Anna might be gazing at the full moon, from which, so to speak, the message of her cabaletta would emanate and b) effective use might be made of the Neoplatonic contrast between the music of the spheres which her "spiritual" ear catches from the moon and the carnal music of this world as represented by the supper music. The stage direction in the piano score we were using says *A darkened chamber*, but there seems to be nothing about the action which makes this necessary. Why shouldn't the chamber have an uncurtained open window through which the moon could be seen? Accordingly, we changed the stage direction and wrote the aria as follows:

RECIT: Disdain you, Hear me, my dearest! None can foretell what the rising sun may bring, a day of sorrow or a day of rejoicing. But, hear me! Remember, when the jealous

misgivings of a lover beset you, all the
stars shall fall down 'ere I forget you!

CAVATINA: Let yonder moon, chaste eye of heaven
Cool desire and calm your soul;
May the bright stars their patience lend you
As their constellations roll,
Turn, turn, turn about the Pole.
Far, too far they seem from our dying,
Cold we call them to our sighing;
We, too, proud, too evil-minded,
By sin are blinded.
See, how bright the moon shines yonder,
Silent witness to all our wrong:
Ah! but hearken! O blessed wonder!
Out of silence comes a music,
And I can hear her song.

CABALETTA: "God will surely, surely, wipe away thy
tears, my daughter,
On thy dark His light shall break.
God is watching thee, hath not forgotten
thee,
On thy dark His light shall break."
God will heed me, sustain me, console me.
On my dark His light shall break.

Any one who attempts to translate from one tongue into another will know moods of despair when he feels he is wasting his time upon an impossible task but, irrespective of success or failure, the mere attempt can teach a writer much about his own language which he would find it hard to learn elsewhere. Nothing else can more naturally correct our tendency to take our own language for granted. Translating compels us to notice its idiosyncracies and limitations, it makes us more attentive to the sound of what we write and, at the same time, if we are inclined to fall into it, will cure us of the heresy that poetry is a kind of music in which the relations of vowels and consonants have an absolute value, irrespective of the meaning of the words.

MUSIC IN SHAKESPEARE

Musick to heare, why hear'st thou musick sadly,
Sweets with sweets warre not, joy delights in joy:
Why lov'st thou that which thou receav'st not
gladly,
Or else receav'st with pleasure thine annoy?

Professor Wilson Knight and others have pointed out the important part played in Shakespeare's poetry by images related to music, showing, for instance, how music occupies the place in the cluster of good symbols which is held in the bad cluster by the symbol of the Storm.

His fondness for musical images does not, of course, necessarily indicate that Shakespeare himself was musical—some very good poets have been musically tone deaf. Any poet of the period who used a musical imagery would have attached the same associations to it, for they were part of the current Renaissance theory of the nature of music and its effects.

Anyone at the time, if asked, "What is music?" would have

given the answer stated by Lorenzo to Jessica in the last scene of *The Merchant of Venice*. Mr. James Hutton in an admirable article in the *English Miscellany* on "Some English Poems in praise of Music" has traced the history of this theory from Pythagoras to Ficino and shown the origin of most of Lorenzo's images. The theory may be summarized thus:

1) Music is unique among the arts for it is the only art practiced in Heaven and by the unfallen creatures. Conversely, one of the most obvious characteristics of Hell is its discordant din.
2) Human reason is able to infer that this heavenly music exists because it can recognize mathematical proportions. But the human ear cannot hear it, either because of man's Fall or simply because the ear is a bodily organ subject to change and death. What Campanella calls the *molino vivo* of the self drowns out the celestial sounds. In certain exceptional states of ecstasy, however, certain individuals have heard it.
3) Man-made music, though inferior to the music which cannot be heard, is a good for, in its mortal way, it recalls or imitates the Divine order. In consequence, it has great powers. It can tame irrational and savage beasts, it can cure lunatics, it can relieve sorrow. A dislike of music is a sign of a perverse will that defiantly refuses to submit to the general harmony.
4) Not all music, however, is good. There is a bad kind of music which corrupts and weakens. "The Devil rides a fiddlestick." Good is commonly associated with old music, bad with new.

Nobody today, I imagine, holds such a theory, i.e., nobody now thinks that the aesthetics of music have anything to do with the science of acoustics. What theory of painting, one wonders, would have developed if Pythagoras had owned a spectroscope and learned that color relations can also be expressed in mathematical proportions.

But if he has never heard of the theory, there are many

things in Shakespeare which the playgoer will miss. For example, the dramatic effect of the recognition scene in *Pericles*.

PERICLES: But what music?
HELICANUS: My lord, I hear none.
PERICLES: None! The music of the spheres! List, my Marina!
LYSIMACHUS: It is not good to cross him: give him way.
PERICLES: Rarest sounds! Do ye not hear?
HELICANUS: My Lord, I hear.
(Act V, Scene 1.)

or even such a simple little joke as this from *Othello:*

CLOWN: If you have any music that may not be heard, to't again; but, as they say, to hear music the general does not greatly care.
1ST. MUS.: We have none such, sir.
(Act III, Scene 1.)

Music is not only an art with its own laws and values; it is also a social fact. Composing, performing, listening to music are things which human beings do under certain circumstances just as they fight and make love. Moreover, in the Elizabethan age, music was regarded as an important social fact. A knowledge of music, an ability to read a madrigal part were expected of an educated person, and the extraordinary output of airs and madrigals between 1588 and 1620 testifies to both the quantity and quality of the music making that must have gone on. When Bottom says, "I have a reasonable good ear in music: let's have the tongs and the bones," it is not so much an expression of taste as a revelation of class, like dropping one's aitches; and when Benedick says, "Well, a horn for my money when all's done," he is being deliberately *épatant*.

Whether he personally cared for music or not, any dramatist of the period could hardly have failed to notice the part played by music in human life, to observe, for instance, that the kind of music a person likes or dislikes, the kind of way in which he listens to it, the sort of occasion on which he wants to hear or make it, are revealing about his character.

A dramatist of a later age might notice the same facts, but it would be difficult for him to make dramatic use of them unless he were to write a play specifically about musicians.

But the dramatic conventions of the Elizabethan stage permitted and encouraged the introduction of songs and instrumental music into the spoken drama. Audiences liked to hear them, and the dramatist was expected to provide them. The average playgoer, no doubt, simply wanted a pretty song as part of the entertainment and did not bother about its dramatic relevance to the play as a whole. But a dramatist who took his art seriously had to say, either, "Musical numbers in a spoken play are irrelevant episodes and I refuse to put them in just to please the public," or, "I must conceive my play in such a manner that musical numbers, vocal or instrumental, can occur in it, not as episodes, but as essential elements in its structure."

If Shakespeare took this second line, it should be possible, on examining the occasions where he makes use of music, to find answers to the following questions:

1) Why is this piece of music placed just where it is and not somewhere else?
2) In the case of a song, why are the mood and the words of this song what they are? Why this song instead of another?
3) Why is it this character who sings and not another? Does the song reveal something about his character which could not be revealed as well in any other way?
4) What effect does this music have upon those who listen to it? Is it possible to say that, had the music been omitted, the behavior of the characters or the feelings of the audience would be different from what they are?

II

When we now speak of music as an art, we mean that the elements of tone and rhythm are used to create a structure of sounds which are to be listened to for their own sake. If it be asked what such music is "about," I do not think it too controversial to say that it presents a virtual image of our experience of living as temporal, with its double aspect of recurrence and becoming. To "get" such an image, the listener must for the time being banish from his mind all immediate desires and practical concerns and only think what he hears.

But rhythm and tone can also be used to achieve non-musical ends. For example, any form of physical movement, whether in work or play, which involves accurate repetition is made easier by sounded rhythmical beats, and the psychological effect of singing, whether in unison or in harmony, upon a group is one of reducing the sense of diversity and strengthening the sense of unity so that, on all occasions where such a unity of feeling is desired or desirable, music has an important function.

> If the true concord of well-tuned sounds
> By unions marred do offend thine ear,
> They do but sweetly chide thee, who confounds
> In singleness the parts that thou shouldst bear.
> Mark how one string, sweet husband to another,
> Strikes each in each by mutual ordering;
> Resembling sire and child and happy mother,
> Who all in one, one pleasing note do sing;
> Whose speechless song, being many, seeming one,
> Sings this to thee, "Thou single wilt prove none."
>
> (Sonnet VIII.)

The oddest example of music with an extramusical purpose is the lullaby. The immediate effect of the rocking rhythm and the melody is to fix the baby's attention upon an ordered pattern so that it forgets the distractions of arbitrary noises, but its final intention is to make the baby fall asleep, that is to say, to hear nothing at all.

Sounds, instrumental or vocal, which are used for social purposes, may of course have a musical value as well but this is usually secondary to their function. If one takes, say, a sea-shanty out of its proper context and listens to it on the gramophone as one might listen to a *lied* by Schubert, one is very soon bored. The beauty of sound which it may have been felt to possess when accompanied by the sensation of muscular movement and visual images of sea and sky cannot survive without them.

The great peculiarity of music as an art is that the sounds which comprise its medium can be produced in two ways, by playing on specially constructed instruments and by using the human vocal cords in a special way. Men use their vocal cords for speech, that is, to communicate with each other, but also, under certain conditions, a man may feel, as we say, "like singing." This impulse has little, if anything, to do with communication or with other people. Under the pressure of a certain mood, a man may feel the need to express that mood to himself by using his vocal cords in an exceptional way. If he should sing some actual song he has learned, he chooses it for its general fitness to his mood, not for its unique qualities.

None of the other arts seem suited to this immediate self-expression. A few poets may compose verses in their bath—I have never heard of anyone trying to paint in his bath—but almost everyone, at some time or other, has sung in his bath.

In no other art can one see so clearly a distinction, even a rivalry, between the desire for pattern and the desire for personal utterance, as is disclosed by the difference between instrumental and vocal music. I think I can see an analogous distinction in painting. To me, vocal music plays the part in music that the human nude plays in painting. In both there is an essential erotic element which is always in danger of being corrupted for sexual ends but need not be and, without this element of the erotic which the human voice and the nude have contributed, both arts would be a little lifeless.

In music it is from instruments that rhythmical and tonal precision and musical structure are mostly derived so that, without them, the voice would have remained tied to impromptu and personal expression. Singers, unchastened by the orchestral discipline, would soon lose interest in singing and wish only to show off their voices. On the other hand, the music of a dumb race who had invented instruments would be precise but dull, for the players would not know what it means to strive after expression, to make their instruments "sing." The kind of effect they would make is the kind we condemn in a pianist when we say: "He just plays the notes."

Lastly, because we do not have the voluntary control over our ears that we have over our eyes, and because musical sounds do not denote meanings like words or represent objects like lines and colors, it is far harder to know what a person means, harder even for himself to know, when he says, "I like this piece of music," than when he says, "I like this book or this picture." At one extreme there is the professional musician who not only thinks clearly and completely what he hears but also recognizes the means by which the composer causes him so to think. This does not mean that he can judge music any better than one without his technical knowledge who has trained himself to listen and is familiar with music of all kinds. His technical knowledge is an added pleasure, perhaps, but it is not itself a musical experience. At the other extreme is the student who keeps the radio playing while he studies because he finds that a background of sound makes it easier for him to concentrate on his work. In his case the music is serving the contradictory function of preventing him from listening to anything, either to itself or to the noises in the street.

Between these two extremes, there is a way of listening which has been well described by Susanne Langer.

> There is a twilight zone of musical enjoyment when tonal appreciation is woven into daydreaming. To the

entirely uninitiated hearer it may be an aid in finding expressive forms at all, to extemporise an accompanying romance and let the music express feelings accounted for by its scenes. But to the competent it is a pitfall, because it obscures the full vital import of the music, noting only what comes handy for a purpose, and noting only what expresses attitudes and emotions the listener was familiar with before. It bars everything new and really interesting in a world, since what does not fit the *petit roman* is passed over, and what does fit is the dreamer's own. Above all it leads attention, not only to the music, but away from it—via the music to something else that is essentially an indulgence. One may spend a whole evening in this sort of dream and carry nothing away from it, no musical insight, no new feeling, and actually nothing heard.

(*Feeling and Form,* Chap. X.)

It is this kind of listening, surely, which is implied by the Duke in *Twelfth Night,* "If music be the food of love, play on," and by Cleopatra, "Give me some music—music, moody food/Of us that trade in love," and which provoked that great music-lover, Bernard Shaw, to the remark, "Music is the brandy of the damned."

III

Shakespeare uses instrumental music for two purposes: on socially appropriate occasions, to represent the voice of this world, of collective rejoicing as in a dance, or of mourning as in a dead march and, unexpectedly, as an auditory image of a supernatural or magical world. In the last case the music generally carries the stage direction, "Solemn."

It may be directly the voice of Heaven, the music of the spheres heard by Pericles, the music under the earth heard by Antony's soldiers, the music which accompanies Queen Katharine's vision, or it may be commanded, either by spirits of the intermediate world like Oberon or Ariel, or by wise men like Prospero and the physicians in *King Lear* and *Pericles,* to exert a magical influence on human beings. When doctors order music, it is, of course, made by human musicians, and to the healthly it may even sound "rough and woeful," but in the ears of the patient, mad Lear or unconscious Thaisa, it seems a platonic imitation of the unheard celestial music and has a curative effect.

"Solemn" music is generally played off stage. It comes, that is, from an invisible source which makes it impossible for those on stage to express a *voluntary* reaction to it. Either they cannot hear it or it has effects upon them which they cannot control. Thus, in Act II, Scene 1 of *The Tempest,* it is an indication of their villainy, the lack of music in their souls, that Antonio and Sebastian are not affected by the sleeping-spell music when Alonso and the others are, an indication which is forthwith confirmed when they use the opportunity so created to plan Alonso's murder.

On some occasions, e.g., in the vision of Posthumus (*Cymbeline,* Act V, Scene 4), Shakespeare has lines spoken against an instrumental musical background. The effect of this is to depersonalize the speaker, for the sound of the music blots out the individual timbre of his voice. What he says to music seems not *his* statement but a message, a statement that has to be made.

Antony and Cleopatra (Act IV, Scene 3) is a good example of the dramatic skill with which Shakespeare places a supernatural musical announcement. In the first scene of the act we have had a glimpse of the cold, calculating Octavius refusing Antony's old-fashioned challenge to personal combat and deciding to give battle next day. To Octavius, chivalry is one aspect of a childish lack of self-control and "Poor Antony" is his contemptuous comment on his opponent. Whereupon we are shown Antony talking to his friends in a wrought-up state of self-dramatization and self-pity:

Give me thy hand,
Thou hast been rightly honest; so hast thou;
Thou—and thou—and thou; you have serv'd me well.
Perchance to-morrow

You'll serve another master. I look on you
As one that takes his leave. Mine honest friends,
I turn you not away; but like a master
Married to your good service, stay till death:
Tend me to-night two hours, I ask no more,
And the gods yield you for't.

We already know that Enobarbus, who is present, has decided to desert Antony. Now follows the scene with the common soldiers in which supernatural music announces that

The god Hercules whom Antony lov'd
Now leaves him.

The effect of this is to make us see the human characters, Octavius, Antony, Cleopatra, Enobarbus, as agents of powers greater than they. Their personalities and actions, moral or immoral, carry out the purposes of these powers but cannot change them. Octavius' self-confidence and Antony's sense of doom are justified though they do not know why.

But in the ensuing five scenes it appears that they were both mistaken, for it is Antony who wins the battle. Neither Octavius nor Antony have heard the music, but we, the audience, have, and our knowledge that Antony must lose in the end gives a pathos to his temporary triumph which would be lacking if the invisible music were cut.

Of the instances of mundane or carnal instrumental music in the plays, the most interesting are those in which it is, as it were, the wrong kind of magic. Those who like it and call for it use it to strengthen their illusions about themselves.

So Timon uses it when he gives his great banquet. Music stands for the imaginary world Timon is trying to live in, where everybody loves everybody and he stands at the center as the source of this universal love.

TIMON: Music, make their welcome!
FIRST LORD: You see, my lord, how ample y'are beloved.
(*Timon of Athens,* Act I, Scene 2.)

One of his guests is the professional sneerer, Apemantus, whose conceit is that he is the only one who sees the world as it really is, as the absolutely unmusical place where nobody loves anybody but himself. "Nay," says Timon to him, "an you begin to rail on society once, I am sworn not to give regard to you. Farewell, and come with better music."

But Timon is never to hear music again after this scene.

Neither Timon nor Apemantus have music in their souls but, while Apemantus is shamelessly proud of this, Timon wants desperately to believe that he has music in his soul, and the discovery that he has not destroys him.

To Falstaff, music, like sack, is an aid to sustaining the illusion of living in an Eden of childlike innocence where nothing serious can happen. Unlike Timon, who does not love others as much as he likes to think, Falstaff himself really is loving. His chief illusion is that Prince Hal loves him as much as he loves Prince Hal and that Prince Hal is an innocent child like himself.

Shakespeare reserves the use of a musical background for the scene between Falstaff, Doll, Poinz, and Hal (*Henry IV, Part II,* Act II, Scene 4). While the music lasts, Time will stand still for Falstaff. He will not grow older, he will not have to pay his debts, Prince Hal will remain his dream-son and boon companion. But the music is interrupted by the realities of time with the arrival of Peto. Hal feels ashamed.

> By heaven, Poinz, I feel me much to blame
> So idly to profane the present time. . . .
> Give me my sword and cloak. Falstaff, good-night!

Falstaff only feels disappointed:

> Now comes in the sweetest morsel of the night, and we must hence, and leave it unpick'd.

In Prince Hal's life this moment is the turning point; from now on he will become the responsible ruler. Falstaff will not change because he is incapable of change but, at this moment, though he is unaware of it, the most important thing in his life, his friendship with Hal, ceases with the words "Good-night." When they meet again, the first words Falstaff will hear are—"I know thee not, old man."

Since music, the virtual image of time, takes actual time to perform, listening to music can be a waste of time, especially for those, like kings, whose primary concern should be with the unheard music of justice.

> Ha! Ha! keep time! How sour sweet music is
> When time is broke and no proportion kept!
> So is it in the music of men's lives.
> And here have I the daintiness of ear
> To check time broke in a disordered string;
> But, for the concord of my time and state,
> Had not an ear to hear my true time broke.
>
> (*Richard II*, Act V, Scene 5.)

IV

We find two kinds of songs in Shakespeare's plays, the called-for and the impromptu, and they serve different dramatic purposes.

A called-for song is a song which is sung by one character at the request of another who wishes to hear music, so that action and speech are halted until the song is over. Nobody is asked to sing unless it is believed that he can sing well and, little as we may know about the music which was actually used in performances of Shakespeare, we may safely assume from the contemporary songs which we do possess that they must have made demands which only a good voice and a good musician could satisfy.

On the stage, this means that the character called upon to sing ceases to be himself and becomes a performer; the audience is not interested in him but in the quality of his singing. The songs, it must be remembered, are interludes embedded in a play written in verse or prose which is spoken; they are not arias in an opera where the dramatic medium is itself song, so that we forget that the singers are performers just as we forget that the actor speaking blank verse is an actor.

An Elizabethan theatrical company, giving plays in which such songs occur, would have to engage at least one person for his musical rather than his histrionic talents. If they had not been needed to sing, the dramatic action in *Much Ado, As You Like It* and *Twelfth Night* could have got along quite well without Balthazar, Amiens and the Clown.

Yet, minor character though the singer may be, he has a character as a professional musician and, when he gets the chance, Shakespeare draws our attention to it. He notices the mock or polite modesty of the singer who is certain of his talents.

DON PEDRO: Come, Balthazar, we'll hear that song again.
BALTHAZAR: O good my lord, tax not so bad a voice
To slander music any more than once.
DON PEDRO: It is the witness still of excellency
To put a strange face on his own perfection.

He marks the annoyance of the professional who must sing for another's pleasure whether he feels like it or not.

JAQUES: More, I prithee, more.
AMIENS: My voice is ragged: I know I cannot please you.
JAQUES: I do not desire you to please me: I desire you to sing. Will you sing?
AMIENS: More at your request than to please myself.

In the dialogue between Peter and the musicians in *Romeo and Juliet,* Act IV, Scene IV, he contrasts the lives and motives of ill-paid musicians with that of their rich patrons. The musicians have been hired by the Capulets to play at Juliet's marriage to Paris. Their lives mean nothing to the Capulets; they are things which make music: the lives of the Capulets mean nothing to the musicians; they are things which pay money. The musicians arrive only to learn that Juliet is believed to be dead and the wedding is off. Juliet's life means nothing to them, but her death means a lot; they will not get paid. Whether either the Capulets or the musicians actually like music is left in doubt. Music is something you have to have at a wedding; music is something you have to play if that is your job. With a felicitous irony Shakespeare introduces a quotation from Richard Edwardes' poem, "In Commendation of Musick"

PETER: When gripping grief the heart doth wound
And doleful dumps the mind oppress
Then music with her silver sound—
Why "silver sound"? Why "music with her silver sound"?
What say you, Simon Catling?

1ST MUS: Marry, sir, because silver hath a sweet sound.

PETER: Pretty! What say you, Hugh Rebeck?

2ND MUS: I say, "silver sound," because musicians sound for silver.

(*Romeo and Juliet,* Act IV, Scene 5.)

The powers the poet attributes to music are exaggerated. It cannot remove the grief of losing a daughter or the pangs of an empty belly.

Since action must cease while a called-for song is heard, such a song, if it is not to be an irrelevant interlude, must be placed at a point where the characters have both a motive for wanting one and leisure to hear it. Consequently we find few called-for songs in the tragedies, where the steady advance of the hero to his doom must not be interrupted, or in the historical plays in which the characters are men of action with no leisure.

Further, it is rare that a character listens to a song for its own sake since, when someone listens to music properly, he forgets himself and others which, on the stage, means that he forgets all about the play. Indeed, I can only think of one case where it seems certain that a character listens to a song as a song should be listened to, instead of as a stimulus to a *petit roman* of his own, and that is in *Henry VIII*, Act III, Scene 1, when Katharine listens to *Orpheus with his lute.* The

Queen knows that the King wants to divorce her and that pressure will be brought upon her to acquiesce. But she believes that it is her religious duty to refuse, whatever the consequences. For the moment there is nothing she can do but wait. And her circumstances are too serious and painful to allow her to pass the time daydreaming:

> Take thy lute, wench; my soul grows sad with troubles;
> Sing and disperse them, if thou canst; leave working.

The words of the song which follows are not about any human feelings, pleasant or unpleasant, which might have some bearing on her situation. The song, like Edwardes' poem, is an *encomium musicae*. Music cannot, of course, cure grief, as the song claims, but in so far that she is able to attend to it and nothing else, she can forget her situation while the music lasts.

An interesting contrast to this is provided by a scene which at first seems very similar, Act IV, Scene I of *Measure for Measure*. Here, too, we have an unhappy woman listening to a song. But Mariana, unlike Katharine, is not trying to forget her unhappiness; she is indulging it. Being the deserted lady has become a rôle. The words of the song, *Take, O take, those lips away,* mirrors her situation exactly, and her apology to the Duke when he surprises her gives her away.

> I cry you mercy, sir; and well could wish
> You had not found me here so musical:
> Let me excuse me, and believe me so—
> My mirth it much displeas'd, but pleas'd my woe.

In his reply, the Duke, as is fitting in this, the most puritanical of Shakespeare's plays, states the puritanical case against the heard music of this world.

> 'Tis good; though music oft hath such a charm
> To make bad good, and good provoke to harm.

Were the Duke to extend this reply, one can be sure that he would speak of the unheard music of Justice.

On two occasions Shakespeare shows us music being used with conscious evil intent. In *The Two Gentlemen of Verona,* Proteus, who has been false to his friend, forsworn his vows to his girl and is cheating Thurio, serenades Silvia while his forsaken Julia listens. On his side, there is no question here of self-deception through music. Proteus knows exactly what he is doing. Through music which is itself beautiful and good, he hopes to do evil, to seduce Silvia.

Proteus is a weak character, not a wicked one. He is ashamed of what he is doing and, just as he knows the difference between good and evil in conduct, he knows the difference between music well and badly played.

HOST: How do you, man? the music likes you not?
JULIA: You mistake; the musician likes me not.
HOST: Why, my pretty youth?
JULIA: He plays false, father.
HOST: How? Out of tune on the strings?
JULIA: Not so; but yet so false that he grieves my very heart-strings . . .
HOST: I perceive you delight not in music.
JULIA: Not a whit, when it jars so.
HOST: Hark, what a fine change is in the music!
JULIA: Ay, that change is the spite.
HOST: You would have them always play but one thing?
JULIA: I would always have one play but one thing.
(*Two Gentlemen of Verona,* Act IV, Scene 2.)

The second occasion is in *Cymbeline,* when Cloten serenades Imogen. Cloten is a lost soul without conscience or shame. He is shown, therefore, as someone who does not know one note from another. He has been told that music acts on women as an erotic stimulus, and wishes for the most erotic music that money can buy:

First a very excellent, good, conceited thing; after, a wonderful sweet air, with admirable rich words to it, and then let her consider.

For, except as an erotic stimulus, music is, for him, worthless:

> If this penetrate, I will consider your music the better; if it do not, it is a vice in her ears which horse-hairs and calves' guts, nor the voice of the unpaved eunuch to boot can never amend.
>
> (*Cymbeline*, Act II, Scene 3.)

V

The called-for songs in *Much Ado About Nothing, As You Like It* and *Twelfth Night* illustrate Shakespeare's skill in making what might have been beautiful irrelevancies contribute to the dramatic structure.

Much Ado About Nothing
Act II, Scene 3.
Song. Sigh no more, ladies.
Audience. Don Petro, Claudio, and Benedick (in hiding).

In the two preceding scenes we have learned of two plots, Don Pedro's plot to make Benedick fall in love with Beatrice, and Don John's plot to make Claudio believe that Hero, his wife-to-be, is unchaste. Since this is a comedy, we, the audience, know that all will come right in the end, that Beatrice and Benedick, Don Pedro and Hero will get happily married.

The two plots of which we have just learned, therefore, arouse two different kinds of suspense. If the plot against Benedick succeeds, we are one step nearer the goal; if the plot against Claudio succeeds, we are one step back.

At this point, between their planning and their execution, action is suspended, and we and the characters are made to listen to a song.

The scene opens with Benedick laughing at the thought of the lovesick Claudio and congratulating himself on being heart-whole, and he expresses their contrasted states in musical imagery.

> I have known him when there was no music in him, but the drum and the fife; and now had he rather hear

> the tabor and the pipe. . . . Is it not strange that sheeps' guts should hale souls out of men's bodies?—Well, a horn for my money when all's done.

We, of course, know that Benedick is not as heart-whole as he is trying to pretend. Beatrice and Benedick resist each other because, being both proud and intelligent, they do not wish to be the helpless slaves of emotion or, worse, to become what they have often observed in others, the victims of an imaginary passion. Yet whatever he may say against music, Benedick does not go away, but stays and listens.

Claudio, for his part, wishes to hear music because he is in a dreamy, lovesick state, and one can guess that his *petit roman* as he listens will be of himself as the ever-faithful swain, so that he will not notice that the mood and words of the song are in complete contrast to his daydream. For the song is actually about the irresponsibility of men and the folly of women taking them seriously, and recommends as an antidote good humor and common sense. If one imagines these sentiments being the expression of a character, the only character they suit is Beatrice.

> She is never sad but when she sleeps; and not even sad then; for I have heard my daughter say, she hath often dream'd of happiness and waked herself with laughing. She cannot endure hear tell of a husband. Leonato by no means: she mocks all her wooers out of suit.

I do not think it too far-fetched to imagine that the song arouses in Benedick's mind an image of Beatrice, the tenderness of which alarms him. The violence of his comment when the song is over is suspicious:

> I pray God, his bad voice bode no mischief! I had as lief have heard the night-raven, come what plague could have come after it.

And, of course, there *is* mischief brewing. Almost immediately he overhears the planned conversation of Claudio and Don Pedro, and it has its intended effect. The song may not have compelled his capitulation, but it has certainly softened him up.

More mischief comes to Claudio who, two scenes later, shows himself all too willing to believe Don John's slander before he has been shown even false evidence, and declares that, if it should prove true, he will shame Hero in public. Had his love for Hero been all he imagined it to be, he would have laughed in Don John's face and believed Hero's assertion of her innocence, despite apparent evidence to the contrary, as immediately as her cousin does. He falls into the trap set for him because as yet he is less a lover than a man in love with love. Hero is as yet more an image in his own mind than a real person, and such images are susceptible to every suggestion.

For Claudio, the song marks the moment when his pleasant illusions about himself as a lover are at their highest. Before he can really listen to music he must be cured of imaginary listening, and the cure lies through the disharmonious experiences of passion and guilt.

As You Like It
Act II, Scene 5.
Song. Under the Greenwood Tree.
Audience. Jaques.

We have heard of Jaques before, but this is the first time we see him, and now we have been introduced to all the characters. We know that, unknown to each other, the three groups—Adam, Orlando; Rosalind, Celia, Touchstone; and the Duke's court—are about to meet. The stage is set for the interpersonal drama to begin.

Of Jaques we have been told that he is a man who is always in a state of critical negation, at odds with the world, ever prompt to strike a discordant note, a man, in fact, with no music in his soul. Yet, when we actually meet him, we find him listening with pleasure to a merry song. No wonder the Duke is surprised when he hears of it:

> If he, compact of jars, grows musical,
> We shall have shortly discord in the spheres.

The first two stanzas of the song are in praise of the pastoral life, an echo of the sentiments expressed earlier by the Duke:

> Hath not old custom made this life more sweet
> Than that of painted pomp? Are not these woods
> More free from peril than the envious court?

The refrain is a summons, *Come Hither,* which we know is being answered. But the characters are not gathering here because they wish to, but because they are all exiles and refugees. In praising the Simple Life, the Duke is a bit of a humbug, since he was compelled by force to take to it.

Jaques' extemporary verse which he speaks, not sings, satirizes the mood of the song.

> If it so pass
> That any man turn ass,
> Leaving his wealth and ease,
> A stubborn will to please,
> Ducdamé, ducdamé, ducdamé:
> Here shall he see
> Gross fools as he,
> An if he will come to me.

At the end of the play, however, Jaques is the only character who chooses to leave his wealth and ease—it is the critic of the pastoral sentiment who remains in the cave. But he does not do this his stubborn will to please, for the hint is given that he will go further and embrace the religious life. In Neoplatonic terms he is the most musical of them all for he is the only one whom the carnal music of this world cannot satisfy, because he desires to hear the unheard music of the spheres.

Act II, Scene 7.
Song. Blow, blow, thou winter wind.
Audience. The Court, Orlando, Adam.

Orlando has just shown himself willing to risk his life for his faithful servant, Adam. Adam, old as he is, has given up everything to follow his master. Both were expecting hostility but have met instead with friendly kindness.

The Duke, confronted with someone who has suffered an injustice similar to his own, drops his pro-pastoral humbug and admits that, for him, exile to the forest of Arden is a suffering.

The song to which they now listen is about suffering, but about the one kind of suffering which none of those present has had to endure, ingratitude from a friend. The behavior of their brothers to the Duke and Orlando has been bad, but it cannot be called ingratitude, since neither Duke Frederick nor Oliver ever feigned friendship with them.

The effect of the song upon them, therefore, is a cheering one. Life may be hard, injustice may seem to triumph in the world, the future may be dark and uncertain, but personal loyalty and generosity exist and make such evils bearable.

TWELFTH NIGHT

I have always found the atmosphere of *Twelfth Night* a bit whiffy. I get the impression that Shakespeare wrote the play at a time when he was in no mood for comedy, but in a mood of puritanical aversion to all those pleasing illusions which men cherish and by which they lead their lives. The comic convention in which the play is set prevents him from giving direct expression to this mood, but the mood keeps disturbing, even spoiling, the comic feeling. One has a sense, and nowhere more strongly than in the songs, of there being inverted commas around the "fun."

There is a kind of comedy, *A Midsummer Night's Dream* and *The Importance of Being Earnest* are good examples, which take place in Eden, the place of pure play where suffering is unknown. In Eden, Love means the "Fancy engendered in the eye." The heart has no place there, for it is a world ruled by wish not by will. In *A Midsummer Night's Dream* it does not really matter who marries whom in the end, provided that the adventures of the lovers form a beautiful pattern; and Titania's fancy for Bottom is not a serious illusion in contrast to reality, but an episode in a dream.

To introduce will and real feeling into Eden turns it into an ugly place, for its native inhabitants cannot tell the difference between play and earnest and in the presence of the earnest they appear frivolous in the bad sense. The trouble, to my mind, about *Twelfth Night* is that Viola and Antonio are strangers to the world which all the other characters inhabit. Viola's love for the Duke and Antonio's love for Sebastian are much too strong and real.

Against their reality, the Duke, who up till the moment of recognition has thought himself in love with Olivia, drops her like a hot potato and falls in love with Viola on the spot, and Sebastian, who accepts Olivia's proposal of marriage within two minutes of meeting her for the first time, appear contemptible, and it is impossible to believe that either will make a good husband. They give the impression of simply having abandoned one dream for another.

Taken by themselves, the songs in this play are among the most beautiful Shakespeare wrote and, read in an anthology, we hear them as the voice of Eden, as "pure" poetry. But in the contexts in which Shakespeare places them, they sound shocking.

Act II, Scene 3.

SONG: O mistress mine, where are you roaming?
AUDIENCE: Sir Toby Belch, Sir Andrew Aguecheek.

Taken playfully, such lines as

> What's to come is still unsure:
> In delay there lies no plenty;
> Then come kiss me, sweet-and-twenty.
> Youth's a stuff will not endure

are charming enough, but suppose one asks, "For what kind of person would these lines be an expression of their true feelings?" True love certainly does not plead its cause by telling the beloved that love is transitory; and no young man, trying to seduce a girl, would mention her age. He takes her youth and his own for granted. Taken seriously, these lines are the voice of elderly lust, afraid of its own death. Shakespeare forces this awareness on our consciousness by making the audience to the song a couple of seedy old drunks.

Act II, Scene 4.

SONG: Come away, come away, death.
AUDIENCE: The Duke, Viola, courtiers.

Outside the pastures of Eden, no true lover talks of being slain by a fair, cruel maid, or weeps over his own grave. In real life, such reflections are the daydreams of self-love which is never faithful to others.

Again, Shakespeare has so placed the song as to make it seem an expression of the Duke's real character. Beside him sits the disguised Viola, for whom the Duke is not a playful fancy but a serious passion. It would be painful enough for her if the man she loved really loved another, but it is much worse to be made to see that he only loves himself, and it is this insight which at this point Viola has to endure. In the dialogue about the difference between man's love and woman's which follows on the song, Viola is, I think, being anything but playful when she says:

We men say more, swear more; but, indeed,
Our vows are more than will; for still we prove
Much in our vows, but little in our love.

VI

The impromptu singer stops speaking and breaks into song, not because anyone else has asked him to sing or is listening, but to relieve his feelings in a way that speech cannot do or to help him in some action. An impromptu song is not art but a form of personal behavior. It reveals, as the called-for song cannot, something about the singer. On the stage, therefore, it is generally desirable that a character who breaks into impromptu song should not have a good voice. No producer, for example, would seek to engage Madame Callas for the part of Ophelia, because the beauty of her voice would distract the audience's attention from the real dramatic point which is that Ophelia's songs are to the highest degree *not* called-for. We are meant to be horrified both by what she sings and by the fact that she sings at all. The other characters are affected but not in the way that people are affected by music. The King is terrified, Laertes so outraged that he becomes willing to use dirty means to avenge his sister.

Generally, of course, the revelation made by an impromptu song is comic or pathetic rather than shocking. Thus the Gravedigger's song in *Hamlet* is, firstly, a labor song which helps to make the operation of digging go more smoothly and, secondly, an expression of the *galgenhumor* which suits his particular mystery.

Singing is one of Autolycus' occupations, so he may be allowed a good voice, but *When daffodils begin to peer* is an impromptu song. He sings as he walks because it makes walking more rhythmical and less tiring, and he sings to keep up his spirits. His is a tough life, with hunger and the gallows never very far away, and he needs all the courage he can muster.

One of the commonest and most deplorable effects of alcohol is its encouragement of the impromptu singer. It is not the least tribute one could pay to Shakespeare when one says that he manages to extract interest from this most trivial and boring of phenomena.

When Silence gets drunk in Shallow's orchard, the maximum pathos is got out of the scene. We know Silence is an old, timid, sad, poor, nice man, and we cannot believe that, even when he was young, he was ever a gay dog; yet, when he is drunk, it is of women, wine, and chivalry that he sings. Further, the drunker he gets, the feebler becomes his memory. The first time he sings, he manages to recall six lines, by the fifth time, he can only remember one:

And Robin Hood, Scarlet, and John.

We are shown, not only the effect of alcohol on the imagination of a timid man, but also its effect on the brain of an old one.

Just as the called-for song can be used with conscious ill-intent, so the impromptu song can be feigned to counterfeit good fellowship.

The characters assembled on Pompey's galley at Misenum

who sing *Come, thou monarch of the Vine,* are anything but pathetic; they are the lords of the world. The occasion is a feast to celebrate a reconciliation, but not one of them trusts the others an inch, and all would betray each other without scruple if it seemed to their advantage.

Pompey has indeed refused Menas' suggestion to murder his guests, but wishes that Menas had done it without telling him. The fact that Lepidus gets stinking and boasts of his power, reveals his inferiority to the others, and it is pretty clear that the Machiavellian Octavius is not quite as tight as he pretends.

Again, when Iago incites Cassio to drink and starts singing

And let the can clink it

we know him to be cold sober, for one cannot imagine any mood of Iago's which he would express by singing. What he sings is pseudo-impromptu. He pretends to be expressing his mood, to be Cassio's buddy, but a buddy is something we know he could never be to anyone.

VII

Ariel's songs in *The Tempest* cannot be classified as either called-for or impromptu, and this is one reason why the part is so hard to cast. A producer casting Balthazar needs a good professional singer; for Stephano, a comedian who can make as raucous and unmusical a noise as possible. Neither is too difficult to find. But for Ariel he needs not only a boy with an unbroken voice but also one with a voice far above the standard required for the two pages who are to sing *It was a lover and his lass.*

For Ariel is neither a singer, that is to say, a human being whose vocal gifts provide him with a social function, nor a nonmusical person who in certain moods feels like singing. Ariel *is* song; when he is truly himself, he sings. The effect when he speaks is similar to that of *recitativo secco* in opera, which we listen to because we have to understand the action, though our real interest in the characters is only aroused when they start to sing. Yet Ariel is not an alien visitor from the world of opera who has wandered into a spoken drama by mistake. He cannot express any human feelings because he has none. The kind of voice he requires is exactly the kind that opera does not want, a voice which is as lacking in the personal and the erotic and as like an instrument as possible.

If Ariel's voice is peculiar, so is the effect that his songs have on others. Ferdinand listens to him in a very different way from that in which the Duke listens to *Come away, come away, death,* or Mariana to *Take, O take those lips away.* The effect on them was not to change them but to confirm the mood they were already in. The effect on Ferdinand of *Come unto these yellow sands* and *Full fathom five,* is more like the effect of instrumental music on Thaisa: direct, positive, magical.

Suppose Ariel, disguised as a musician, had approached Ferdinand as he sat on a bank, "weeping against the king, my father's wrack," and offered to sing for him; Ferdinand would probably have replied, "Go away, this is no time for music"; he might possibly have asked for something beautiful and sad; he certainly would not have asked for *Come unto these yellow sands.*

As it is, the song comes to him as an utter surprise, and its effect is not to feed or please his grief, not to encourage him to sit brooding, but to allay his passion, so that he gets to his feet and follows the music. The song opens his present to expectation at a moment when he is in danger of closing it to all but recollection.

The second song is, formally, a dirge, and, since it refers to his father, seems more relevant to Ferdinand's situation than the first. But it has nothing to do with any emotions which a son might feel at his father's grave. As Ferdinand says, "This is no mortal business." It is a magic spell, the effect of which is, not to lessen his feeling of loss, but to change his attitude towards his grief from one of rebellion—"How could this bereavement happen to me?"—to one of awe and reverent acceptance. As long as a man refuses to accept whatever he suffers as given, without pretending he can understand why, the past from which it came into being is an obsession which makes him deny any value to the present. Thanks to the music, Ferdinand is able to accept the past, symbolized by his father, as past, and at once there stands before him his future, Miranda.

The Tempest is full of music of all kinds, yet it is not one of the plays in which, in a symbolic sense, harmony and concord finally triumph over dissonant disorder. The three romantic comedies which precede it, *Pericles, Cymbeline,* and *The Winter's Tale,* and which deal with similar themes, injustice, plots, separation, all end in a blaze of joy—the wrongers repent, the wronged forgive, the earthly music is a true reflection of the heavenly. *The Tempest* ends much more sourly. The only wrongdoer who expresses genuine repentance is Alonso; and what a world of difference there is between Cymbeline's "Pardon's the word to all," and Prospero's

> For you, most wicked sir, whom to call brother
> Would even infect my mouth, I do forgive
> Thy rankest fault—all of them; and require
> My dukedom of thee, which perforce I know
> Thou must restore.

Justice has triumphed over injustice, not because it is more harmonious, but because it commands superior force; one might even say because it is louder.

The wedding masque is peculiar and disturbing. Ferdinand and Miranda, who seem as virginal and innocent as any fairy story lovers, are first treated to a moral lecture on the danger of anticipating their marriage vows, and the theme of the masque itself is a plot by Venus to get them to do so. The masque is not allowed to finish, but is broken off suddenly by Prospero, who mutters of another plot, "that foul conspiracy of the beast Caliban and his confederates against my life." As an entertainment for a wedding couple, the masque can scarcely be said to have been a success.

Prospero is more like the Duke in *Measure for Measure* than any other Shakespearian character. The victory of Justice which he brings about seems rather a duty than a source of joy to himself.

> I'll bring you to your ship and so to Naples
> Where I have hope to see the nuptials
> Of these our dear-beloved solemnis'd
> And thence retire me to my Milan, where
> Every third thought shall be my grave.

The tone is not that of a man who, putting behind him the vanities of mundane music, would meditate like Queen Katharine "upon that celestial harmony I go to," but rather of one who longs for a place where silence shall be all.

About the Author

WYSTAN HUGH AUDEN was born in York, England, on February 21, 1907. He studied at Gresham's School, Holt, and Christ Church, Oxford, after which he lived for a year in a Berlin slum. In the early nineteen-thirties he taught school at Helensburgh, in Scotland, and then at the Downs School, near Malvern. In the later thirties he worked as a free-lance writer, and published travel books on Iceland (with Louis MacNeice) and the Sino-Japanese War (with Christopher Isherwood). Also in collaboration with Isherwood, he wrote three plays for the Group Theatre, London: *The Dog Beneath the Skin, The Ascent of F6,* and *On the Frontier.* In 1939 he left England for the United States, where he became a citizen in 1946. In America he lived in New York until 1941, then taught at Michigan and Swarthmore. In 1945 he served in Germany with the U.S. Strategic Bombing Survey, and, when he returned, again took an apartment in New York. From 1948 to 1972 he spent his winters in America and his summers in Europe, first in Ischia, then, from 1958, in a house he owned in Kirchstetten, Austria. During this period he wrote four opera libretti with Chester Kallman: *The Rake's Progress* (for Igor Stravinsky), *Elegy for Young Lovers* and *The Bassarids* (both for Hans Werner Henze), and *Love's Labour's Lost* (for Nicolas Nabokov). From 1956 to 1960 he spent a few months of each year in Oxford as the elected Professor of Poetry. In 1972 he left his winter home in New York to return to Oxford. He died in Vienna on September 29, 1973.

EDWARD MENDELSON, the editor of this volume, is the literary executor of the Estate of W. H. Auden.